Fodor's

MAINE, VERMONT & NEW HAMPSHIRE

Excerpted from *Fodor's New England*

WELCOME TO MAINE, VERMONT, AND NEW HAMPSHIRE

Maine, Vermont, and New Hampshire are iconic New England, with the quaint towns, brilliant fall foliage, and picturesque landscapes the region is famous for. It's easy to enjoy the outdoors by hiking a section of the Appalachian Trail, skiing the Green Mountains, or taking a scenic drive In Acadia National Park. Shopping for antiques or browsing at a farmer's market are equally inviting pastimes. Smaller cities offer their own pleasures: boutiques and galleries, dockside lobster shacks, and Colonial architecture. All these charms keep visitors coming back.

TOP REASONS TO GO

★ **Fall Foliage:** Leaf peepers gather for the country's best festival of colors.

★ **Regional Food:** Vermont maple syrup and cheese, Maine lobster and blueberries.

★ **Outdoor Fun:** Hiking, boating, biking, or simply taking in a magnificent view.

★ **Small Towns:** A perfect day includes strolling a town green and locavore dining.

★ **Fantastic Skiing:** All three states have wonderful winter retreats with superb slopes.

★ **The Coast:** Iconic lighthouses and harbors, plus whale-watching and sailing.

Fodor's MAINE, VERMONT & NEW HAMPSHIRE

Publisher: Amanda D'Acierno, *Senior Vice President*

Editorial: Arabella Bowen, *Editor in Chief*; Linda Cabasin, *Editorial Director*

Design: Fabrizio La Rocca, *Vice President, Creative Director*; Tina Malaney, *Associate Art Director*; Chie Ushio, *Senior Designer*; Ann McBride, *Production Designer*

Photography: Melanie Marin, *Associate Director of Photography*; Jessica Parkhill and Jennifer Romains, *Researchers*

Maps: Rebecca Baer, *Senior Map Editor*; Mark Stroud (Moon Street Cartography) and David Lindroth, *Cartographers*

Production: Linda Schmidt, *Managing Editor*; Evangelos Vasilakis, *Associate Managing Editor*; Angela L. McLean, *Senior Production Manager*

Sales: Jacqueline Lebow, *Sales Director*

Marketing & Publicity: Heather Dalton, *Marketing Director*; Katherine Punia, *Senior Publicist*

Business & Operations: Susan Livingston, *Vice President, Strategic Business Planning*; Sue Daulton, *Vice President, Operations*

Fodors.com: Megan Bell, *Executive Director, Revenue & Business Development*; Yasmin Marinaro, *Senior Director, Marketing & Partnerships*

Copyright © 2015 by Fodor's Travel, a division of Random House LLC

Writers: Mike Dunphy, Debbie Hagan, Brian Kevin, Josh Rogol, Mary Ruoff

Editors: Salwa Jabado (*lead project editor*), Mark Sullivan

Editorial Contributors: Róisín Cameron, Amanda Sadlowski

Production Editor: Jennifer DePrima

14th Edition

ISBN 978-0-8041-4336-3

ISSN 1073-6581

All details in this book are based on information supplied to us at press time. Always confirm information when it matters, especially if you're making a detour to visit a specific place. Fodor's expressly disclaims any liability, loss, or risk, personal or otherwise, that is incurred as a consequence of the use of any of the contents of this book.

SPECIAL SALES

This book is available at special discounts for bulk purchases for sales promotions or premiums. For more information, e-mail specialmarkets@randomhouse.com

PRINTED IN THE UNITED STATES OF AMERICA

10 9 8 7 6 5 4 3 2 1

CONTENTS

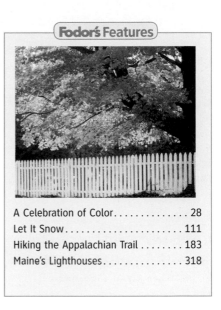

MAPS

ABOUT
THIS GUIDE

Fodor's Recommendations

Everything in this guide is worth doing—we don't cover what isn't—but exceptional sights, hotels, and restaurants are recognized with additional accolades. Fodor$Choice★ indicates our top recommendations. Care to nominate a new place? Visit Fodors.com/contact-us.

Trip Costs

We list prices wherever possible to help you budget well. Hotel and restaurant price categories from $ to $$$$ are noted alongside each recommendation. For hotels, we include the lowest cost of a standard double room in high season. For restaurants, we cite the average price of a main course at dinner or, if dinner isn't served, at lunch. For attractions, we always list adult admission fees; discounts are usually available for children, students, and senior citizens.

Hotels

Our local writers vet every hotel to recommend the best overnights in each price category, from budget to expensive. Unless otherwise specified, you can expect private bath, phone, and TV in your room. For expanded hotel reviews, facilities, and deals visit Fodors.com.

Restaurants

Unless we state otherwise, restaurants are open for lunch and dinner daily. We mention dress code only when there's a specific requirement and reservations only when they're essential or not accepted. To make restaurant reservations, visit Fodors.com.

Credit Cards

The hotels and restaurants in this guide typically accept credit cards. If not, we'll say so.

Top Picks
★ Fodor$Choice

Listings
⊠ Address
⊠ Branch address
☎ Telephone
🖷 Fax
⊕ Website
✍ E-mail
✎ Admission fee
◷ Open/closed times
Ⓜ Subway
✛ Directions or Map coordinates

Hotels & Restaurants
⌂ Hotel
⌙ Number of rooms
⦿ Meal plans
✕ Restaurant
⌒ Reservations
⌂ Dress code
⊟ No credit cards
Ⓢ Price

Other
⇨ See also
☞ Take note
⚐ Golf facilities

EXPERIENCE MAINE, VERMONT, AND NEW HAMPSHIRE

1

WHAT'S WHERE

The following numbers refer to chapters.

3 Vermont. Southern Vermont has farms, freshly starched New England towns, quiet back roads, and bustling ski resorts. Central Vermont's trademarks include famed marble quarries, and large dairy herds and pastures that create the quilted patchwork of the Champlain Valley. The heart of the area is the wilderness of the Green Mountain National Forest. Both the state's largest city (Burlington) and the nation's smallest state capital (Montpelier) are in northern Vermont, as are some of the most rural and remote areas of New England. With Montréal only an hour from the border, the Canadian influence is strong here.

4 New Hampshire. Portsmouth, the star of New Hampshire's 18-mile coastline, has great shopping, restaurants, music, and theater, as well as one of the best historic districts in the nation. The Lakes Region, rich in historic landmarks, also has good restaurants, several golf courses, hiking trails, and antiques shops. People come to the White Mountains to hike and climb, to photograph the dramatic vistas and the vibrant foliage, and to ski. Western and central New

Hampshire have managed to keep the waterslides and the outlet malls at bay. The lures here include Lake Sunapee, the charming college town of Hanover, and Mt. Monadnock, the second-most-climbed mountain in the world.

5 Inland Maine. Maine is by far the largest state in New England. At its extremes it measures 300 miles by 200 miles; all the other New England states could fit within its perimeter. The Western Lakes and vast North Woods regions attract skiers, hikers, campers, anglers, and other outdoors enthusiasts.

6 Coastal Maine. Classic townscapes, rocky shore-lines punctuated by sandy beaches, and picturesque downtowns draw vacationing New Englanders to Maine like a magnet. Maine's southern-most coastal towns are too overdeveloped to give you the rugged, Down East experience, but the Kennebunks will. Purists hold that the Maine Coast begins at Penobscot Bay, where the vistas over the water are wider and bluer, the shore a jumble of granite boulders. East of the bay is Acadia National Park, with waterfront Bar Harbor being the park's main gateway town, for both motorists and cruise ship passengers.

MAINE, VERMONT, AND NEW HAMPSHIRE PLANNER

When to Go

Northern New England is a largely year-round destination, with winter popular with skiers, summer a draw for families and beach lovers, and fall a delight to those who love the bursts of autumnal color. Spring can also be a great time, with sugar shacks transforming maple sap into all sorts of tasty things and lilacs scenting the air. But, take note that you'll probably want to avoid rural areas during mud season (April) and black-fly season (mid-May to mid-June).

Average Temperatures

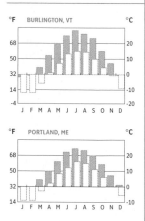

Getting Here

Most travelers visiting northern New England head for a major gateway, such as Boston or Manchester, New Hampshire, and then rent a car to explore the region. The northern New England states form a fairly compact region, with few important destinations more than six hours apart by car.

Air Travel: Boston's Logan Airport is one of the nation's most important domestic and international airports, with direct flights arriving from all over North America and across the globe. New England's other major airports receive few international flights (mostly from Canada) but do offer a wide range of direct domestic flights to East Coast and Midwest destinations, and to a lesser extent to the western United States. Times from U.S. destinations are similar, if slightly shorter, to Albany and Hartford, assuming you can find direct flights.

Airports: The main gateway to northern New England is Boston's Logan International Airport (BOS), the region's largest. Manchester Boston Regional Airport (MHT), about an hour north of Boston in New Hampshire, is another major airport. Additional northern New England airports served by major carriers include Portland International Jetport (PWM) in Maine and Burlington International Airport (BTV) in Vermont. Other airports are in Albany, New York (ALB, near Vermont), and Bangor, Maine (BGR).

Train Travel: Amtrak offers frequent daily service along its Northeast Corridor route from Washington, Philadelphia, and New York to Boston. Amtrak's high-speed *Acela* trains link Boston and Washington, with a stop at Penn Station in New York and other communities along the way. The *Downeaster* connects Boston with Portland, Maine, with stops in coastal New Hampshire.

Other Amtrak services include the *Vermonter* between Washington, D.C., and St. Albans, Vermont, and the *Ethan Allen Express* between New York and Rutland, Vermont. These trains run on a daily basis. To avoid last-minute confusion, allow 15 to 30 minutes to make train connections.

Getting Around

Car Travel: Northern New England is best explored by car. Areas in the interior are largely without heavy traffic and congestion, and parking is consistently easy to find, even in cities. Coastal New England is considerably more congested, and parking can be hard to find in resort towns along the coast. Still, a car is typically the best way to get around even on the coast (though you may want to park it at your hotel and use it as little as possible, exploring on foot, on a bike, or by local transit and cabs once you arrive). In the interior, public transportation options are more limited and a car is almost necessary. Morning and evening rush-hour traffic isn't usually much of a problem, except in larger cities and along the coast. Note that Interstate 95 is a toll highway throughout northern New England. If you rent a car at Logan International Airport, allow plenty of time to return it—as much as 60 minutes to be comfortable.

See the Getting Here and Around section in the planner at the beginning of each chapter and Travel Smart Maine, Vermont & New Hampshire for more information on transportation.

Boat Travel: Ferry routes provide access to many islands off the Maine Coast. In addition, ferries cross Lake Champlain between Vermont and upstate New York. International service between Portland and Bar Harbor, Maine, and Yarmouth, Nova Scotia, is also available. With the exception of the Lake Champlain ferries—which are first-come, first-served—car reservations are always advisable.

TRAVEL TIMES FROM BOSTON TO				
	BY AIR	BY CAR	BY BUS	BY TRAIN
Acadia National Park, ME	1 hour	5 hours	not applicable	not applicable
Burlington, VT	no direct flight	3½ hours	4½–5 hours	8¾ hours
New York, NY	¾–1 hour	4 hours	4½–7 hours	3½–4¼ hours
Portland, ME	no direct flight	2 hours	2¼ hours	2½ hours

Online Resources

Check out the official home page of each northern New England state for information on state government, as well as for links to state agencies with information on doing business, working, studying, living, and traveling in these areas. GORP is a terrific general resource for just about every kind of recreational activity; just click on the state link under "Destinations" and you'll be flooded with links to myriad topics, from wildlife refuges to ski trips to backpacking advice.

Yankee, New England's premier regional magazine, also publishes an informative travel website. Another great Web resource is Visit New England.

Online Info GORP (⊕ *www. gorp.com*). **Visit New England** (⊕ *www.visitnewengland.com*). **Yankee Magazine** (⊕ *www. yankeemagazine.com/travel*).

Visitor Info Maine Office of Tourism (☎ *888/624–6345* ⊕ *www.visitmaine.com*). **State of New Hampshire Division of Travel and Tourism Development** (☎ *800/386–4664 or 603/271–2665* ⊕ *www.visitnh. gov*). **Vermont Department of Tourism and Marketing** (☎ *802/828–3237, 800/837–6668* brochures ⊕ *www. vermontvacation.com*).

QUINTESSENTIAL MAINE, VERMONT & NEW HAMPSHIRE

Artisans

Northern New England's independent artisans have built a thriving cottage industry. Some of the finest potters spin their wheels on the coast, and one-off, often whimsical jewelry is wrought in silver, pewter, and other metals. Modern furniture makers take classic simple New England designs, including those of the Shakers and Quakers, and refine them for buyers the world over who are willing to pay thousands for craftsmanship that has withstood the test of time. The varied landscapes throughout the three states have patiently sat for thousands of painters, whose canvases are sold in small shops and local museums. Visitors who come to Maine, Vermont, and New Hampshire to create their own art have plenty to paint or photograph. Photographers especially focus their lens on classic New England architecture, colorful lobster buoys, and the mighty windjammers.

The Coast

The coast of Maine and New Hampshire is both workplace and playground. Starting in the 17th century, boat builders sprang up in one town after another to support the shipping and fishing trades. Today, the boatyards are far fewer than in historical times, but shipping and especially fishing remain important to the economy on the coast and beyond. But it's not all work and no play—some of the classic wooden sailboats now serve cruise goers, and some fishermen have traded in their lobster boats for whale-watching vessels. Maine's Reid and Popham Beach state parks are a beachcomber's paradise, and the relatively chilly waters of the North Atlantic don't scare away swimmers come summertime.

If you want to get a sense of northern New England culture and indulge in some of its pleasures, start by familiarizing yourself with the rituals of daily life.

Fall Foliage

It's impossible to discuss northern New England without mentioning that time of year when the region's deciduous trees explode in reds, yellows, oranges, and other rich hues. The season can be finicky, defined as much by the weather as it is by the species of trees—a single rainstorm can strip trees of their grandeur. But what happens in one region doesn't necessarily happen in another, and if you have the time you can follow the colors from one area to the next. Remember, you'll be competing with thousands of other likeminded leaf peepers, so be sure to book lodging early on for the hot spots. Your preparedness will pay off the first time you drive down a winding country road aflame in the bright sun of a crisp northern New England autumn day.

Food, Glorious Food

Maine will forever be famous for its delectable lobsters, and Vermont equally known for its maple treats. But Maine lobster and Vermont Grade A maple syrup are just samples to whet your appetite. Dining in northern New England is a feast for the gastronomist to behold, and it runs the gamut from the simply prepared to the most artistic of presentations; from blueberry pie just like Grandma used to make to slow-cooked Long Island duck with kumquat, glazed carrots, and long pepper. Beyond lobsters, also delicious are the area's shellfish—shrimp, clams, scallops, crab, and mussels—and in Vermont, famous local cheddar and high-quality, grass-fed beef. Chefs who grew up here may leave to learn their trade, but often return and enrich the dining scene; the region is known for attracting newcomers as well.

MAINE, VERMONT & NEW HAMPSHIRE TOP ATTRACTIONS

Acadia National Park

(A) Hosting more than 2 million visitors annually, this wonder of the Maine coast was the first national park established east of the Mississippi River. In the warmer months, take a drive around Mount Desert Island's 27-mile Park Loop Road to acquaint yourself with the area and indulge in spectacular views of the mountains and the sea. Head to the top of Cadillac Mountain (especially popular at sunrise) or bike the scenic 45-mile carriage-road system, or go on a park ranger–led boat trip in search of local wildlife such as porpoises, seals, and seabirds. Adorable Bar Harbor is the park's gateway town.

Appalachian Trail

(B) The 2,180-mile Appalachian Trail, running from Springer Mountain, Georgia, to Katahdin, Maine, cuts through five New England states: Connecticut, Massachusetts, New Hampshire, Vermont, and

Maine. Though the trail is best known as a weeks-long endurance test for expert hikers, many portions can be walked in a few hours. "AT" terrain in Maine and New Hampshire can be quite challenging.

Baxter State Park

(C) Baxter State Park's 200,000 acres contain numerous lakes and streams, plus Mt. Katahdin, Maine's tallest peak and the northern terminus of the Appalachian Trail. Offering frequent sightings of moose, white-tailed deer, and black bear, and attracting only 60,000 visitors a year, Baxter State Park provides a wilderness experience not found elsewhere in New England.

Green Mountains

(D) Vermont takes its nickname (the Green Mountain State) and its actual name (*verts monts* is "green mountains" in French) from this 250-mile-long mountain range that forms the spine of the state. Part of the Appalachian Mountains, the Green

Mountains are a wild paradise filled with rugged hiking trails (most notably the Long Trail and the Appalachian Trail), unspoiled forests, quaint towns, and some of the East Coast's best ski resorts.

Lake Winnipesaukee

(E) As fun to fish as it is to pronounce, the largest (and longest) lake in New Hampshire is home to three species of trout, small- and largemouth bass, bluegill, and more. The 72-square-mile lake and its more than 250 islands also contain beaches, arcades, water parks, and countless other fun family diversions.

Maine Coast

(F) Counting all its nooks, crannies, and crags, Maine's coast would stretch for thousands of miles if you could pull it straight. The southern Coast is the most visited section, stretching north from Kittery to just outside Portland, but don't let that stop you from heading farther "Down East" (Maine-speak for "up the coast"). Despite the cold waters, beachgoers enjoy miles of sandy—or, more frequently, rocky—beaches, with sweeping views of lighthouses, forested islands, and the wide-open sea.

Mt. Washington

(G) New England's highest mountain, this New Hampshire peak has been scaled by many a car (as the bumper stickers will attest). You can also take a cog railway to the top or, if you're an intrepid hiker, navigate a maze of trails. Bundle up if you make the trek—the average temperature at the summit is below freezing.

Portland Head Light

(H) One of the most photographed lighthouses in the nation, the historic white stone Portland Head Light features an informative museum in the Victorian-style innkeeper's cottage. The lighthouse is in Fort Williams Park, about 2 miles from the town center of Cape Elizabeth, at the southwest entrance of Portland harbor.

TOP EXPERIENCES IN MAINE, VERMONT, AND NEW HAMPSHIRE

Peep a Leaf

Tourist season in most of New England is concentrated in the late spring and summer, but there's a resurgence in September and October, especially in the northern states, when leaf peepers from all corners descend by the car- and busload to see the leaves turn red, yellow, orange, and all shades in between. Foliage season can be fragile and unpredictable—temperature, winds, and rain all influence when the leaves turn and how long they remain on the trees—but that makes the season even more precious. Apple picking at a local orchard and searching for the perfect pumpkin for a jack-o'-lantern among the falling leaves are quintessential New England experiences.

Comb a Beach

Whether sandy or rocky, New England beaches can be filled with flotsam and jetsam. Anything from crab traps unmoored by heavy waves to colored sea glass worn smooth by the water to lost watches, jewelry, and the like can appear at your feet. Also common are shells of sea urchins, clams, and other bivalves. During certain times of the year sand dollars of all sizes and colors are plentiful—you may even find one still whole.

Hit the Slopes

Though the mountain snow in New England is not as legendary as the powder out west (and, in fact, can be downright unpleasant when packed snow becomes crusty ice), skiing is quite popular here. Vermont has several ski areas, with Killington ranking among the largest resorts in the Northeast: its nearly 200 trails span seven mountains. New Hampshire's White Mountains and Massachusetts's Berkshires also cater to snow-sport lovers, while Sunday River and Sugarloaf in Maine are perennial favorites with advanced-intermediate and expert skiers. Beginners (and lift-ticket bargain hunters) can choose from a number of small but fun hills throughout northern New England.

Eat a Maine Lobster

Maine lobsters are world renowned, and lobstermen and fish markets all along the coast will pack a live lobster in seaweed for overnight shipment to almost anywhere nationwide. These delectable crustaceans are available throughout New England, but without a doubt the best place to eat them is near the waters of origin. Lobster meat is sweet, especially the claws, and most agree that simple preparation is the best way to go: steamed and eaten with drawn butter or pulled into chunks and placed in a toasted hot dog bun—the famous New England lobster roll. There are two types of lobster rolls to try: traditional Maine style features a cold lobster salad with a leaf of lettuce and the barest amount of mayonnaise, while the Connecticut lobster roll is served warm with drawn butter and no mayo. Don't forget to save room for New England's other culinary treasure: *chowdah*. No two clam chowders taste the same, but they're all delicious.

Rise and Shine at a B&B

New England's distinctive architecture, much of it originating in the 18th and 19th centuries, has resulted in beautiful buildings of all shapes and sizes, many of which have been restored as bed-and-breakfasts. These inns typify the cozy, down-home, and historic feel of New England, and are an ideal lodging choice. This is especially true when the weather is cold, and the warm ambience of many of these inns more than justifies the slightly

higher prices you'll pay here versus a hotel or motel.

Watch a Whale

The deep, cold waters of the North Atlantic serve as feeding grounds and migration routes for a variety of whales, including the fin, humpback, the occasional blue, and endangered white whales. Maine's southern coast and midcoast regions are the best places to hop aboard a whale-watching boat, but tours also depart from Boston Harbor. Some boat captains go so far as to guarantee at least a single sighting. The tours head to the whale feeding grounds about 20 miles offshore, where the majestic animals are numerous. The whale-watching season varies by tour skipper, but generally runs from April through October.

Fair Thee Well

New Englanders love their fairs and festivals. Maine-iacs celebrate the moose, clam, lobster, and blueberry. Maple sugar and maple syrup are feted in Vermont, while "live free or die" New Hampshire honors American independence. Many rural communities throughout New England hold agricultural fairs in late August and September.

Get Up Close and Personal with Nature

New England might be known for its flashy foliage in the fall and spectacular slopes in the winter, but the outdoors in the spring and summer delights all the senses as well. You can breathe in the ocean air as you drive along the Maine Coast or enjoy the fragrance of the mountains and forests in the Berkshires, Vermont's Green Mountains, and New Hampshire's White Mountains while hiking along the Appalachian Trail. You may observe such animals as moose and

bear. Close to the ocean there are numerous chances to see birds, seals, dolphins, and whales.

Savor Sweet Stuff

Summer vacations in New England go hand in hand with sweet treats; it's difficult to visit without sampling homemade fudge at an old-fashioned candy store, buying an ice cream for your sweetie, or bringing home some saltwater taffy to share with the folks back at the ranch. Be sure to try a Maine specialty—the whoopie pie. Made from two chocolate circles of cake with vanilla cream filling in between, it's a delectable Maine tradition. If you are visiting Maine when the tiny wild blueberry is in season, take every opportunity to savor this flavorful fruit, whether in pie, muffin, or pancake form, and you'll understand its legendary culinary status. In Vermont, go on a factory tour at Ben & Jerry's, and have a delicious cone afterward.

Find the Perfect Souvenir

Artists and craftspeople abound in New England, meaning that finding the perfect souvenir of your vacation will be an enjoyable hunt. Whether you choose a watercolor of a picturesque fishing village, a functional and beautiful piece of handmade pottery, or a handcrafted piece of jewelry, you'll be supporting the local economy while taking a little piece of the region home with you.

Check Out Lighthouses

Maine's long and jagged coastline is home to more than 60 lighthouses, perched high on rocky ledges or on the tips of wayward islands. Though modern technology in navigation has made many of the lights obsolete, preservation groups restore and maintain many of them and often make them accessible to the public. Some of the

state's more famous lights include Portland Head Light, commissioned by President George Washington in 1787 and immortalized in one of Edward Hopper's paintings; Two Lights, a few miles down the coast in Cape Elizabeth; and West Quoddy Head, on the easternmost tip of land in the United States. Some lighthouses are privately owned and others accessible only by boat, but plenty are within easy reach and open to the public, some with museums and tours. At the Maine Lighthouse Museum in Rockland, visitors can view a collection of Fresnel lenses and Coast Guard artifacts.

Sail the Coast

The coastline of northern New England is a sailor's paradise, complete with hidden coves, windswept islands, and picture-perfect harbors where you can pick up a mooring for the night. With nearly 3,500 miles of undulating, rocky shoreline, you could spend a lifetime of summers sailing the waters off the Maine Coast and never see it all. If you're not one of the lucky few with a sailboat to call your own, there are many companies that offer sailboat charters, whether for day trips or weeklong excursions. It might sound like an expensive getaway, but as meals and drinks are usually included, an overnight sailing charter might not cost any more than a seaside hotel room, plus you have an experienced captain to provide history and insight along the voyage.

Get the First Sight of First Light

At 1,530 feet, Cadillac Mountain, in Maine's Acadia National Park, is the highest mountain on the New England coast—so what better place to view the sunrise? Drive the winding and narrow 3½-mile road to the summit before dawn (not accessible when the Loop Road is closed in the winter), and you could be the first person in the United States to see the summer sun's rays. (Note that this depends on the time of year; sometimes the first sunrise is at West Quoddy Head Lighthouse in Lubec, Maine).

MAINE, VERMONT, AND NEW HAMPSHIRE TODAY

The People

The idea of the self-reliant, thrifty, and often stoic New England Yankee has taken on almost mythic proportions in American folklore, but in some parts of New England—especially in rural Maine, Vermont, and New Hampshire—there still is some truth to this image, which shouldn't come as a surprise. You need to be independent if you farm an isolated field, live in the middle of a vast forest, or work a fishing boat miles off the coast. Like any part of the country, there are stark differences between urban New Englanders and those you encounter outside the cities. Both, though, are usually fiercely proud of the region, its rugged beauty, and its contributions to the nation.

The Politics

Though they're often portrayed as a bunch of loony liberals, the political views of New Englanders are actually more complex. The region's representation in both the United States Senate and the House of Representatives is heavily Democratic, even in those states that elect a Republican governor. Voters in New Hampshire, which now hosts the nation's first primary each presidential election season, tend to lean conservative but with a distinctly libertarian slant, as do residents in many rural portions of New England. Five states that allow same-sex marriage are in New England (Massachusetts, Vermont, New Hampshire, Connecticut, and Maine).

The Economy

Long gone are the days since New England's shoe and textile industries sailed overseas, when many a mill town suffered blows to employment and self-image. In Maine, the lobster-fishing industry (about 70% of the state's seafood industry) is hoping to rebound after a number of tough years. Between 2005 and 2009 lobster prices dropped nearly two dollars per pound, however prices have recovered somewhat since 2010, and in 2011 Maine fishermen hauled in lobster at a record-setting pace.

Exports are a major part of the modern New England economy, consisting heavily of computer and other electronics, chemicals, and specialized machinery. The service industries also are strong, especially in the insurance and financial sectors. Some towns are known for a particular export: Bath, Maine, has naval shipyards supplying the military with high-technology fighting ships; Barre, Vermont, quarries granite. Assorted foods produced include maple syrup, blueberries, lobster, and other seafood.

The Language

As people move around, the local accents have begun to blend, creating more of a general New England accent. (In fact, in some urban areas, you may not hear any accent.) Linguistic differences, however, are still evident in some places, especially close to the coast.

Maine has a Boston-like accent (lengthened vowels, dropped Rs in certain places) but with nuanced differences. True Mainers drop or soften their Rs—making their favorite dish "lobstah"; they also often accentuate the vowel, so a one-word syllable can be pronounced like two, meaning "here" may become "hee-yuh."

In New Hampshire the accent is not nearly as strong, but it comes out in certain words, like the locals' pronunciation of their capital "Cahn-cuhd."

FLAVORS OF MAINE, VERMONT, AND NEW HAMPSHIRE

FOOD FESTIVALS

Wilton Blueberry Festival, Wilton, Maine. You can pick your own wild blueberries and sample baked goods from pancakes to pies at this festival (⊕ *www.wiltonbbf. com*), which takes place in early August.

Keene Pumpkin Festival, Keene, New Hampshire. Locals attempt to set the world record for most lighted pumpkins at this celebration (⊕ *pumpkinfestival2011.org*), which takes place in mid-to-late October. Enjoy hayrides and contests from pie eating to pumpkin-seed spitting.

Maine Lobster Festival, Rockland, Maine. Stuff your face with lobster tails and claws during this lobstravaganza (⊕ *www. mainelobsterfestival.com*) in late July and early August. With almost 20,000 pounds of delicious crustacean at your finger tips, leaving hungry is unthinkable.

Vermont Cheesemakers Festival, Shelburne, Vermont. Artisanal cheeses and local beer and wine highlight this daylong festival (⊕ *www.vtcheesefest.com*) in late July. Sample more than 200 cheese varieties from 40 local cheese makers in the Coach Barn of Shelburne Farms.

SPECIALTIES BY STATE

Vermont

Vermonters are big on **maple syrup,** but dairy products take top billing in this state. Milk and cream from the region's dairy farms are used in cheeses, like the famous **cheddars;** and in **ice cream,** like Ben & Jerry's. Willow Hill Farm in Milton, Vermont, is famous for its sheep's milk cheeses. Try the savory Vaquero Blue, a blue cheese made from both sheep and cow's milk. For a family-friendly stop, check out Shelburne Farms' children's farmyard. On the shore of Lake Champlain, Shelburne Farms uses only purebred Brown Swiss cows to make its famous farmhouse cheddar. In addition to the Vermont Cheesemakers Festival, Shelburne attracts visitors year-round to taste mouthwatering cheeses and explore walking trails.

New Hampshire

Northern New Hampshire's cuisine carries a heavy French-Canadian influence. One of the most enticing francophone creations is *poutine* (french fries covered with cheese curds and gravy). The local **corn chowder** substitutes corn for clams and bacon, putting a twist on a Northeastern classic. **Smuttynose Brewing Company,** a craft brewery in Portsmouth, offers tours and tastings.

Maine

Lobster classics include **boiled lobster**—a staple at "in the rough" picnic-bench-and-paper-plate spots along the Maine Coast—and **lobster rolls,** a lobster meat–and-mayo or melted-butter preparation served in a toasted hot dog bun.

Blueberries, strawberries, raspberries, and **blackberries** grow wild (and on farms) all over the Northeast in the summer. Blueberry pancakes with maple syrup, blueberry muffins, and blueberry pies are popular, especially in coastal Maine. Mainers also love **whoopie pies,** cakelike cookies sandwiched with frosting.

Portland's waterfront Commercial Street is bookended by two typical Maine diners, Gilbert's Chowderhouse and Becky's Diner. The former has one of the state's finest lobster rolls and homemade clam cakes; the latter opens for breakfast at 4 am to feed the fishermen before they head out to sea. Order a slice of fresh pie or buy one whole to take with you.

OUTDOOR ADVENTURES

BEACHCOMBING AND SWIMMING

Long, wide beaches edge the northern New England coast from New Hampshire to southern Maine. Many of the beaches have lifeguards on duty in season; some have picnic facilities, restrooms, changing facilities, and concession stands. Depending on the locale, you may need a parking sticker to use the lot.

When to Go

The waters are at their warmest in August, though they're cold even at the height of summer along much of Maine. Inland, small lake beaches abound, most notably in New Hampshire and Vermont. The best time to beachcomb is after the tide has gone out, when the retreating water has left behind its treasures. Early spring is an especially good time to see sand dollars washed up on beaches.

What to Look For

The best part of beachcombing is that you never quite know what you'll find at your feet. Sea glass—nothing more than man-made glass worn smooth from its seaward journeys—is common and most prized in rare shades of blue. You'll also find shells in abundance: blue mussels, tiny periwinkles, razor, or "jackknife" clams, ridged scallops, and oysters, with their rough outside shell and lovely mother-of-pearl interiors.

Best Beaches

Hampton Beach State Park, New Hampshire. The Granite State's ocean shore is short, but this state park along historic Route 1 takes full advantage of the space it has. In addition to swimming and fishing, there are campsites with full hookups for RVs and an amphitheater with a band shell for fair-weather concerts.

Old Orchard Beach, Maine. Think Coney Island on a smaller scale. There's a white-sand beach to be sure (lapped by cold North Atlantic waters), but many come to ride the Pirate Ship at Palace Playland, drop quarters at the arcade, and browse the multitude of trinket-and-T-shirt shops.

Reid State Park, Maine. The water is cold much of the year, but this beach just west of Sheepscot Bay on Georgetown Island is a beautiful and quiet place to look for sand dollars or climb the rocks at low tide, exploring tidal pools. Great views can be had from the park's rocky Griffith Head.

BICYCLING

Biking on a road through northern New England's countryside is an idyllic way to spend a day. Many ski resorts allow mountain bikes in summer.

Bike Tours

There are a multitude of tour operators and magnificent trails throughout northern New England and many bike shops rent and repair bicycles. Bike New England offers cycling routes and maps throughout the Northeast.

Safety

On the road, watch for trucks and stay as close as possible to the side of the road, in single file. On the trail, ride within your limits and keep your eyes peeled for hikers and horses (both of which have the right of way), as well as dogs. Always wear a helmet and carry plenty of water.

Best Rides

Acadia National Park, Maine. At the heart of this popular park is the 45-mile network of historic carriage roads covered in crushed rock that bicyclists share only with equestrians and hikers. Hybrid or

mountain bikes are the way to go here, so leave your road bike at home. Fit and experienced riders can ascend the road to the top of Cadillac Mountain, but take caution: heavy traffic in high season can make this a dangerous proposition.

All Along the Coast. U.S. 1, Maine. The major road that travels along the Maine Coast is only a narrow two-lane highway for most of its route, but it is still one of the country's most historic highways. As a result, it's very popular in spring, summer, and fall with serious long-distance bike riders.

Killington Resort, Vermont. Following the lead of many ski resorts in the western United States, Killington allows fat-tire riders on many of its ski trails after the snow has melted. Stunt riders can enjoy the jumps and bumps of the mountain-bike park.

Portland, Maine. The paved Eastern Prom Trail extends from the edge of the Old Port to East End Beach, then to Back Bay for a 6-mile loop, before returning.

BOATING

Along many of northern New England's larger lakes, sailboats, rowboats, canoes, kayaks, and outboards are available for rent at local marinas. Sailboats are available for rent at a number of seacoast locations, but you may be required to prove your seaworthiness. Lessons are frequently available.

What to Wear

It can get cold on the water, especially while sailing, so dress in layers and bring along a windbreaker and fleece even if it's warm on land. Don't wear cotton or jeans: once they get wet, they stay wet and will leave you chilled. Sunscreen, sunglasses (with Croakies so they don't fall overboard), and a hat are also musts, as are drinking water and high-energy snacks, especially for canoe and kayak expeditions.

Best Boating

Allagash Wilderness Waterway, Maine. This scenic and remote waterway—92 miles of lakes, ponds, rivers, and streams—is part of the 740-mile Northern Forest Canoe Trail, which also floats through New York, Vermont, and New Hampshire.

Lake Champlain, Vermont. Called by some the sixth Great Lake, 435-square-mile Lake Champlain is bordered by Vermont's Green Mountains to the east and the Adirondacks of New York to the west. Burlington, Vermont, is the largest lakeside city and a good bet for renting a boat—be it canoe, kayak, rowboat, skiff, or motorboat. Attractions include numerous islands and deep-blue water that's often brushed by pleasant New England breezes.

Lakes Region, New Hampshire. Lake Winnipesaukee is the largest lake in New Hampshire, but there are many puddles large and small worth dipping a paddle into. Squam Lake is a tranquil lake made famous by *On Golden Pond*, Lake Wentworth has a state park with a boat launch, bathhouse, and picnic tables.

Rockland, Maine. For a guided trip on the water, consider a windjammer excursion out of Rockland, Camden, or Rockport. From day sails to multiday cruises, trips cost between $50 and $1,000, and include meals. Check The Maine Windjammer Association (⊕ *www.sailmainecoast. com*) or Windjammer Cruises (⊕ *www. mainewindjammercruises.com*) for more information.

HIKING

Probably the most famous trails in the region are the 270-mile Long Trail, which runs north–south through the center of Vermont, and the Maine-to-Georgia Appalachian Trail, which runs through northern New England on both private and public land. The Appalachian Mountain Club (AMC) maintains a system of staffed huts in New Hampshire's Presidential Range, with bunk space and meals available by reservation. State parks throughout the region afford good hiking.

Safety

There are few real hazards to hiking, but a little preparedness goes a long way. Know your limits, and make sure the terrain you are about to embark on doesn't exceed your abilities. Check the trail map carefully and pay attention to elevation changes, which make a huge difference in the difficulty of a hike (a steep 1-mile-long trail is much tougher to negotiate than a flat 2- or even 3-mile trail). Bring layers of clothing to accommodate changing weather and always carry enough drinking water. Before you go, be sure to tell someone where you're going and how long you expect to be gone.

Best Hikes

Appalachian Trail, Maine, Vermont, New Hampshire. This path from Georgia to Maine is as great for a short day hike as it is for a challenging six-month endurance test. The popular trail is marked by rectangular white blazes which are kept up and relatively easy to follow. ⇨ *For a guide to the best day hikes and more information on hiking the AT, see "Hiking the Appalachian Trail" feature in Chapter 4.*

Mt. Washington, New Hampshire. The cog railroad and the auto road to the summit are popular routes up New England's highest mountain, but for those with stamina and legs of steel it's one heck of a hike. There are a handful of trails to the top, the most popular beginning at Pinkham Notch Visitor Center. Be sure to dress in layers and have some warm clothing for the frequent winds toward the peak.

The Long Trail, Vermont. Following the main ridge of the Green Mountains from one end of Vermont to the other, this is the nation's oldest long-distance trail. In fact, some say it was the inspiration for the Appalachian Trail. Hardy hikers make a go of its 270-mile length, but day hikers can drop in and out at many places along the way.

MAINE, VERMONT, AND NEW HAMPSHIRE WITH KIDS

Northern New England is ideally suited for family vacations, offering historic sites, beaches, sports and recreation, outdoor adventures, and some of the most beautiful mountain and coastal scenery around.

Children's Museum & Theater of Maine, Portland, Maine. Located in the heart of Portland's Arts District, this is a hands-on children's museum A first-floor exhibit called Our Town includes a lobster boat, car repair shop, and supermarket. Upstairs is a kid-sized rock wall and tidepool touch tank.

Hampton Beach, New Hampshire. This seaside diversion draws families to its almost Coney Island–like fun. Along the boardwalk, kids enjoy arcade games, parasailing, live music, and an annual children's festival. They can even learn how saltwater taffy is made. **Montshire Museum of Science,** Norwich, Vermont. This interactive museum uses more than 60 hands-on exhibits to explore nature and technology. The building sits amid 110 acres of woodlands and nature trails. Live animals are on-site as well. **Shelburne Farms,** Shelburne, Vermont. This working dairy farm is also an educational and cultural resource center. Visitors can watch artisans make the farm's famous cheddar cheese from the milk of more than 100 purebred and registered Brown Swiss cows. A children's farmyard and walking trails round out the experience. **Southworth Planetarium,** Portland, Maine. This University of Southern Maine facility offers classes such as night-sky mythology and introductory astronomy. The 30-foot dome houses a star theater complete with lasers, digital sounds, and a star projector that displays more than 5,000 heavenly bodies. **Story Land,** Glen, New Hampshire. This fantasyland theme park has been entertaining young children and their parents since 1954. The $32 per person admission (ages three and older) covers all 22 rides, which include a flume ride, roller coaster, and river-raft ride. When summer gets too hot, kids can enjoy the Oceans of Fun Sprayground.

Whale-watching, Maine. Few things speak of the great, deep, blue unknown like a whale, and any sighting of these magnificent creatures is dramatic and not soon forgotten. The whale-watching season varies by tour skipper, but generally is contained between the months of April and October. The best spots to hop aboard a whale-watching tour are Boothbay Harbor, Portland, and Bar Harbor.

BEST FALL FOLIAGE DRIVES & ROAD TRIPS

A CELEBRATION

Picture this: one scarlet maple offset by the stark white spire of a country church, a whole hillside of brilliant foliage foregrounded by a vintage barn or perhaps a covered bridge that straddles a cobalt river. Such iconic scenes have launched a thousand postcards and turned New England into the ultimate fall destination for leaf peepers.

OF COLOR

By Susan MacCallum-Whitcomb

Mother Nature, of course, puts on an annual autumn performance elsewhere, but this one is a showstopper. Like the landscape, the mix of deciduous (leaf-shedding) trees is remarkably varied here and creates a broader than usual palette. New England's abundant evergreens lend contrast, making the display even more vivid. Every September and October, leaf peepers arrive to cruise along country lanes, join outdoor adventures, or simply stroll on town greens.

Did you know the brilliant shades actually lurk in the leaves all year long? Leaves contain three pigments. The green chlorophyll, so dominant in summer that it obscures the red anthocyanins and orangey-yellow carotenoids, decreases in fall and reveals a crayon box of color.

Above, Vermont's Green Mountains are multicolored in the fall (and often white in winter).

PREDICTING THE PEAK

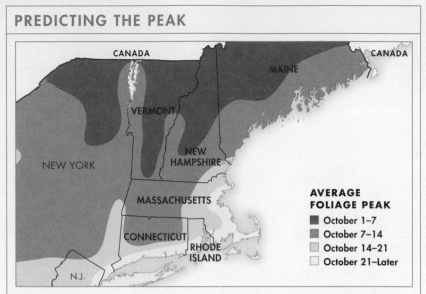

AVERAGE
FOLIAGE PEAK

- ■ October 1–7
- ■ October 7–14
- ☐ October 14–21
- ☐ October 21–Later

LOCATION

Pinning down precisely when colors will appear remains an inexact science, although location plays a major role. Typically, the transformation begins in the highest and northernmost parts of New England in mid-September, then moves steadily into lower altitudes and southern sectors throughout October.

For trip planning, think in terms of regions rather than states. In Maine (a huge state that runs north–south) leaf color can peak anytime from the fourth week of September to the third week of October, depending on the locale.

WEATHER

Early September weather is another deciding factor. From the foliage aficionado's perspective, the ideal scenario is calm, temperate days capped by nights that are cool but still above freezing. If the weather is too warm, it delays the onset of the season. If it's too dry or windy, the leaves shrivel up or blow off.

COLOR CHECK RESOURCES

Curious about current conditions? In season, each state maintains a dedicated Web site reporting on foliage conditions. Weather Channel has peak viewing maps and Foliage Network uses a network of spotters to chart changes.

- ■ **Connecticut:** ☎ *800/282–6863* ⊕ *www.ct.gov/dep*
- ■ **Foliage Network:** ⊕ *www. foliagenetwork.com*
- ■ **Maine:** ☎ *888/624–6345* ⊕ *www. maine.gov/doc/foliage*
- ■ **Massachusetts:** ☎ *617/973–8500* ⊕ *www.massvacation.com*
- ■ **New Hampshire:** ☎ *800/258–3608* ⊕ *www.visitnh.gov*
- ■ **Rhode Island:** ☎ *800/556–2484* ⊕ *www.visitri.com*
- ■ **Vermont:** ☎ *800/837–6668* ⊕ *www. foliage-vermont.com*
- ■ **Weather Channel:** ⊕ *www.weather.com*

TOP TREES FOR COLOR

Ⓐ AMERICAN BEECH. This tree's smooth, steel-gray trunk is crowned with gold, copper, and bronze-tinted leaves in autumn, giving it a metallic sheen. Though the elliptical leaves sometimes hang on all winter, its "fruit" goes fast because beechnuts are a popular snack for birds, squirrels, and even bears.

Ⓑ NORTHERN RED OAK. The upside of oaks is that they retain their fall shading until late in the season—the downside is that, for most species, that color is a boring brown. Happily, the northern red isn't like other members of the oak family. Its elongated, flame-shaped leaves turn fiery crimson and incandescent orange.

Ⓒ QUAKING ASPEN. Eyes and ears both prove useful when identifying this aspen. Look for small, ovate leaves that usually become almost flaxen. Or listen for the leaves' quake: a sound, audible in even a gentle breeze, which the U.S. Forest Service likens to that made by "thousands of fluttering butterfly wings."

Ⓓ SUGAR MAPLE. The leaf of the largest North American maple species is so lovely that Canada put it on its national flag. Each generally has five multi-pointed lobes—plus enough anthocyanin to produce a deep red color. The tree itself produces plentiful sap and is the cornerstone of New England's syrup industry.

Ⓔ WHITE ASH. This tall tree typically grows to between 65 to 100 feet. Baseball enthusiasts admire the wood (which is used to craft bats); while foliage fans admire the compound leaves, each consisting of five to nine slightly serrated, tapering leaflets. They range in hue from burgundy and purple to amber.

Ⓕ WHITE BIRCH. A papery, light, bright bark makes this slender hardwood easily recognizable. Centuries ago, Native Americans used birch wood to make everything from canoes to medicinal teas. Today's photographers know the bark also makes great pictures since it provides a sharp contrast to the tree's vibrant yellow leaves.

FANTASTIC FALL ITINERARY

The Berkshires

Fall is the perfect time to visit New England—country roads wind through dense forests exploding into reds, oranges, yellows, and purples. For inspiration, here is an itinerary for the truly ambitious that links the most stunning foliage areas; choose a section to explore more closely. Like autumn itself, this route works its way south from northern Vermont into Connecticut, with one or two days in each area.

VERMONT

NORTHWEST VERMONT
In Burlington, the elms will be turning colors on the University of Vermont campus. You can ride the ferry across Lake Champlain for great views of Vermont's Green Mountains and New York's Adirondacks. After visiting the resort town of Stowe, detour off Route 100 beneath the cliffs of Smugglers' Notch. The north country's palette unfolds in Newport, where the blue waters of Lake Memphremagog reflect the foliage. (⇨ *Northern Vermont in Chapter 3.*)

NORTHEAST KINGDOM
After a side trip along Lake Willoughby, explore St. Johnsbury, where the Fairbanks Museum and St. Johnsbury Athenaeum reveal Victorian tastes in art and natural-history collecting. In Peacham, stock up for a picnic at the Peacham Store. (⇨ *Northern Vermont in Chapter 3.*)

NEW HAMPSHIRE

WHITE MOUNTAINS AND LAKES REGION
In New Hampshire, Interstate 93 narrows as it winds through craggy Franconia Notch. Get off the interstate for the sinuous Kancamagus Highway portion of Route 112 that passes through the mountains to Conway. In Center Harbor, in the Lakes Region, you can ride the *MS Mount Washington* for views of the Lake Winnipesaukee shoreline, or ascend to Moultonborough's Castle in the Clouds for a falcon's-eye look at the colors. (⇨ *The White Mountains and Lakes Region in Chapter 4.*)

MT. MONADNOCK
In Concord, stop at the Museum of New Hampshire History and the State House. Several trails climb Mt. Monadnock, near Jaffrey Center, and colorful vistas extend as far as Boston. (⇨ *The Monadnocks and Merrimack Valley in Chapter 4.*)

⇨ For local drives perfect for an afternoon, also see our Fall Foliage Drive Spotlights on Vermont, New Hampshire, and Inland Maine.

THE MOOSE IS LOOSE!

Take "Moose Crossing" signs seriously because things won't end well if you hit an animal that stands six feet tall and weighs 1,200 pounds. Some 40,000 reside in northern New England. To search out these ungainly creatures in the wild, consider an organized moose safari in northern New Hampshire or Maine.

MASSACHUSETTS

THE MOHAWK TRAIL

In Shelburne Falls, Massachusetts, the Bridge of Flowers displays the last of autumn's blossoms. Follow the Mohawk Trail section of Route 2 as it ascends into the Berkshire Hills—and stop to take in the view at the hairpin turn just east of North Adams (or drive up Mt. Greylock, the tallest peak in New England, for more stunning vistas). In Williamstown, the Sterling and Francine Clark Art Institute houses a collection of impressionist works.

THE BERKSHIRES

The scenery around Lenox, Stockbridge, and Great Barrington has long attracted the talented and the wealthy. Near U.S. 7, you can visit the homes of novelist Edith Wharton (the Mount, in Lenox), sculptor Daniel Chester French (Chesterwood, in Stockbridge), and diplomat Joseph Choate (Naumkeag, in Stockbridge).

CONNECTICUT

THE LITCHFIELD HILLS

This area of Connecticut combines the feel of upcountry New England with exclusive urban polish. The wooded shores of Lake Waramaug are home to country inns and wineries in pretty towns. Litchfield has a perfect village green—an idealized New England town center.

FOLIAGE PHOTO HINT

Don't just snap the big panoramic views. Look for single, brilliantly colored trees with interesting elements nearby, like a weathered gray stone wall or a freshly painted white church. These images are often more evocative than big blobs of color or panoramic shots.

LEAF PEEPER PLANNER

Hot-air balloons and ski-lift rides give a different perspective on fall's color.

Enjoying fall doesn't necessarily require a multistate road trip. If you are short on time (or energy), a simple autumnal stroll might be just the ticket: many state parks even offer free short ranger-led rambles.

HIKE AND BIKE ON A TOUR

You can sign on for foliage-focused hiking holidays with **Country Walkers** (☎ 800/464–9255 ⊕ www.countrywalkers.com) and **Boundless Journeys** (☎ 800/941–8010 ⊕ www.boundlessjourneys.com); or cycling ones with **Bike Vermont** (☎ 800/257–2226 ⊕ www.bikevt.com) and **VBT Bicycling Vacations** (☎ 800/245–3868, ⊕ www.vbt.com). Individual state tourism boards list similar operators elsewhere.

SOAR ABOVE THE CROWDS

New Hampshire's Cannon Mountain (☎ 603/823–8800 ⊕ www.cannonmt.com) is only one of several New England ski resorts that provides gondola or aerial tram rides during foliage season. Area hot-air balloon operators, like **Balloons of Vermont, LLC** (☎ 802/369–0213 ⊕ www.balloonsofvermont.com), help you take it in from the top.

ROOM AT THE INN?

Accommodations fill quickly in autumn. Vermont's top lodgings sell out months in advance for the first two weeks in October. So book early and expect a two-night minimum stay requirement. If you can't find a quaint inn, try basing yourself at a B&B or off-season ski resort. Also, be prepared for some sticker shock; if you can travel midweek, you'll often save quite a bit.

RIDE THE RAILS OR THE CURRENT

Board the **Essex Steam Train** for a ride through the Connecticut countryside (☎ 800/377–3987 ⊕ www.essexsteamtrain.com) or float through northern Rhode Island on the **Blackstone Valley Explorer** riverboat (☎ 401/724–2200 ⊕ www.rivertourblackstone.com).

DID YOU KNOW?

Fall foliage in Stowe, Vermont begins the last week in September and lasts until the second week in October. You can take a gondola up to the peak of the state's highest mountain for an aerial view or stroll down Main Street for a view of the beautiful Stowe Community Church.

VERMONT FALL FOLIAGE DRIVE

Nearly 80% of Vermont is forested, with cities few and far between. The interior of Vermont is a rural playground for leaf peepers, and it's widely considered to have the most intense range of foliage colors anywhere on the continent. The few distractions from the dark reds, yellows, oranges, and russets—the tiny towns and hamlets—are as pristine as nature itself.

Begin this drive in Manchester Village, along the old-fashioned, well-to-do homes lining Main Street, and drive south to Arlington, North Bennington, and Old Bennington. Stop first just a mile south along 7A at **Hildene**, the Lincoln family home. The 412 acres of explorable grounds here are ablaze with color, and the views over the Battenkill Valley are as good as any you can find anywhere. Continue south another mile along 7A to **Equinox Nursery**, where you can pick your own pumpkin from a huge patch, try delicious apple cider and cider doughnuts, and take in the stunning countryside. A few more miles south along 7A is the small town of Arlington.

BEST TIME TO GO

Late September and early October are the times to go, with the southern area peaking about a week later than the north. Remember to book hotels in advance. The state has a Fall Foliage Hotline and an online interactive map (☎ *800/828–3239* ⊕ *www. foliage-vermont.com*). The drive from Manchester to Bennington outlined here is just 30 minutes, but a relaxed day is best to take in all the sights.

2

From 7A in Arlington you can take two adventurous and stunning detours. One is pure foliage: follow 313 west a few miles to the New York State border for more beautiful views. Or head east a mile to East Arlington where delightful stores await you, including a chocolate emporium. (You can continue even farther east from this spot to Kelly Stand Road leading into the Green Mountains; this is a little-known route that can't be beat.) Back on 7A South in Arlington, stop at the **Cheese House**, the delightfully cheesy roadside attraction.

Farther south into Shaftsbury is **Clear Brook Farm**, a brilliant place for cider and fresh produce and pumpkins. Robert Frost spent much of his life in South Shaftsbury, and you can learn about his life at his former home, the **Stone House**. From South Shaftsbury take Route 67 through North Bennington and continue on to Route 67A in Old Bennington. Go up the 306-foot-high **Bennington Battle Monument** to survey the seasonal views across four states. Back down from the clouds, walk a few serene blocks to the cemetery of the **Old First Church**, where Robert Frost is buried, and contemplate his autumnal poem, "Nothing Gold Can Stay."

NEED A BREAK?

Equinox Valley Nursery. This nursery carries fresh produce, seasonal snacks, and is full of family-friendly fall activities—a corn maze, pumpkin golf (mini golf played with small pumpkins), hay rides, and pumpkin carving. ⊠ *1158 Main St., Manchester* ☎ *802/362–2610* ⊕ *www. equinoxvalleynursery.com* ⊠ *Free.*

Clear Brook Farm. Set on more than 25 acres, Clear Brook Farm sells its own organic produce, in addition to baked goods and other seasonal treats. ⊠ *47 Hidden Valley Rd., Manchester* ☎ *802/442–4273* ⊕ *www. clearbrookfarm.com.*

The Cheese House. Get your Vermont cheddar fix at the The Cheese House, which also sells maple syrup and other local products and gifts. ⊠ *5187 Vermont Rte. 7A, Arlington* ☎ *802/375–9033* ⊕ *www. thevermontcheesehouse. com* ⊠ *Free* ⊙ *Closed Tues.*

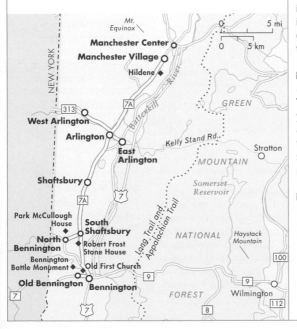

NEW HAMPSHIRE FALL FOLIAGE DRIVE

With its quaint villages graced with green commons, white town halls, and covered bridges, southwestern New Hampshire is dominated by the imposing rocky summit of Mt. Monadnock and brilliant colors in fall. The Kancamagus Highway is another classic foliage route, but for more solitude and less traffic, try this more accessible route that peaks a few weeks later than the state's far north.

The Granite State is the second-most forested state in the nation; by Columbus Day the colors of the leaves of its maple, birch, elm, oak, beech, and ash trees range from green to gold, purple to red, and orange to auburn. Routes 12, 101, 202, and 124 compose a loop around Mt. Monadnock. Start in Keene with a cup of coffee at Prime Roast; for New Hampshire–made products, take a walk on Main Street or detour west on Route 9 to reach **Stonewall Farm** for something more country.

BEST TIME TO GO

Early October is best time to view foliage in southern New Hampshire, but the time can vary by up to four weeks. For daily leaf changes, contact **Visit New Hampshire** (☎ *800/258-3608* ⊕ *www. visitnh.gov*).

PLANNING YOUR TIME

Expect to travel about 55 miles. The journey can take up to a full day if you stop to explore along the way.

2

From Keene, travel east on Route 101 through Dublin and over Pack Monadnock, a 2,290-foot peak (not to be confused with the 3,165-foot Grand, or Mt. Monadnock). In quaint **Peterborough**, browse the local stores, whose attitude and selection mirror the state's independent spirit.

Then turn south on Route 202 toward Jaffrey Village. Just west on Route 124, in historic Jaffrey Center, be sure to visit the **Meeting House Cemetery,** where author Willa Cather is buried. A side trip, 4 miles south on Route 202, leads to the majestic **Cathedral of the Pines** in Rindge, one of the best places in the region for foliage viewing because the evergreens offset the brilliant shades of red.

Heading west on Route 124, you can take Dublin Road to the main entrance of **Monadnock State Park** or continue along to the Old Toll Road parking area for one of the most popular routes up the mountain, the **Halfway House Trail**. All the hiking trails have great views, including the area's many lakes. Continuing on Route 124, you come to Fitzwilliam and Route 12; turn north back to Keene.

NEED A BREAK?

Stonewall Farm. This nonprofit working farm teaches about the importance of agriculture. The farm offers an active schedule of events, including maple sugaring and seasonal horse-drawn hayrides. Walking trails wind throughout the farm—in winter you can borrow snowshoes for free. Young children love the discovery room, and the interactive greenhouse is geared for all ages.
✉ *242 Chesterfield Rd., Keene* ☎ *603/357–7278* ⊕ *www.stonewallfarm.org* ⊙ *Weekdays 9–4:30.*

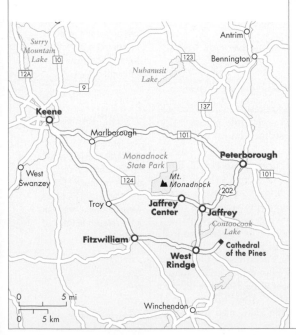

INLAND MAINE FALL FOLIAGE DRIVE

Swaths of pine, spruce, and fir trees offset the red, orange, and yellow of maples and birches along this popular foliage drive through Western Maine's mountains, but hardwoods largely dominate the landscape.

Wending its way to the four-season resort town of Rangeley, near its northern terminus, the route passes by or near stunning overlooks, forest-lined lakes, waterfalls, hiking trails, and a state park.

From Mexico, Route 17 heads north from U.S. 2, flowing past old homesteads and fields along the Swift River Valley before making the winding, mountainous ascent to **Height of Land**, the drive's literal pinnacle. This must-stop overlook has off-road parking, interpretive panels, stone seating, and a path to the nearby **Appalachian Trail**. Mountain vistas are reflected in the many (and often connected) lakes, ponds, rivers, and streams. On a clear day you can see west to New Hampshire and Canada. **Mooselookmeguntic Lake** and **Upper Richardson Lake** seem to float in the sea of forestland below. A few miles north of here is an overlook for Rangeley Lake, also with interpretive panels.

BEST TIME TO GO

Fall color usually peaks in the Rangeley area in the first or second week of October. Get fall foliage updates at ⊕ *www.mainefoliage.com*.

PLANNING YOUR TIME

The Rangeley Lakes National Scenic Byway (⊕ *www.byways.org*) makes up much of this 59-mile drive (1½ hours without stops), but plan for a relaxed full day of exploring.

2

In tiny, welcoming Oquossoc, where Routes 17 and 4 meet, **The Farmer's Daughter** welcomes passersby with displays of pumpkins and mums during autumn. Inside the seasonal specialty foods store you can pick up apple cider and picnic items. Or stop at the **Gingerbread House Restaurant** for a meal, or just ice cream or baked goods. The hamlet is also home to the **Rangeley Outdoor Sporting Heritage Museum**, where you can learn why visitors have come here to fish, hunt, and enjoy the outdoors since the mid-1800s.

Rangeley, 7 miles east on Route 4, has restaurants, inns, waterfront parks, and outdoorsy shops. The countryside sweeps into view along public hiking trails at both **Saddleback Maine** ski resort and the 175-acre **Wilhelm Reich Museum**.

The road to **Rangeley Lake State Park** is accessible from both Routes 4 and 17, as is the **Appalachian Trail**. Overhanging foliage frames waterfalls at the scenic rest areas at or near each end of the drive: Smalls Falls on Route 4, the byway's eastern terminus, and Coos Canyon on Route 17 en route to Height of Land. Both spots have several falls, swimming holes, and paths with views of the drops. Coos Canyon is along the Swift River, a destination for recreational gold panning. You can rent or buy panning equipment at **Coos Canyon Rock and Gift**, across from its namesake. It also sells sandwiches and snacks.

NEED A BREAK?

The Farmer's Daughter. At The Farmer's Daughter, much of the produce—including pumpkins and gourds come fall—is from the family farm. At the bakery counter you can buy a cup of coffee or apple cider in season. ✉ *13 Rumford Rd., Oquossoc* ☎ *207/864-2492.*

Wilhelm Reich Museum. This museum showcases the life and work of controversial physician-scientist Wilhelm Reich (1897–1957). There are magnificent views from the observatory and the many trails on the 175-acre grounds. ✉ *19 Orgonon Circle, off Rte. 4, Rangeley* ☎ *207/864-3443* ⊕ *www.wilhelmreichtrust.org* ▣ *Museum $6, grounds free* ☉ *Museum July and Aug., Wed.–Sun. 1-5; Sept., Sat. 1-5. Grounds daily 9–5.*

Rangeley Lakes Heritage Trust. This trust protects 13,000 acres of area land. It has trail maps and information about outdoor activities in the area. ✉ *52 Carry Rd., Oquossoc* ☎ *207/864-7311* ⊕ *www.rlht.org.*

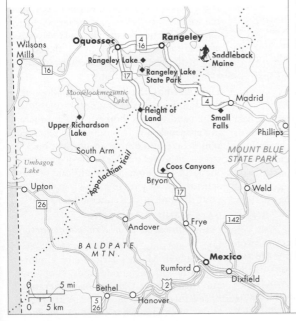

GREAT ITINERARIES

NEW HAMPSHIRE AND MAINE

The Coast and Mountains, 7 Days

Revel in the coastlines of two New England states—New Hampshire and Maine—on the path from the region's smallest shoreline, to the its highest peak, Mt. Washington. An assortment of New England's coastal treasures are at your fingertips as you pilot the ins and outs of the jagged northeastern coastline, before ascending the heights of the White Mountains.

DAY 1: NEW HAMPSHIRE COAST

Kick off your trek in the southeastern corner of the Granite State. New Hampshire fronts the Atlantic for a scant 18 miles, but its coastal landmarks range from honky-tonk **Hampton Beach** to quiet **Odiorne Point State Park** in Rye and pretty Portsmouth, where the cream of pre-Revolutionary society built Georgian- and Federal-style mansions—visit a few at the **Strawbery Banke Museum.** Stay the night in **Portsmouth** at the centrally located **Ale House Inn.**

DAY 2: THE YORKS
(30-minute drive from Portsmouth)

Much of the appeal of the Maine Coast lies in its geographical contrasts, from its long stretches of swimming and walking beaches in the south to the cliff-edged, rugged, rocky coasts in the north. And not unlike the physical differences of the shoreline, each town along the way reveals a slightly different character, starting with **York.**

In **York Village** take a leisurely stroll through the seven buildings of the **Old York Historical Society,** getting a glimpse of 18th-century life in this gentrified town. Spend time wandering amid the shops or walking the nature trails and beaches around York

Harbor. There are several grand lodging options here, most with views of the harbor. If you prefer a livelier pace, continue on to **York Beach,** a haven for families with plenty of entertainment venues. Stop at **Fox's Lobster House** after visiting **Nubble Light** for a seaside lunch or dinner.

DAYS 3: OGUNQUIT AND THE KENNEBUNKS
(35-minute drive from York)

For well over a century, **Ogunquit** has been a favorite vacation spot for those looking to combine the natural beauty of the ocean with a sophisticated environment. Take a morning walk along the **Marginal Way** to see the waves crashing on the rocks. In **Perkins Cove,** have lunch, stroll the shopping areas, or sign on with a lobster-boat cruise to learn about Maine's most important fishery—the state's lobster industry supplies more than 90% of the world's lobster intake. See the extraordinary collection at the **Ogunquit Museum of American Art,** take in a performance at one of the several theater venues, or just spend time on the beach.

Head north to the Kennebunks, allowing at least two hours to wander through the shops and historic homes of **Dock Square** in **Kennebunkport.** This is an ideal place to rent a bike and amble around the backstreets, head out on Ocean Avenue to view the large mansions, or ride to one of the several beaches to relax awhile. Spend your third night in Kennebunkport.

DAYS 4 AND 5: PORTLAND
(45-minute drive from Kennebunkport)

If you have time, you can easily spend several days in Maine's largest city, exploring its historic neighborhoods, shopping and eating in the **Old Port,** or visiting one of several excellent museums. A brief side trip to **Cape Elizabeth** takes you to **Portland**

Head Light, Maine's first lighthouse, which was commissioned by George Washington in 1787. The lighthouse is on the grounds of **Fort Williams Park** and is an excellent place to bring a picnic. Be sure to spend some time wandering the ample grounds. There are also excellent walking trails (and views) at nearby **Two Lights State Park.** If you want to take a boat tour while in Portland, get a ticket for Casco Bay Lines and see some of the islands that dot the bay. Spend two nights in Portland.

DAY 6: BRETTON WOODS
(3-hour drive from Portland)

Wake up early and drive to Bretton Woods, where you will spend nights six and seven. The driving time from Portland to Bretton Woods is approximately three hours, due to two-lane, steep mountain roads. ■TIP→ Be sure to drive a four-wheel-drive vehicle in winter. Drive northwest along U.S. 302 toward **Sebago Lake,** a popular water-sports area in the summer, and continue on toward the time-honored New England towns of Naples and Bridgton. Just 15 miles from the border of New Hampshire, and nearing Crawford Notch, U.S. 302 begins to thread through New Hampshire's **White Mountains,** passing beneath brooding **Mt. Washington** before arriving in Bretton Woods.

DAY 7: THE WHITE MOUNTAINS

In Bretton Woods, the **Mt. Washington Cog Railway** still chugs to the summit, and the **Mount Washington Hotel** recalls the glory days of White Mountain resorts. Beloved winter activities here include snowshoeing and skiing on the grounds of the Mount Washington Resort. Afterwards, defrost with a cup of steaming hot cider while checking out vintage photos of the International Monetary Conference, held here in 1944.

MAINE'S NORTHERN COAST

Portland to Acadia
National Park, 6 Days

Lighthouses, beaches, lobster rolls, and water sports—Maine's northern coast has something for everyone. Quaint seaside villages and towns line the shore as U.S. 1 winds its way toward the easternmost swath of land in the United States at Quoddy Head State Park. Maine's only National Park, Acadia, is a highlight of the tour, drawing more than 2 million visitors per year.

DAY 1: PORTLAND TO BRUNSWICK

Use Maine's maritime capital as your jumping-off point to head farther up the Maine Coast, or, as Mainers call it, "Down East." Plan to spend half of your

first day in Portland, then head to Brunswick for the night.

Portland shows off its restored waterfront at the **Old Port**. From there, before you depart, you can grab a bite at either of two classic Maine eateries: **Gilbert's Chowderhouse** or **Becky's Diner**. For a peek at the freshest catch of the day, wander over to the **Harbor Fish Market,** a Portland institution since 1968, and gaze upon Maine lobsters and other delectable seafood. Two lighthouses on nearby **Cape Elizabeth, Two Lights** and **Portland Head,** still stand vigil.

Following U.S. 1, travel northeast along the ragged, island-strewn coast of Down East Maine and make your first stop at the retail outlets of **Freeport,** home of **L.L. Bean.** More than 3 million people visit the massive flagship store every year, where you can find everything from outerwear to camping equipment. Just 10 miles north of Freeport on U.S. 1, **Brunswick,** Maine is home to the campus of **Bowdoin College** and also features a superb coastline for kayaking. Spend the night in Brunswick at one of the many inns that line U.S. 1.

DAY 2: BATH
(1-hour-and-45-minute drive from Brunswick to Rockland)

From Brunswick, head to **Bath,** Maine's shipbuilding capital, and tour the **Maine Maritime Museum,** stopping for lunch on the waterfront. Check out the boutiques and antiques shops, or take in the plenitude of beautiful homes. From here it's a 30-minute drive down Route 127 to **Reid State Park,** where you will find a quiet beach lining Sheepscot Bay, and maybe even a sand dollar or two to take home if you arrive at low tide. For a stunning vista, make your way to **Griffith Head.**

Drive north on Georgetown Island and reconnect with U.S. 1. Continue through the towns of **Wiscasset** and **Damariscotta,** where you may find yourself pulling over to stop at the outdoor flea markets and intriguing antiques shops that line the road. Another hour from here is **Rockland,** Maine, where you'll spend your second night.

DAY 3: ROCKLAND, CAMDEN, AND CASTINE
(1½-hour drive from Rockland to Castine)

From Rockland, spend the day cruising on one of the majestic schooners that set sail from here or reserve a tee time at **Somerset Resorts'** 18-hole championship course that overlooks the Rockland Harbor. If you're an art lover, save some time for Rockland's **Farnsworth Art Museum** and the **Wyeth Center.**

In **Camden** and Castine, exquisite inns occupy homes built from inland Maine's gold and timber. These are perfect places to stay overnight as you make your way closer to Acadia National Park. Camden is a beautiful seaside town with hundreds of boats bobbing in the harbor, immaculately kept antique homes, streets lined with boutiques and specialty stores, and restaurants serving lobster at every turn. The modest (by Maine standards, anyway) hills of nearby Mt. Battie offer good hiking and a great spot from which to picnic and view the surrounding area. Camden is one of the hubs for the beloved and historic windjammer fleet—there is no better way to see the area than from the deck of one of these graceful beauties.

DAYS 4 AND 5: MOUNT DESERT ISLAND AND ACADIA NATIONAL PARK
(1-hour-and-15-minute-drive from Castine to Bar Harbor)

On Day 4, head out early for **Bar Harbor** and plan to spend two nights here, using the bustling village as jumping-off point for the park—Bar Harbor is less than 5 miles from the entrance to **Mount Desert Island**'s 27-mile Park Loop Road. Spend at least a day exploring **Acadia National Park**, Maine's only national park and its most popular tourist destination. Popular ways of enjoying the island's natural beauty include kayaking along the coast, biking the 45-mile, historic, unpaved, carriage-road system, and driving to the summit of **Cadillac Mountain** to enjoy the stunning panorama.

DAY 6: BAR HARBOR TO QUODDY HEAD STATE PARK
(2½-hour drive from Bar Harbor)

About 100 miles farther along U.S. 1 and "Way Down East" is **Quoddy Head State Park** in Lubec, Maine. Here, on the easternmost tip of land in the United States, sits the **West Quoddy Head Lighthouse,** one of 60 lighthouses that dot Maine's rugged coastline. Depending on the time of year, you might be lucky enough to catch the East Coast's first sunrise.

VERMONT

Best of the Green Mountain State, 7 Days

Following roads that weave through the Green Mountains and charming towns, this 200-mile journey is ideal for all seasons. It has Vermont covered from top to bottom.

DAY 1: BRATTLEBORO

Artsy **Brattleboro** is the perfect place to begin a tour of Vermont and is worth a day to do some shopping and exploring. Take in a movie at the art-deco **Latchis Theatre,** browse in a bookstore, or simply grab a cup of joe and people-watch. For dinner, make a reservation well in advance at tiny **T.J. Buckley's,** one of the best restaurants in the state. Spend one night in Brattleboro.

DAY 2: BRATTLEBORO TO KILLINGTON
(2½-hour drive from Brattleboro)

Depart from Brattleboro heading west on Route 9 and link up with Route 100 in Wilmington. As you travel north along the eastern edge of **Green Mountain National Forest,** you'll pass a plethora of panoramic overlooks and delightful ski towns. Stop to snap a photo or take a moment to peruse what's for sale at a funky general store, as you meander toward gigantic Killington Peak. Spend the night in **Killington,** the largest ski resort in Vermont. Skiers: one of the closest places to the slopes to stay is **The Mountain Top Inn & Resort.**

DAYS 3 AND 4: KILLINGTON

Wake up early to carve the mountain's fresh powder in winter. In summer, enjoy trails long after the ground has thawed, when they are opened to mountain bikers and hikers. For a more leisurely activity, try your hand at the 18-hole disc-golf course. Spend two nights here exploring Killington's more than 20 lifts and 140 trails.

DAY 5: KILLINGTON TO BURLINGTON
(2½-hour drive from Killington)

Continue on Route 100 north until you reach Hancock and then head west onto Route 125 as you enter the land of poet Robert Frost. Frost spent almost 40 years living in Vermont, and summered in the nearby tiny mountain town of Ripton, where he wrote numerous poems. Plaques along the 1.2-mile **Robert Frost Interpretive Trail,** a quiet woodland walk that takes about 30 minutes, display commemorative quotes from his poems, including his timeless piece, "The Road Not Taken." After your stroll, head north on U.S. 7 until you hit Burlington.

Burlington, Vermont's largest city and home to the **University of Vermont,** is located on the eastern shore of Lake Champlain. Bustling in the summer and fall, the **Burlington Farmers' Market** is filled with everything from organic meats and cheeses to freshly cut flowers and maple syrup. Spend the night in Burlington. At night, check out **Nectar's,** where the band Phish played its first bar gig, or wander into any of the many other pubs and cafés that attract local musicians.

DAY 6: SHELBURNE AND LAKE CHAMPLAIN
(10-minute drive from Burlington to Magic Hat; 20-minute drive from Burlington to Shelburne Farms)

Basing yourself in Burlington, you can take a day trip south to the **Magic Hat Brewing Company,** in operation since 1994, on your second day in the area. It was at the forefront of Vermont's microbrewery explosion. Take a free half-hour guided or self-guided tour of the Artifactory (even dogs are welcome), and wet your whistle by filling a growler from one of the 48 taps pumping out year-round, seasonal, and experimental brews. With one brewery for about every 24,000 Vermonters, the Green Mountain State is tops in the United States. A stone's throw farther down U.S. 7, in **Shelburne,** is family-friendly **Shelburne Farms.** Watch the process of making cheese from start to finish

2

or wander the gorgeous 1,400-acre estate designed by Frederick Law Olmsted, co-creator of New York's Central Park. The grounds overlook beautiful **Lake Champlain** and are the perfect place to picnic. If you're visiting in late July, don't miss the **Vermont Cheesemakers Festival,** showcasing more than 200 varieties of cheese crafted by 40 local purveyors. If you can't get enough, you can opt to spend the night at Shelburne Farms.

DAY 7: STOWE
(1-hour drive from Burlington to Stowe)

A 30-minute drive down Interstate 89 from Burlington reunites you with Route 100 in the small town of Waterbury. Head north toward Stowe, and, in under 2 miles you can make the obligatory pit stop at **Ben & Jerry's Ice Cream Factory.** The factory tour offers a behind-the-scenes look at how the ice cream is made; you can taste some of the limited-release creations only available at the factory.

Next, set out for the village of **Stowe.** Proximity to Mt. Mansfield, Vermont's highest peak at 4,395 feet, has made Stowe a popular ski destination since the 1930s. If there's snow on the ground, hit the slopes, hitch a ride on a one-horse open sleigh, or simply put your feet up by the fire and enjoy a Heady Topper beer (an unfiltered, hoppy, American Double IPA beloved by Vermonters). In warmer weather, pop into the cute shops and art galleries that line the town's main street and sample some of the finest cheddar cheese and maple syrup that Vermont has to offer. Rejuvenate yourself at **Topnotch Resort and Spa,** which offers more than 100 different treatments. Spend your final night here.

VERMONT

WELCOME TO VERMONT

TOP REASONS TO GO

★ **Small-Town Charm:** Vermont rolls out a seemingly never-ending supply of tiny, charming towns made of steeples, general stores, village squares, red barns, and B&Bs.

★ **Ski Resorts:** The East's best skiing takes place in uncrowded, modern facilities, with great views and lots and lots of fresh snow.

★ **Fall Foliage:** Perhaps the most vivid colors in North America wave from the trees in September and October, when the whole state is ablaze.

★ **Gorgeous Landscapes:** This sparsely populated, heavily forested state is an ideal place to find peace and quiet amid the mountains, valleys, and lakes.

★ **Tasty and Healthy Eats:** The state's rich soil and focus on local farming and ingredients yields great cheeses, dairies, orchards, vineyards, local food resources, and restaurants.

1 Southern Vermont. Most people's introduction to the state is southern Vermont, accessible by car from New York and Boston. As elsewhere across the state, you'll find unspoiled towns, romantic B&Bs, rural farms, and pristine forests. There are two notable exceptions: sophisticated Manchester has upscale shopping, and independent Brattleboro remains a hippie outpost and environmentally conscious town.

2 Central Vermont. Similar to southern Vermont in character and geography, central Vermont's star is Stowe, the quintessential ski town east of the Mississippi. Woodstock, Waitsfield, and Middlebury are among its charming small towns.

3 Northern Vermont. The northernmost part of the state is a place of contrasts. Burlington, with dramatic views of Lake Champlain and the Adirondacks, is the state's most populous city at around 60,000 residents; it's an arts-loving, laid-back college town with a sophisticated local food scene. To the east, the landscape becomes increasingly rural, with stupendous natural beauty and almost no significant population, making the Northeast Kingdom a refuge for nature lovers and aficionados of getting away from it all.

GETTING ORIENTED

Vermont can be divided into three regions. The southern part of the state, flanked by Bennington on the west and Brattleboro on the east, played an important role in Vermont's Revolutionary War–era drive to independence (yes, there was once a Republic of Vermont) and its eventual statehood. The central part is characterized by rugged mountains and the gently rolling dairy lands near Lake Champlain. Northern Vermont is home to the state's capital, Montpelier, and its largest city, Burlington, as well as its most rural area, the Northeast Kingdom. The Green Mountains run north to south in the center of the state and are covered in protected national forest.

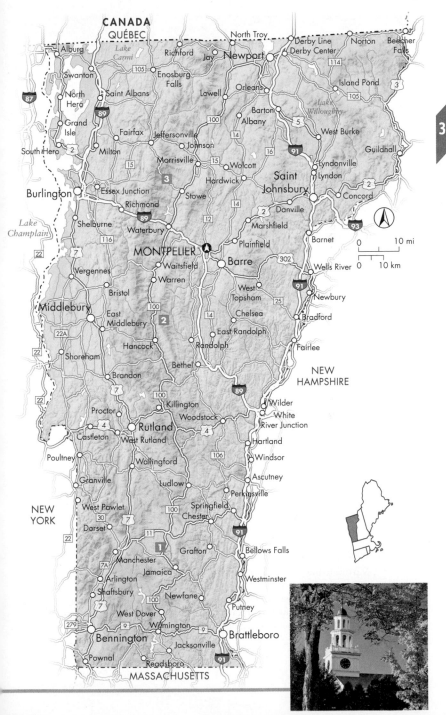

CANADA
QUÉBEC

North Troy
Alburg
Lake
Carmi
Richford
Jay
Newport
Derby Line
Derby Center
Norton
Beecher
Falls

Swanton
Enosburg
Falls
114
3

87
North
Hero
Saint Albans
Lowell
Orleans
Island Pond
105

Grand
Isle
Fairfax
Jeffersonville
Barton
Albany
West Burke
5

89
Johnson
14
Guildhall

South Hero
2
Milton
Morrisville
15
Wolcott
Lyndonville
Lyndon

15
Hardwick
Saint
Johnsbury
2
Concord

Burlington
Essex Junction
3
Stowe
14
Danville

Richmond
12
Marshfield
Barnet
93

Lake
Champlain
Shelburne
Waterbury
2
Plainfield
Wells River

116
MONTPELIER
Waitsfield
Barre
302
0   10 mi

22
7
Warren
West
Topsham
91
Newbury
0   10 km

Vergennes
Bristol
100
Chelsea
Bradford

Middlebury
East
Middlebury
2
14
Fairlee
NEW
HAMPSHIRE

22A
Hancock
Randolph
East Randolph

22
Shoreham
Bethel
89

Brandon
7
Killington
Woodstock
Wilder
White
River Junction

22
Proctor
4
Rutland
4
Hartland

Castleton
West Rutland
106
Windsor

Poultney
Wallingford
Ascutney

Granville
Ludlow
Perkinsville

NEW
YORK
West Pawlet
30
7
100
Springfield
Chester
91

22
Dorset
11
Grafton
Bellows Falls

7A
Manchester
Jamaica
Westminster

Arlington
Shaftsbury
100
Newfane
Putney

7
West Dover
Wilmington
Brattleboro

279
9
9

Bennington
Jacksonville

Pownal
Readsboro
91

MASSACHUSETTS

3

Updated by
Mike Dunphy

Vermont is an entire state of hidden treasures and unspoiled scenery. Wander anywhere in the state—nearly 80% is forest—and you'll travel a pristine countryside dotted with farms and framed by mountains. Tiny towns with picturesque church steeples, village greens, and clapboard Colonial-era houses are perfect for exploring.

Sprawl has no place here. Highways are devoid of billboards by law, and on some roads cows still stop traffic twice a day en route to and from the pasture. In spring, sap boils in sugarhouses, some built generations ago, and up the road a chef trained at the New England Culinary Institute in Montpelier might use the resulting maple syrup to glaze a pork tenderloin.

It's the landscape, for the most part, that attracts people to Vermont. The rolling hills belie the rugged terrain underneath the green canopy of forest growth. In summer, clear lakes and streams provide ample opportunities for swimming, boating, and fishing; the hills attract hikers and mountain bikers. The more than 14,000 miles of roads, many of them only intermittently traveled by cars, are great for biking. In fall the leaves have their last hurrah, painting the mountainsides a stunning show of yellow, gold, red, and orange. Vermont has the best ski resorts in the eastern United States, centered along the spine of the Green Mountains running north to south. The traditional heart of skiing is the town of Stowe. Almost anywhere you go, any time of year, it will make you reach for your camera.

Vermont may seem locked in time, but technological sophistication appears where you least expect it: wireless Internet access in a 19th-century farmhouse-turned-inn and cell phone coverage from the state's highest peaks. Like an old farmhouse under renovation, Vermont's historic exterior is still the main attraction.

PLANNING

WHEN TO GO

In summer the state is lush and green, although in winter the hills and towns are blanketed with snow and skiers travel from around the world to challenge Vermont's peaks. Fall, however, is always the most amazing time to come. If you have never seen the kaleidoscope of Vermont's autumn colors, it's well worth braving the slow-moving traffic and paying the extra money for fall lodging. The only time things really slow down is during "mud" season—otherwise known as late spring. Even innkeepers have told guests to come another time. Activities in the Champlain Islands essentially come to a halt in the winter, except for ice fishing and snowmobiling. Two of the state's biggest attractions, Shelburne Farms and the Shelburne Museum, are closed mid-October through April. Otherwise, Vermont is open for business all year.

PLANNING YOUR TIME

There are many ways to take advantage of Vermont's beauty: skiing or hiking its mountains, biking or driving its back roads, fishing or sailing its waters, shopping for local products, visiting its museums and sights, or simply finding the perfect inn and never leaving the front porch.

Distances are relatively short, yet the mountains and back roads will slow a traveler's pace. You can see a representative north–south section of Vermont in a few days; if you have up to a week, you can hit the highlights. Note that many inns have two-night-minimum stays on weekends and holidays.

GETTING HERE AND AROUND

AIR TRAVEL

Delta, JetBlue, United, Porter Airlines, and US Airways fly into Burlington International Airport. Rutland State Airport has daily service to and from Boston on Cape Air.

BOAT TRAVEL

Lake Champlain Ferries. This company operates three ferry routes between the Vermont and New York shores: Grand Isle–Plattsburgh, NY; Burlington–Port Kent, NY; and Charlotte–Essex, NY. ☎ *802/864–9804* ⊕ *www.ferries.com.*

CAR TRAVEL

Vermont is divided by a mountainous north–south middle, with a main highway on either side: scenic Route 7 on the western side and Interstate 91 (which begins in New Haven and runs through Hartford, central Massachusetts, and along the Connecticut River in Vermont to the Canadian border) on the east. Interstate 89 runs from New Hampshire across central Vermont from White River Junction to Burlington and up to the Canadian border. For current road conditions, call ☎ *800/429–7623.*

TRAIN TRAVEL

Amtrak. Amtrak has daytime service linking Washington, D.C., with Brattleboro, Bellows Falls, White River Junction, Montpelier, Waterbury, Essex Junction, and St. Albans via the *Vermonter.* Amtrak's *Ethan Allen Express* connects New York City with Castleton and Rutland. ☎ *800/872–7245* ⊕ *www.amtrak.com.*

RESTAURANTS

Everything that makes Vermont good and wholesome is distilled in its eateries, making the regional cuisine much more defined than that in neighboring states. With an almost political intensity, farmers and chefs have banded together to insist on utilizing Vermont's wonderful bounty. Especially in summer, the produce and meats are impeccable. Many of the state's restaurants belong to the **Vermont Fresh Network** (⊕ *www. vermontfresh.net*), a partnership that encourages chefs to create menus from local produce.

Great chefs are coming to Vermont for the quality of life, and the New England Culinary Institute is a recruiting ground for new talent. Seasonal menus use local fresh herbs and vegetables along with native game. Look for imaginative approaches to native New England foods such as maple syrup (Vermont is the largest U.S. producer), dairy products (especially cheese), native fruits and berries, "new Vermont" products such as salsa and salad dressings, and venison, quail, pheasant, and other game.

Your chances of finding a table for dinner vary with the season: lengthy waits are common in tourist centers at peak times (a reservation is always advisable); the slow months are April and November. Some of the best dining is at country inns. *Prices in the reviews are the average cost of a main course at dinner or, if dinner is not served, at lunch.*

HOTELS

Vermont's only large chain hotels are in Burlington and Rutland. Elsewhere it's just quaint inns, bed-and-breakfasts, and small motels. The many lovely and sometimes quite luxurious inns and B&Bs provide what many people consider the quintessential Vermont lodging experience. Most areas have traditional base ski condos; at these you sacrifice charm for ski-and-stay deals and proximity to the lifts. Rates are highest during foliage season, from late September to mid-October, and lowest in late spring and November, although many properties close during these times. Winter is high season at Vermont's ski resorts. *Prices in the reviews are the lowest cost of a standard double room in high season.*

TOURS

Country Inns Along the Trail. This company arranges guided and self-guided hiking, skiing, and biking trips from inn to inn in Vermont. ✉ *52 Park St., Brandon* ☎ *802/247–3300, 800/838–3301* ⊕ *www.inntoinn. com.*

P.O.M.G. Bike Tours of Vermont. This outfitter, whose name is short for "Peace Of Mind Guaranteed," leads weekend and multiday bike tours around the state. ☎ *802/434–2270, 888/635–2453* ⊕ *www.pomgbike. com.*

Ski Vermont/Vermont Ski Areas Association. For skiing information, contact Ski Vermont/Vermont Ski Areas Association. ✉ *26 State St., Montpelier* ☎ *802/223–2439* ⊕ *www.skivermont.com.*

Vermont Bicycle Touring. This guide company leads bike tours across the state. ☎ *802/453–4811, 800/245–3868* ⊕ *www.vbt.com.*

VISITOR INFORMATION

Vermont Seasonal Hotline. This useful hotline has tips on peak foliage viewing locations and times, up-to-date snow conditions, and seasonal events. ☎ *802/828–3239.*

Vermont Department of Tourism and Marketing ✉ *6 Baldwin St., Drawer 33, Montpelier* ☎ *802/828–3237, 800/837–6668* ⊕ *www.vermontvacation.com.*

Regional Contacts Northeast Kingdom Travel and Tourism Association ☎ *802/626–8511, 800/884–8001* ⊕ *www.travelthekingdom.com.*

SOUTHERN VERMONT

Cross into the Green Mountain State from Massachusetts on Interstate 91, and you might feel as if you've entered a new country. There isn't a town in sight. What you see are forested hills punctuated by rolling pastures. When you reach Brattleboro, no fast-food joints or strip malls line the exits to signal your arrival at southeastern Vermont's gateway city. En route to downtown, you pass by Victorian-era homes on tree-lined streets. From Brattleboro you can cross over the spine of the Green Mountains toward Bennington and Manchester.

The state's southwest corner is the southern terminus of the Green Mountain National Forest, dotted with lakes, threaded with trails and old forest roads, and home to four big ski resorts: Bromley, Stratton, Mount Snow, and Haystack Mountain.

BRATTLEBORO

60 miles south of White River Junction.

Brattleboro has drawn political activists and earnest counter-culturists since the 1960s. Today the arty town of 12,000 is still politically and culturally active, making it Vermont's most offbeat outside of Burlington.

GETTING HERE AND AROUND

Brattleboro is near the intersection of Route 9, the principal east–west highway also known as the Molly Stark Trail, and Interstate 91. For downtown, use Exit 2 from Interstate 91.

ESSENTIALS

Visitor Information Brattleboro Area Chamber of Commerce ✉ *180 Main St.* ☎ *802/254–4565, 877/254–4565* ⊕ *www.brattleborochamber.org.*

EXPLORING

Brattleboro Museum and Art Center. Downtown is the hub of Brattleboro's art scene, with this museum in historic Union Station at the forefront. It presents changing exhibits created by locally, nationally, and internationally renowned artists. ✉ *10 Vernon St.* ☎ *802/257–0124* ⊕ *www. brattleboromuseum.org* 🎫 *$8* ⊙ *Sun., Mon., Wed., Thurs., 11–5; Fri., 11–7; Sat., 10–5.*

OFF THE BEATEN PATH

Putney. Nine miles upriver, this small town, with a population just short of 3,000, is the country cousin of bustling Brattleboro and is a haven for writers, artists, and craftspeople. There are dozens of pottery studios to visit and a few orchards. Each November dozens of artisans and

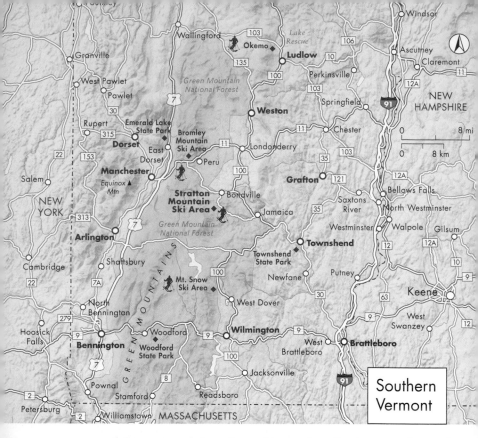

Southern Vermont

craftsmen open their studios and homes for a live demonstrations and plenty of fun during the Putney Craft Tour. ✉ *Putney*.

WHERE TO EAT

$
AMERICAN
✕ **Brattleboro Food Co-op.** This foodie hot spot has many charms, including different grades of self-serve maple syrup and reusable containers to store your bounty. Pick up a plate of curry chicken at the deli counter, then eat it in the glassy café area or out on the river-view patio. Local and organic is the focus in dishes like beef *satay* (skewered grilled meat). The newly expanded deli serves fabulous sandwiches. $ *Average main: $8* ✉ *2 Main St.* ☎ *802/257–0236* ⊕ *www.brattleborofoodcoop.com*.

$$
ITALIAN
✕ **Fireworks.** Stop by this trendy, airy, and colorful trattoria-style restaurant for flatbread pizzas, pastas, and salads any night of the week. In nice weather, check out the back patio. Try the daily specials and well-mixed cocktails. $ *Average main: $16* ✉ *69-73 Main St.* ☎ *802/254-2073* ⊕ *www.fireworksrestaurant.net/brattleboro* ☽ *No lunch*.

$$$$
AMERICAN
Fodor's Choice
★
✕ **Peter Havens.** Since coming under the ownership of chef Zachary Corbin, Peter Havens has added a new layer of polish to its already sterling reputation. This chic little bistro seems to know just how to perfectly prepare and present everything on the menu, drawing heavily on local sources. One room is painted a warm red, another in sage; both are punctuated by a rotating exhibitions of paintings, creating a look

OUTDOOR ACTIVITIES

Biking: Vermont, especially the often-deserted roads of the Northeast Kingdom, is great bicycle-touring country. Many companies lead weekend tours and weeklong trips throughout the state. If you'd like to go it on your own, most chambers of commerce have brochures highlighting good cycling routes in their area.

Canoeing and Kayaking: Getting on Vermont's many rivers and lakes is a great way to experience nature. Outfitters can be found almost anywhere there's water.

Fishing: Central Vermont is the heart of the state's warm-water lake and pond fishing area. Lake Champlain, stocked annually with salmon and lake trout, has become the state's ice-fishing capital.

Hiking: Vermont is an ideal state for hiking—nearly 80% of the state is forest, and trails are everywhere. The Long Trail runs the length of the state. It was the first portion of the Appalachian Tral to be completed and inspired the rest of the trail. Many bookstores in the state have numerous volumes dedicated to local hiking.

Skiing: The Green Mountains run through the middle of Vermont like a bumpy spine, visible from almost every point in the state; generous accumulations of snow make them an ideal site for skiing. Route 100 is also known as Skier's Highway, passing by 13 of the state's ski areas.

that is one of the most sophisticated in the state. Whatever your main dish, start off with the fabulous tuna tartare and a seasonal cocktail or glass from the superb wine list. [$] *Average main: $30* ✉ *32 Elliot St.* ☎ *802/257–3333* 🌐 *www.peterhavens.com* 🕒 *Closed Mon. and Tues. No lunch.*

$$$$ AMERICAN Fodor's Choice ★ 🍴 **T.J. Buckley's.** It's easy to miss this tiny restaurant, but it's worth seeking out as one of the most romantic eateries in Vermont. Open the doors to the sleek black 1920s diner and enter what amounts to a very intimate theater, with a mere 18 seats for the show. The stage is an open kitchen, the flames a few feet away, and working under the whisper of jazz and candlelight is the star of the show: Michael Fuller, the dashing owner and sole chef, who has been at the helm for 30 years. The contemporary menu is conveyed verbally each day and is based on locally available ingredients. [$] *Average main: $40* ✉ *132 Elliot St.* ☎ *802/257–4922* 🌐 *www.tjbuckleys.com* ✍ *Reservations essential* 🕒 *Closed Mon.–Wed.*

$$ BARBECUE 🍴 **Top of the Hill Grill.** Don't let the diminutive size of this roadside smokehouse deceive you. It houses some big flavors that locals line up for: hickory-smoked ribs, apple-smoked turkey, beef brisket, and pulled pork, to name a few. Homemade pecan pie is the dessert of choice. The restaurant probably has the best view in town, with outdoor picnic tables and a cozy enclosed area overlooking the West River. [$] *Average main: $15* ✉ *632 Putney Rd.* ☎ *802/258–9178* 🌐 *www.topofthehillgrill.com* 💳 *No credit cards* 🕒 *Closed Nov.–Mar.*

The rolling green hills of Putney are home to many organic farm operations.

WHERE TO STAY

$$$$
B&B/INN
Fodor's Choice
★

🏨 **Forty Putney Road.** Realizing her dream to run an inn, Rhonda Calhoun took over this French-style manse and has added her own colorful touch to the original features. **Pros:** caring host makes you feel like a guest, not a customer **Cons:** tight parking. $ *Rooms from: $239* ✉ *192 Putney Rd.* ☎ *802/254–6268, 800/941–2413* ⊕ *www.fortyputneyroad. com* 🛏 *5 rooms, 1 suite* ❙○❙ *Breakfast.*

$$$
B&B/INN
Fodor's Choice
★

🏨 **Hickory Ridge House.** If you're looking for a relaxing country getaway, this 1808 Federal-style mansion, a former sheep farm set on a wide meadow, is a sure bet. **Pros:** peaceful, property; great breakfast; quintessential B&B experience. **Cons:** not walking distance from town. $ *Rooms from: $175* ✉ *53 Hickory Ridge Rd., 11 miles north of Brattleboro, Putney* ☎ *802/387–5709, 800/380–9218* ⊕ *www. hickoryridgehouse.com* 🛏 *6 rooms, 1 cottage* ❙○❙ *Breakfast.*

$
HOTEL

🏨 **Latchis Hotel.** To stay in the heart of town, you won't find a more economical option than the three-story Latchis. **Pros:** heart-of-town location; lots of personality; reasonable rates. **Cons:** limited breakfast. $ *Rooms from: $110* ✉ *50 Main St.* ☎ *802/254–6300, 800/798–6301* ⊕ *www.latchis.com* 🛏 *30 rooms, 3 suites* ❙○❙ *Breakfast.*

NIGHTLIFE AND THE ARTS

THE ARTS

Latchis Theater. This art-deco movie theater, complete with statues and frescoes, shows four films at a time and hosts art exhibits. ✉ *50 Main St.* ☎ *802/254–6300* ⊕ *www.latchis.com.*

NIGHTLIFE

Metropolis Wine Bar & Cocktail Lounge. This popular lounge serves up signature infused cocktails, wine, and local beer, as well as finger food and live music. It has a hip, festive atmosphere. ⊠ *55 Elliot St.* ☎ *802/254–8500* ⊕ *www.metropoliswinebar.com.*

NEED A BREAK?

Mocha Joe's Cafe. This gathering spot for coffee and conversation takes great care in sourcing beans from places like Kenya, Ethiopia, and Guatemala. This is ground zero for Brattleboro's contemporary bohemian spirit. ⊠ *82 Main St., at Elliot St.* ☎ *802/257-5637* ⊕ *www.mochajoes.com*

> **BILLBOARDS AND VERMONT**
>
> Did you know that there are no billboards in Vermont? The state banned them in 1967 (similar laws exist in Maine, Alaska, and Hawaii), and the last one came down in 1975, so when you look out your window, you see trees and other scenic sights, not advertisements. (It may make playing the alphabet game with your child a bit difficult.)

3

SPORTS AND THE OUTDOORS

BIKING

Brattleboro Bicycle Shop. This shop rents hybrid bikes and does repair work. Maps and equipment are available. ⊠ *165 Main St.* ☎ *802/254–8644* ⊕ *www.bratbike.com.*

CANOEING

Vermont Canoe Touring Center. Canoes and kayaks are available for rent here. ⊠ *451 Putney Rd.* ☎ *802/257–5008* ⊕ *www.vermontcanoetouringcenter.com.*

SHOPPING

ART

Gallery in the Woods. This funky three-floor store sells art, jewelry, and light fixtures from around the world. Rotating shows take place in the upstairs and downstairs galleries. ⊠ *145 Main St.* ☎ *802/257–4777* ⊕ *www.galleryinthewoods.com.*

Vermont Artisan Designs. Ceramics, glass, wood, clothing, jewelry, and furniture from more than 300 artists are on display here. Rotating shows are in the small gallery upstairs. ⊠ *106 Main St.* ☎ *802/257–7044* ⊕ *www.vtart.com.*

BOOKS

Brattleboro Books. With more than 25,000 used books, this is a great spot to browse. ⊠ *36 Elliot St.* ☎ *802/257–7777* ⊕ *brattleborobooks. com* ⊙ *Mon.–Sat. 10–6, Sun. 11–5.*

FOOD

Serenity Herbs and Teas. Even if you're not an avid tea drinker, it's hard not to admire the passion and expertise of the proprietors of this elegant shop. Ask what makes a true Earl Grey and you'll learn more than you ever thought possible. All teas are hand-blended in the back. ⊠ *60 Elliot St.* ⊕ *www.serenityherbsandteas.com* ⊙ *Wed.–Sat. 11–5.*

WILMINGTON

18 miles west of Brattleboro.

The village of Wilmington, with its classic Main Street lined with 18th- and 19th-century buildings, anchors the Mount Snow Valley. Most of the valley's lodging and dining establishments, however, line Route 100, which travels 5 miles north to West Dover and Mount Snow, where skiers flock on winter weekends. The area abounds with cultural activity year-round, from concerts to art exhibits.

GETTING HERE AND AROUND

Wilmington is at the junction of Routes 9 and 100. West Dover and Mount Snow are a few miles to the north along Route 100.

ESSENTIALS

Visitor Information Mount Snow Valley Chamber of Commerce ✉ *21 W. Main St.* ☎ *802/464–8092, 877/887–6884* 🌐 *www.visitvermont.com.*

EXPLORING

FAMILY **Adams Farm.** At this working farm you can collect fresh eggs from the chicken coop, feed a rabbit, milk a goat, ride a tractor or a pony, or take sleigh rides in winter. A livestock barn is open November to mid-June; the animals roam free the rest of the year. ✉ *15 Higley Hill Rd., off Rte. 100* ☎ *802/464–3762* 🌐 *www.adamsfamilyfarm.com* 🎟 *$6.95* 🕒 *Mid-June–Oct., daily 10–4; Nov.–mid-June, Wed.–Sun. 10–4.*

FAMILY **Southern Vermont Natural History Museum.** This museum, 5 miles east of Wilmington, houses one of New England's largest collections of mounted birds, including three extinct species and a complete collection of mammals native to the Northeast. The museum also has live hawk and owl exhibits. There's also an adjacent 600-acre nature preserve. ✉ *7599 Rte. 9* ☎ *802/464–0048* 🌐 *www.vermontmuseum.org* 🎟 *$5* 🕒 *Weekdays 10–4, weekends 10–5.*

WHERE TO EAT

$$$ EUROPEAN 🍴 **Inn at Sawmill Farm.** No other restaurant in Vermont aims as high with its haute Continental food, wine, and service as the restaurant at Sawmill. Order a beer and the bottle is served chilled in a small ice bucket, as if it were champagne. This reverent service and deference to potables come from the top: chef-owner Brill Williams passionately cares for his 17,000-bottle cellar, the biggest restaurant collection in the state. Try the potato-crusted fish of the day served in beurre blanc or grilled loin of venison. Gourmands of Mount Snow, this is your place. [$] *Average main: $23* ✉ *7 Crosstown Rd., at Rte. 100, West Dover* ☎ *802/464–8131, 800/493–1133* 🌐 *www.theinnatsawmillfarm.com* 🕒 *Closed early Apr.–late May. No lunch.*

WHERE TO STAY

$$$ B&B/INN 🏨 **Deerhill Inn.** The picture of a quintessential New England inn, this is a truly charming spot. **Pros:** great restaurant; nicely renovated rooms. **Cons:** must drive to town and resort. [$] *Rooms from: $185* ✉ *14 Valley View Rd., West Dover* ☎ *802/464–3100, 800/993–3379* 🌐 *www.deerhill.com* 🛏 *10 rooms, 3 suites* 🍽 *Breakfast.*

CLOSE UP

Vermont Maple Syrup

Vermont is one of the country's smallest states, but it's the largest producer of maple syrup. A visit to a maple farm is a great way to learn all about sugaring, the process of taking maple tree sap and making syrup. Sap is stored in a sugar maple tree's roots in the winter, and in the spring when conditions are just right, the sap runs up and is capable of being tapped. Tapping season takes place in March and April, which is when all maple in the state is produced.

Maple sap is collected in buckets.

One of the best parts of visiting a maple farm is getting to taste the four grades of syrup. As the sugaring season goes on and days get warmer, the sap becomes progressively darker and stronger flavored. Color, clarity, and flavor define the four grades of syrup. Is one grade better than another? Nope. It's just a question of taste. Sap drawn early in the season produces the lightest color, and has the most delicate flavor: this is called Vermont Fancy. Vermont Grade A Medium Amber has a mellow flavor. Vermont Grade A Dark Amber is much more robust, and Vermont Grade B is the most flavorful, making it often the favorite of first-time tasters.

Is one syrup better than another? Can you actually tell the difference? You'd need an exceptionally nuanced palate to discern between one Vermont syrup and another, but aesthetics can alter taste, and authenticity counts. So when visiting a maple farm, make sure that this is a place that actually makes its own syrup, as opposed to just bottling or selling someone else's.

Morse Farm Maple Sugarworks. There's no better introduction to Vermont mapling than a visit to Morse Farm Maple Sugarworks in Montpelier, Vermont. Burr Morse's family has been mapling for more than 200 years, longer than anyone else in the state. Attractions here include a free tour of a sugar house, tastings, and an outdoor museum and woodshed theater. ⌧ *1168 County Rd., Montpelier* ☎ *800/242–2740* ⊕ *www. morsefarm.com.*

Vermont Maple Syrup. There are approximately 50 maple farms that are free and open all year to the public. The official industry Web site for Vermont Maple Syrup is a great resource that has a map of maple farms that host tours, a directory of producers open year-round, and a list of places you can order maple by mail. In addition, you can learn about the Annual Maple Open House weekend, which is when sugarhouses throughout the state open their doors to the public. ⊕ *www.vermontmaple. org.*

—Michael de Zayas

During the spring sugaring season water is boiled off the maple sap to concentrate the syrup's flavor.

$$$$ 🏨 **Grand Summit Hotel.** The hotel at Mount Snow is an easy choice
RESORT for skiers who don't care about anything but getting on the slopes
FAMILY as quickly as possible. **Pros:** easy ski access; modern property. **Cons:**
somewhat bland decor. $ *Rooms from: $328* ✉ *89 Grand Summit Way,
West Dover* ☎ *800/245-7669* ⊕ *www.mountsnow.com* ⇥ *104 rooms,
93 suites* ❍ *No meals.*

$$$ 🏨 **The Inn at Sawmill Farm.** Full of character and charm, this inn in a
B&B/INN converted barn has common rooms elegantly accented with English
chintzes, antiques, and Oriental rugs. **Pros:** spacious grounds; atten-
tive service. **Cons:** overload of floral prints in some rooms; room size
varies. $ *Rooms from: $175* ✉ *7 Crosstown Rd., at Rte. 100, West
Dover* ☎ *802/464–8131, 800/493–1133* ⊕ *www.theinnatsawmillfarm.
com* ⇥ *21 rooms* ⊙ *Closed early-Apr.–late May* ❍ *Multiple meal plans.*

$$$ 🏨 **White House of Wilmington.** It's hard to miss this 1915 Federal-style
B&B/INN mansion standing imposingly atop a high hill east of Wilmington. **Pros:**
intriguing property; intimate dining. **Cons:** not in town, so you have
to drive to everything; no children under eight. $ *Rooms from: $220*
✉ *178 Rte. 9* ☎ *802/464–2135, 800/541–2135* ⊕ *www.whitehouseinn.
com* ⇥ *15 rooms, 1 suite* ❍ *Breakfast.*

SPORTS AND THE OUTDOORS
BOATING
Green Mountain Flagship Company. Canoes and kayaks are available for
rent from May through Columbus Day on Lake Whitingham. ✉ *389
Rte. 9, 2 miles west of Wilmington* ☎ *802/464–2975.*

Molly Stark State Park. Molly Stark State Park is home to some of the
state's most popular snowshoe trails. Mount Olga Trail is a relatively

easy 1.7-mile hike climaxing with a 360-degree view of southern Vermont and northern Massachusetts. ✉ *705 Rte. 9 East* ☎ *802/464–5460* ⊕ *www.vtstateparks.com/htm/ mollystark.htm.*

SKI AREAS

Mount Snow. The closest major ski area to all of the Northeast's big cities, Mount Snow has a full roster of year-round activities. It prides itself on its 253 snowmaking fan guns, more than any other resort in North America. There are four major downhill areas. The main mountain is mostly intermediate terrain, while the north face includes the majority of the expert terrain. The south face, Sunbrook,

has wide, sunny trails. The trails are served by 20 lifts, including three high-speed quads and a six-passeger bubble lift called the Bluebird Express. The ski school's instruction program is designed to help skiers of all abilities, including kids. In summer, the 800-acre resort has an 18-hole golf course, 45 miles of mountain-biking trails, and an extensive network of hiking trails. ✉ *39 Mount Snow Rd., West Dover* ☎ *802/464–3333, 802/464–2151 snow conditions* ⊕ *www.mountsnow. com.*

Timber Creek. North of Snow Mountain, this appealingly small cross-country skiing and snowshoeing center has 4½ miles of groomed loops, equipment rentals, and ski lessons. ✉ *R1 Tomber Creek Rd., at Rte. 100, West Dover* ☎ *802/464–0999* ⊕ *www.timbercreekxc.com.*

SHOPPING

Quaigh Design Centre. For half a century, this store has been seling great pottery and artwork from Britain and New England, including works by Vermont woodcut artist Mary Azarian. Scottish woolens are also on offer. ✉ *11 W. Main St.* ☎ *802/464–2780.*

BENNINGTON

21 miles west of Wilmington.

Bennington is the commercial focus of Vermont's southwest corner and home to the renowned Bennington College. It's really three towns in one: Downtown Bennington, Old Bennington, and North Bennington. Downtown Bennington has retained much of the industrial character it developed in the 19th century, when paper mills, gristmills, and potteries formed the city's economic base. The outskirts of town are commercial and not worth a stop, so make your way right into Downtown and Old Bennington to appreciate the true charm of the area.

The poet Robert Frost is buried in Bennington at the Old First Church, "Vermont's Colonial Shrine."

GETTING HERE AND AROUND

The heart of modern Bennington is at the intersection of U.S. 7 and Route 9. Old Bennington is a couple of miles west on Route 9, at Monument Avenue. North Bennington is a few miles north on Route 67A.

ESSENTIALS

Visitor Information Bennington Area Chamber of Commerce ⊠ *100 Veterans Memorial Dr.* ☎ *802/447–3311, 800/229–0252* ⊕ *www.bennington.com.*

EXPLORING

TOP ATTRACTIONS

FAMILY **Bennington Battle Monument.** This 306-foot stone obelisk—with an elevator to the top—commemorates General John Stark's victory over the British, who attempted to capture Bennington's stockpile of supplies. Inside the monument you can learn all about the battle, which took place near Walloomsac Heights in New York state on August 16, 1777, and helped bring about the surrender of the British commander "Gentleman Johnny" Burgoyne two months later. The summit provides commanding views of the Massachusetts Berkshires, the New York Adirondacks, and the Vermont Green Mountains. ⊠ *15 Monument Circle, Old Bennington* ☎ *802/447–0550* ⊕ *www.historicsites.vermont. gov* ⊠ *$3* ☉ *Mid-Apr.–Oct., daily 9–5.*

Bennington Museum. The rich collections at this museum include military artifacts, early tools, dolls, and the Bennington Flag, one of the oldest of the Stars and Stripes in existence. One room is devoted to early Bennington pottery, and another examines life here during the Gilded Age. There's glass and metalwork by Tiffany, but the museum's highlight may still remain the largest public collection of the work of Grandma Moses

(1860–1961), the popular self-taught artist who lived and painted in the area. ⊠ *75 Main St., Old Bennington* ☎ *802/447–1571* ⊕ *www. benningtonmuseum.com* ⊡ *$10* ⊘ *July–Oct. daily 10–5; Nov., Dec., and Feb.–June, Thurs.–Tues. 10–5.*

Robert Frost Stone House Museum. It was to the town of Shaftsbury that poet Robert Frost came in 1920 "to plant a new Garden of Eden with a thousand apple trees of some unforbidden variety." The museum tells the story of the nine years (1920–29) Frost spent living in the house with his wife and four children. (He passed the 1930s in a house up the road in Shaftsbury, now owned by a producer Norman Lear.) It was here that he penned "Stopping by Woods on a Snowy Evening" and published two books of poems. Seven of the Frost family's original 80 acres can be wandered. Among the apple boughs you just might find inspiration of your own. ⊠ *121 Historic Rte. 7A, Shaftsbury* ☎ *802/447–6200* ⊕ *www.frostfriends.org* ⊡ *$5* ⊘ *May–Nov., daily 10–5.*

WORTH NOTING

Old Bennington. West of downtown, this National Register Historic District is well endowed with stately Colonial and Victorian mansions. The famous Catamount Tavern, where Ethan Allen organized the Green Mountain Boys to capture Fort Ticonderoga in 1775, now contains a bronze statue of Vermont's now-extinct indigenous mountain lion. ⊠ *Monument Ave., Old Bennington.*

The Old First Church. In the graveyard of this church, the tombstone of the poet Robert Frost proclaims, "I had a lover's quarrel with the world." ⊠ *1 Monument Cir, at Monument Ave., Old Bennington* ☎ *802/447– 1223* ⊕ *www.oldfirstchurchbenn.org* ⊡ *Free.*

WHERE TO EAT

$ ✕ **Blue Benn Diner.** Breakfast is served all day in this authentic diner,
DINER where the eats include turkey hash and breakfast burritos with scrambled eggs, sausage, and chilies, plus pancakes of all imaginable varieties. The menu lists many vegetarian selections. Lines may be long, especially on weekends: locals and tourists alike can't stay away. $ *Average main: $10* ⊠ *314 North St.* ☎ *802/442–5140* ⚖ *Reservations not accepted* ▭ *No credit cards.*

WHERE TO STAY

$$ 🛏 **The Eddington House Inn.** You can thank Patti Eddington for maintaining
B&B/INN ing this three-bedroom house, the best value in all of Vermont. **Pros:** budget prices for great B&B; privacy and gentle service. **Cons:** slightly off usual tourist track; only three rooms so it fills up fast. $ *Rooms from: $139* ⊠ *21 Main St., North Bennington* ☎ *802/442–1511* ⊕ *www. eddingtonhouseinn.com* ⟿ *3 suites* ⏐⊘⏐ *Breakfast.*

$$ 🛏 **Four Chimneys Inn.** One of the best inns in Vermont, this three-story
B&B/INN 1915 neo-Georgian looks out over a substantial lawn and a wonderful
Fodor's Choice old stone wall. **Pros:** stately mansion that's extremely well kept; formal
★ dining; nicely renovated rooms. **Cons:** common room/bar closes early. $ *Rooms from: $149* ⊠ *21 West Rd., Old Bennington* ☎ *802/447–3500* ⊕ *www.fourchimneys.com* ⟿ *9 rooms, 2 suites* ⏐⊘⏐ *Breakfast.*

THE ARTS

Vermont Arts Exchange. The fun and funky "basement music series" is presented in a lower-level cabaret space in an old factory building. Buy tickets in advance for the best contemporary music performances in town. ⊠ *29 Sage St., North Bennington* ☎ *802/442–5549* ⊕ *www. vtartxchange.org/bms.php.*

Bennington Center for the Arts. Cultural events, including exhibitions by local and national artists, take place here. It's home to the Oldcastle Theatre Company, whose season runs April to November. ⊠ *44 Gypsy La.* ☎ *802/442–7158* ⊕ *www.thebennington.org.*

SPORTS AND THE OUTDOORS

Lake Shaftsbury State Park. You'll find a swimming beach, nature trails, boat and canoe rentals, and a snack bar at this pretty park. ⊠ *262 Shaftsbury State Park Rd., 10½ miles north of Bennington* ☎ *802/375– 9978* ⊕ *www.vtstateparks.com/htm/shaftsbury.htm.*

Woodford State Park. This park has an activities center on Adams Reservoir, a playground, boat and canoe rentals, and nature trails. ⊠ *142 State Park Rd., 10 miles east of Bennington* ☎ *802/447–7169* ⊕ *www. vtstateparks.com/htm/woodford.htm.*

SHOPPING

The Apple Barn & Country Bake Shop. This shop sells home-baked goodies, fresh cider, Vermont cheeses, maple syrup, and 30 varieties of apples. You can pick berries here too, making it a fun family stop. You can watch them making cider donuts at the bakery and café on weekends. ⊠ *604 Rte. 7S, 1½ miles south of downtown Bennington* ☎ *802/447– 7780* ⊕ *theapplebarn.com.*

The Bennington Bookshop. The state's oldest independent bookstore sells the latest releases an offers free Wi-Fi. ⊠ *467 Main St.* ☎ *802/442–5059.*

Bennington Potters Yard. The showroom at the Bennington Potters Yard stocks goods from the famed Bennington Potters. Take a self-guided tour to see the potters working in the yard. ⊠ *324 County St.* ☎ *802/447– 7531, 800/205–8033* ⊕ *www.benningtonpotters.com* ⊙ *Weekdays 9–6.*

Now & Then Books. This great used bookstore, located in an upstairs shop, has nearly 45,000 volumes in stock. ⊠ *439 Main St.* ☎ *802/442– 5566* ⊕ *www.nowandthenbooksvt.com.*

ARLINGTON

15 miles north of Bennington.

Smaller than Bennington and more down-to-earth than upper-crust Manchester to the north, Arlington exudes a certain Rockwellian folksiness, and it should. Illustrator Norman Rockwell lived here from 1939 to 1953, and many of his neighbors served as models for his portraits of small-town life.

GETTING HERE AND AROUND

Arlington is at the intersection of Routes 313 and 7A. Take 313 West to reach West Arlington.

3

EXPLORING

West Arlington. A covered bridge leads to the quaint town green of West Arlington, where Norman Rockwell once lived. River Road runs along the south side of the Battenkill River, a scenic drive. If you continue west along Route 313, you'll come to the Wayside Country Store, a real charmer, where you can pick up sandwiches and chat with locals. The store is frequently mentioned in the Vermont columns written by Christopher Kimball, editor of *Cooks Illustrated.* ✉ *Rte. 313 W.*

WHERE TO STAY

$$$ B&B/INN 🏨 **The Arlington Inn.** Greek Revival columns at this 1847 home lend it an imposing presence in the middle of town, but the atmosphere is friendly and old-fashioned. **Pros:** heart-of-town location; friendly atmosphere. **Cons:** expensive dining. [$] *Rooms from: $199* ✉ *3904 Historic Rte. 7A* ☎ *802/375–6532* 🌐 *www.arlingtoninn.com* 🛏 *13 rooms, 5 suites* 🍴 *Multiple meal plans.*

$$$ B&B/INN FAMILY 🏨 **West Mountain Inn.** This 1810 farmhouse sits on 150 acres on the side of a mountain, offering hiking trails and easy access to the Battenkill River, where you can canoe or go tubing. **Pros:** mountainside location; lots of activities; great if you have kids. **Cons:** outdated bathrooms. [$] *Rooms from: $195* ✉ *144 West Mountain Inn Rd., at Rte. 313* ☎ *802/375–6516* 🌐 *www.westmountaininn.com* 🛏 *14 rooms, 6 suites* 🍴 *Multiple meal plans.*

SPORTS AND THE OUTDOORS

BattenKill Canoe. This outfitter rents canoes for trips along the Battenkill River, which runs directly behind the shop. If you're hooked, they also run bigger white-water trips as well as inn-to-inn tours. ✉ *6328 Historic Rte. 7A* ☎ *802/362–2800, 800/421–5268* 🌐 *www.battenkill.com.*

SHOPPING

ANTIQUES

East Arlington Antiques Center. More than 70 dealers display their wares at East Arlington Antiques Center, which is in a converted 1930s movie theater. Among the finds is one of the country's best stoneware collections. ✉ *1152 East Arlington Rd., East Arlington* ☎ *802/375–6144* 🕒 *Daily 10–5.*

GIFTS

FAMILY **Village Peddler.** This shop has a "chocolatorium" where you can learn all about cocoa. It sells fudge and other candies and stocks a large collection of teddy bears. ✉ *261 Old Mill Rd., East Arlington* ☎ *802/375–6037* 🌐 *www.villagepeddlervt.com.*

MANCHESTER

9 miles northeast of Arlington.

Well-to-do Manchester has been a popular summer retreat since the mid-19th century, when city dwellers traveled north to take in the cool clean air at the foot of 3,816-foot Mt. Equinox. Manchester Village's tree-shaded marble sidewalks and stately old homes—Main Street here could hardly be more picture perfect—reflect the luxurious resort lifestyle of more than a century ago. A mile north on 7A, Manchester

The formal gardens and mansion at Robert Todd Lincoln's Hildene are a far cry from his father's log cabin.

Center is the commercial twin to Colonial Manchester Village, as well as where you'll find the town's famed upscale factory outlets doing business in attractive faux-Colonial shops.

Manchester Village also houses the world headquarters of Orvis, the outdoor goods brand that began here in the 19th century and has greatly influenced the town ever since. Its complex includes a fly-fishing school with lessons in its casting ponds and the Battenkill River.

GETTING HERE AND AROUND
Manchester is the main town for the ski resorts of Stratton and Bromley and is roughly 15 minutes from either on Routes 11 and 30. It's 15 minutes north of Arlington, 30 minutes north of Bennington and south of Rutland on Routes 7 and 7A. Take 7A for a more scenic drive.

ESSENTIALS
Visitor Information Green Mountain National Forest Visitor Center ⊠ *2538 Depot St.* ☎ *802/362-2307* ⊕ *www.fs.fed.us/r9/gmfl* ⊙ *Weekdays 8–4:30.* **Manchester and the Mountains Regional Chamber of Commerce** ⊠ *39 Bonnet St.* ☎ *802/362-6313, 800/362-4144* ⊕ *www.visitmanchestervt.com.*

EXPLORING
American Museum of Fly Fishing. This museum houses the world's largest collection of angling art and angling-related objects. Rotating exhibitions draw from a permanent collection of more than 1,500 rods, 800 reels, 30,000 flies, and the tackle of notables like Winslow Homer, Bing Crosby, and Jimmy Carter. Every August, a fly-fishing festival has vendors selling antique equipment. You can also practice your casting

out back. ✉ *4104 Main St.* ☎ *802/362–3300* 🌐 *www.amff.com* 🎟 *$5* ⏲ *Tues.–Sat 10–4.*

FAMILY
Fodor's Choice ★
Hildene. The Lincoln Family Home is a twofold treat, providing historical insight into the life of the Lincolns while escorting you through the lavish Manchester life of the 1900s. Abraham had only one son who survived to adulthood, Robert Todd Lincoln, who served as secretary of war and head of the Pullman Company. Robert bought the beautifully preserved 412-acre estate and built a 24-room mansion where he and his descendants lived from 1905 to 1975. The sturdy Georgian Revival house holds many of the family's prized possessions, including one of three surviving stovepipe hats owned by Abraham and a Lincoln Bible. When the 1,000-pipe aeolian organ is played, the music reverberates as though from the mansion's very bones.

Rising from a 10-acre meadow, the new Hildene Farm, which opened in 2008, is magnificent. The agriculture center is built in a traditional style—post-and-beam construction of timber felled and milled on the estate—and has informative farming displays that recall the family's use of this land. Best of all, you can meet the resident goats and watch goat cheese being made.

The highlight, though, may be the elaborate formal gardens: in June a thousand peonies bloom. When conditions permit, you can cross-country ski and snowshoe on the property. Robert's carriage house now houses a gorgeous museum store and welcome center that showcase, among other things, a live bee exhibit. In good weather Jessie Lincoln's 1928 vintage Franklin car is parked out front. Allow half a day for exploring Hildene. ✉ *1005 Hildene Rd., at Rte. 7A* ☎ *802/362–1788* 🌐 *www.hildene.org* 🎟 *Tour $16* ⏲ *Daily 9:30–4:30.*

Fodor's Choice ★
Southern Vermont Arts Center. At the end of a long, winding driveway, this complex houses rotating exhibits and a permanent collection of more than 800 19th- and 20th-century American artworks. The original building, a graceful Georgian mansion set on 100 acres, now is home to 10 galleries with pieces by more than 600 artists, many of them from Vermont. The building also hosts concerts, performances, and film screenings. In summer and fall, lunch at the pleasant restaurant with magnificent views. ✉ *930 SVAC Dr., West Rd.* ☎ *802/362–1405* 🌐 *www.svac.org* 🎟 *$6* ⏲ *Tues.–Sat. 10–5, Sun. noon–5.*

WHERE TO EAT

$$$$
FRENCH
🍴 **Bistro Henry.** The presence of chef-owner Henry Bronson accounts for the continual popularity of this friendly place, as does the fact that dishes are about $5 cheaper than at the town's other upscale restaurants. The bistro menu includes classics like a peppery steak au poivre and a medium-rare duck breast served with a crispy leg, then mixes things up with eclectic dishes like tuna with wasabi and soy, crab cakes in a Cajun rémoulade, and delicious seared scallops with lemon-ginger risotto. The wine list is extensive, and Dina Bronson's desserts are memorable—indulge in the "gooey chocolate cake," a great molten treat paired with a homemade malt ice cream. [$] *Average main: $29* ✉ *1942 Depot St., 3 miles east of Manchester Center* ☎ *802/362–4982* 🌐 *www.bistrohenry.com* ⏲ *Closed Mon. No lunch.*

$$$$ EUROPEAN 🍴 **Chantecleer.** There is something wonderful about eating by candlelight in an old barn. Chantecleer's dining rooms (in winter ask to sit by the great fieldstone fireplace) are wonderfully romantic, especially with the collection of roosters atop the wooden beams. The menu leans toward the Continental with starters like a fine escargots glazed with Pernod in a hazelnut and parsley butter. Crowd pleasers include Colorado rack of lamb and whole Dover sole filleted table-side. A recipe from the chef's Swiss hometown makes a winning winter dessert: Basel Rathaus Torte, a delicious hazelnut layer cake. [$] *Average main: $38* ✉ *8 Reed Farm La., 3½ miles north of Manchester, East Dorset* ☎ *802/362–1616* 🌐 *www.chantecleerrestaurant.com* ✍ *Reservations essential* 🕘 *Closed Nov., Apr., and Sun.–Tues. No lunch.*

$$$$ STEAKHOUSE 🍴 **Chop House.** Walk to the very back room of the Equinox's Marsh Tavern, past a velvet curtain, and you'll have entered a different eatery—a wonderful, very expensive steak house called the Chop House. The dining room has a bit of history—the marble above the fireplace is chiseled L. L. ORVIS 1832 (and way before he claimed the spot, the Green Mountain Boys gathered here to plan their resistance). Today, you'll yield to aged corn- or grass-fed beef broiled at 1,700 degrees and finished with herb butter. The New York strip, rib eye, filet mignon, milk-fed veal chops, and seafood are delicious, a must for deep-pocketed carnivores. [$] *Average main: $44* ✉ *3567 Main St.* ☎ *802/362–4700* 🌐 *www.equinoxresort.com* 🕘 *No lunch.*

$$ PIZZA 🍴 **Depot 62 Bistro.** The best pizzas in town are topped with terrific fresh ingredients and served in the middle of a high-end antiques showroom, making this Turkish-Mediterranean restaurant a local secret worth knowing about. The wood-fired oven yields masterful results—like the arugula pizza, a beehive of fresh greens atop a thin crust. This a great place for lunch or an inexpensive but satisfying dinner. Sit on your own or at the long communal table. [$] *Average main: $18* ✉ *515 Depot St.* ☎ *802/366–8181* 🌐 *www.depot62.us.*

$$$ FRENCH 🍴 **Mistral's at Toll Gate.** This classic French restaurant is tucked in a grotto on the climb to Bromley Mountain. The two dining rooms are perched over the Bromley Brook, and at night lights magically illuminate a small waterfall. Ask for a window table. Specialties include Chateaubriand béarnaise and rack of lamb with rosemary for two. Chef Dana Markey's crispy sweetbreads with Dijonnaise sauce are a favorite. [$] *Average main: $25* ✉ *10 Toll Gate Rd., off Rte. 11/30* ☎ *802/362–1779* 🌐 *www.mistralsattollgate.com* 🕘 *Closed Wed. Closed Tues. Nov.–June. No lunch.*

$$$ ECLECTIC Fodor's Choice ★ 🍴 **Perfect Wife.** Owner-chef Amy Chamberlain, a Manchester native, creates a fun, freestyle atmosphere with dishes like Peking duck rolled in Mandarin pancakes and sesame-crusted yellowfin tuna topped with crispy rice sticks. There are two entrances: one to the charming restaurant on the lower level and another to the Other Woman Tavern above. The tavern is one of the livelier local spots in town, with live music on weekends and a pub menu with burgers, potpies in winter, and Vermont microbrews on tap. [$] *Average main: $27* ✉ *2594 Depot St., 2½ miles east of Manchester Center* ☎ *802/362–2817* 🌐 *www.perfectwife.com* 🕘 *Closed Sun. No lunch.*

$$$$
AMERICAN
✕ **The Reluctant Panther Inn & Restaurant.** The dining room at this luxurious inn is a large, modern space where rich woods and high ceilings meld into a kind of nouveau Vermont aesthetic. The contemporary American cuisine emphasizes farm-to-table ingredients and has earned the restaurant "Gold Barn" honors from the Vermont Fresh Network. The dinner menu includes grilled Hollandeer Farm venison and pan-roasted pheasant breast. You can pair your choice with a bottle from the award-winning wine list. In the warmer months, sit outside on the lovely landscaped patio, which has a raw bar on Thursday to Saturday evenings. $ *Average main: $36* ✉ *39 West Rd.* ☎ *800/822–2331, 802/362–2568* ⊕ *www.reluctantpanther.com* ⊘ *No lunch.*

$$$$
ECLECTIC
Fodor's Choice
★
✕ **The Silver Fork.** This popular, intimate bistro with Caribbean flair is owned by husband-and-wife team Mark and Melody French. The owners spent years living in Puerto Rico, and the flavors of the island are reflected in their menu. Start with savory olive tapenade and warm rosemary flatbread, then sample the salmon seared on mango with greens, or dig into crispy crab cakes. There are also more Continental offerings on the sophisticated international menu like veal ragu and warm apple-cinnamon beignets. Be sure to reserve one of the six tables ahead of time, or sit at the wine bar for a casual and romantic dinner with a bottle from the impressive wine list or a maple martini. $ *Average main: $29* ✉ *4201 Main St., across from Orvis Flagship Store* ☎ *802/768–8444* ⊕ *www.thesilverforkvt.com* ⌒ *Reservations essential* ⊘ *Closed Sun. No lunch.*

$$
AMERICAN
✕ **Ye Olde Tavern.** This circa-1790 Colonial inn serves up Yankee favorites like pot roast and cheddar-and-ale onion soup along with plenty of local New England charm. A favorite of regulars and visitors alike, the tavern serves excellent food in a casual, colorful setting with fireplaces. The cozy tap room is a nice spot to stop for a drink and a taste of Vermont. $ *Average main: $20* ✉ *5183 Main St.* ☎ *802/362–0611* ⊕ *www.yeoldetavern.net.*

WHERE TO STAY

$$$$
RESORT
▦ **The Equinox.** The Equinox defines the geographic center and historic heart of Manchester Village, and has been *the* fancy hotel in town—and in the state—since the 18th century. **Pros:** heart-of-town location; full-service hotel; great golf and spa. **Cons:** corporate feel; spotty service; overrun by New Yorkers on weekends. $ *Rooms from: $294* ✉ *3567 Main St.* ☎ *802/362–4700, 888/367–7625* ⊕ *www.equinoxresort.com* ⇆ *164 rooms, 29 suites* ⦿ *No meals.*

$$$
B&B/INN
Fodor's Choice
★
▦ **Wilburton Inn.** Stepping into this hilltop 1902 Tudor style mansion, you might think you've walked into a lavish film set. **Pros:** beautiful setting with easy access to Manchester; fine dining. **Cons:** limited indoor facilities; popular wedding site. $ *Rooms from: $190* ✉ *257 River Rd.* ☎ *802/362–2500, 800/648–4944* ⊕ *www.wilburton.com* ⇆ *30 rooms, 4 suites* ⦿ *Breakfast.*

3

NIGHTLIFE AND THE ARTS

Falcon Bar. This sophisticated bar at the Equinox Resort has live music on weekends. Don't miss the wonderful outdoor deck—in winter, the place to be is around the giant Vermont slate fire pit. ⊠ *Equinox Resort, 3567 Main St.* ☎ *800/362–4747* ⊕ *www.equinoxresort.com.*

SPORTS AND THE OUTDOORS

BIKING

Battenkill Sports Bicycle Shop. This shop rents, sells, and repairs bikes and provides maps and route suggestions. ⊠ *1240 Depot St., off Rte. 7* ☎ *802/362–2734, 800/340–2734* ⊕ *www.battenkillsports.com.*

FISHING

Battenkill Anglers. Teaching the art and science of fly-fishing, Battenkill Anglers offers both private and group lessons. ⊠ *6204 Main St.* ☎ *802/379–1444* ⊕ *www.battenkillangler.com.*

Orvis Fly-Fishing School. This nationally renowned school offers courses mid-April to mid-October, ranging from two-hour pond trips with casting lessons and fishing with private instructors to two-day advanced classes on the Battenkill. ⊠ *6204 Rte. 7A, Manchester Center* ☎ *802/ 362–4604* ⊕ *www.orvis.com/schools.*

HIKING

There are bountiful hiking trails in the Green Mountain National Forest. Shorter hikes begin at the Equinox Resort, which owns about 1,000 acres of forest and has a great trail system open to the public.

Long Trail. One of the most popular segments of Vermont's Long Trail leads to the top of Bromley Mountain. The strenuous 5.4-mile round-trip takes about four hours. ⊠ *Rte. 11/30* ⊕ *www.greenmountainclub.org.*

Lye Brook Falls. This 4.6-mile hike starts off Glen Road and ends at Vermont's most impressive cataract, Lye Brook Falls. The moderate hike takes four hours. ⊠ *Manchester East Rd.*

Mountain Goat. Stop here for hiking, cross-country-skiing, and snowshoeing equipment, as well as lots of warm clothing. ⊠ *4886 Main St.* ☎ *802/362–5159* ⊕ *mountaingoat.com.*

ICE-SKATING

Riley Rink at Hunter Park. This Olympic-size indoor ice rink has skate rentals and a concession stand. ⊠ *410 Hunter Park Rd.* ☎ *802/362–0150, 866/866–2086* ⊕ *www.rileyrink.com.*

SHOPPING AND SPAS

ART AND ANTIQUES

Long Ago & Far Away. This store specializes in fine indigenous artwork, including Inuit stone sculpture. ⊠ *Green Mountain Village Shops, 4963 Main St.* ☎ *802/362–3435* ⊕ *www.longagoandfaraway.com.*

Tilting at Windmills Gallery. This large gallery displays the paintings and sculpture of nationally known artists. ⊠ *24 Highland Ave.* ☎ *802/362–ac 3022* ⊕ *www.tilting.com.*

Manchester Designer Outlets' Colonial-style architecture helps blend upscale discount shopping with the surrounding town.

BOOKS

FAMILY **Northshire Bookstore.** The heart of Manchester Center, this bookstore is adored by visitors and residents for its ambience, selection, and service. Up the iron staircase is a second floor dedicated to children's books, toys, and clothes. Connected to the bookstore is the Spiral Press Café, where you can sit for a grilled pesto-chicken sandwich or a latte and scone. ✉ *4869 Main St.* ☎ *802/362–2200, 800/437–3700* ⊕ *www. northshire.com.*

CLOTHING

Manchester Designer Outlets. This is the most upscale collection of stores in northern New England—and every store is a discount outlet. The architecture reflects the surrounding homes, so the place looks a bit like a Colonial village. The long list of upscale clothiers here includes Kate Spade, Yves DeLorme, Michael Kors, Ann Taylor, Tumi, BCBG, Armani, Coach, Polo Ralph Lauren, Brooks Brothers, and Theory. ✉ *97 Depot St.* ☎ *802/362–3736, 800/955–7467* ⊕ *www. manchesterdesigneroutlets.com.*

Orvis Flagship Store. The lodge-like Orvis Flagship Store has a trout pond as well as the company's latest clothing, fly-fishing gear, and pet supplies. It's a required shopping destination for many visitors—the Orvis name is pure Manchester. There are demonstrations of how fly rods are constructed and tested. ✉ *4200 Rte. 7A* ☎ *802/362–3750* ⊕ *www. orvis.com.*

SPAS

Spa at Equinox. With mahogany doors and beadboard wainscoting, this spa feels like a country estate. At one end is an indoor pool and outdoor hot tub; at the other end are the treatment rooms. The signature 80-minute Spirit of Vermont combines Reiki, reflexology, and massage. In the co-ed relaxation room, you can nestle into overstuffed chairs next to a two-sided fireplace made of Vermont gneiss. The locker rooms, with marble accents and pottery-bowl wash basins, have steam rooms and saunas. ✉ *Equinox Resort, 3567 Rte. 7A, Manchester* ☎ *802/362–4700* ⊕ *www.equinoxresort.com.*

DORSET

7 miles north of Manchester.

Lying at the foot of many mountains and with a village green surrounded by white clapboard homes and inns, Dorset has a solid claim to the title of Vermont's most picture-perfect town. The town has just 2,000 residents, but two of the state's best and oldest general stores.

The country's first commercial marble quarry opened here in 1785. Dozens followed suit, providing the marble for the main research branch of the New York City Public Library and many Fifth Avenue mansions, among other notable landmarks, as well as the sidewalks here and in Manchester. A remarkable private home made entirely of marble can be seen on Dorset West Road, a beautiful residential road west of the town green. The marble Dorset Church on the green features two Tiffany stained-glass windows.

EXPLORING

FAMILY
Fodor's Choice
★

Dorset Quarry. On hot summer days the sight of dozens of families jumping, swimming, and basking in the sun around this massive 60-foot-deep swimming hole makes it one of the most wholesome and picturesque recreational spots in the region. First mined in 1785, the stone from the country's oldest commercial marble quarry went to build the main branch of the New York Public Library and Montreal Museum of Fine Arts. ✉ *Rte. 30* 🎫 *Free.*

FAMILY
Merck Forest & Farmland Center. This 3,100-acre educational center has 30 miles of nature trails for hiking, cross-country skiing, snowshoeing, and horseback riding. You can visit the 60-acre farm, which grows organic fruit and vegetables (and purchase them at the farm stand), and check out the horses, cows, sheep, pigs, and chickens. You're even welcome to help out with the chores. ✉ *3270 Rte. 315, Rupert* ☎ *802/394–7836* ⊕ *www.merckforest.org* 🎫 *Free* ☉ *Visitor center daily 9–4.*

WHERE TO EAT

$$$
AMERICAN

✕ **The Dorset Inn.** Built in 1796, this inn has been continuously operating ever since. The comfortable tavern, which serves the same menu as the more formal dining room, is popular with locals, and Patrick, the amiable veteran bartender, will make you feel at home. Popular choices include the Taylor Farm Gouda fondue and the maple-glazed duck breast. A member of the Vermont Fresh Network, the restaurant benefits greatly from its strong connections with local farmers and chefs.

$ *Average main: $22* ✉ *Dorset Green, 8 Church St.* ☎ *802/867–5500* ⊕ *www.dorsetinn.com.*

$$$$
ECLECTIC

✕ **Inn at West View Farm.** Chef-owner Raymond Chen was the lead line cook at New York City's Mercer Kitchen under Jean-Georges Vongerichten before opening this local-ingredient-friendly restaurant. You'll find traditional floral wallpaper and soft classical music, but that's where the similarities to Dorset's other eateries end. Chen's dishes are skillful and practiced, starting with an amuse-bouche such as salt cod over pesto. French influences are evident in the sautéed mushrooms and mascarpone ravioli in white truffle oil. Asian notes are evident, too, as in the lemongrass ginger soup with shiitake mushrooms that's ladled over grilled shrimp. A tavern serves enticing, inexpensive small dishes. $ *Average main: $31* ✉ *2928 Rte. 30* ☎ *802/867–5715, 800/769–4903* ⊕ *www.westviewfarm.com* ⊘ *Closed Tues. and Wed.*

WHERE TO STAY

$$$$
HOTEL

⊞ **Barrows House.** If you've had enough of the ubiquitous floral fabrics found in many New England inns, this renovated 19th-century manse, once the residence of the town's pastor, is a pleasant alternative. **Pros:** perhaps the best bar and restaurant in town; chintz-free decor. **Cons:** rooms can become drafty in cold weather. $ *Rooms from: $245* ✉ *3156 Rte. 30* ☎ *802/867–4455* ⊕ *www.barrowshouse.com* ⇆ *18 rooms, 9 suites, 3 cottages* ¶◎¶ *Breakfast.*

$$$
B&B/INN

⊞ **Squire House Bed & Breakfast.** On a wonderfully quiet road, this inn has three rooms that combine modern comforts and antique fixtures. **Pros:** big estate feels like your own; well-maintained rooms. **Cons:** bathrooms less exciting than rooms; no credit cards. $ *Rooms from: $210* ✉ *3395 Dorset West Rd.* ☎ *802/867–0281* ⊕ *www.squirehouse.com* ⇆ *2 rooms, 1 suite* ▭ *No credit cards* ¶◎¶ *Breakfast.*

THE ARTS

Dorset Playhouse. Dorset is home to a prestigious summer theater troupe that presents the annual Dorset Theater Festival. Plays are presented in a wonderful converted pre-Revolutionary War barn. ✉ *Dorset Playhouse, 104 Cheney Rd.* ☎ *802/867–5777* ⊕ *www.dorsetplayers.org.*

SPORTS AND THE OUTDOORS

Emerald Lake State Park. This park has a marked nature trail, a small beach, boat rentals, and a snack bar. ✉ *65 Emerald Lake La., East Dorset* ☎ *802/362–1655* ⊕ *www.vtstateparks.com/htm/emerald.htm* ▧ *$3.*

SHOPPING

Dorset Union Store. Dating from 1816, this general store makes good prepared dinners, has a big wine selection, and sells interesting gifts. ✉ *Dorset Green, Church St.* ☎ *802/867–4400* ⊕ *www.dorsetunionstore. com* ⊘ *Mon.–Sat. 7–6, Sun. 8–5.*

H. N. Williams General Store. Started in 1840 by William Williams, this authentic country store has been run by the same family for six generations. This is one of those unique places where you can buy both maple syrup and ammo and catch up on posted town announcements. A farmers' market is held outside on Sundays in summer. ✉ *2732 Rte. 30* ☎ *802/867–5353* ⊕ *www.hnwilliams.com.*

3

STRATTON

26 miles southeast of Dorset.

Stratton is really Stratton Mountain Resort—a mountaintop ski resort with a self-contained "town center" of shops, restaurants, and lodgings clustered at the base of the slopes. When the snow melts, golf, tennis, and a host of other summer activities are big attractions, but the ski village remains quiet. For those arriving from the north along Route 30, Bondville is the town at the base of the mountain. At the junction of Routes 30 and 100 is the tiny Vermont village of Jamaica, with its own cluster of inns and restaurants on the east side of the mountain.

GETTING HERE AND AROUND

From Manchester or Route 7, follow Route 11/30 east until they split. Route 11 continues past Bromley ski mountain while Route 30 turns south 10 minutes toward Bondville, the town closest to Stratton Mountain.

WHERE TO EAT

$$$$
AMERICAN

✕ **The Red Fox Inn.** This two-level converted barn has the best nightlife in southern Vermont and a fun dining room to boot. The upper level is the restaurant—the big A-frame has wagon wheels and a carriage suspended from the ceiling. Settle in near the huge fireplace for beef tenderloin, roasted half duckling, or penne alla vodka. The apple pie was served at the 2009 and 2013 presidential inaugurations. Downstairs in the tavern, open year-round, there's Irish music, half-price Guinness, and fish-and-chips on Wednesday. On the premises are some relaxed, no-frills accommodations. $ *Average main: $30* ⊠ *103 Winhall Hollow Rd., Bondville* ☎ *802/297–2488* ⊕ *www.redfoxinn.com* ⊗ *No lunch. Closed Mon.–Wed. June–Oct.*

WHERE TO STAY

$$
RENTAL

▥ **Long Trail House.** Directly across the street from the ski village, this condo complex is one of the closest to the slopes. **Pros:** across from skiing; reasonable rates available; outdoor heated pool. **Cons:** room decor varies; two-night stay required on weekends. $ *Rooms from: $165* ⊠ *5 Village Lodge Rd.* ☎ *802/297–4000, 800/787–2886* ⊕ *www.stratton. com* ⌂ *100 units* ⦿ *No meals.*

$$$$
B&B/INN
Fodor's Choice
★

▥ **Three Mountain Inn.** A 1780s tavern, the romantic Three Mountain Inn in downtown Jamaica feels authentically Colonial, from the wide-plank paneling to the low ceilings. **Pros:** charming B&B; well-kept rooms; great dinners. **Cons:** can be expensive. $ *Rooms from: $234* ⊠ *30 Depot St., 10 miles northeast of Stratton, Jamaica* ☎ *802/874–4140* ⊕ *www.threemountaininn.com* ⌂ *14 rooms, 1 suite* ⦿ *Breakfast.*

NIGHTLIFE AND THE ARTS

Fodor's Choice
★

Johnny Seesaw's. Near Bromley Mountain, Johnny Seesaw's is a classic rustic ski lodge with two huge fireplaces and a relaxed attitude. There's live acoustical music on weekends, a separate games room, and an excellent comfort-food menu. ⊠ *3574 Rte. 11, Peru* ☎ *802/824–5533, 800/424–2729* ⊕ *www.jseesaw.com.*

Mulligan's. Popular Mulligan's hosts bands or DJs in the downstairs Green Door Pub on weekends. ✉ *Stratton Village Sq. 11B, Mountain Rd., Bondville* ☎ *802/297–9293.*

SPORTS AND THE OUTDOORS
SKI AREAS
Bromley. About 20 minutes from Stratton, Bromley is a favorite with families. The 46 trails are evenly divided between beginner, intermediate, and expert. The resort runs a child-care center for kids ages 6 weeks to 6 years and hosts children's programs for ages 3 to 17. Beginning skiers and snowboarders have expanded access to terrain-based training in the dedicated Learning Zone, while everyone can unwind in the newly renovated base lodge. An added bonus: the trails face south, making for glorious skiing in spring and on warm winter days. ✉ *3984 Vermont Rte. 11, Peru* ☎ *802/824–5522, 800/865–4786* ⊕ *www.bromley.com.*

Stratton Mountain. About 30 minutes from Manchester, sophisticated Stratton Mountain draws affluent families and young professionals. An entire village, with a covered parking structure for 700 cars, sits at the base of the mountain. In summer Stratton has 15 outdoor clay tennis courts, 27 holes of golf, and hiking trails accessed by a gondola. The sports center, open year-round, has a 25-meter indoor pool, a hot tub, a steam room, and a fitness facility.

In terms of downhill skiing, Stratton prides itself on its immaculate grooming, making it excellent for cruising. The lower part of the mountain is beginner to low-intermediate, served by several chairlifts, including one high-speed six passenger. The upper mountain is served by several chairlifts, including a six passenger and a 12-passenger gondola. Down the face are the expert trails, and on either side are intermediate cruising runs with a smattering of wide beginner slopes. The third sector, the Sun Bowl, is off to one side with two six-passenger lifts serving two expert trails and plenty of intermediate terrain. Snowmaking covers 95% of the slopes. In all, Stratton has 12 lifts that service 94 trails and more than 115 acres of glades. There's also 11 miles of cross-country skiing. An on-site day-care center takes children from six weeks to five years old for indoor activities and outdoor excursions. Children also love careening down one of four groomed lift-serviced lanes at the resort's Coca Cola Tube Park. ✉ *5 Village Rd., Bondville* ☎ *802/297–4211 snow conditions, 800/787–2886* ⊕ *www.stratton.com.*

WESTON

17 miles north of Stratton.

Best known for the Vermont Country Store, Weston was one of the first Vermont towns to discover its own intrinsic loveliness—and marketability. With its summer theater, classic town green with a Victorian bandstand, and an assortment of shops, the little village really lives up to its vaunted image.

WHERE TO STAY

$$$$ B&B/INN 🏨 **The Inn at Weston.** Highlighting the country elegance of this 1848 inn, a short walk from the town green and a stone's throw from four ski mountains, is innkeeper Bob Aldrich's collection of 500 orchid species—rare and beautiful specimens surround the dining table in the gazebo. **Pros:** great rooms; terrific town location. **Cons:** top-end rooms are expensive. [$] *Rooms from: $235* ✉ *630 Main St.* ☎ *802/824–6789* 🌐 *www.innweston.com* 🛏 *13 rooms* 🍴 *Breakfast.*

THE ARTS

Weston Playhouse. The oldest professional theater in Vermont produces plays, musicals, and other works. The season runs from late June to early September. ✉ *703 Main St., off Rte. 100* ☎ *802/824–5288* 🌐 *www.westonplayhouse.org.*

SHOPPING

The Vermont Country Store. This store opened in 1946 and is still run by the Orton family, though it has become something of an empire, with a large catalog and online business. One room is set aside for Vermont Common Crackers and bins of fudge and other candy. In others you'll find nearly forgotten items such as Lilac Vegetol aftershave, as well as practical items such as sturdy outdoor clothing. Nostalgia-evoking implements dangle from the rafters. There's a second location on Route 103 in Rockingham. ✉ *657 Main St.* ☎ *802/824–3184* 🌐 *www.vermontcountrystore.com.*

LUDLOW

9 miles northeast of Weston.

Ludlow is a largely nondescript industrial town whose major draw is Okemo, one of Vermont's largest and most popular ski resorts.

WHERE TO EAT

$$ AMERICAN ✕ **Coleman Brook Tavern.** Slopeside at the Jackson Gore Inn, Coleman Brook is the fanciest and most expensive of Okemo's 19 places to eat, but it's not formal—you'll find ski-boot-wearing diners crowding the tables at lunch. Big wing chairs and large banquettes line window bays. Ask to sit in the Wine Room, a separate section where tables are surrounded by the noteworthy collection of wines. Start with a pound of mussels steamed in butter, garlic, white wine, and fresh herbs. Then move on to the sesame seed–crusted ahi tuna served over green-tea soba noodles in a ginger-miso broth. The s'mores dessert is cooked with a tabletop "campfire." [$] *Average main: $20* ✉ *111 Jackson Gore Rd., Okemo* ☎ *802/228–1435.*

$ PIZZA FAMILY ✕ **Goodman's American Pie.** This pizzeria has the best wood-fired oven pizza in town. It also has character to spare—sit in chairs from old ski lifts and order from a counter that was once a purple VW bus. Though it's on Main Street, it's set back and kind of hidden—you may consider it your Ludlow secret. Locals and Okemo regulars already in the know stop by to design their own pizza from 25 ingredients; there is also a section of six specials. The Rip Curl has mozzarella, Asiago, ricotta, chicken, fresh garlic, and fresh tomatoes. Slices are available.

You never know what you'll find at a rambling general store like Weston's Vermont Country Store.

Arcade games are in the back. $ *Average main: $8* ✉ *106 Main St.* ☎ *802/228–4271* ▭ *No credit cards* ⊘ *Closed Wed.*

$$
ECLECTIC

✕ Harry's. The local favorite when you want to eat a little out of town, this casual roadside restaurant 5 miles northwest of Ludlow has a number of international influences. Traditional contemporary entrées such as pork tenderloin are at one end of the menu and Mexican dishes at the other. The large and tasty burrito, made with fresh cilantro and black beans, is one of the best bargains around. Chef-owner Trip Pearce also owns the equally popular Little Harry's in Rutland. $ *Average main: $19* ✉ *3621 Rte. 103, Mount Holly* ☎ *802/259–2996* ⊕ *www.harryscafe.com* ⊘ *Closed Mon. and Tues. No lunch.*

$$
ECLECTIC
Fodor's Choice
★

✕ The Inn at Weathersfield. One of Vermont's best restaurants, this is a culinary gem inside an 18th-century countryside inn. A chalkboard in the foyer lists the farms that grow the food you'll eat here on any given night. Executive chef Jean-Luc Matecap, who has extensive experience cooking for top restaurants in France, Nantucket, and his native Vermont, is passionate about local ingredients. The inn's farm-to-table cuisine is showcased in an à la carte tavern menu, chalkboard specials, and two nightly prix-fixe menus in the formal dining room. The first ($59) includes meats such as roasted Cavendish game birds and dry-aged Black Watch Farm sirloin; the second ($45) offers vegetarian and gluten-free dishes. Service is excellent, and the wine list is large and reasonably priced. If it's summer, enjoy your meal on the patio. $ *Average main: $20* ✉ *1342 Rte. 106, 15 miles east of Ludlow, Perkinsville* ☎ *802/263–9217* ⊕ *www.innatweathersfield.com* ⊘ *No lunch. Closed Mon., Tues., and Apr. and beginning of Nov.*

CLOSE UP

Vermont Artisanal Cheese

Vermont is the artisanal cheese capital of the country, with more than 40 creameries (and growing fast) that are open to the public—carefully churning out hundreds of different cheeses. Many creameries are "farmstead" operations, meaning that the animals that provide the milk are on-site where their milk is made into cheese. If you eat enough cheese during your time in the state, you may be able to differentiate between the many types of milk (cow, goat, sheep, or even water buffalo), as well as make associations between the geography and climate of where you are and the taste of the cheese you eat.

This is one of the reasons why taking a walk around a dairy is a great idea: you can see the process in action, from grazing to aging to eating. Almost all dairies welcome visitors, though it's universally recommended that you call ahead to plan your visit.

Vermont sheep's milk cheese.

Vermont Cheese Council. This group has developed the Vermont Cheese Trail, a map of 44 creameries with contact information for each. ☎ *866/261–8595* 🌐 *www.vtcheese.com.*

Vermont Cheesemakers Festival. If you're a real cheese lover, definitely plan your trip to Vermont around the state's world-class food event, the annual Vermont Cheesemakers Festival—each July over 40 cheesemakers gather in Shelburne to sell and sample their various cheeses. 🌐 *www.vtcheesefest.com.*

—Michael de Zayas

WHERE TO STAY

$$$ B&B/INN 🏨 **Inn at Water's Edge.** Former Long Islanders Bruce and Tina Verdrager converted their old ski house and barns into this comfortably refined haven, perfect for those who want to ski but don't want to stay in town. **Pros:** bucolic setting on a lakefront; interesting house. **Cons:** ordinary B&B rooms. [$] *Rooms from: $175* ✉ *45 Kingdom Rd., 5 miles north of town* ☎ *802/228–8143, 888/706–9736* 🌐 *www.innatwatersedge.com* 🛏 *9 rooms, 2 suites* 🍴 *Multiple meal plans.*

$$$ B&B/INN 🏨 **Inn at Weathersfield.** This is the kind of place where relaxation rules—unless you want to take advantage of year-round seasonal sports like hiking, cross-country skiing, and even apple picking. **Pros:** dynamite restaurant and tavern; laid-back inn; quiet setting. **Cons:** 15-mile drive from the Okemo slopes. [$] *Rooms from: $179* ✉ *1342 Rte. 106, Perkinsville* ☎ *802/263–9217* 🌐 *www.innatweathersfield.com* 🛏 *12 rooms* 🕒 *Closed first two weeks in Nov.* 🍴 *Breakfast.*

$$ HOTEL FAMILY 🏨 **Jackson Gore Village.** This slope-side base lodge is the place to stay if your aim is convenience to Okemo's slopes. **Pros:** ski-in ski-out at base of mountain; good for families. **Cons:** chaotic and noisy on weekends; expensive. [$] *Rooms from: $162* ✉ *77 Okemo Ridge Rd., off Rte. 103* ☎ *802/228–1400, 800/786–5366* 🌐 *www.okemo.com* 🛏 *263 rooms.*

SPORTS AND THE OUTDOORS
SKI AREAS
Okemo Mountain Resort. Family-owned since 1982 and still run by Tim and Diane Mueller, Okemo Mountain Resort has evolved into a major year-round resort, now with two base areas. At 2,200 feet, Okemo has the highest vertical drop of any resort in southern Vermont. Beginner trails extend above both base areas, with more challenging terrain higher on the mountains. Intermediate trails are the theme here, but experts will find steep trails and glades at Jackson Gore and on the South Face. The total 120 trails are served by an efficient system of 24 lifts, including nine quads, three triple chairlifts, and seven surface lifts; 96% of the trails are covered by snowmaking. Okemo has six terrain parks for skiers and snowboarders, including one for beginners, a progression park, and 500-foot-long superpipe. For cross-country skiing, the Okemo Valley Nordic Center has 14 miles of groomed cross-country trails and 8 miles dedicated to snowshoeing. For ice-skating, the resort's roofed Ice House rink near the Jackson Gore base area is open mid-December to April, with rentals and entry costing $4 each. A tubing facility can also be found there, with four groomed lanes serviced by a conveyor-style lift Friday and Saturday 3-6 pm.

If you're looking for non-snow-related activities, you can play basketball and tennis at the Ice House next to Jackson Gore Inn or perfect your swing at the 18-hole course at the Okemo Valley Golf Club. The Spring House, next to the entrance of Jackson Gore Inn, has a great kids' pool with slides, a racquetball court, fitness center, and sauna. ⊠ *77 Okemo Ridge Rd.* ☎ *802/228–4041, 802/228–5222 snow conditions* ⊕ *www.okemo.com.*

GRAFTON

20 miles south of Ludlow.

Out-of-the-way Grafton is as much a historical museum as a town. During its heyday, citizens grazed some 10,000 sheep and spun their wool into sturdy yarn for locally woven fabric. When the market for wool declined, so did Grafton. Then in 1963 the Windham Foundation—Vermont's second-largest private foundation—commenced the town's rehabilitation. Not only was the Old Tavern preserved (now called The Grafton Inn), but so were many other commercial and residential structures in the village center.

EXPLORING
Historical Society Museum. The Historical Society Museum documents the town's history with exhibits that change yearly. ⊠ *147 Main St.* ☎ *802/843–2584* ⊕ *www.graftonhistory.info* ⊠ *$3* ⊙ *Memorial Day–Columbus Day, Thurs.–Mon. 10–4. Closed Tues. and Wed.*

WHERE TO STAY
$$$$
B&B/INN
🏨 **The Grafton Inn.** One of the country's oldest operating inns, this 1801 classic encourages you to linger on the wraparound porches, in the authentically Colonial common rooms, or with a book by the fire in the old-fashioned library. **Pros:** classic Vermont inn and tavern;

professionally run; appealing common areas. **Cons:** rooms are attractive but not stellar. $ *Rooms from: $225* ⊠ *92 Main St.* ☎ *802/843–2231, 800/843–1801* ⊕ *www.graftoninnvermont.com* ⇲ *38 rooms, 7 suites* ⟨◯⟩ *Breakfast.*

SHOPPING

Gallery North Star. Inside this restored 1877 home original oil paintings, watercolors, lithographs, and sculptures by more than 30 New England artists are on display. ⊠ *151 Townshend Rd.* ☎ *802/843–2465* ⊕ *www. gnsgrafton.com* ⊙ *Daily 10–5.*

Grafton Village Cheese Company. Sample the best of Vermont cheddar at the Grafton Village Cheese Company's downtown wine and cheese shop. ⊠ *56 Townshend Rd.* ☎ *800/472–3866, 802/843–2221* ⊕ *www. graftonvillagecheese.com.*

TOWNSHEND

9 miles south of Grafton.

One of a string of attractive villages along the banks of the West River, Townshend embodies the Vermont ideal of a lovely town green presided over by a gracefully proportioned church spire. The spire belongs to the 1790 Congregational Meeting House, one of the state's oldest houses of worship. North on Route 30 is the Scott Bridge, the state's longest single-span covered bridge. It makes for a pretty photo although it is closed to foot and vehicle traffic.

OFF THE BEATEN PATH

Newfane. With a village green surrounded by pristine white buildings, Newfane, 6 miles southeast of Townshend, is sometimes described as the quintessential New England small town. The 1839 First Congregational Church and the Windham County Court House, with 17 green-shuttered windows and a rounded cupola, are often open. The building with the four-pointed spire is Union Hall, built in 1832. ⊠ *Newfane* ⊕ *www.newfanevt.com.*

WHERE TO EAT

$

DINER

✕ **Townshend Dam Diner.** Folks come from miles around to enjoy traditional fare such as meat loaf, roast beef, chili, and croquettes, as well as Townshend-raised bison burgers and creative daily specials. Breakfast, served all day, includes such tasty treats as raspberry-chocolate-chip walnut pancakes and homemade French toast. You can sit at any of the collection of 1930s enamel-top tables or in the big swivel chairs at the U-shaped counter. The diner is a few miles northwest of the village on Route 30. $ *Average main: $8* ⊠ *5929 Rte. 30, West Townshend* ☎ *802/874–4107* ⊟ *No credit cards* ⊙ *Closed Tues.*

WHERE TO STAY

$

B&B/INN

⛫ **Boardman House.** This handsome Greek Revival home on the town green combines modern comfort with the relaxed charm of a 19th-century farmhouse. **Pros:** inexpensive; perfect village green location. **Cons:** no phone, and cell-phone reception is bad. $ *Rooms from: $80* ⊠ *Grafton Rd.* ☎ *802/365–4086* ⇲ *4 rooms, 1 suite* ⊟ *No credit cards* ⟨◯⟩ *Breakfast.*

$$$$
B&B/INN
🛏 **Windham Hill Inn.** As there's not too much to do nearby, you might find yourself sitting by a fire or swimming in the outdoor pool at this inn, part of the Relais & Chateau collection. **Pros:** lovely views; exceedingly cozy spa. **Cons:** extremely expensive; staff not always helpful. $ *Rooms from: $305* ✉ *311 Lawrence Dr., West Townshend* ☎ *802/874–4080, 800/944–4080* ⊕ *www.windhamhill.com* ⇄ *11 rooms, 10 suites, 1 cottage* �‖ *Breakfast.*

SPORTS AND THE OUTDOORS
Townshend State Park. At Townshend State Park you'll find a sandy beach on the West River and a trail that parallels the river for almost 2 miles, topping out on Bald Mountain Dam. Up the dam, the trail follows switchbacks literally carved into the stone apron. ✉ *2755 State Forest Rd.* ☎ *802/365–7500* ⊕ *www.vtstateparks.com/htm/townshend.htm.*

SHOPPING
Newfane Country Store. You'll find delicious homemade fudge, locally made jams and jellies, and colorful quilts—which can also be custom ordered—at this pleasant shop. ✉ *598 Rte. 30, Newfane* ☎ *802/365–7916* ⊕ *www.newfanecountrystore.com.*

CENTRAL VERMONT

Central Vermont's economy once centered on marble quarrying and mills. But today, as in much of the rest of the state, tourism drives the economic engine. The center of the dynamo is Killington, the East's largest downhill resort, but there's more to discover in central Vermont than high-speed chairlifts and slope-side condos. The old mills of Quechee and Middlebury are now home to restaurants and shops, giving wonderful views of the waterfalls that once powered the mill turbines. Woodstock has upscale shops and a national historic park. Away from these settlements, the protected (except for occasional logging) lands of the Green Mountain National Forest are laced with hiking trails.

Our coverage of towns begins with Norwich, on U.S. 5 near Interstate 91 at the state's eastern edge, winds west toward U.S. 7, then continues north to Middlebury before heading over the spine of the Green Mountains to Waitsfield.

NORWICH

6 miles north of White River Junction.

On the bank of the Connecticut River, Norwich boasts beautifully maintained 18th- and 19th-century homes set about a handsome green. Norwich is the Vermont sister to sophisticated Hanover, New Hampshire (home of Dartmouth College), over the river.

GETTING HERE AND AROUND
Most attractions are off Interstate 91; the town sits a mile to the west.

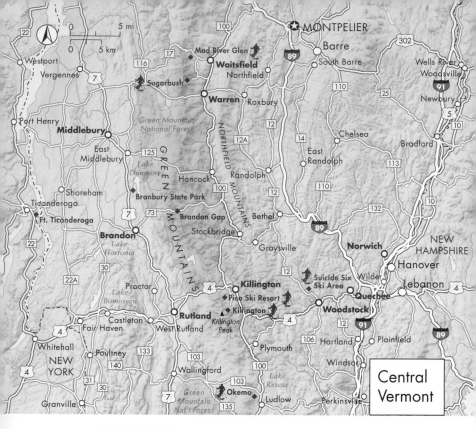

Central Vermont

EXPLORING

Montshire Museum of Science. Numerous hands-on exhibits at this science museum explore nature and technology. Kids can make giant bubbles, see images from NASA space telescopes, watch marine life swim in aquariums, and explore a maze of outdoor trails by the river. Adults will happily join the fun. An ideal destination for a rainy day, this is one of the finest museums in New England. ⊠ *1 Montshire Rd.* ☎ *802/649–2200* ⊕ *www.montshire.org* ⊠ *$14* ⊙ *Daily 10–5.*

SPORTS AND THE OUTDOORS

Lake Morey Ice Skating Trail. For the most fun you can have on skates, head to American's longest ice-skating trail. From January to March the lake freezes over and is groomed for ice-skating, providing a magical 4½-mile route amid forested hillsides. Bring your own skates or rent them at the Lake Morey Resort, which maintains the trail. ⊠ *1 Clubhouse Rd., Fairlee* ☎ *800/423–1211* ⊕ *www.lakemoreyresort.com.*

SHOPPING

King Arthur Flour Baker's Store. This shop is a must-see for those who love bread. The shelves are stocked with all the ingredients and tools in the company's *Baker's Catalogue,* including flours, mixes, and local jams and syrups. The bakery has a viewing area where you can watch products being made, and you can buy baked goods or sandwiches. ⊠ *135*

U.S. 5 S ☎ *802/649–3881, 800/827–6836* ⊕ *www.kingarthurflour.com* ⊗ *Weekdays 8 am–9 pm, weekends 9–5.*

QUECHEE

11 miles southwest of Norwich, 6 miles west of White River Junction.

A historic mill town, Quechee sits just upriver from its namesake gorge, an impressive 165-foot-deep canyon cut by the Ottauquechee River. Most people view the gorge from U.S. 4. To escape the crowds, hike along the gorge or scramble down one of several trails to the river.

EXPLORING

FAMILY

Fodor's Choice

★

Simon Pearce. The main attraction in the village is this glassblowing factory, store, and restaurant, set in a restored woolen mill by a waterfall. Water power still drives the factory's furnace. Take a free self-guided tour of the downstairs factory floor and see the amazing glassblowers at work (great for kids, too!). The store sells beautifully crafted contemporary glass and ceramic tableware. Seconds and discontinued items are available on a first-come, first-served basis. An excellent, sophisticated restaurant with outstanding views of the falls uses the Simon Pearce glassware and is justly popular. ⊠ *The Mill, 1760 Quechee Main St.* ☎ *802/295–1470* ⊕ *www.simonpearce.com* ⊗ *Daily 10–9.*

FAMILY

Vermont Institute of Natural Science Nature Center. Next to Quechee Gorge, this science center has 17 raptor exhibits, including bald eagles, peregrine falcons, and owls. All the caged birds have been found injured and are unable to survive in the wild. "Raptors up Close," a 30-minute live bird program, starts daily at 1:30. ⊠ *6565 Woodstock Rd.* ☎ *802/359–5000* ⊕ *www.vinsweb.org* 💲*$13* ⊗ *Late June–Oct., daily 10–5:30; Nov.–early Apr., daily 10–4; mid-Apr.–mid-June, daily 10–5.*

WHERE TO EAT AND STAY

$$$

AMERICAN

Fodor's Choice

★

✕ **Simon Pearce.** Sparkling glassware from the studio downstairs, exposed brick, flickering candles, and large windows overlooking the falls of the roaring Ottauquechee River create an ideal setting for contemporary American cuisine. The food is widely considered to be worthy of a pilgrimage. Horseradish-crusted blue cod with crispy leeks, herb mashed potatoes, and balsamic shallot reduction as well as roast duck with mango chutney sauce are house specialties; the wine cellar holds several hundred vintages. 💲 *Average main: $28* ⊠ *The Mill, 1760 Main St.* ☎ *802/295–1470* ⊕ *www.simonpearce.com.*

$$$$

B&B/INN

The Parker House Inn. This beautiful 1857 house on the National Historic Register was once home to Senator Joseph Parker, who also owned the textile mill next door. **Pros:** riverfront location; spacious rooms. **Cons:** no yard. 💲 *Rooms from: $245* ⊠ *1792 Main St.* ☎ *802/295–6077* ⊕ *www.theparkerhouseinn.com* ⇆ *7 rooms, 1 suite* ⊗ *Breakfast.*

$$$

B&B/INN

Quechee Inn at Marshland Farm. Each room in this handsomely restored 1793 country home has Queen Anne–style furnishings and period antiques. **Pros:** historic house; spacious grounds. **Cons:** some bathrooms are dated. 💲 *Rooms from: $175* ⊠ *1119 Main St.* ☎ *802/295–3133, 800/235–3133* ⊕ *www.quecheeinn.com* ⇆ *22 rooms, 3 suites* ⊗ *Breakfast.*

SPORTS AND THE OUTDOORS

Wilderness Trails and the Vermont Fly Fishing School. This school leads fly-fishing workshops, rents mountain bikes, and arranges canoe and kayak trips. In winter the company conducts cross-country and snowshoe treks. ⊠ *1119 Quechee Main St.* ☎ *802/295–7620* ⊕ *www. scenesofvermont.com/wildernesstrails.*

SHOPPING

ANTIQUES AND CRAFTS

Quechee Gorge Village. Hundreds of dealers sell their wares at the Quechee Gorge Village, an antiques and crafts mall in a reconstructed barn that also houses a country store and a classic diner. A merry-go-round and a small-scale working railroad operate when weather permits. ⊠ *573 Woodstock Rd., U.S. 4* ☎ *802/295–1550, 802/295–1550* ⊕ *www.quecheegorge.com.*

CLOTHING AND MORE

Scotland by the Yard. This store sells all things Celtic, from kilts to Argyle jackets and tartan ties. ⊠ *8828 Woodstock Rd.* ☎ *802/295–5351, 800/295–5351* ⊕ *www.scotlandbytheyard.com.*

WOODSTOCK

4 miles west of Quechee.

Woodstock is a Currier & Ives print come to life. Well-maintained Federal-style houses surround the tree-lined village green, which is not far from a covered bridge. The town owes much of its pristine appearance to the Rockefeller family's interest in historic preservation and land conservation and to native George Perkins Marsh, a congressman, diplomat, and conservationist who wrote the pioneering book *Man and Nature* (1864) about humanity's use and abuse of the land. Only busy U.S. 4 detracts from the town's quaintness.

ESSENTIALS

Visitor Information Woodstock Vermont Area Chamber of Commerce ⊠ *59 Central St.* ☎ *802/457–3555, 888/496–6378* ⊕ *www.woodstockvt.com.*

EXPLORING

FAMILY **Billings Farm and Museum.** Founded by Frederick Billings in 1871, this is one of the oldest operating dairy farms in the country. In addition to watching the herds of Jersey cows, horses, and other farm animals at work and play, you can tour the restored 1890 farm house and learn about 19th-century farming and domestic life in the adjacent barns. The biggest takeaway, however, is a renewed belief in sustainable agriculture and stewardship of the land. ⊠ *69 Old River Rd., ½ mile north of Woodstock* ☎ *802/457–2355* ⊕ *www.billingsfarm.org* 🖀 *$12* ⊗ *May– late Oct., daily 10–5; Nov.–Feb., weekends 10–3:30.*

Marsh-Billings-Rockefeller National Historical Park. This 555-acre park is Vermont's only national park and the nation's first to focus on conserving natural resources. The pristine and stunning park includes Frederick Billings's mansion, gardens, and carriage roads. The entire property was the gift of Laurance S. Rockefeller, who lived here with his late wife Mary, Billings's granddaughter. You can learn more at the visitor

Simon Pearce is a glassblowing factory, store, and restaurant; the factory's furnace is still powered by hydroelectricity from Quechee Falls.

center, tour the residential complex with a guide every hour on the hour, and explore the 20 miles of trails and old carriage roads that climb Mt. Tom. ✉ *54 Elm St.* ☎ *802/457–3368* 🌐 *www.nps.gov/mabi* 🎟 *Tour $8* 🕒 *May–Oct., mansion and garden tours 10–5; grounds daily dawn–dusk.*

WHERE TO EAT

$$$$ AMERICAN 🍴 **Barnard Inn Restaurant and Max's Tavern.** The dining room in this 1796 brick farmhouse exudes 18th-century charm, but the food is decidedly from the 21st century. Former San Francisco restaurant chef-owners Will Dodson and Ruth Schimmelpfennig create inventive three- and four-course prix-fixe menus ($65 to $75) with such delicacies as venison medallions and chili and house-made chive-and-nutmeg potato gnocchi. In the back is a local favorite, Max's Tavern, which serves upscale pub fare such as beer-battered oysters and dry-rubbed pulled pork. [$] *Average main: $65* ✉ *5518 Rte. 12, 8 miles north of Woodstock, Barnard* ☎ *802/234–9961* 🌐 *barnardinn.com* ✍ *Reservations essential* 🕒 *Closed Sun. and Mon. No lunch.*

$$$$ AMERICAN 🍴 **Cloudland Farm.** Representative of the wildly popular local food scene in Vermont, Cloudland Farm offers thrice-weekly prix-fixe dinners—Thursday, Friday, and Saturday—with all the seasonal ingredients fresh from the farm or other growers. Cloudland's own pork and beef feature in such main dishes as maple-glazed ham roast with an apple-and-onion compote or beef shank osso bucco with sauteed kale and beef bacon. Desserts, such as homemade carrot cake with red wine caramel and carrot jam, are delicious. With the table literally on the farm, this is a unique farm-to-table experience and worth the short drive

from Woodstock. $ *Average main: $30* ✉ *1101 Cloudland Rd., North Pomfret* ☎ *802/457–2599* ⊕ *www.cloudlandfarm.com* ⚄ *Reservations essential* ⊘ *Closed Mar. and Sun.–Wed. No lunch.*

$$$ ✕ **Keeper's Café.** Creatively prepared, moderately priced fare draws cus-
CAFÉ   tomers from all over the region to this cozy café. Chef Chris Loucka's menus include such organic dishes as the char-grilled kielbasa and the arugula-and-beet salad. Blackboard specials change daily. Housed inside a former general store, the three dining rooms feel relaxed, with locals table-hopping to chat with friends. $ *Average main: $22* ✉ *3685 Rte. 106, 12 miles south of Woodstock, Reading* ☎ *802/484–9090* ⊕ *www. keeperscafe.com* ⊘ *Closed Sun. and Mon. No lunch.*

$$$ ✕ **Pane e Saluto.** Don't let the size fool you—meals at this little upstairs
ITALIAN   restaurant are exciting and memorable, thanks to young couple Deirdre
Fodor's Choice   and Caleb Barber. Reserve well in advance, as the small space fills up
★   fast. Hip decor, an intimately small space, and Heekin's discreetly pas-
sionate front-of-house direction all come together to complement the Barbers' slow-food-inspired passion for flavorful, local and farm-raised dishes. Try *ragu d'agnello e maiale* (spaghetti with an *abruzzese* ragu from roasted pork and lamb) followed by *cotechino e lenticche* (garlic sausage with lentils). You might expect such an *osteria* in Berkeley or Brooklyn, but this tiny spot pumps life into the blood of old Woodstock. $ *Average main: $21* ✉ *61 Central St.* ☎ *802/457–4882* ⊕ *www. osteriapaneesalute.com* ⚄ *Reservations essential* ⊘ *Closed Mon., Tues., and Wed. and Apr. and Nov. No lunch.*

$$$ ✕ **The Prince & The Pauper.** Modern French and American fare with a
FRENCH   Vermont accent is the focus of this candlelit Colonial restaurant off the town green. The grilled duck breast might have an Asian five-spice sauce, and the boneless rack of lamb is wrapped in puff pas-try and splashed with Bordelaise sauce. A three-course prix-fixe menu is available for $49; a less expensive bistro menu is available in the lounge. If you like the artwork hanging above your table, feel free to buy it. $ *Average main: $21* ✉ *24 Elm St.* ☎ *802/457–1818* ⊕ *www. princeandpauper.com* ⊘ *No lunch.*

WHERE TO STAY

$$$ ⊡ **The Fan House.** If you're searching for an authentic inn in the heart of
B&B/INN   a small, quaint Vermont town, consider this Colonial-style house dating from 1840. **Pros:** center of old town; plenty of creature comforts; good library. **Cons:** upstairs rooms can be cool in winter. $ *Rooms from: $200* ✉ *6297 Rt. 12 N* ☎ *802/234–6704* ⊕ *www.thefanhouse.com* ⤴ *3 rooms* ▭ *No credit cards* ⊘ *Closed Apr.* ⦿*Breakfast.*

$$$$ ⊡ **Kedron Valley Inn.** You're likely to fall in love at the first sight of
B&B/INN   this 1828 three-story brick building, which forms the centerpiece of a 15-acre retreat. **Pros:** good food; quiet setting. **Cons:** 5 miles south of Woodstock. $ *Rooms from: $259* ✉ *4778 South Rd., South Woodstock* ☎ *802/457–1473, 800/836–1193* ⊕ *www.kedronvalleyinn.com* ⤴ *24 rooms, 1 suites* ⊘ *Closed Apr.* ⦿*Breakfast.*

$$ ⊡ **The Shire Riverview Motel.** Many rooms in this immaculate motel have
HOTEL   decks, and almost all have fabulous views of Ottauquechee River, which runs right along the building. **Pros:** inexpensive access to the heart of Woodstock; views. **Cons:** basic rooms; unexciting exterior. $ *Rooms*

The upscale Woodstock area is known as Vermont's horse country.

from: $158 ✉ 46 Pleasant St. ☎ 802/457–2211 🌐 www.shiremotel.com 🛏 42 rooms, 1 suite 🍴 No meals.

$$$$ ALL-INCLUSIVE Fodor's Choice ★ 🏨 **Twin Farms.** Let's just get it out: Twin Farms is the best lodging in Vermont. And if you can afford it—stays begin at well over $1,000 a night—you'll want to experience it. Each incredible accommodation is furnished with a blend of high art (Jasper Johns, Milton Avery, Cy Twombly), gorgeous folk art, and furniture that goes beyond comfortable sophistication. **Pros:** impeccable service; stunning rooms; sensational meals. **Cons:** incredibly steep prices [$] *Rooms from: $1600 ✉ 452 Royalton Tpke., Barnard ☎ 802/234–9999 🌐 www.twinfarms.com 🛏 10 rooms, 10 cottages 🕓 Closed Apr. 🍴 All-inclusive.*

$$$$ RESORT Fodor's Choice ★ 🏨 **The Woodstock Inn & Resort.** This resort sits in the middle of it all. **Pros:** attractive and historic property; excellent food; soothing spa. **Cons:** can lack intimacy. [$] *Rooms from: $300 ✉ 14 The Green ☎ 802/457–1100, 800/448–7900 🌐 www.woodstockinn.com 🛏 135 rooms, 7 suites 🍴 No meals.*

SPORTS AND THE OUTDOORS

GOLF

Woodstock Inn & Resort Golf Club. Robert Trent Jones Sr. designed this challenging course at the Woodstock Inn & Resort. *✉ Woodstock Inn & Resort, 14 The Green ☎ 802/457–1100 🌐 www.woodstockinn.com 🎟 Greens fee: $89 weekdays, $109 weekends ⛳ 18 holes, 6000 yards, par 70.*

SHOPPING AND SPAS

CRAFTS

Collective. This funky and attractive shop sells local jewelry, glass, pottery, and clothing. ⊠ *47 Central St.* ☎ *802/457–1298* ⊕ *www.collectivetheartofcraft.com* ⊙ *Mon.–Sat.10–5, Sun. 11–4.*

FOOD

Sugarbush Farm. Take the Taftsville Covered Bridge to Sugarbush Farm, where you'll learn how maple sugar is made and get to sample as much maple syrup as you'd like. The farm also makes excellent cheeses. ⊠ *591 Sugarbush Farm Rd., off Rte. 4* ☎ *802/457–1757, 800/281–1757* ⊕ *www.sugarbushfarm.com* ⊙ *Daily 10–5.*

Taftsville Country Store. East of town, the Taftsville Country Store sells a wide selection of Vermont cheeses, moderately priced wines, and Vermont specialty foods. ⊠ *404 Woodstock Rd., Taftsville* ☎ *802/457–1135, 800/854–0013* ⊕ *www.taftsville.com.*

Village Butcher. This emporium of Vermont edibles has great sandwiches, cheeses, local beers, and delicious baked goods—perfect for a picnic or lunch-on-the-go. ⊠ *18 Elm St.* ☎ *802/457–2756.*

Woodstock Farmers' Market. The market is a year-round buffet of local produce, fresh fish, and excellent sandwiches and pastries. The maplewalnut scones go fast, so get there early. ⊠ *468 Woodstock Rd. (U.S. 4)* ☎ *802/457–3658* ⊕ *www.woodstockfarmersmarket.com* ⊙ *Tues.–Sat. 7:30–7, Sun. 9–6.*

GALLERIES

Gallery on the Green. This corner gallery in one of Woodstock's oldest buildings showcases paintings depicting regional landscapes by more than 26 New England artists. ⊠ *One the Green* ☎ *802/457–4956* ⊕ *www.galleryonthegreen.com.*

SPAS

Out of the Woods Spa at Twin Farms. A visit to Twin Farms is a trip to another world, and a treatment at the on-site spa completes the journey. Set in the woods of the charming estate of Nobel Prize–winning writer Sinclair Lewis, the spa expounds a philosophy of wellness that goes well beyond the realm of massages and skin treatments. Employing an organic product line by Vermont-based Tata Harper and Lunaroma, the spa offers a range of facials, polishes, aromatherapy, and mud wraps, but the star remains the 120-minute Ultimate Body Treatment, which administers a heavenly reboot to your skin and muscles. ⊠ *Twin Farms, 452 Royalton Tpke., Barnard* ☎ *802/234–9999* ⊕ *www. twinfarms.com/experience/spa.*

Spa at the Woodstock Inn and Resort. The spa features a stunning 10,000-square-foot nature-inspired facility with 10 treatment rooms, a full-service salon, and sophisticated shop dedicated to wellness and relaxation. The elegant, minimalist design accentuates its beautiful setting: natural light pours into the sparking dressing rooms and the comfortable firelit Great Room. An outdoor meditation courtyard has a soaking pool and a Scandinavian-style sauna that face the sky. The mood is peaceful, quiet and serene; choose from a wide array of treatments and organic products. Each season has its own 100-minute signature treatment. ✉ *Woodstock Inn and Resort, 14 The Green, Woodstock* ☎ *802/457–6697* ⊕ *www.woodstockinn.com/Activities/Spa.*

KILLINGTON

15 miles east of Rutland.

With only a gas station, post office, motel, and a few shops at the intersection of Routes 4 and 100, it's difficult to tell that the East's largest ski resort is nearby. The village of Killington is characterized by unfortunate strip development along the access road to the ski resort. But the 360-degree views atop Killington Peak, accessible by the resort's gondola, make it worth the drive.

WHERE TO STAY

$$

B&B/INN

Birch Ridge Inn. A slate-covered carriageway about a mile from the Killington ski resort leads to one of the area's most popular off-mountain stays, a former executive retreat in two renovated A-frames. **Pros:** quirky design; well-maintained property; tasty cuisine. **Cons:** oddly furnished; outdated style. $ *Rooms from: $150* ✉ *37 Butler Rd.* ☎ *802/422–4293, 800/435–8566* ⊕ *www.birchridge.com* ⊸ *10 rooms* ☾ *Closed May* ⦿ *Breakfast.*

$$$$

RESORT

FAMILY

The Mountain Top Inn & Resort. This cross-country skiing and horseback riding haven has stunning views and laid-back yet luxurious accommodations. **Pros:** family-friendly vibe; a great spot for outdoor activities. **Cons:** expensive for what it is. $ *Rooms from: $275* ✉ *195 Mountain Top Rd., Chittenden* ☎ *802/483–2311* ⊕ *www.mountaintopinn.com* ⊸ *32 rooms, 4 cabins, 3 cottages, 18 homes* ⦿ *Breakfast.*

$$$$

RESORT

The Woods Resort & Spa. These upscale two- and three-bedroom town houses stand in wooded lots along a winding road leading to the spa. **Pros:** contemporary facility; spacious rooms; lots of layout choices. **Cons:** lacks traditional Vermont feel. $ *Rooms from: $250* ✉ *53 Woods La.* ☎ *802/422–3139, 866/785–8904* ⊕ *www.woodsresortandspa.com* ⊸ *107 units* ⦿ *No meals.*

NIGHTLIFE

Inn at Long Trail. On weekends, listen to live Irish music and sip draft Guinness at the Inn at Long Trail. ✉ *709 Rte. 4* ☎ *800/325–2540* ⊕ *www.innatlongtrail.com.*

Pickle Barrel Night Club. During ski season the Pickle Barrel Night Club has live music on Friday and Saturday. After 8 the crowd moves downstairs for dancing, sometimes to big-name bands. ✉ *1741 Killington Rd.* ☎ *802/422–3035* ⊕ *www.picklebarrelnightclub.com.*

Outback. This friendly place serves an all-you-can-eat pizza buffet on Monday nights. With a focus on live music, it's open year-round. ✉ *2841 Killington Rd.* ☎ *802/422–9885.*

Wobbly Barn. Twentysomethings dance at the Wobbly Barn, open during ski season. ✉ *2229 Killington Rd.* ☎ *802/422–6171* ⊕ *www. wobblybarn.com.*

SPORTS AND THE OUTDOORS

BIKING

True Wheels Bike Shop. This shop rents bicycles and has information on local routes. ✉ *2886 Killington Rd.* ☎ *802/422–3234, 877/487–9972* ⊕ *www.truewheels.com.*

CROSS-COUNTRY SKIING

The Mountain Top Inn & Resort. This resort has 37 miles of hilly trails groomed for cross-country skiing, 24 miles of which can be used for skate skiing. You can also enjoy snowshoeing, ice skating, and snowmobile and sleigh rides. In the summer there's horseback riding, clay-bird shooting, fishing, hiking, sand volleyball, and water sports. ✉ *195 Mountaintop Rd., Chittenden* ☎ *802/483–6089, 802/483–2311* ⊕ *www.mountaintopinn.com.*

FISHING

Gifford Woods State Park. Kent Pond in Gifford Woods State Park is a terrific fishing spot. ✉ *34 Gifford Woods Rd., ½ mile north of U.S. 4* ☎ *802/775–5354* ⊕ *www.vtstateparks.com/htm/gifford.cfm.*

GOLF

Killington Golf Course. At its namesake resort, the Killington Golf Course has a challenging layout. ✉ *4763 Killington Rd.* ☎ *802/422–6200* ⊕ *www.killington.com/summer/golf_course* ▨ *Greens fee: $50 weekdays, $60 weekends* ⌁ *18 holes, 6,186 yards, par 72.*

HIKING

Deer Leap Trail. This 3-mile round-trip hike leads to a great view overlooking Sherburne Gap and Pico Peak. ✉ *Rte. 4, near Inn at Long Trail, Rutland* ⊕ *www.greenmountainhikingtrails.com/deerleap.html.*

SKI AREAS

Fodor's Choice ★ **Killington.** "Megamountain" aptly describes Killington. Thanks to its extensive snowmaking system, the resort typically opens in early November, and the lifts often run into late April or early May. Après-ski activities are plentiful and have been rated the best in the region by national ski magazines. Killington ticket holders can also ski at Pico Mountain: a shuttle connects the two areas.

In terms of downhill skiing, it would probably take weeks to test all 212 trails on the seven mountains of the Killington complex. There are 29 lifts, including 2 gondolas, 11 quads (including 7 high-speed express quads), 5 triples, and a Magic Carpet. The K-1 Express Gondola goes to the area's highest elevation, 4,241-foot Killington Peak. The Skyeship Gondola starts on U.S. 4, far below Killington's main base lodge. ■ **TIP➜** Savvy skiers park at the base of the Skyeship Gondola to avoid the more crowded access road.

Although Killington has a vertical drop of 3,050 feet, only gentle trails like the Juggernaut go from top to bottom. The skiing includes everything from Outer Limits, the East's steepest and longest mogul trail, to 6½-mile Great Eastern. In the glades, underbrush and low branches have been cleared to provide tree skiing. Killington's 22-foot Superpipe is one of the best rated in the East. Instruction programs are available for youngsters ages 3 to 8; those 6 to12 can join an all-day program. The Killington–Pico complex also has a host of summer activities,

including mountain biking, hiking, and golf. ⊠ *4763 Killington Rd.*
☎ *802/422–6200, 802/422–6200 snow conditions* ⊕ *www.killington.*
com.

Pico. When weekend hordes hit Killington, the locals head to Pico.
One of Killington's "seven peaks," Pico is physically separated from
its parent resort. The 57 trails range from elevator-shaft steep to challenging intermediate trails near the summit, with easier terrain near
the bottom of the mountain's 2,000-foot vertical. The learning slope is
separated from the upper mountain, so hotshots won't bomb through
it. The lower express quad can get crowded, but the upper one rarely
has a line. ⊠ *73 Alpine Dr., Mendon* ☎ *802/422–6200, 866/667–7426*
⊕ *www.picomountain.com.*

SNOWMOBILE TOURS

Snowmobile Vermont. Blazing down forest trails on a snowmobile is one
way Vermonters embrace the winter landscapes. Rentals are available
through Snowmobile Vermont at several locations including Killington and Okemo. Both have hour-long guided tours across groomed
ski trails ($99). If you're feeling more adventurous, take the two-hour
backcountry tour through 25 miles of Calvin Coolidge State Forest ($149). ⊠ *170 Rte. 100, Bridgewater Corners* ☎ *802/422–2121*
⊕ *www.snowmobilevermont.com.*

RUTLAND

15 miles southwest of Killington, 32 miles south of Middlebury.

On and around U.S. 7 in Rutland are strips of shopping centers and a
seemingly endless row of traffic lights—very un-Vermont. Two blocks
west, however, stand the mansions of the marble magnates. The county
farmers' market is held in Depot Park Saturdays 9–2. Note: while Rutland is a good central base to grab a bite and see some interesting
marble, it's not a place to spend too much time sightseeing.

ESSENTIALS

Visitor Information Rutland Region Chamber of Commerce ⊠ *50 Merchants*
Row ☎ *802/773–2747, 800/756–8880* ⊕ *www.rutlandvermont.com.*

EXPLORING

Chaffee Art Center. Housed in a beautiful mansion, this arts center exhibits the work of more than 200 Vermont artists. A second location is
open downtown on Merchants Row. ⊠ *16 S. Main St.* ☎ *802/775–0356*
⊕ *www.chaffeeartcenter.org* ⊡ *Free* ☉ *Thurs.–Sat. 10–6.*

New England Maple Museum. Maple syrup is Vermont's signature product,
and this museum north of Rutland explains the history and process of
turning sap into syrup. If you don't get a chance to visit a sugarhouse,
this is a fine place to sample the different grades and pick up some sou-
venirs. ⊠ *4578 U.S. 7, 9 miles south of Brandon, Pittsford* ☎ *802/483–*
9414 ⊕ *www.maplemuseum.com* ⊡ *Museum $5* ☉ *Late May–Oct.,*
daily 9:30–5:30; Nov., Dec., and mid-Mar.–late May, daily 10–4.

Paramount Theatre. The highlight of downtown is this 838-seat gilded
playhouse, an architectural gem dating from 1913. The gorgeous theater

is home to music, theater, and films, as well as stand-up comedy. ✉ *30 Center St.* ☎ *802/775–0570* 🌐 *www.paramountvt.org.*

Vermont Marble Museum. This monument to marble highlights one of the main industries in this region. The hall of presidents has a carved bust of each U.S. president, and in the marble chapel is a replica of Leonardo da Vinci's *Last Supper.* Elsewhere you can watch a sculptor-in-residence at work, compare marble from around the world, and check out the Vermont Marble Company's original "stone library." A short walk away is the original quarry, which helped finish the U.S. Supreme Court. ✉ *52 Main St., off Rte. 3, Proctor* ☎ *802/459–2300, 800/427–1396* 🌐 *www.vermont-marble.com* 🎟 *$7* 🕓 *Mid-May–Oct., daily 9–5:30.*

Wilson Castle. Completed in 1867, this 32-room mansion was built over the course of eight years by a Vermonter who married a British aristocrat. Within the opulent setting are 84 stained-glass windows (one inset with 32 Australian opals), hand-painted Italian frescoes, and 13 fireplaces. It's magnificently furnished with European and Asian objets d'art. ✉ *2708 West St., Proctor* ☎ *802/773–3284* 🌐 *www.wilsoncastle.com* 🎟 *$10* 🕓 *Daily 9–5; last tour at 5.*

WHERE TO EAT AND STAY

$$ ECLECTIC

🍴 **Little Harry's.** Locals have packed this restaurant ever since chef-owners Trip Pearce and Jack Mangan brought Vermont cheddar ravioli and lamb lo mein to downtown Rutland in 1997. This place is " Little" compared to the bigger Harry's, near Ludlow. The 17 tabletops are adorned with laminated photos of the regulars. If you have a big appetite but a small budget, try the vegetarian red curry—it's under $12. [$] *Average main: $18* ✉ *121 West St.* ☎ *802/747–4848* 🌐 *littleharrys.com* 🕓 *No lunch.*

SPORTS AND THE OUTDOORS

BOATING

Lake Bomoseen Marina. Rent pontoon boats, speedboats, paddleboards, and kayaks at Lake Bomoseen Marina. ✉ *145 Creek Rd., off Rte. 4A* ☎ *802/265–4611* 🌐 *www.woodardmarine.com.*

HIKING

Mountain Travelers. This place sells hiking, sporting, and boating equipment; gives advice on local hikes; and rents skis. ✉ *147 Rte. 4 E* ☎ *802/775–0814.*

BRANDON

15 miles northwest of Rutland.

Thanks to an active artists' guild, tiny Brandon is making a name for itself. In 2003 the Brandon Artists Guild, led by American folk artist Warren Kimble, auctioned 40 life-size fiberglass pigs painted by local artists. The "Really Really Pig Show" raised money for the guild and has brought small-town fame ever since to this community through its yearly shows. Brandon is also home to the Basin Bluegrass Festival, held in July.

3

ESSENTIALS

Visitor Information Brandon Visitor Center ✉ *4 Grove St.* ☎ *802/247–6401* 🌐 *brandon.org.*

EXPLORING

Brandon Museum at the Stephen A. Douglas Birthplace. The famous Early American statesman was born in this house in 1813. He left 20 years later to establish himself as a lawyer, becoming a three-time U.S. senator and arguing more cases before the U.S. Supreme Court than anyone else. This museum recounts the early Douglas years, early Brandon history, and the antislavery movement in Vermont—the first state to abolish it. ✉ *4 Grove St., at U.S. 7* ☎ *802/247–6401* 🌐 *www.brandon.org* 🎟 *Free* ⏲ *Mid-May–mid-Oct., daily 11–4.*

WHERE TO EAT AND STAY

$$ CAFÉ 🍴 **Café Provence.** Robert Barral, former director of the New England Culinary Institute, graces Brandon with this informal eatery named after his birthplace. One story above the main street, the café with hints of Provence—flowered seat cushions and dried-flower window valences—specializes in eclectic farm-fresh dishes. Goat-cheese cake with mesclun greens, braised veal cheeks and caramelized endive, and a portobello pizza from the restaurant's hearth oven are just a few of the choices. Breakfast offerings include buttery pastries, eggs Benedict, and breakfast pizza. Outdoor seating can be had under large umbrellas. [$] *Average main: $20* ✉ *11 Center St.* ☎ *802/247–9997* 🌐 *www.cafeprovencevt.com.*

$$$$ B&B/INN Fodor's Choice ★ 🏨 **Blueberry Hill Inn.** In Green Mountain National Forest, 5½ miles off a mountain pass on a dirt road, you'll find this secluded inn with lush gardens and a pond with a wood-fired sauna on its bank. **Pros:** peaceful setting within the national forest; lots of activities; great food. **Cons:** fills up with wedding parties. [$] *Rooms from: $269* ✉ *1307 Goshen–Ripton Rd., Goshen* ☎ *802/247–6735, 800/448–0707* 🌐 *www.blueberryhillinn.com* 🛏 *12 rooms* 🍽 *Some meals.*

$$$ B&B/INN 🏨 **The Lilac Inn.** The best B&B in town has spacious, cheery, and comfortable rooms in a central setting half a block from the heart of Brandon. **Pros:** big manor house; walking distance to town; charming rooms. **Cons:** busy in summer with weddings. [$] *Rooms from: $220* ✉ *53 Park St.* ☎ *802/247–5463, 800/221–0720* 🌐 *www.lilacinn.com* 🛏 *8 rooms, 1 suite* 🍽 *Breakfast.*

SPORTS AND THE OUTDOORS

PARKS

Moosalamoo National Recreation Area. Covering more than 20,000 acres of the Green Mountain National Forest, this recreation area northeast of Brandon delights the hikers, mountain bikers, and cross-country skiers who enjoy the 60-plus miles of trails through gorgeous terrain. If there is anywhere to stop and smell the flowers in Vermont, this is it. ☎ *800/448–0707* 🌐 *www.moosalamoo.org.*

GOLF

Neshobe Golf Club. This bent-grass course has terrific views of the Green Mountains. Several local inns offer golf packages. ⌧ *224 Town Farm Rd.* ☎ *802/247–3611* ⊕ *www.neshobe.com* ⌧ *Greens fee: $49–$60* 🏌 *18 holes, 6,500 yards, par 72.*

HIKING

Branbury State Park. On the shores of Lake Dunmore, Branbury State Park sits near Moosalamoo National Recreation Area. A large turnout on Route 53 marks a moderate trail to the Falls of Lana. ⌧ *Rte. 53.*

Mt. Horrid. For great views from a vertigo-inducing cliff, hike up the Long Trail to Mt. Horrid. The steep, hour-long hike starts at the top of Brandon Gap, about 8 miles east of Brandon. ⌧ *Rte. 73.*

Mt. Independence State Historic Site. West of Brandon, four trails—two short ones of less than 1 mile each and two longer ones—lead to the abandoned Revolutionary War fortifications at Mt. Independence State Historic Site. To reach them, take the first left turn off Route 73 west of Orwell and go right at the fork. The parking lot is on the left at the top of the hill. ⌧ *28 Shoales Dr., Orwell* ⊕ *www.historicsites.vermont. gov/directory/mount_independence.*

SHOPPING

The Inside Scoop and Antiques by the Falls. A husband-and-wife team runs these two separate and equally fun-loving businesses under one roof: a colorful ice cream stand and penny candy store and an antiques store filled floor to ceiling with Americana. ⌧ *22 Park St., East Brandon* ☎ *802/247–6600.*

MIDDLEBURY

17 miles north of Brandon, 34 miles south of Burlington.

In the late 1800s Middlebury was the largest Vermont community west of the Green Mountains, an industrial center of river-powered wool and grain mills. This is Robert Frost country: Vermont's late poet laureate spent 23 summers at a farm east of Middlebury. Still a cultural and economic hub amid the Champlain Valley's serene pastoral patchwork and the home of top-notch Middlebury College, the picturesque town and rolling countryside invite a day of exploration.

EXPLORING

Middlebury College. Founded in 1800, Middlebury College was conceived as a more godly alternative to the worldly University of Vermont, but has no religious affiliation today. In the middle of town, the early-19th-century stone buildings contrast provocatively with the postmodern architecture of the **Mahaney Center for the Arts,** which offers music, theater, and dance performances throughout the year. ⌧ *131 College St.* ☎ *802/443–5000* ⊕ *www.middlebury.edu.*

Robert Frost Interpretive Trail. About a mile west of Middlebury College's Bread Loaf campus, this easy 1.2-mile trail winds through quiet woodlands. Plaques along the way bear quotations from Frost's poems. A picnic area is across the road from the trailhead. ⌧ *Rte. 125, 10 miles east of downtown.*

3

FAMILY **University of Vermont Morgan Horse Farm.** The Morgan horse—Vermont's official state animal—has an even temper, stamina, and slightly truncated legs in proportion to its body. This farm, about 2½ miles west of Middlebury, is a breeding and training center where in summer you can tour the stables and paddocks. ⊠ *74 Battell Dr., off Morgan Horse Farm Rd., Weybridge* 🕾 *802/388–2011* ⊕ *www.uvm.edu/morgan* ⊠ *$5* ☉ *May–Oct., daily 9–4.*

Vermont Folklife Center. In the Masonic Hall, exhibits include photography, antiques, folk paintings, manuscripts, and other artifacts and contemporary works that examine facets of Vermont life. ⊠ *88 Main St.* 🕾 *802/388–4964* ⊕ *www.vermontfolklifecenter.org* ⊠ *Donations accepted* ☉ *Tues.–Sat. 10–5.*

OFF THE
BEATEN
PATH

Fort Ticonderoga Ferry. Established in 1759, the Fort Ti cable ferry crosses Lake Champlain between Shoreham and Fort Ticonderoga, New York, at one of the oldest ferry crossings in North America. The trip takes seven minutes. ⊠ *4831 Rte. 74W, Shoreham* 🕾 *802/897–7999* ⊕ *www. forttiferry.com* ⊠ *Cars $9; bicycles $2; pedestrians $1* ☉ *May, June, Sept., and Oct., daily 7–6; July–Sept., 7–7.*

WHERE TO EAT

$$
PIZZA

✕ **American Flatbread Middlebury Hearth.** On weekends this is the most happening spot in town, and no wonder: the pizza is extraordinary, and the attitude is pure Vermont. Wood-fired clay domes create masterful thin crusts from organically grown wheat. Besides the innovative, delicious pizzas, try an organic mesclun salad tossed in the house ginger-tamari vinaigrette. If you love pizza, you're in for a treat. There are also locations in Waitsfield and Burlington. $ *Average main: $20* ⊠ *137 Maple St.* 🕾 *802/388–3300* ⊕ *www.americanflatbread.com* ⊠ *Reservations not accepted* ☉ *No lunch. No dinner Sun. and Mon.*

$$
AMERICAN

✕ **The Bobcat Cafe & Brewery.** Worth the drive from Middlebury to the small, quaint town of Bristol, The Bobcat is the place to be in the area. Fun, funky, and hip, this charming eatery is nice enough for a date but casual enough for the whole family. Choose from a wide range of great offerings from burgers to cornmeal-crusted haddock and wash it down with excellent house-brewed beer. For something special, try the maple-brined pork loin or the peach upside-down cake for dessert. $ *Average main: $18* ⊠ *5 Main St., Bristol* 🕾 *802/453–3311* ⊕ *www. bobcatcafe.com* ☉ *No lunch.*

$$$
AMERICAN
Fodor's Choice
★

✕ **Mary's at Baldwin Creek.** People drive from the far reaches of Vermont to dine at this restaurant just beyond the charming, little-known town of Bristol, 13 miles northeast of Middlebury. Plan time to visit the sprawling gardens that surround this beautiful property—they represent the slow approach to cooking that earned this restaurant its stellar reputation. Seasonal fare bursts to life here with hearty fare like the summer lasagna packed with vegetables and the near-legendary garlic soup, a creamy year-round staple that seems genetically engineered to please. Desserts, however, are hit or miss. $ *Average main: $25* ⊠ *1868 North Rte. 116, Bristol* 🕾 *802/453–2432* ⊕ *www.innatbaldwincreek. com* ☉ *Closed Mon. and Tues.*

$$　✕ **The Storm Cafe.** There's no setting in town quite like this restaurant's
MODERN　deck, overlooking Otter Creek Falls at one end of a long footbridge.
AMERICAN　Even if you're not here in summer, the eclectic, ever-changing menu at
this small restaurant in the old Frog Hollow Mill makes it worth a visit
any time of year. Spicy calamari and vegetable curry are favorites, as
are the large salads. $ *Average main: $20* ✉ *3 Mill St.* ☎ *802/388–1063*
⊕ *www.thestormcafe.com* ⊘ *No dinner Sun. and Mon.*

WHERE TO STAY

$$　▦ **Inn on the Green.** On the National Register of Historic Places, this
B&B/INN　1803 inn and carriage house sit in the center of bucolic Middlebury near
the stunning campus of Middlebury College. **Pros:** ideal location; great
breakfast. **Cons:** rooms can be small and close together. $ *Rooms from:*
$170 ✉ *71 S. Pleasant St.* ☎ *802/388–7512* ⊕ *www.innonthegreen.com*
⥅ *9 rooms, 2 suites* ❍| *Breakfast.*

$$　▦ **Swift House Inn.** The 1814 Georgian home of a 19th-century governor
B&B/INN　showcases white-panel wainscoting, mahogany furnishings, and marble
fireplaces. **Pros:** attractive, spacious, well-kept rooms; professionally
run. **Cons:** near to but not quite in the heart of town. $ *Rooms from:*
$169 ✉ *25 Stewart La.* ☎ *866/388–9925* ⊕ *www.swifthouseinn.com*
⥅ *20 rooms* ❍| *Breakfast.*

SHOPPING

Edgewater Gallery. This gallery alongside Otter Creek is about as pictur-
esque as you can get. However, there are plenty of impressive paintings,
jewelry, ceramics, and pieces of furniture inside the bright, airy space to
steal your attention as well. Exhibitions rotate regularly, demonstrating
the owner's ambition to be more gallery than shop (although all pieces
are for sale). ✉ *1 Mill St.* ☎ *802/458–0098* ⊕ *www.edgewatergallery-vt.*
com.

Historic Marble Works. This renovated marble manufacturing facility has
a collection of shops and eateries set amid quarrying equipment and
factory buildings. ✉ *2 Maple St.* ☎ *802/388–3701.*

　Danforth Pewter. In addition to the lovely handcrafted pewter vases,
lamps, and jewelry, this store offers you a front-row seat to the art of
pewter spinning in the back workshop. There's also a small museum.
✉ *52 Seymour St.* ☎ *800/222–3142* ⊕ *www.danforthpewter.com*

WAITSFIELD AND WARREN

32 miles northeast (Waitsfield) and 25 miles east (Warren) of Middlebury.

Skiers discovered the high peaks overlooking the pastoral Mad River
Valley in the 1940s. Now the valley and its two towns, Waitsfield and
Warren, attract the hip, the adventurous, and the low-key. Warren is
tiny and adorable, with a general store that attracts tour buses. The
gently carved ridges cradling the valley and the swell of pastures and
fields lining the river seem to keep notions of ski-resort sprawl at bay.
With a map from the Sugarbush Chamber of Commerce you can inves-
tigate back roads off Route 100 that have exhilarating valley views.

Sheep's cheese is just one of the many food products that contribute to great fresh local meals in Vermont.

ESSENTIALS

Visitor Information Mad River Valley Chamber of Commerce ✉ *4061 Main St.* ☎ *802/496–3409, 800/828–4748* 🌐 *www.madrivervalley.com.*

WHERE TO EAT

$$ PIZZA Fodor's Choice ★ 🍴 **American Flatbread Waitsfield.** Is this the best pizza experience in the world? It just may be. In summer you can dine outside around fire pits in the beautiful valley. The organically grown flour and vegetables and the wood-fired clay ovens transform the pizza into something magical. One of our favorites is the maple-fennel sausage pie topped with sun-dried tomatoes, caramelized onions, cheese, and herbs; it's a dream, as are the more traditional flavors. This is the original American Flatbread location—plan your trip around it. Seats can be hard to come by, but if you stay at the adjoining inn, they're reserved. [$] *Average main: $18* ✉ *46 Lareau Rd., off Rte. 100* ☎ *802/496–8856* 🌐 *www.americanflatbread.com* ✍ *Reservations not accepted* ⏲ *Closed Mon.–Wed. No lunch.*

$$$ MODERN AMERICAN 🍴 **Common Man.** This restaurant is in a big 1800s barn with hand-hewn rafters and crystal chandeliers hanging from the beams. That's the Common Man for you: fancy and après-ski all at once. Bottles of Moët & Chandon signed by the customers who ordered them sit atop the beams. The eclectic, sophisticated New American cuisine highlights locally grown produce and meats. The menu might include a roasted beet salad with goat cheese and fennel in an orange vinaigrette, duck breast with butternut squash puree, or seared black bass with sticky rice and bok choy. Dinner is served by candlelight. Couples sit by the big fireplace. [$] *Average main: $25* ✉ *3209 German Flats Rd., Warren*

☎ *802/583–2800* 🌐 *www.commonmanrestaurant.com* ⏲ *Closed Sun. and Mon. No lunch.*

WHERE TO STAY

$$$ B&B/INN

🏨 **The Inn at Round Barn Farm.** A Shaker-style round barn (one of only five in Vermont) is the centerpiece of this B&B, but what you'll remember when you leave is how comfortable a stay here is. **Pros:** great trails, gardens, and rooms; tasty breakfasts; unique architecture. **Cons:** no restaurant; fills up for wedding parties. [$] *Rooms from: $205* ✉ *1661 E. Warren Rd.* ☎ *802/496–2276* 🌐 *www.theroundbarn.com* 🛏 *11 rooms, 1 suite* 🍴 *Breakfast.*

$$$$ B&B/INN Fodor's Choice ★

🏨 **The Pitcher Inn.** Sublime is a word which comes to mind when thinking about a night at the elegant Pitcher Inn, one of Vermont's trio of Relais & Châteaux properties. **Pros:** exceptional service; fabulous restaurant; beautiful location. **Cons:** at some point, you have to go home. [$] *Rooms from: $425* ✉ *275 Main St., Warren* ☎ *802/496–6350, 888/867–4824* 🌐 *www.pitcherinn.com* 🛏 *9 rooms, 2 suites* 🍴 *Breakfast.*

NIGHTLIFE AND THE ARTS

THE ARTS

Green Mountain Cultural Center. The Green Mountain Cultural Center hosts concerts, art exhibits, and educational workshops. ✉ *Inn at Round Barn Farm, 1661 E. Warren Rd.* ☎ *802/496-4759* 🌐 *www.theroundbarn.com.*

NIGHTLIFE

Purple Moon Pub. Live bands play most weekends at Purple Moon Pub. ✉ *6163 Main St.(Rte. 100)* ☎ *802/496–3422* 🌐 *www.purplemoonpub.com.*

Fodor's Choice ★

Tracks. Downstairs at the Pitcher Inn, this comfortable tavern has a tasteful lodge-style setting complete with a crackling fireplace. It has a terrific bar menu—try the seared scallops over sweet potatoes and bacon or the local pork chops. There's also an excellent wine selection, billiard tables, dart boards, and a fun shuffleboard game played on a long table. ✉ *Pitcher Inn, 275 Main St, ., Warren* ☎ *802/493–6350* 🌐 *www.pitcherinn.com.*

SPORTS AND THE OUTDOORS

GOLF

Sugarbush Resort Golf Club. Great views and challenging play are the trademarks of the Robert Trent Jones Sr.–designed mountain course. ✉ *Sugarbush, 1840 Sugarbush Access Rd., Warren* ☎ *802/583–6300* 🌐 *www.sugarbush.com* 🎫 *Greens fee: $40–$100* ⛳ *18 holes, 6,464 yards, par 72.*

MULTI-SPORT OUTFITTER

Clearwater Sports. This outfitter rents canoes and kayaks and leads guided river trips in the warmer months. When the weather turns cold it offers snowshoe and backcountry ski tours. ✉ *4147 Main St.* ☎ *802/496–2708* 🌐 *clearwatersports.com.*

SKI AREAS

Blueberry Lake Cross Country and Snowshoeing Center. This ski area has 18 miles of trails through thickly wooded glades. ⊠ *424 Plunkton Rd., East Warren* ☎ *802/496–6687* ⊕ *www.blueberrylakeskivt.com.*

Mad River Glen. A pristine alpine experience, Mad River attracts rugged individualists looking for less polished terrain. The area was developed in the late 1940s, and has changed relatively little since then. It remains one of only three resorts in the country that ban snowboarding. Mad River is steep, with natural slopes that follow the mountain's fall lines. The terrain changes constantly on the 45 interconnected trails, of which 33% are beginner, 27% are intermediate, and 41% are expert. Five lifts—including one of two surviving single chairlifts in the country— service the mountain's 2,037-foot vertical drop. Most of Mad River's trails are covered only by natural snow. The kids' ski school runs classes for little ones ages 4 to 12.

Known as the capital of free-heel skiing, Mad River Glen sponsors Telemark programs throughout the season. Every March the North America Telemark Organization Festival attracts up to 1,400 visitors. Snowshoeing is also an option. There is a $5 fee to use the snowshoe trails, and rentals are available. ⊠ *Rte. 17* ☎ *802/496–3551, 802/496–2001 snow conditions* ⊕ *www.madriverglen.com.*

Sugarbush. Sugarbush has remade itself as a true skier's mountain, with steep, natural snow glades and fall-line drops. Not as rough around the edges as Mad River Glen, Sugarbush also has well-groomed intermediate and beginner terrain. A computer-controlled system for snowmaking has increased coverage to 70%. At the base of the mountain are condominiums, restaurants, shops, bars, and a sports center.

Sugarbush is two distinct, connected mountain complexes connected by the Slide Brook Express quad. Lincoln Peak, with a vertical drop of 2,400 feet, is known for formidable steeps, especially on Castlerock. Mount Ellen has more beginner runs near the bottom, with steep fall-line pitches on the upper half of the 2,650 vertical feet. There are 111 trails in all: 22% beginner, 46% intermediate, 32% expert. The resort has 18 lifts: seven quads (including four high-speed versions), three triples, four doubles, and four surface lifts. There's half- and full-day instruction available for children ages 4 to 12 and supervised ski-and-ride programs for teens. Sugarbear Forest, a terrain garden, has fun bumps and jumps. ⊠ *1840 Sugarbush Access Rd., accessible from Rte. 100 or 17, Warren* ☎ *802/583–6300, 802/583–7669 snow conditions* ⊕ *www.sugarbush.com.*

SHOPPING

All Things Bright and Beautiful. This eccentric Victorian house is jammed to the rafters with stuffed animals of all shapes, sizes, and colors, as well as folk art, European glass, and Christmas ornaments. ⊠ *27 Bridge St.* ☎ *802/496–3997* ⊕ *www.allthingsbright.com.*

The Warren Store. This general store has everything you'd hope to find in tiny but sophisticated Vermont: a nice selection of local beer and wine, cheeses, baked goods, strong coffee, and delicious sandwiches and prepared foods. In summer, grab a quick lunch on the small deck by the water; in winter, warm up at the woodstove. ■TIP→ Don't forget to head upstairs for an eclectic selection of warm, wooly clothing and accessories. ✉ *284 Main St., Warren* ☎ *802/496–3864* ⊕ *www. warrenstore.com* ۞ *Mon.–Sat. 8–7, Sun. 8–6.*

NORTHERN VERMONT

Vermont's northernmost region presents the state's greatest contrasts. To the west, Burlington and its suburbs have grown so rapidly that rural wags now say that Burlington's greatest advantage is that it's "close to Vermont." The north country also harbors Vermont's tiny but charming capital, Montpelier, and its highest mountain, Mt. Mansfield, site of the famous Stowe and Smugglers' Notch ski resorts. To the northeast of Montpelier is a sparsely populated and heavily wooded territory that former Senator George Aiken dubbed the "Northeast Kingdom." It's the domain of loggers, farmers, and avid outdoors enthusiasts.

MONTPELIER

38 miles southeast of Burlington, 115 miles north of Brattleboro.

With only about 8,000 residents, little Montpelier is the country's smallest capital city. But it has a youthful energy—and certainly an independent spirit—that makes it seem almost as large as Burlington. The well-preserved downtown bustles with state and city workers walking to meetings and restaurants, or students heading to one of the funky coffee shops.

EXPLORING

Hope Cemetery. The "Granite Capital of the World," Barre lies just 7 miles east of Montpelier. On a hilltop north of town you'll find one of the world's most gorgeous cemeteries. Many of the superbly crafted tombstones were carved by the stonecutters themselves to demonstrate their skill. A few embrace the avant-garde, while others take defined shapes like a racecar, biplane, and soccer ball. ✉ *201 Maple Ave, Barre.*

FAMILY
Fodor's Choice
★
Morse Farm Maple Sugarworks. With eight generations of sugaring, the Morses may be the oldest maple family in existence, so you're sure to find an authentic maple farm experience here. Burr Morse heads up the operation now, along with his son Tom, but you can still see Burr's father hamming it up in a hilarious video playing in the Woodshed Theater. More than 3,000 trees produce the syrup (sample all the grades), candy, cream, and sugar in their gift shop. Surrounding trails offer pleasant strolls in summer and prime cross-country skiing in winter. ✉ *1168 County Rd.* ☎ *800/242–2740* ⊕ *www.morsefarm.com* ⌦ *Free.*

Vermont History Museum. The collection here was begun in 1838 and features all things Vermont, from a catamount (the now-extinct local cougar) to Ethan Allen's shoe buckles. The museum store has a great collection of books, prints, and gifts. ✉ *109 State St.* ☎ *802/828–2291* ⊕ *www.vermonthistory.org* ⌦ *$5* ۞ *Tues.–Sat. 10–4.*

QUICK
BITES
✕ **La Brioche Bakery. This is a great downtown stop for breakfast and lunch. New England Culinary Institute students are up at 4 am preparing breads for thankful locals. There's a nice selection of soups, salads, and**

sandwiches, but it's the pastries that are the most tempting. $ *Average main: $425* ✉ *89 Main St.* ☎ *802/229–0443* ⊕ *www.neci.edu/labrioche.*

Vermont State House. The regal capitol building surrounded by forest is emblematic of this proudly rural state. With the gleaming dome topped by the goddess of agriculture and columns of Barre granite measuring 6 feet in diameter, the statehouse is home to the country's oldest legislative chambers still in their original condition. Half-hour tours take you through the governor's office and the house and senate chambers. Interior paintings and exhibits make much of Vermont's sterling Civil War record. ✉ *115 State St.* ☎ *802/828–2228* 💲 *Donations accepted* ⊙ *Weekdays 8–4; tours July–mid-Oct., weekdays every ½ hr 10–3:30, Sat. 11–3.*

OFF THE BEATEN PATH

Rock of Ages Granite Quarry. The attractions here range from the awe-inspiring (the quarry resembles the Grand Canyon in miniature) to the mildly ghoulish (you can consult a directory of tombstone dealers throughout the country) to the whimsical (an outdoor granite bowling alley). You might recognize the sheer walls of the quarry from *Batman and Robin,* the film starring George Clooney and Arnold Schwarzenegger. At the crafts center, skilled artisans sculpt monuments and blast stone, while at the quarries themselves 25-ton blocks of stone are cut from sheer 475-foot walls by workers who clearly earn their pay. ✉ *560 Graniteville Rd., off I–89, Graniteville* ☎ *802/476–3119* ⊕ *www.rockofages.com* 💲 *Tours $5* ⊙ *Visitor center May–Oct., Mon.–Sat. 9–5.*

WHERE TO EAT

$$$
ECLECTIC

✕ **Ariel's.** Well off the beaten path, this small restaurant overlooking a lake is worth the drive down a dirt road. The chef prepares small, medium, and large plates of New England–inspired cuisine based on local sources. Favorites include herb-crusted lamb loin and line-caught swordfish. Don't leave without ordering a board of Vermont cheeses, which pair especially well with the excellent wine selection. $ *Average main: $26* ✉ *29 Stone Rd., 18 miles south of Montpelier, Brookfield* ☎ *802/276–3939* ⊕ *www.arielsrestaurant.com* ⊙ *Closed Nov. and Apr.; Mon. and Tues. May–Oct.; Sun.–Thurs. Dec.–Mar. No lunch.*

$$
AMERICAN

✕ **NECI on Main.** Nearly everyone working here is a student at the New England Culinary Institute, but the quality and inventiveness of the food is anything but beginner's luck. The menu changes seasonally, but soups and Misty Knoll Farm free-range chicken are reliable winners. The lounge downstairs offers the same menu, but in a more casual atmosphere. Sunday brunch is very popular, and reservations are strongly recommended. $ *Average main: $20* ✉ *118 Main St.* ☎ *802/223–3188* ⊕ *www.neci.edu* ⊙ *Closed Mon. No dinner Sun.*

$$
ITALIAN

✕ **Sarducci's.** Legislative lunches have been a lot more leisurely since Sarducci's came along to fill the trattoria void in Vermont's capital. These bright, cheerful rooms alongside the Winooski River are a local favorite for pizza fresh from wood-fired ovens, wonderfully textured homemade Italian breads, and imaginative dishes like pasta *pugliese,* which marries penne with basil, black olives, roasted eggplant, portobello mushrooms, and sun-dried tomatoes. $ *Average main: $17* ✉ *3 Main St.* ☎ *802/223–0229* ⊕ *www.sarduccis.com* ⊙ *No lunch Sun.*

$ ✕ **The Skinny Pancake.** This dine-in creperie makes a great stop for break-
CAFÉ fast, lunch, or an easy dinner. The Breakfast Monster, made with eggs
and local Cabot cheddar, is a winner. For lunch, try the spinach and
feta crepes, the Veggie Monster, or the Lamb Fetatastic, made with
local lamb sausage, baby spinach, Vermont feta, and kalamata olives.
If you're in the mood for dessert, sample the Nutella crepe or the Pooh
Bear served with warm local honey and cinnamon. ⓢ *Average main:
$9* ✉ *89 Main St., Monpelier* ☎ *802/262–2253* ⊕ *www.skinnypancake.
com.*

$$ ✕ **That's Life Soup.** As the name indicates, soup is the focus of this tiny,
INTERNATIONAL bright restaurant. The selections here are delicious and warming, per-
haps the best in the state. The ever-changing menu incorporates a truly
global influence and a lot of quirkiness, with flavors like South Ameri-
can chipotle pork stew and Tuscan ribollita. There are few tables, so
it's best to aim for off-peak hours. ⓢ *Average main: $18* ✉ *41 Elm St.,
Montpelier* ☎ *802/223–5333.*

$$ ✕ **Three Penny Taproom.** This hip, lively taproom is quickly becoming one
ECLECTIC of the best in Vermont. The Three Penny serves a wide array of craft
Fodor's Choice beers, including the coveted and hard-to-get Hill Farmstead. Now with
★ a full menu and expanded seating, the pub is a dining destination as
well, sharing an award for the state's best burger. The vibe feels straight
out of an artsy neighborhood in Brussels but with the earthiness of Vermont. ⓢ *Average main: $15* ✉ *108 Main St* ☎ *802/223–8277* ⊕ *www.
threepennytaproom.com.*

WHERE TO STAY

$$ 🛏 **Inn at Montpelier.** The town's most charming lodging option, this lov-
B&B/INN ingly tended inn dating from 1830 has rooms filled with antique four-
poster beds and Windsor chairs. **Pros:** beautiful home; relaxed central
setting; amazing porch. **Cons:** some rooms are small. ⓢ *Rooms from:
$150* ✉ *147 Main St.* ☎ *802/223–2727* ⊕ *www.innatmontpelier.com*
↩ *19 rooms* ⊙ *Breakfast.*

SHOPPING

Artisans Hand Craft Gallery. For more than 30 years, Maggie Neale has
been celebrating and supporting Vermont's craft community. Her store
houses jewelry, textiles, sculpture, and paintings by many local artists.
✉ *89 Main St.* ☎ *802/229-9492* ⊕ *www.artisanshand.com.*

Vermont Butter & Cheese Creamery. One of the leaders of the artisanal
cheese movement, Vermont Butter & Cheese invites curious cheese afi-
cionados to visit its 4,000-square-foot creamery where gem-like goat
cheeses such as Bonne Bouche—a perfectly balanced, cloud-like cheese—
are made weekdays. It's in Websterville, southwest of the city. ✉ *40 Pit-
man Rd., Websterville* ☎ *800/884–6287* ⊕ *www.vermontcreamery.com.*

Zutano. For hip newborn, baby, and toddler clothing designed in Vermont,
head to Zutano. ✉ *79 Main St.* ☎ *802/223–2229* ⊕ *www.zutano.com.*

**EN
ROUTE**
Ben & Jerry's Ice Cream Factory. On your way to Stowe, be sure to stop
at Ben & Jerry's Ice Cream Factory. Ben Cohen and Jerry Greenfield
began selling ice cream from a renovated gas station in Burlington in
the 1970s. The tour only skims the surface of the behind-the-scenes
goings-on at the plant—a flaw forgiven when the free samples are dished

out. ✉ *1281 Waterbury-Stowe Rd., 1 mile north of I–89, Waterbury* ☎ *802/846–1500* 🌐 *www.benjerry.com* 🎟 *Tour $4* 🕒 *Late Oct.–June, daily 10–6; July–mid-Aug., daily 9–9; mid-Aug.–late Oct., daily 9–7. Tours run every half hour.*

Cabot Creamery. The state's biggest cheese producer, Cabot Creamery has a visitor center where you can learn about the dairy industry. ✉ *2878 Main St., 5 miles north of U.S. 2, Cabot* ☎ *800/837–4261* 🌐 *www.cabotcheese.coop* 🎟 *$2* 🕒 *June–Oct., daily 9–5; Nov., Dec., and Feb.–May, Mon.–Sat. 9–4; Jan., Mon.–Sat. 10–4.*

3

STOWE

22 miles northwest of Montpelier, 36 miles east of Burlington.

Fodor's Choice ★

Long before skiing came to Stowe in the 1930s, the rolling hills and valleys beneath Vermont's highest peak, 4,395-foot Mt. Mansfield, attracted summer tourists looking for a reprieve from city heat. Most stayed at one of two inns in the village of Stowe. When skiing made the town a winter destination, the arriving skiers outnumbered the hotel beds, so locals took them in. This spirit of hospitality continues, and many of these homes are now lovely country inns. The village itself is tiny, just a few blocks of shops and restaurants clustered around a picture-perfect white church with a lofty steeple, but it serves as the anchor for Mountain Road, which leads north past restaurants, lodges, and shops on its way to Stowe's fabled slopes.

ESSENTIALS

Visitor Information Stowe Area Association ☎ *802/253–7321, 877/467–8693* 🌐 *www.gostowe.com.*

EXPLORING

Trapp Family Lodge. Built by the von Trapp family of *The Sound of Music* fame, this Tyrolean lodge and its grounds are the site of a popular outdoor music series in the summer. You can hike along the trails in warm weather, or go cross-country skiing in winter. The lodge's café, overlooking a breathtaking mountain vista, serves tasty food and local beers; a ski-in cabin offers homemade soups, sandwiches, and hot chocolate. There's also a fine-dining restaurant on the premises. ✉ *700 Trapp Hill Rd.* ☎ *802/253–8511, 800/826–7000* 🌐 *www.trappfamily.com.*

Vermont Ski and Snowboard Museum. The state's skiing and snowboarding history is documented here with myriad exhibits. ✉ *1 S. Main St.* ☎ *802/253–9911* 🌐 *www.vtssm.com* 🎟 *$5* 🕒 *Wed.–Mon. noon–5.*

WHERE TO EAT

$$ AMERICAN

🍴 **Harrison's Restaurant.** For an excellent dinner at a warm and unpretentious American bistro, go no further than Harrison's in downtown Stowe. A lively local scene, cozy booths by the fireplace, and a creative menu paired with a variety of fine wines and local beers make this a perfect stop for couples and families alike. Stop in for braised short ribs in blackberry-chipotle barbecue sauce, sirloin bistro steak, or lobster mac 'n' cheese made with Cabot cheddar. The bar is also inviting—it's a nice place to dine alone or chat over a drink with a local. [$] *Average* *main: $20* ✉ *25 Main St., behind TD Bank* ☎ *802/253–7773* 🌐 *www.harrisonsstowe.com* ✍ *Reservations essential* 🕒 *No lunch.*

$$$ ECLECTIC Fodor's Choice ★ 🍴 **Hen of the Wood.** Ask Vermont's great chefs where they go for a tremendous meal, and Hen of the Wood inevitably tops the list. The setting is riveting: a converted 1835 grist mill beside a waterfall. Inside the underground level of the mill, a sunken pit formerly housing the grindstone is now filled with tables, thick wood beams, and uneven stone walls dotted with tiny candles that make the ambience decidedly romantic. Sophisticated dishes showcase the abundance of local produce, meat, and cheese. A typical plate on the daily changing menu may feature goat's milk dumplings, a local farm pork loin, grass-fed rib eye, and a wild Alaskan halibut. This is very nearly the perfect Vermont dining experience. In the warmer months, beg for a coveted patio table overlooking a dramatic series of falls. A second branch of the restaurant is in Burlington. [$] *Average main: $25* ✉ *92 Stowe St., Waterbury* ☎ *802/244–7300* 🌐 *www.henofthewood.com* ✍ *Reservations essential* 🕒 *Closed Sun. No lunch.*

$$$$ EUROPEAN 🍴 **Michael's on the Hill.** Swiss-born chef Michael Kloeti trained in Europe and New York before opening this dining establishment in a 19th-century farmhouse outside Stowe. In addition to à la carte options, Michael's two four-course prix-fixe menus ($47 and $67) highlight European cuisine with farm-to-table earthiness, perhaps best seen in dishes like spice-roasted duck breast and venison navarin. The menu changes seasonally. [$] *Average main: $32* ✉ *4182 Stowe-Waterbury Rd., 6 miles south of Stowe, Waterbury Center* ☎ *802/244–7476* 🌐 *www.michaelsonthehill.com* 🕒 *Closed Tues. No lunch.*

$ AMERICAN 🍴 **Prohibition Pig.** The Alchemist, a very popular downtown restaurant, closed a few years back, but new owners have brought the place roaring back to life. Prohibition Pig is just as good, with more or less the same hip look and layout of the previous incarnation. It also still serves the same fabulous local brews and barbecue-friendly bistro cuisine like duck-fat fries, roasted brisket, and pit-smoked chicken. A young, energetic crowed creates a fun vibe. [$] *Average main: $12* ✉ *23 S. Main St., Waterbury* ☎ *802/244–4120* 🌐 *prohibitionpig.com* 🕒 *No lunch Mon.–Thurs.*

$ CAFÉ 🍴 **Red Hen Baking Co.** If you're a devotee of artisanal bakeries, it'd be a mistake not to trek the 15 miles away from Stowe to have lunch, pick up fresh baked bread, or sample a sweet treat here. Try the ham-and-cheese croissants, sticky buns, homemade soups, and savory sandwiches. Red Hen supplies bread to some of the state's best restaurants, including Hen of the Wood, and is open daily. [$] *Average main: $8* ✉ *961 Rte. 2, Middlesex* ☎ *802/223–5200* 🌐 *www.redhenbaking.com* ✍ *Reservations not accepted* 🕒 *No dinner.*

WHERE TO STAY

$$$ B&B/INN 🏨 **Green Mountain Inn.** Welcoming guests since 1833, this classic redbrick inn gives you access to the buzz of downtown. **Pros:** fun location; lively tavern; and lots of character. **Cons:** farther from skiing than other area hotels. [$] *Rooms from: $189* ✉ *18 Main St.* ☎ *802/253–7301, 800/253–7302* 🌐 *www.greenmountaininn.com* 🛏 *103 rooms* 🍽 *No meals.*

Continued on page 118

LET IT SNOW

WINTER ACTIVITIES IN VERMONT

by Elise Coroneos

SKIING AND SNOWBOARDING IN VERMONT

Less than 5 mi from the Canadian border, Jay Peak is Vermont's northernmost ski resort.

Ever since America's first ski tow opened in a farmer's pasture near Woodstock in January 1934, skiers have headed en masse to Vermont in winter. Today, 19 alpine and 30 nordic ski areas range in size and are spread across the state, from Mount Snow in the south to Jay Peak near the Canadian border. The snow-making equipment has also become more comprehensive over the years, with more than 75% of the trails in the state using man-made snow. Here are some of the best ski areas by various categories:

GREAT FOR KIDS Smugglers' Notch, Okemo, and **Bromley Mountain** all offer terrific kids' programs, with classes organized by age categories and by skill level. Kids as young as 3 (4 at some ski areas) can start learning. Child care, with activities like stories, singing, and arts and crafts, are available for those too young to ski; some ski areas, like Smuggler's Notch, offer babysitting with no minimum age daytime and evening.

BEST FOR BEGINNERS Beginner terrain makes up nearly half of the mountain at **Stratton**, where options include private and group lessons for first-timers. Also good are small but family-friendly **Bolton Valley** and **Bromley Mountains,** which both designate a third of their slopes for beginners.

EXPERT TERRAIN The slopes at **Jay Peak** and massive **Killington** are most notable for their steepness and pockets of glades. About 40% of the runs at these two resorts are advanced or expert. Due to its far north location, Jay Peak tends to get the most snow, making it ideal for those skilled in plowing through fresh powder. Another favorite with advanced skiers is Central Vermont's **Mad River Glen**, where many slopes are ungroomed (natural) and the motto is "Ski it if you can." In addition, **Sugarbush, Stowe,** and **Smugglers' Notch** are all revered for their challenging untamed side country.

Mount Mansfield is better known as Stowe.   Stratton Mountain clocktower

NIGHT SKIING Come late afternoon, **Bolton Valley** is hopping. That's because it's the only location in Vermont for night skiing. Ski and ride under the lights from 4 until 8 Wednesday through Saturday, followed by a later après-ski scene.

APRÈS-SKI The social scenes at **Killington, Sugarbush,** and **Stowe** are the most noteworthy (and crowded). Warm up after a day in the snow in Killington with all-you-can-eat pizza on Monday nights and daily happy hour specials at the Outback, or stop by the always popular Wobbly Barn. For live music, try Castlerock Pub in Sugarbush or the Matterhorn Bar in Stowe.

SNOWBOARDING Boarders (and some skiers) will love the latest features for freestyle tricks in Vermont. **Stratton** has a half pipe, rail garden, and four other parks. **Mount Snow's** Carinthia Peak is an all-terrain park—dedicated mountain, the only of its kind in New England. Head to **Killington** for Burton Stash, another beautiful all-natural features terrain park. **Okemo** has a superpipe and eight terrain parks and a gladed park with all-natural features. Note that snowboarding is not allowed at skiing cooperative **Mad River Glen.**

CROSS-COUNTRY To experience the best of cross-country skiing in the state, simply follow the Catamount Trail, a 300-mile nordic route from southern Vermont to Canada. **The Trapp Family Lodge** in Stowe has 37 miles of groomed cross-country trails and 62 miles of back-country trails. Another top option is **The Mountain Top Inn & Resort,** just outside of Killington. Its Nordic Ski and Snowshoe Center provides instruction for newcomers, along with hot drinks and lunches when it is time to take a break and warm up.

TELEMARK Ungroomed snow and tree skiing are a natural fit with free-heel skiing at **Mad River Glen. Bromley** and **Jay Peak** also have telemark rentals and instruction.

MOUNTAIN-RESORT TRIP PLANNER

TIMING

■ **Snow Season.** Winter sports time is typically from Thanksgiving through April, weather permitting. Holidays are the most crowded.

■ **March Madness.** Most of the season's snow tends to come in March, so that's the time to go if you want to ski on fresh, nature-made powder. To increase your odds, choose a ski area in the northern part of the state.

■ **Summer Scene.** During summertime, many ski resorts reinvent themselves as prime destinations for golfers, zipline and canopy tours, mountain bikers, and weddings. Other summer visitors come to the mountains to enjoy hiking trails, climbing walls, aquatic centers, chairlift and horse-back rides, or a variety of festivals.

■ **Avoid Long Lift Lines.** Try to hit the slopes early—many lifts start at 8 or 9 am, with ticket windows opening a half-hour earlier. Then take a mid-morning break as lines start to get longer and head out again when others come in for lunch.

SAVINGS TIPS

■ **Choose a Condo.** Especially if you're planning to stay for a week, save money on food by opting for a condominum unit with a kitchen. You can shop at the supermarket and cook breakfast and dinner.

■ **Rent Smart.** Consider ski rental options in the villages rather than those at the mountain. Renting right at the ski area may be more convenient, but it may also cost more.

■ **Discount Lift Tickets.** Online tickets are often the least expensive; multi-day discounts and and ski-and-stay packages will also lower your costs. Good for those who can plan ahead, early-bird tickets often go on sale before the ski season even starts.

■ **Hit the Peaks Off-peak.** In order to secure the best deals at the most competitive rates, avoid booking during school holidays. President's Week in February is the busiest, because that's when Northeastern schools have their spring break.

Top left, Killington's six mountains make up the largest ski area in Vermont. Top right, Stratton has a Snowboard-cross course.

THINK WARM THOUGHTS

It can get cold on the slopes, so be prepared. Consider proper face warmth and smart layering, plus ski-specific socks, or purchase a pair each of inexpensive hand and feet warmers that fit easily in your gloves and boots. Helmets, which can also be rented, provide not only added safety but warmth.

VERMONT SKI AREAS BY THE NUMBERS

Okemo's wide slopes attract snowbirds to Ludlow in Central Vermont.

Numbers are a helpful way to compare mountains, but remember that each resort has a distinct personality. This list is composed of ski areas in Vermont with at least 100 skiable acres. For more information, see individual resort listings.

SKI AREA	Vertical Drop	Skiable Acres	# of Trails & Lifts	Terrain Type ● ■ ◆/◆◆			Snowboarding Options
Bolton Valley	1,704	300	70/6	36%	37%	27%	Terrain park
Bromley	1,334	178	46/10	32%	37%	31%	Terrain park
Burke Mountain	2,011	270	50/6	10%	44%	46%	Terrain park
Jay Peak	2,153	385	78/22	22%	39%	41%	Terrain park
Killington	3,050	752	155/22	28%	33%	39%	Terrain park, Half-pipe
Mad River Glen	2,037	115	45/9	30%	30%	40%	Snowboarding not allowed
Mount Snow	1,700	588	80/20	14%	73%	13%	Terrain park, Half-pipe
Okemo	2,200	655	120/19	31%	38%	31%	Terrain park, Superpipe, RossCross terrain cross park
Pico Mountain	1,967	468	57/7	18%	46%	36%	Triple Slope, terrain park
Smugglers' Notch	2,610	311	78/8	19%	50%	31%	Terrain park
Stowe	2,160	485	116/13	16%	59%	25%	Terrain park, Half-pipe
Stratton	2,003	625	97/11	42%	31%	27%	Terrain park, Half-pipe, Snowboardcross course
Sugarbush	2,600	578	111/16	20%	45%	35%	Terrain park

CONTACT THE EXPERTS

Ski Vermont (☎ *802/223-2439* ⊕ *www. skivermont.com*), a non-profit association in Montpelier, Vermont, and **Vermont Department of Tourism** (⊕ *www.vermontvacation. com*) are great resources for travelers planning a wintertime trip to Vermont.

KNOW YOUR SIGNS

On trail maps and the mountains, trails are rated and marked:

 Beginner   Advanced

■ Intermediate   ◆◆ Expert

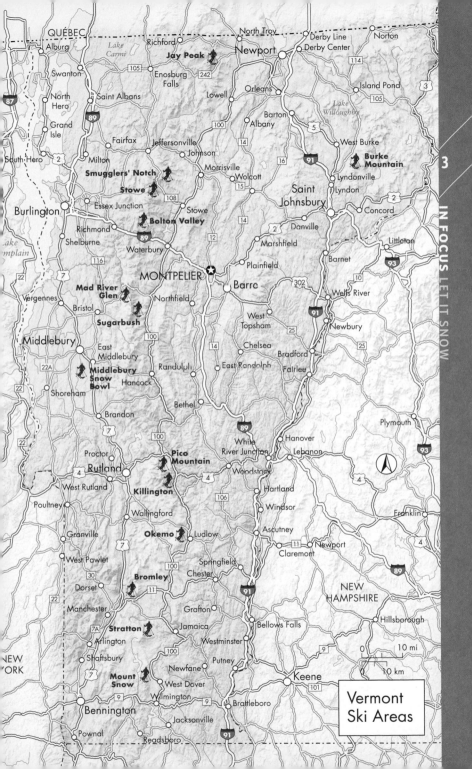

**Vermont
Ski Areas**

$$$$ B&B/INN **Stone Hill Inn.** A contemporary B&B where classical music plays in the hallways, the Stone Hill Inn has rooms with two-sink vanities and two-person whirlpools in front of double-sided fireplaces. **Pros:** very comfortable rooms; convenient location. **Cons:** grounds could use a bit of grooming. [$] *Rooms from: $380* ✉ *89 Houston Farm Rd.* ☎ *802/253–6282* 🌐 *www.stonehillinn.com* 🛏 *9 rooms* 🍴 *Breakfast.*

$$$$ RESORT **Stoweflake Mountain Resort and Spa.** With one of the largest spas in the area, Stowflake lets you enjoy a hydrotherapy waterfall that cascades into a hot tub, an herb and flower labyrinth, and a fitness center reached via a covered bridge. **Pros:** nice spa; wide range of rooms. **Cons:** mazelike layout can make rooms a bit hard to find. [$] *Rooms from: $279* ✉ *1746 Mountain Rd.* ☎ *802/253–7355* 🌐 *www.stoweflake.com* 🛏 *120 rooms, 60 town houses* 🍴 *No meals.*

$ HOTEL FAMILY **Stowe Motel & Snowdrift.** This family-owned motel sits on 16 acres across the river from one of the area's favorite hiking trails. **Pros:** inexpensive rates; complimentary bikes; friendly game room. **Cons:** motel-style accommodations. [$] *Rooms from: $120* ✉ *2043 Mountain Rd.* ☎ *802/253–7629, 800/829–7629* 🌐 *www.stowemotel.com* 🛏 *52 rooms, 4 suites, 4 houses* 🍴 *Breakfast.*

$$$$ RESORT Fodor's Choice ★ **Stowe Mountain Lodge.** At the base of the ski slopes, Stowe Mountain Lodge would be king of the hill for location alone, but a stay here also treats to you many perks. **Pros:** perfect setting; great concierge; activities galore. **Cons:** somewhat sterile feel; no separate kids' pool. [$] *Rooms from: $350* ✉ *7412 Mountain Rd.* ☎ *802/253–3560* 🌐 *www.stowemountainlodge.com* 🛏 *312 rooms* 🍴 *No meals.*

$$$$ RESORT Fodor's Choice ★ **Topnotch Resort.** On 120 acres overlooking Mt. Mansfield, this posh property has a contemporary look and an outstanding spa. **Pros:** outdoor heated pool facing the mountains; impeccable service; family-friendly atmosphere. **Cons:** boutique style may not be for everyone. [$] *Rooms from: $250* ✉ *4000 Mountain Rd.* ☎ *802/253–8585, 800/451–8686* 🌐 *www.topnotchresort.com* 🛏 *71 rooms, 9 suites, 14 town houses* 🍴 *Multiple meal plans.*

NIGHTLIFE AND THE ARTS

THE ARTS

Spruce Peak Performing Arts Center. This center hosts a wide variety of visual and performing arts, including theater, music, and dance. ✉ *122 Hourglass Dr.* ☎ *802/760–4634* 🌐 *www.sprucepeakarts.org.*

NIGHTLIFE

Matterhorn. This nightspot hosts live music and dancing on weekends during the ski season. If you'd rather just watch, there's a separate martini bar. ✉ *4969 Mountain Rd.* ☎ *802/253–8198* 🌐 *www.matterhornbar.com.*

SPORTS AND THE OUTDOORS

CANOEING AND KAYAKING

Umiak Outdoor Outfitters. This full-service outfitter rents canoes and kayaks. It has outposts on the Winooski River in Waterbury, at North Beach in Burlington, and on the Lamoille River in Jeffersonville. ✉ *849 S. Main St.* ☎ *802/253–2317* 🌐 *www.umiak.com.*

FISHING

The Fly Rod Shop. This shop provides a guide service, offers fly-tying and casting classes, and rents tackle and other equipment. ✉ *2703 Waterbury Rd., 1½ miles south of Stowe* ☎ *802/253–7346* ⊕ *www. flyrodshop.com.*

GOLF

Stowe Country Club. A scenic 18-hole golf course, a driving range, and a putting green are available at Stowe Country Club. ✉ *744 Cape Cod Rd.* ☎ *802/253–4893* ⛳ *Greens fee: $65–$115* ⊙ *18 holes, 6,185 yards, par 72.*

HIKING

Mt. Mansfield. Ascending Mt. Mansfield makes for a challenging day hike. Trails lead from Mountain Road to the summit, where they meet the north-to-south Long Trail. Views take in New Hampshire's White Mountains, New York's Adirondacks, and southern Québec. The Green Mountain Club publishes a trail guide. ✉ *Mountain Rd.* ☎ *802/244– 7037* ⊕ *www.greenmountainclub.org.*

SLEDDING

FAMILY **Peacepups Dog Sledding.** This company offers two-hour day tours and one-hour night tours using a team of eight Siberian huskies. You can ride inside a padded toboggan or join in the driving using a two-person tandem sled. The cost is $275 per day or $175 at night. If you prefer to walk the trails yourself, snowshoe rentals are also available. ✉ *239 Cross Rd., Lake Elmore* ☎ *802/888–7733* ⊕ *www.peacepupsdogsledding.com* ⊙ *Mid-Dec.–Mar., Wed. and Fri.–Sun. at 10, noon, and 2.*

SKI AREA

Stowe Mountain Resort. The name of the village is Stowe and the name of the mountain is Mt. Mansfield, but to generations of skiers, the area, it's all just plain Stowe. The area's mystique attracts as many serious skiers as social ones. Improved snowmaking, new lifts, and free shuttle buses that gather skiers from lodges, inns, and motels along Mountain Road have made Stowe much more convenient. Yet the traditions remain: the Winter Carnival in January and the Sugar Slalom in April, to name two. Three base lodges provide the essentials, including two on-mountain restaurants.

The resort has 27 miles of groomed cross-country trails and 18 miles of backcountry trails. Four interconnecting cross-country ski areas have more than 90 miles of groomed trails within the town of Stowe. Mt. Mansfield, with an elevation of 4,395 feet and a vertical drop of 2,360 feet, is one of the giants among Eastern ski mountains. Its symmetrical shape allows skiers of all abilities long, satisfying runs from the summit. The famous Front Four (National, Liftline, Starr, and Goat) are the intimidating expert runs, yet there is plenty of intermediate skiing and one long beginner trail. Mansfield's satellite sector is a network of intermediate trails and one expert trail off a basin served by a gondola. Spruce Peak, separate from the main mountain, is a teaching hill and offers a pleasant experience for intermediates and beginners.

In addition to the high-speed, eight-passenger gondola, Stowe has 13 lifts, including two quads, two triples, and four double chairlifts, a carpet lift, plus one handle tow, to service its 116 trails. Night-skiing trails are accessed by the gondola. The resort has 80% snowmaking coverage. Snowboard facilities include a half pipe and two terrain parks—one for beginners, at Spruce Pcak, and one for experts, on the Mt. Mansfield side. Children's programs are headquartered at Spruce Peak, with ski-school programs for ages 3 to 12. ✉ *5781 Mountain Rd.* ☎ *802/253–3000, 802/253–3600 snow conditions ⊕ www.stowe.com.*

SHOPPING AND SPAS

In Stowe, Mountain Road is lined with shops from town up toward the ski area. North of Stowe, shops line Route 100 from Interstate 89.

FOOD

Cabot Cheese Annex Store. In addition to the shelves of Vermont-made jams, mustards, crackers, and maple products, the store features a long central table with samples of a dozen Cabot cheeses. ✉ *2657 Waterbury-Stowe Rd., 2½ miles north of I–89* ☎ *802/244–6334* ⊕ *www.cabotcheese.coop.*

FAMILY
Fodor's Choice
★

Cold Hollow Cider Mill. Watch apples pressed into fabulous cider at the Cold Hollow Cider Mill. The on-site store also sells apple butter, jams and jellies, and Vermont-made handicrafts. Kids get free cider popsicles. ✉ *3600 Waterbury-Stowe Rd., 3 miles north of I–89, Waterbury Center* ☎ *800/327–7537* ⊕ *www.coldhollow.com.*

SPAS

Spa at Stoweflake. One of the largest spas in New England, the Spa at Stoweflake features a massaging hydrotherapeutic waterfall, a Hungarian mineral pool, 30 treatment rooms, and 120 services like the Bingham Falls Renewal, named after a local waterfall. This treatment begins with a body scrub and a Vichy shower, followed by an aromatherapy oil massage. The spacious men's and women's sanctuaries have saunas, steam rooms, and whirlpool tubs. ✉ *Stoweflake Mountain resort and Spa, 1746 Mountain Rd.* ☎ *802/760–1083* ⊕ *www.stoweflake.com.*

Spa at Topnotch. An aura of calm pervades the Spa at Topnotch, with its birchwood doors and accents, natural light, and cool colors. Signature services include the Mount Mansfield Saucha, a three-stage herbal body treatment, and the Little River Stone Massage, which uses's the resort's own wood-spice oil. Locker areas are spacious and spotless, with saunas, steam rooms, and whirlpool tubs. Classes in tai chi, yoga, and Pilates are offered throughout the day in the nearby fitness center. ✉ *Topnotch Resort and Spa, 4000 Mountain Rd.* ☎ *802/253–6463* ⊕ *www.topnotchresort.com.*

Spa and Wellness Center at Stowe Mountain Lodge. This 21,000-square-foot facility has 19 treatment rooms, a fitness center, and an outdoor pool and hot tub. In addition to the expected array of facials, scrubs, and massages for adults, the spa offers a separate program for kids. ✉ *Stowe Mountain Lodge, 7412 Mountain Rd.* ☎ *802/253–3560* ⊕ *www.stowemountainlodge.com.*

JEFFERSONVILLE

30 miles west of Craftsbury, 18 miles north of Stowe.

Jeffersonville is just over Smugglers' Notch from Stowe but miles away in feel and attitude. In summer you can drive over the notch road as it curves precipitously around boulders that have fallen from the cliffs above, then pass open meadows and old farmhouses and sugar shacks on the way down to town. Below the notch, Smugglers' Notch Ski Resort is the hub of activity year-round. Downtown Jeffersonville, once home to an artists' colony, is quiet but has excellent dining and nice art galleries.

3

EXPLORING

Boyden Valley Winery. West of Jeffersonville, this winery conducts tours and tastings and showcases an excellent selection of Vermont specialty products and local handicrafts. The winery's Big Barn Red is satisfyingly full-bodied, but the real fun may be in the ice wines, maple creme liqueur, and hard cider. ⊠ *Junction of Rtes. 15 and 104, Cambridge* ☎ *802/644–8151* ⊕ *www.boydenvalley.com* ☉ *Daily 10–5.*

WHERE TO EAT AND STAY

$$
\text{AMERICAN}
$$

$$ ✕ **158 Main Restaurant & Bakery.** The best and most popular restaurant in Jeffersonville, 158 Main easily earns its accolades. For breakfast, locals love the "Two Eggs Basic," which comes with two eggs any style, homemade toast, and home fries for $4. Portions are big; prices are not. Menu selections for dinner range from sesame-seared yellowfin tuna with wok-seared vegetables to hanger steak with a maple-chipotle sauce. Sunday brunch is very popular. $ *Average main: $16* ⊠ *158 Main St.* ☎ *802/644–8100* ⊕ *www.158Main.com* ☚ *Reservations not accepted* ☉ *Closed Mon. No dinner Sun.*

$$$$
RESORT
FAMILY
Fodor'sChoice
★

Smugglers' Notch Resort. With four giant water parks for summer fun and just about every winter activity imaginable, this family resort has amenities other places can only dream about. **Pros:** great place for families to learn to ski. **Cons:** not a romantic getaway for couples. $ *Rooms from: $388* ⊠ *4323 Rte. 108 S* ☎ *802/644–8851, 800/419–4615* ⊕ *www.smuggs.com* ☚ *600 condominiums* ☉ *No meals.*

SPORTS AND THE OUTDOORS

KAYAKING

Vermont Canoe and Kayak. This outfitter rents canoes and kayaks for use on the Lamoille River and leads guided canoe trips to Boyden Valley Winery. ⊠ *4807 Rte. 15* ☎ *802/644–8336* ⊕ *www.vermontcanoeandkayak. com.*

LLAMA RIDES

Applecheek Farm. Applecheek Farm runs daytime and evening hay and sleigh rides, llama treks, and farm tours. ⊠ *567 McFarlane Rd., Hyde Park* ☎ *802/888–4482* ⊕ *www.applecheekfarm.com.*

Northern Vermont Llama Co. These llamas carry everything, including snacks and lunches for half-day treks along the trails of Smugglers' Notch. Advance reservations are essential for the trips, offered from late May to Labor Day. ⊠ *766 Lapland Rd., Waterville* ☎ *802/644–2257* ⊕ *www.northernvermontllamaco.com.*

SKI AREA

FAMILY   **Smugglers' Notch.** The "granddaddy of all family resorts," Smuggler's Notch consistently wins accolades for its family programs. Its children's ski school is one of the best in the country—possibly *the* best—but there are challenges for skiers of all levels. This was the first ski area in the East to designate a triple-black-diamond run, the Black Hole.

The self-contained village has outdoor ice-skating and snow tubing. For Nordic skiing, the area has 18 miles of groomed and tracked trails and 12 miles of snowshoe trails. For downhill skiing, the resort has three mountains. The highest, Madonna, with a vertical drop of 2,610 feet, has trails connecting it to 1,500-foot Sterling. The third mountain, 1,150-foot Morse, can be reached via trails and a shuttle bus.

The tops of each of the mountains have expert terrain—a couple of double-black diamonds and a triple-black-diamond make Madonna memorable. Intermediate trails fill the lower sections, and Morse has many beginner trails. The 78 trails are served by eight lifts, including six chairs and two surface lifts. Top-to-bottom snowmaking allows for 62% coverage. There are five terrain parks, including one for beginners. A snowboarding park is for kids three to six. There's a full roster of summertime amenities, including waterslides, hiking programs, a treetop obstacle course, a zipline canopy tour, and crafts workshops. ⊠ *4323 Rte. 108 S* ☎ *802/644–8851, 800/419–4615* ⊕ *www.smuggs.com.*

SHOPPING

ANTIQUES

Route 15 between Jeffersonville and Johnson is dubbed the "antiques highway."

Smugglers' Notch Antiques. In a rambling barn, this shop sells antiques, collectibles, and custom-made furniture from 60 dealers. ⊠ *906 Rte. 108 S* ☎ *802/644–2100* ⊕ *smugglersnotchantiques.com.*

CLOTHING

Fodor'sChoice   **Johnson Woolen Mills.** This factory store has great deals on woolen blankets, household goods, and the famous Johnson outerwear. ⊠ *51 Lower Main St. E, 9 miles east of Jeffersonville, Johnson* ☎ *802/635–2271* ⊕ *www.johnsonwoolenmills.com.*

BURLINGTON

31 miles southwest of Jeffersonville, 76 miles south of Montreal, 349 miles north of New York City, 223 miles northwest of Boston.

Fodor'sChoice   As you drive along Main Street toward downtown Burlington, it's easy to see why this four-college city is so often called one of the most livable small cities in the United States. Downtown is filled with hip restaurants and bars, art galleries, and the Church Street Marketplace—a bustling pedestrian mall with trendy shops, crafts vendors, street performers, and sidewalk cafés. Just beyond, Lake Champlain shimmers beneath the towering Adirondacks on the New York shore. On the shores of the lake, Burlington's revitalized waterfront teems with outdoors enthusiasts who bike or stroll along its recreation path, picnic on the grass, and ply the waters in sailboats and motor craft in summer.

BURLINGTON'S LOCAL FOOD MOVEMENT

Burlington is exploding on the national food scene as one of the hubs of the local food movement. Known for its excellent soil and abundance of local organic farms—as showcased in its huge weekly farmers' market (Saturday, May through October) and popular outdoor summertime farm suppers—this health-conscious and liberal city is home to restaurants and markets with a foodie's focus on fresh, high-quality ingredients rivaling those of a much larger city. Burlington residents are likely to be seen biking to pick up their weekly CSA share at the Intervale (the city's huge web of community gardens), doing some weeding in their own urban garden plots, or stopping by one of the farms to pick berries or flowers on their way to a dinner party.

EXPLORING

FAMILY **ECHO Lake Aquarium and Science Center.** This center gives kids and adults a chance to learn about the Lake Champlain region through more than 100 interactive exhibits. You can also get an up-close look at 70 species of indigenous animals. ⊠ *1 College St.* ☎ *802/864–1848* ⊕ *www. echovermont.org* ☜ *$13.50* ⊙ *Daily 10–5.*

Ethan Allen Homestead Museum. When Vermont hero Ethan Allen retired from his revolutionary activities, he purchased 350 acres along the Winooski River and built this modest cabin in 1787. The original structure is a real slice of 18th-century life, including such frontier hallmarks as saw-cut boards and an open hearth for cooking. A kitchen garden resembles the one the Allens would have had. There's also a visitor center and miles of biking and hiking trails. In warmer months, climb Ethan Allen Tower at the west end of the property for stupendous views of Lake Champlain and the Green Mountains. Don't forget mosquito repellent. ⊠ *1 Ethan Allen Homestead, off Rte. 127* ☎ *802/865–4556* ⊕ *www.ethanallenhomestead.org* ☜ *$7* ⊙ *May–Oct., Thurs.–Mon. 10–4.*

Magic Hat Brewing Company. You can tour the Magic Hat brewery, which puts out 400 bottles a minute. The free tour includes free beer samples and the Growler Bar has 48 beers on tap. ⊠ *5 Bartlett Bay Rd., South Burlington* ☎ *802/658–2739* ⊕ *magichat.net* ☜ *Free* ⊙ *Mon.–Sat. 10–6, Sun. noon–5.*

University of Vermont. Crowning the hilltop above Burlington is the University of Vermont, known as UVM for the abbreviation of its Latin name, Universitas Viridis Montis, meaning the University of the Green Mountains. With more than 10,000 students, this is the state's principal institution of higher learning. The most architecturally impressive buildings face the green and have gorgeous lake views, as does the statue of founder Ira Allen, Ethan's brother. ⊠ *85 South Prospect St.* ☎ *802/656–3131* ⊕ *www.uvm.edu.*

WHERE TO EAT

$$ PIZZA Fodor's Choice ★ 🍴 **American Flatbread Burlington.** It might be worth going to college in Burlington just to be able to gather with friends at this wildly popular organic pizza place. Seating is first-come, first-served, and the scene is bustling with locals and visitors sipping house-made brews. The wood-fired clay dome is where the cooks create delicious pies like the Punctuated Equilibrium, which has kalamata olives, roasted red peppers, goat cheese, fresh rosemary, red onions, mozzarella, and garlic. Fresh salads topped with locally made cheese are also popular. Here's to the college life! [$] *Average main: $17* ✉ *115 St. Paul St.* ☎ *802/861–2999* 🌐 *americanflatbread.com* ✍ *Reservations not accepted.*

$$$ MODERN AMERICAN 🍴 **Bluebird Tavern.** Hidden away off the main downtown drag, this trendy bistro is a foodie favorite, with a chic French-bistro setting, open-air kitchen, and a fabulous bar serving some of the best cocktails in town. It's also one of the few places in town to serve the coveted Hill Farmstead beer. Try the Sunday night suppers for local comfort food, or come any night for mussels, oysters, burgers, and homemade pasta. If you prefer a more intimate feel, dine at the bar. [$] *Average main: $25* ✉ *86 St Paul St.* ☎ *802/540–1786* 🌐 *www.bluebirdvermont.com.*

$ ITALIAN 🍴 **Bove's.** Since 1941, this petite old-school eatery has been feeding Burlingtonians tasty and affordable Italian cuisine. Now in the third generation, the family and its fabulous lasagna and spaghetti are held deep in the hearts of locals. The dishes have remained mostly unchanged, making them the city's most time-tested fare. [$] *Average main: $8* ✉ *68 Pearl St.* ☎ *802/864–6651* 🌐 *www.boves.com* ⏲ *Closed Sun. and Mon. No lunch Tues.–Thurs.*

$$ AMERICAN Fodor's Choice ★ 🍴 **Farmhouse Tap & Grill.** This is one of the most popular restaurants in town, so don't be put off by the line on a typical weekend night. Known for using only local beef, cheese, and produce, this farm-to-table experience is laid-back in style but one of the finest meals in the area. Specialities include excellent burgers, chicken and biscuits, wonderful local cheese and charcuterie plates, and a great wine and craft-beer selection. ■ **TIP→ Put your name on the list and have a drink at the cozy downstairs Tap Room or the outdoor beer garden while you wait.** If the wait feels too long, try El Cortijo, its small taqueria down the street, for locally raised beef or chicken tacos and terrific margaritas. [$] *Average main: $18* ✉ *160 Bank St.* ☎ *802/859–0888* 🌐 *www.farmhousetg.com.*

$$$$ STEAKHOUSE 🍴 **Guild and Company Steakhouse.** Vermont's best steak can be found roasting over hardwood coals in the open kitchens of Guild and Company. All the meat is sourced from local farms, dry-aged a minimum of 21 days, and cooked to absolute perfection. The space itself is also a treat, with antique chicken feeders serving as light fixtures and a soapstone-topped bar in the center. Lighter fare is available, but make sure at least one person in your party orders the rib eye. [$] *Average main: $48* ✉ *1633 Williston Rd.* ☎ *802/497–1207* 🌐 *www.guildandcompany.com* ⏲ *No lunch.*

$$$ MODERN AMERICAN Fodor's Choice ★ 🍴 **Hen of the Wood Burlington.** Arguably Vermont's best restaurant, Hen of the Wood has yielded to the desires of its ravenous fans with a branch in Burlington. With a more urban feel than that of the original location in Waterbury, the restaurant serves the same inventive yet down-to-earth cuisine that sets diners' hearts aflutter and tongues wagging. Drop your

Vermont by Bike

CLOSE UP

Road biking in the Green Mountains.

Vermont has more than 16,000 miles of roads, and almost 80% of them are town roads that see little high-speed traffic, making them ideal for scenic bike rides. More than half are dirt roads, making them especially suitable for mountain biking. Although mountain-bike trails and old farm and logging roads wind through the Green Mountain State, most are on private property and are, therefore, not mapped. Several mountain-biking centers around the state have extensive trail networks (and maps) that will keep avid fat-tire fans happy for a few hours or a few days. To road bike in Vermont, you'll want a map and preferably a bicycle with at least 10 gears. The only roads that prohibit cycling are the four-lane highways and Routes 7 and 4 in Rutland.

TOP ROAD BIKING ROUTES:
To make a relatively easy 16-mile loop, begin at the blinker on U.S. 7 in **Shelburne** and follow Mt. Philo Road south to Hinesburg Road, then west

to Charlotte. Lake Road, Orchard Road, and Mouth of River Road go past orchards and berry fields. Bostwick Road returns to U.S. 7.

In the heart of the central Green Mountains is a moderate 18-mile loop on Routes 4, 100, and 100A that passes Calvin Coolidge's home in **Plymouth Notch.**

West of **Rutland** is a beautiful 27-mile ride on Routes 140, 30, and 133 that passes swimming holes, then hugs the shore of Lake St. Catherine. Start in Middletown Springs.

A scenic 43-mile ride in the **Northeast Kingdom** passes through pleasant Peacham and the birches and maples of Groton State Forest. Start in Danville and follow Peacham Road, then Routes 302 and 232 and U.S. 2.

For a real test, try the 48-mile ride over **Middlebury and Brandon Gaps** on Routes 125 and 73, which connect via Routes 153 and 100.

finger anywhere on the menu and you can't go wrong, especially with dishes like brown butter crepes stuffed with chanterelles and smoked bluefish toast in buttermilk. If you ever need to say "I love you," this is the place. $ *Average main: $27* ✉ *55 Cherry St.* ☎ *802/540–0534* ⊕ *www.henofthewood.com* ⊘ *No lunch.*

$$$$
AMERICAN

✕ **Juniper.** The Hotel Vermont has generated excitement not just for its new-school accommodations, but also for its ground-floor restaurant and bar. Its delightful design—a perfect blend of boutique chic and real Vermont, with reclaimed, antique, red-oak floors; black granite walls; and a free-flowing layout—is only part of the fun. The rest is in the inventive menu, which includes juniper-roasted quail and applewood-smoked pickled eggs, and possibly the best cocktail list in town. Weather permitting, you can stay toasty on the outdoor patio with its central fire pit. $ *Average main: $29* ✉ *41 Cherry St.* ☎ *802/651–5027* ⊕ *www. hotelvt.com/dining-drinking/juniper* ⊘ *No lunch.*

$$$
CAFÉ

✕ **Leunig's Bistro & Cafe.** This popular café delivers alfresco bistro cuisine, a friendly European-style bar, and live jazz. Favorite entrées include salade Niçoise, *soupe au pistou,* and beef bourguignon. Fans of crème brûlée: this place makes the best in town. A prix-fixe dinner for two goes for $30, and it's one of the city's best bargains. An expanded upstairs lounge offers cocktails, a nice wine selection, and local cheese plates and other light fare. This is a great spot for weekend brunch. $ *Average main: $28* ✉ *115 Church St.* ☎ *802/863–3759* ⊕ *www.leunigsbistro. com.*

$
AMERICAN
FAMILY

✕ **Penny Cluse Cafe.** This popular breakfast and brunch spot is often busy and buzzing with activity. Weekend lines can be long, but locals think it's worth the wait for the famous gingerbread-blueberry pancakes, warm buscuits with herb gravy, huevos rancheros, and homemade banana bread. $ *Average main: $10* ✉ *169 Cherry St.* ☎ *802/651–8834* ⊕ *www.pennycluse.com* ⊘ *No dinner.*

$$
CHINESE

✕ **A Single Pebble.** The creative, authentic Chinese fare served on the first floor of this charming residential row house includes traditional clay-pot dishes as well as wok specialties like beef with fresh baby bok choy and chicken with peanuts and chili peppers. The dry-fried green beans (sautéed with flecks of pork, black beans, preserved vegetables, and garlic) are a house specialty, as is "mock eel," braised shiitake mushrooms served in a crispy ginger sauce. All dishes can be made without meat. ■ TIP→ Try the dim sum on Sunday from 11:30–1:45. $ *Average main: $20* ✉ *133 Bank St.* ☎ *802/865–5200* ⊕ *www.asinglepebble.com* ⌀ *Reservations essential.*

$$$
ITALIAN

✕ **Trattoria Delia.** If you didn't manage a trip to Umbria this year, the next best thing is this charming Italian country eatery around the corner from City Hall Park. Game and fresh produce are the stars; try the wild boar braised in red wine, tomatoes, rosemary, and sage served on soft polenta. Wood-grilled items are also a specialty. In winter, try to reserve a table near the fire. $ *Average main: $25* ✉ *152 St. Paul St.* ☎ *802/864–5253* ⊕ *www.trattoriadelia.com* ⌀ *Reservations essential* ⊘ *No lunch.*

$
AMERICAN

✕ **Zabby and Elf's Stone Soup.** A perfect place to stop for a delicious and healthful lunch or early dinner, Stone Soup offers all-local produce and organic ingredients showcased in fresh salads, wonderful soups, home-made breads, and a wide array of baked goods. There are many veggie and vegan options. $ *Average main: $12* ⊠ *211 College St.* ☎ *802/862–7616* ⊕ *www.stonesoupvt.com* ☉ *Closed Sun.*

WHERE TO STAY

$$$$
HOTEL
Fodor'sChoice
★

Hotel Vermont. Ever since the Hotel Vermont opened its doors in 2013, guests have been stepping inside with acute curiosity and walking out with copious praise. **Pros:** destination restaurant; gorgeous rooms; unbelievable service. **Cons:** luxury doesn't come cheap. $ *Rooms from: $299* ⊠ *41 Cherry St.* ☎ *802/651–0080* ⊕ *www.hotelvt.com* ⇆ *120 rooms, 5 suites* ⊙| *No meals.*

$$
B&B/INN

The Lang House on Main Street. Within walking distance of downtown but in the historic hill section of town, this grand 1881 Victorian home charms completely with its period furnishings, fine woodwork, plaster detailing, and stained-glass windows. **Pros:** family-friendly vibe; interesting location; well run. **Cons:** no elevator. $ *Rooms from: $165* ⊠ *360 Main St.* ☎ *802/652–2500, 877/919–9799* ⊕ *www.langhouse.com* ⇆ *11 rooms* ⊙| *Breakfast.*

$$
B&B/INN

Willard Street Inn. High in the historic hill section of Burlington, this ivy-covered house with an exterior marble staircase and English gardens incorporates elements of Queen Anne and Georgian Revival styles. **Pros:** innkeepers passionate about their job; lots of friendly attention. **Cons:** a tad old-fashioned; walk to downtown can be a drag in winter. $ *Rooms from: $170* ⊠ *349 S. Willard St.* ☎ *802/651–8710, 800/577–8712* ⊕ *www.willardstreetinn.com* ⇆ *14 rooms* ⊙| *Breakfast.*

NIGHTLIFE AND THE ARTS

THE ARTS

Fodor'sChoice
★

Flynn Center for the Performing Arts. A grandiose art-deco gem, the Flynn Theatre is the cultural heart of Burlington. In addition to being home to Vermont's largest musical theater company, it also hosts the Vermont Symphony Orchestra as well as big-name acts like Neko Case, Elvis Costello, and the like. The adjacent Flynn Space is a coveted spot for more off-beat, experimental performances. ⊠ *153 Main St.* ☎ *802/863–5966* ⊕ *www.flynncenter.org.*

NIGHTLIFE

The Farmhouse Tap & Grill. The Tap Room, downstairs from the hugely popular Farmhouse Tap & Grill, serves a wide range of local artisan beers, wines, and small plates in a cozy and buzzing fireside setting reminiscent of a Colorado lodge tavern. Featuring local foods—try the great cheese plates—and a seasonal outdoor beer garden in summertime, this is the place to see and be seen in downtown Burlington. It's also one of just four places in town to get the coveted Hill Farmstead beer on tap. ⊠ *160 Bank St.* ☎ *802/859–0888* ⊕ *www.farmhousetg.com.*

Higher Ground. When you feel like shaking it up to live music, come to Higher Ground—it gets the lion's share of local and national musicians. ⊠ *1214 Williston Rd., South Burlington* ☎ *802/652–0777* ⊕ *www.highergroundmusic.com.*

Burlington's pedestrian-only Church Street Marketplace and the nearby shores of Lake Champlain are great for exploring.

Nectar's. The band Phish got its start at Nectar's, which is always jumping to the sounds of local bands and never charges a cover. Don't leave without a helping of the bar's famous fries and gravy. ⊠ *188 Main St.* ☎ *802/658–4771* ⊕ *www.liveatnectars.com.*

Vermont Pub & Brewery. Vermont's first brewpub still makes its own beer and remains a popular spot, especially in warm weather when locals head to the outdoor patio. Folk musicians play here regularly. ⊠ *144 College St.* ☎ *802/865–0500* ⊕ *www.vermontbrewery.com.*

SPORTS AND THE OUTDOORS
BEACHES

FAMILY **North Beach.** Along Burlington's "new" North End, a long line of beaches stretches to the Winooski River delta, beginning with North Beach, which has a grassy picnic area, snack bar, and boat rentals. Neighboring Leddy Park offers a more secluded beach. **Amenities:** food and drink; lifeguards; parking (fee); showers; toilets. **Best for:** partiers; swimming; walking; windsurfing. ⊠ *North Beach Park, 52 Institute Rd., off North Ave.* ☎ *802/864–0123* ⊕ *www.enjoyburlington.com/ northbeach.cfm.*

BIKING

FAMILY
Fodor'sChoice
★
Burlington Bike Path. Anyone who's put the rubber to the pedal on the 7.5-mile Burlington Bike Path and its almost equally long northern extension on the Island Line Trail sings its praises. Along the way there are endless postcard views of Lake Champlain and the Adirondack Mountains. The northern end of the trail is slightly more rugged and windswept, so dress accordingly. ☎ *802/864–0123* ⊕ *www.enjoyburlington. com/parks/bikepath1.cfm.*

North Star Sports. In addition to stocking an extensive supply of sports apparel and accessories, this family-owned shop rents bikes and provides maps of cycling routes. ✉ *100 Main St.* ☎ *802/863–3832* ⊕ *northstarsportsvt.com.*

Ski Rack. Burlington's one-stop shop for winter sports equipment, the Ski Rack also rents bikes and sells running gear throughout the year. ✉ *85 Main St.* ☎ *802/658–3313, 800/882–4530* ⊕ *www.skirack.com.*

> ## WORD OF MOUTH
>
> "Art in Burlington is great, which includes galleries, theater and music. The Flynn Theater has many shows, including some great National acts, and the Burlington Waterfront is just precious!"
> —jpigeonuvm

True North Kayak Tours. This company conducts two- and five-hour guided kayak tours of Lake Champlain that include talks about the region's natural history. It also offers customized lessons and runs a kayak camp for kids. ✉ *25 Nash Pl.* ☎ *802/238–7695* ⊕ *www.vermontkayak.com.*

BOATING

Burlington Community Boathouse. This boathouse houses the city's marina and a summertime watering hole called Splash, one of the best places to watch the sun set over the lake. ✉ *Burlington Harbor, College St.* ☎ *802/865–3377* ⊕ *www.enjoyburlington.com/waterfront.cfm.*

Lake Champlain Shoreline Cruises. The three-level *Spirit of Ethan Allen III*, a 363-passenger vessel, offers narrated cruises, themed dinners, and sunset sails with stunning views of the Adirondacks and the Green Mountains. ✉ *Burlington Boat House, 1 College St.* ☎ *802/862–8300* ⊕ *www.soea.com* 🖙 *$16* ⊙ *Late May–mid-Oct., daily 10–9.*

FAMILY **Community Sailing Center.** In addition to renting dinghies, keelboats, and kayaks, the Community Sailing Center offers classes geared to all levels. ✉ *1 Lake St.* ☎ *802/864–2499* ⊕ *www.communitysailingcenter.org.*

SKI AREA

Bolton Valley Resort. About 25 miles from Burlington, Bolton Valley Resort is a family favorite. In addition to 71 downhill ski trails (more than half rated for intermediates and beginners), Bolton has 62 miles of cross-country and snowshoe trails, night skiing, and a sports center. ✉ *4302 Bolton Valley Access Rd., Bolton* ☎ *802/434–3444, 877/926–5866* ⊕ *www.boltonvalley.com.*

SHOPPING

With each passing year, Burlington's industrial South End attracts ever greater numbers of artists and craftspeople, who set up studios, shops, and galleries in the former factories and warehouses along Pine Street. The district's annual "Art Hop" is the city's largest art celebration, and a roaring good time.

CRAFTS

Bennington Potters North. In addition to its popular pottery, Bennington Potters North stocks interesting kitchen items. ✉ *127 College St.* ☎ *802/863–2221* ⊕ *www.benningtonpotters.com.*

Frog Hollow. This nonprofit collective sells contemporary and traditional crafts by more than 200 Vermont artisans. ⊠ *85 Church St.* ☎ *802/863–6458* ⊕ *www.froghollow.org.*

FOOD

Lake Champlain Chocolates. This chocolatier makes sensational truffles, caramels, candies, fudge, and even hot chocolate. The chocolates are all natural, made in Vermont, and make a great edible souvenir. ⊠ *750 Pine St.* ☎ *800/465–5909* ⊕ *www.lakechamplainchocolates.com.*

MARKETS

Fodor'sChoice
★
Burlington Farmers' Market. Burlington's lively farmers' market is an absolute must-see when visiting in summer or fall. Located in the center of town, the Saturday market is jam-packed with local farmers selling a colorful array of organic produce, flowers, baked goods, maple syrup, meats, cheeses, prepared foods, and crafts. There's live music on the green, fresh cider and doughnuts in the fall, and the best people-watching in the state. From November to March it's held every other Saturday at Memorial Auditorium. ⊠ *City Hall Park, corner of College St. and St. Paul St.* ☎ *802/310–5172* ⊕ *www.burlingtonfarmersmarket.org* ⊙ *Late May–Oct., Sat. 8:30–2.*

FAMILY
Fodor'sChoice
★
Church Street Marketplace. For more than 30 years, this pedestrian-only thoroughfare has served as the heartbeat of Burlington, with lots of boutiques, cafés, restaurants, and street vendors during the day and a lively bar and live-music scene at night. On sunny days there are few better places to be in Burlington. ⊠ *2 Church St.* ☎ *802/863–1648* ⊕ *www.churchstmarketplace.com.*

OFF THE
BEATEN
PATH
Green Mountain Audubon Nature Center. This is a wonderful place to discover Vermont's outdoor wonders. The center's 255 acres of diverse habitats are a sanctuary for all things wild, and the 5 miles of trails provide an opportunity to explore the workings of differing natural communities. Events include dusk walks, wildflower and birding rambles, nature workshops, and educational activities for children and adults. The center is 18 miles southeast of Burlington. ⊠ *255 Sherman Hollow Rd., Huntington* ☎ *802/434–3068* ⊕ *vt.audubon.org* ▣ *Donations accepted* ⊙ *Mon.–Sat. 8:30–5.*

SHELBURNE

5 miles south of Burlington.

A few miles south of Burlington, the Champlain Valley gives way to fertile farmland, affording stunning views of the rugged Adirondacks across the lake. In the middle of this farmland is the village of Shelburne (and just farther south, beautiful and more rural Charlotte), chartered in the mid-18th century and partly a bedroom community for Burlington. Stunning Shelburne Farms is worth at least a few hours of exploring, as are Shelburne Orchards in fall when you can pick your own apples and drink fresh cider while admiring breathtaking views of the lake and mountains beyond.

GETTING HERE AND AROUND

Shelburne is south of Burlington after the town of South Burlington, notable for its very un-Vermont traffic and commercial and fast food–franchised stretch of U.S. 7. It's easy to confuse Shelburne Farms—2 miles west of town on the lake, with Shelburne Museum, which is just south of town directly on Route 7, but you'll want to make time for both.

EXPLORING

FAMILY
Fodor's Choice
★

Shelburne Farms. Founded in the 1880s as a private estate for two very rich New Yorkers, this 1,400-acre farm is much more than an exquisite landscape: it's an educational and cultural resource center with a working dairy farm, an award-winning cheese producer, an organic market garden, and a bakery whose aroma of fresh bread and pastries is an olfactory treat. It's a brilliant place for parents to expose their kids to the dignity of farm work and the joys of compassionate animal husbandry—indeed, children and adults alike will get a kick out of hunting for eggs in the oversize coop and milking a cow. Frederick Law Olmsted, co-creator of New York's Central Park, designed the magnificent grounds overlooking Lake Champlain. If you fall in love with the scenery, arrange a romantic dinner at the lakefront mansion or spend the night. ⊠ *1611 Harbor Rd., west of U.S. 7* ☎ *802/985–8498* ⊕ *www.shelburnefarms.org* ☜ *$8* ☉ *Visitor center mid-May–mid-Oct., daily 9–5:30; mid-Oct.–mid-May, daily 10–5.*

FAMILY
Fodor's Choice
★

Shelburne Museum. You can trace much of New England's history simply by wandering through the 45 acres and 38 buildings of this museum. The outstanding 150,000-object collection of art, design, and Americana consists of antique furniture, farm tools, fine and folk art, quilts, trade signs, and weather vanes. There are also more than 200 carriages and sleighs. In total, 25 buildings were moved to the museum, including an old-fashioned jail, an 1871 lighthouse, and even a 220-foot steamboat, the *Ticonderoga*. The Pizzagalli Center for Art and Education is open year-round with changing exhibitions and programs for kids and adults. ⊠ *6000 Shelburne Rd.* ☎ *802/985–3346* ⊕ *www.shelburnemuseum.org* ☜ *$22* ☉ *May–Oct., daily 10–5; Nov.–Apr., Tues.–Sun. 10–5.*

Shelburne Vineyard. On Route 7 you'll see rows and rows of organically grown vines. Visit the attractive tasting room and learn how wine is made. ⊠ *6308 Shelburne Rd.* ☎ *802/985–8222* ⊕ *www. shelburnevineyard.com* ☜ *$5.*

FAMILY

Vermont Teddy Bear Company. On the 30-minute tour of this fun-filled factory you'll hear more puns than you ever thought possible and learn how a few homemade bears, sold from a cart on Church Street, have turned into a multimillion-dollar business. Patrons and children can relax, eat, and play under a large canvas tent in summer or wander the beautiful 57-acre property. ⊠ *6655 Shelburne Rd.* ☎ *802/985–3001* ⊕ *www.vermontteddybear.com* ☜ *Tour $4* ☉ *July–Oct., daily 9:30–5; Nov.–June, daily 10–4.*

WHERE TO EAT

$$ ECLECTIC
🍴 **The Bearded Frog.** This is the top restaurant in the Shelburne area, perfect for a casual dinner in its cozy bar or for a more upscale ambience in the attractive, sophisticated dining room. In the bar, try the soups, burgers, and terrific cocktails, or take them to the somewhat more formal dining room and add the fresh salads topped with local blue cheese, seared scallops, excellent grilled fish, steaks, and decadent desserts. [$] *Average main: $20* ✉ *5247 Shelburne Rd.* ☎ *802/985–9877* 🌐 *www.thebeardedfrog.com* 🕒 *No lunch.*

$$$ AMERICAN Fodor's Choice ★
🍴 **The Dining Room at the Inn at Shelburne Farms.** Dinner here will make you dream of F. Scott Fitzgerald. Piano music wafts from the library, and you can carry a drink through the rooms of this 1880s mansion, gazing across a long lawn and formal gardens on the shore of dark Lake Champlain—you'll swear Jay Gatsby is about to come down the stairs. Count on just-grown ingredients that come from the market gardens as well as flavorful locally grown venison, beef, pork, and chicken. On weekends a spectacular spread of produce is set up next to a cocktail bar with fresh specialties. The dining room overlooks the lake, and the Sunday brunch is the area's best. Breakfast is served as well. [$] *Average main: $27* ✉ *Inn at Shelburne Farms, 1611 Harbor Rd.* ☎ *802/985–8498* 🌐 *www.shelburnefarms.org* 🕒 *Closed mid-May–mid-Oct.*

WHERE TO STAY

$$ B&B/INN
🏨 **Heart of the Village Inn.** Each of the elegantly furnished rooms at this B&B in a restored 1886 Queen Anne Victorian provides coziness and comfort. **Pros:** adorable village B&B; friendly owners; well run. **Cons:** near to but not within Shelburne Farms. [$] *Rooms from: $170* ✉ *5347 Shelburne Rd.* ☎ *802/985–9060, 866/985–9060* 🌐 *www.heartofthevillage.com* 🛏 *9 rooms* 🍽 *Breakfast.*

$$$ B&B/INN Fodor's Choice ★
🏨 **The Inn at Shelburne Farms.** It's hard not to feel a little bit like an aristocrat at this exquisite turn-of-the-20th-century Tudor-style inn, one of the most memorable properties in the country. **Pros:** stately lakefront setting in a fantastic historic mansion; great service; wonderful value; great restaurant. **Cons:** some may miss having a TV in the room; closed in winter; must book far in advance. [$] *Rooms from: $165* ✉ *1611 Harbor Rd.* ☎ *802/985–8498* 🌐 *www.shelburnefarms.org* 🛏 *24 rooms, 17 with bath; 2 cottages; 1 house* 🕒 *Closed mid-Oct.–mid-May* 🍽 *No meals.*

$$$$ B&B/INN Fodor's Choice ★
🏨 **Mt. Philo Inn.** If you've grown tired of the ubiquitous floral wallpaper of so many traditional New England inns, Jane and Dave Garbose's charming Mt. Philo Inn is a good place to check out. **Pros:** space, and lots of it; elegant rooms; great art collection. **Cons:** a bit remote. [$] *Rooms from: $240* ✉ *27 Inn Rd., Charlotte* ☎ *802/425–3335* 🌐 *www.mtphiloinn.com* 🛏 *4 suites* 🍽 *No meals.*

SHOPPING

The Shelburne Country Store. When you enter the The Shelburne Country Store, you'll step back in time. Walk past the potbellied stove and take in the aroma emanating from the fudge neatly piled behind huge antique glass cases. The store specializes in candles, weather vanes, glassware,

Shelburne Museum's many attractions include the *Ticonderoga* steamship and other pieces from New England's past.

and local foods. ✉ *29 Falls Rd., off U.S. 7* ☎ *800/660–3657* ⊕ *www. shelburnecountrystore.com.*

VERGENNES

12 miles south of Shelburne.

Vermont's oldest city, founded in 1788, is also the third oldest in New England. The downtown area is a compact district of restored Victorian homes and public buildings with a few good eateries sprinkled throughout. Main Street slopes down to Otter Creek Falls, where cannonballs were made during the War of 1812. The statue of Thomas MacDonough on the green immortalizes the victor of the Battle of Plattsburgh in 1814.

ESSENTIALS

Visitor Information Addison County Chamber of Commerce ✉ *93 Court St., Middlebury* ☎ *802/388–7951* ⊕ *www.addisoncounty.com.*

OFF THE
BEATEN
PATH

Lake Champlain Maritime Museum. This museum documents centuries of activity on the historically significant lake. Climb aboard a replica of Benedict Arnold's Revolutionary War gunboat moored in the lake, learn about shipwrecks, and watch craftsmen work at traditional boat-building and blacksmithing. ✉ *4472 Basin Harbor Rd., 7 miles west of Vergennes, Basin Harbor* ☎ *802/475–2022* ⊕ *www.lcmm.org* ✍ *$10* ⊙ *May–mid-Oct., daily 10–5.*

WHERE TO EAT AND STAY

$$$ ECLECTIC — 🍴 **Starry Night Café.** This chic restaurant is one of the hottest spots around. The proprietors combine artisanal tableware and furniture with a seasonal, farm-to-table cuisine like grilled pork belly and almond-encrusted salmon. The walls also host rotating shows by local artists. [$] *Average main: $24* ✉ *5371 Rte. 7, 5 miles north of Vergennes, Ferrisburg* ☎ *802/877–6316* 🌐 *www.starrynightcafe.com* ✍ *Reservations essential* 🕘 *Closed Mon. and Tues. No lunch.*

$$$$ RESORT FAMILY Fodor's Choice ★ — 🏨 **Basin Harbor Club.** On 700 acres overlooking Lake Champlain, this ultimate family resort provides luxurious accommodations and a full roster of amenities, including an 18-hole golf course, a 48-foot tour boat, and morning and evening children's programs. **Pros:** gorgeous lakeside property; activities galore. **Cons:** open only half the year; pricey. [$] *Rooms from: $240* ✉ *4800 Basin Harbor Rd.* ☎ *802/475–2311, 800/622–4000* 🌐 *www.basinharbor.com* 🛏 *32 rooms, 14 suites in 3 guesthouses, 73 cottages* 🕘 *Closed mid-Oct.–mid-May* 🍽 *Breakfast.*

SHOPPING

Dakin Farm. Cob-smoked ham, aged cheddar cheese, maple syrup made on-site, and other specialty foods can be found here. You can also visit the ham smokehouse and watch the waxing and sealing of the cheeses. ✉ *5797 Rte. 7, 5 miles north of Vergennes* ☎ *800/993–2546* 🌐 *www.dakinfarm.com.*

LAKE CHAMPLAIN ISLANDS

Lake Champlain stretches more than 100 miles south from the Canadian border and forms the northern part of the boundary between New York and Vermont. Within it is an elongated archipelago composed of several islands—Isle La Motte, North Hero, Grand Isle, South Hero—and the Alburg Peninsula. With a temperate climate, the islands hold several apple orchards and are a center of water recreation in summer and ice fishing in winter. A scenic drive through the islands on U.S. 2 begins at Interstate 89 and travels north to Alburg Center; Route 78 takes you back to the mainland.

ESSENTIALS

Visitor Information Lake Champlain Regional Chamber of Commerce ✉ *60 Main St., Suite 100, Burlington* ☎ *802/863–3489, 877/686–5253* 🌐 *www.vermont.org.* **Lake Champlain Islands Chamber of Commerce** ✉ *3501 US Rte. 2, Suite 100, North Hero* ☎ *802/372–8400, 800/262–5226* 🌐 *www.champlainislands.com.*

EXPLORING

Snow Farm Vineyard and Winery. Vermont's first vineyard was started here in 1996; today the winery specializes in nontraditional botanical hybrid grapes to withstand the local climate. Take a self-guided tour, sip some samples in the tasting room, and picnic and listen to music at the free concerts on the lawn Thursday evenings mid-June through Labor Day. ✉ *190 W. Shore Rd., South Hero* ☎ *802/372–9463* 🌐 *www.snowfarm.com* 🎟 *Free* 🕘 *May–Dec., daily 11–5.*

St. Anne's Shrine. This spot marks the site where French soldiers and Jesuits put ashore in 1665 and built a fort, creating Vermont's first European settlement. The state's first Roman Catholic Mass was celebrated here on July 26, 1666. ✉ *92 St. Anne's Rd., Isle La Motte* ☎ *802/928–3362* 🌐 *www.saintannesshrine.org* 🎫 *Free* 🕒 *Mid-May–mid-Oct., daily 9–4; Nov–Apr., hrs vary.*

WHERE TO STAY

$$ B&B/INN FAMILY 🏨 **North Hero House Inn and Restaurant.** This inn has four buildings right on Lake Champlain, including the 1891 Colonial Revival main house with nine guest rooms, a restaurant, a pub room, library, and sitting room. **Pros:** relaxed complex; superb lakefront setting. **Cons:** closed in winter. [$] *Rooms from: $170* ✉ *3643 U.S. Rural Rte. 2, North Hero* ☎ *802/372–4732, 888/525–3644* 🌐 *www.northherohouse.com* 🛏 *23 rooms, 3 suites* 🕒 *Closed Nov.–Mar.* 🍴 *Breakfast.*

$$ HOTEL 🏨 **Ruthcliffe Lodge & Restaurant.** Good food and splendid scenery make this off-the-beaten-path motel directly on Lake Champlain a great value. **Pros:** inexpensive rates; serene setting; laid-back vibe. **Cons:** rooms simple, not luxurious. [$] *Rooms from: $149* ✉ *1002 Quarry Rd., Isle La Motte* ☎ *802/928–3200* 🌐 *www.ruthcliffe.com* 🛏 *7 rooms* 🕒 *Closed Columbus Day–mid-May* 🍴 *Breakfast.*

SPORTS AND THE OUTDOORS

Apple Island Resort. Apple Island Resort rents pontoon boats, rowboats, canoes, kayaks, and motorboats. ✉ *71 US Rte. 2, South Hero* ☎ *802/372–3922* 🌐 *appleislandresort.com.*

Hero's Welcome. This shop rents bikes, canoes, kayaks, and paddleboats. In winter, there are skates, cross-country skis, and snowshoes. ✉ *3643 U.S. 2, North Hero* ☎ *802/372–4161, 800/372–4376* 🌐 *heroswelcome.com.*

Missisquoi National Wildlife Refuge. On the mainland east of the Alburg Peninsula, the Missisquoi National Wildlife Refuge consists of 6,729 acres of federally protected wetlands, meadows, and woods. It's a beautiful area for bird-watching, canoeing, or walking nature trails. ✉ *29 Tabor Rd., 36 miles north of Burlington, Swanton* ☎ *802/868–4781* 🌐 *www.fws.gov/refuge/missisquoi.*

Sand Bar State Park. One of Vermont's best swimming beaches is at Sand Bar State Park, along with a snack bar, changing room, and boat rentals. ✉ *1215 U.S. 2, South Hero* ☎ *802/893–2825* 🌐 *www.vtstateparks.com/htm/sandbar.htm* 🎫 *$3.50* 🕒 *Memorial Day weekend–Labor Day weekend, daily dawn–dusk.*

SHOPPING

Allenholm Farm. Open May to December, this farm store sells exemplary local produce, has a pick-your-own apple orchard, and features an animal-petting paddock. ✉ *150 South St., South Hero* ☎ *802/372–5566* 🌐 *www.allenholm.com.*

MONTGOMERY AND JAY

51 miles northeast of Burlington.

Montgomery is a small village near the Canadian border and Jay Peak ski resort. Amid the surrounding countryside are seven covered bridges.

DID YOU KNOW?

Long and skinny Lake Champlain is sometimes called the sixth Great Lake. Several small and scenic islands, like Grand Isle, are popular seasonal getaways in warm weather.

OFF THE BEATEN PATH

Lake Memphremagog. Vermont's second-largest body of water, Lake Memphremagog extends from Newport 33 miles north into Canada. Prouty Beach in Newport has tennis courts, boat rentals, and a 9-hole disc golf course. Watch the sun set from the deck of the East Side Restaurant, which serves excellent burgers and prime rib. ✉ *242 Prouty Beach Rd., Newport* ☎ *802/334–6345.*

SPORTS AND THE OUTDOORS

ICE-SKATING

FAMILY **Ice Haus Arena.** The sprawling Ice Haus Arena has a professional-size hockey rink and seating for 400 spectators. You can practice your stick and puck skills, and public skating is available several times a week. If you just want to watch, check out the several tournaments that take place throughout most of the year. ✉ *830 Jay Peak Rd., Jay* ☎ *802/988–2611* 🌐 *www.jaypeakresort.com.*

SKI AREAS

Hazen's Notch Cross Country Ski Center and B&B. Delightfully remote at any time of the year, this center has 40 miles of marked and groomed trails and rents equipment and snowshoes. ✉ *1419 Hazen's Notch Rd.* ☎ *802/326–4799* 🌐 *www.hazensnotch.org.*

Jay Peak. Sticking up out of the flat farmland, Jay Peak averages 380 inches of snow a year—more than any other Vermont ski area. It's renowned for its glade skiing and powder. Jay Peak has two interconnected mountains for downhill skiing, the highest reaching nearly 4,000 feet with a vertical drop of 2,153 feet. The smaller mountain has straight-fall-line, expert terrain that eases mid-mountain into an intermediate pitch. Beginners should stick near the bottom on trails off the Metro quad lift. The area's 78 trails, including 21 glades and two chutes, are served by eight lifts, including Vermont's only tramway and a long detachable quad. The area also has three quads, a triple, and a double chairlift; and two moving carpets. Jay has 80% snowmaking coverage. The area also has four terrain parks, each rated for different abilities, and a state-of-the art ice arena for hockey, figure skating, and curling. There are ski-school programs for children ages 3 to 18.

Jay Peak runs tram rides to the summit from mid-June through Labor Day and mid-September through Columbus Day. In the winter snowshoes can be rented, and guided walks are led by a naturalist. Telemark rentals and instruction are available. ✉ *830 Jay Peak Rd., Jay* ☎ *802/988–2611* 🌐 *www.jaypeakresort.com.*

WHERE TO STAY

$$$ HOTEL FAMILY 🏨 **Hotel Jay & Jay Peak Condominiums.** Centrally located in the ski resort's base area, the hotel and its simply furnished rooms are a favorite for families. **Pros:** great for skiers; wide range of accommodations; kids 14 and under stay and eat free. **Cons:** can get noisy; not very intimate; service isn't always helpful. [$] *Rooms from: $201* ✉ *4850 Rte. 242* ☎ *802/988–2611* 🌐 *www.jaypeakresort.com* 🛏 *172 suites, 94 condominiums* 🍴 *Some meals.*

$$ B&B/INN 🏨 **The INN.** Innkeepers Nick Barletta and Scott Pasfield have transformed this older property into a smart chalet-style lodging with tons of character. **Pros:** walking distance from shops and supplies. **Cons:**

noise from bar can seep into nearby rooms. $ *Rooms from: $159* ⊠ *241 Main St.* ☎ *802/326-4391* ⊕ *www.theinn.us* ⇄ *11 rooms* ⊙ *No meals.*

$$$$

B&B/INN

Phineas Swann Bed & Breakfast Inn. The top-hatted bulldog on the sign of this 1880 farmhouse isn't just a mascot: it reveals the hotel's welcoming attitude to pet owners. **Pros:** walking distance from shops and supplies. **Cons:** decor is a tad old-fashioned. $ *Rooms from: $449* ⊠ *195 Main St.* ☎ *802/326–4306* ⊕ *phineasswann.com* ⇄ *3 rooms, 6 suites* ⊙ *Breakfast.*

EN ROUTE

Northeast Kingdom. Routes 14, 5, 58, and 100 make a scenic drive around the Northeast Kingdom, named for the remoteness and stalwart independence that have helped preserve its rural nature. You can extend the loop and head east on Route 105 to the city of Newport on Lake Memphremagog. Some of the most unspoiled areas in all Vermont are on the drive south from Newport on either U.S. 5 or Interstate 91 (the latter is faster, but the former is prettier).

LAKE WILLOUGHBY

30 miles southeast of Montgomery (summer route; 50 miles by winter route), 28 miles north of St. Johnsbury.

EXPLORING

FAMILY

Bread and Puppet Museum. This ramshackle barn houses a surrealistic collection of props used by the world-renowned Bread and Puppet Theater. The troupe has been performing social and political commentary with the towering (they're supported by people on stilts), eerily expressive puppets for 50 years. In July and August, there are performances on Sunday at 2:30. ⊠ *753 Heights Rd., 1 mile east of Rte. 16, Glover* ☎ *802/525–3031* ⊕ *www.breadandpuppet.org* ▱ *Donations accepted* ⊙ *June–Oct., daily 10–6.*

Lake Willoughby. The cliffs of Mt. Pisgah and Mt. Hor drop to the edge of Lake Willoughby on opposite shores, giving this beautiful, deep, glacially carved lake a striking resemblance to a Norwegian fjord. The trails to the top of Mt. Pisgah reward hikers with glorious views. ⊠ *Westmore.*

EAST BURKE

17 miles south of Lake Willoughby.

Once a sleepy village, East Burke is now the Northeast Kingdom's outdoor-activity hub. The Kingdom Trails attract thousands of mountain bikers in summer and fall. In winter, many trails are groomed for cross-country skiing.

ESSENTIALS

Kingdom Trails Association ☎ *802/626–0737* ⊕ *www.kingdomtrails.org.*

WHERE TO STAY

$$$

RESORT

FAMILY

The Wildflower Inn. The hilltop views are breathtaking at this rambling, family-oriented complex of old farm buildings on 570 acres. **Pros:** kid-friendly resort; relaxed atmosphere; lots of activities. **Cons:** most rooms have basic furnishings. $ *Rooms from: $200* ⊠ *2059 Darling Hill Rd., 5 miles west of East Burke, Lyndonville* ☎ *802/626–8310, 800/627–8310* ⊕ *www.wildflowerinn.com* ⇄ *10 rooms, 13 suites, 1 cottage* ⊙ *Closed Apr. and Nov.* ⊙ *Breakfast.*

Catch a show and some social commentary at the Bread and Puppet Theater in summer, or visit the museum year-round.

SPORTS AND THE OUTDOORS

BIKING

East Burke Sports. This shop rents and repairs mountain bikes, kayaks, skis, snowboards, and snowshoes. ✉ *439 Rte. 114* ☎ *802/626–3215* ⊕ *www.eastburkesports.com.*

Kingdom Trails. Locals maintain this 110-mile network of trails for mountain biking and hiking in the summer, and 37 miles for snowshoeing and cross-country skiing in the winter. ✉ *478 Rte. 114* ☎ *802/626–0737* ⊕ *www.kingdomtrails.com.*

Village Sport Shop. This shop rents bikes, canoes, kayaks, paddleboats, skis, and snowshoes. ✉ *511 Broad St., Lyndonville* ☎ *802/626–8448* ⊕ *www.villagesportshop.com.*

SKI AREA

Burke Mountain. About an hour's drive from Montpelier is Burke Mountain ski resort. Racers stick to the Training Slope, served by its own lift. The other 55 trails and glades are a quiet playground. ✉ *1 Mountain Rd.* ☎ *802/626–7300* ⊕ *www.skiburke.com.*

ST. JOHNSBURY

16 miles south of East Burke, 39 miles northeast of Montpelier.

St. Johnsbury, the southern gateway to the Northeast Kingdom, was chartered in 1786. But its identity was established after 1830, when Thaddeus Fairbanks invented the platform scale, a device that revolutionized weighing methods. The Fairbanks family's philanthropic efforts gave the city a strong cultural and architectural imprint. Today St. J, as the locals call it, is the friendly, adventure-sports-happy hub of the Northeast Kingdom.

EXPLORING

FAMILY **Dog Mountain.** Artist Stephen Huneck was famous for his colorful folk art sculptures and paintings of dogs. Much more than an art gallery–gift shop, this deeply moving place is complete with a chapel where animal lovers can reflect on their beloved pets. Above all, this is a place to bring your dog: there is a swimming pond and hiking trails. ✉ *143 Parks Rd., off Spaulding Rd.* ☎ *800/449–2580* 🌐 *www.dogmt.com* 🎟 *Free* 🕒 *May–August: Daily 10–5; October–May, Thurs.–Mon. 11–4.*

FAMILY Fodor's Choice ★ **Fairbanks Museum and Planetarium.** This odd and deeply thrilling little museum displays the eccentric collection of Franklin Fairbanks, who surely had one of the most inquisitive minds in American history. He built this magnificent barrel-vaulted gallery in 1889 to house the specimens of plants, animals, birds, reptiles, and collections of folk art and dolls—and a seemingly unending variety of beautifully mounted curios—he had picked up around the world. The museum showcases over 175,000 items, but it's surprisingly easy to feast your eyes on everything here without getting a museum headache. There's also a popular 45-seat planetarium, the state's only public planetarium; as well the Eye on the Sky Weather Gallery, home to live NPR weather broadcasts. ✉ *1302 Main St.* ☎ *802/748–2372* 🌐 *www.fairbanksmuseum.org* 🎟 *Museum $8; planetarium $5* 🕒 *Apr.–Oct., Mon.–Sat. 9–5, Sun. 1–5; Nov.–Mar., Tues.–Sat. 9–5, Sun. 1–5.*

Fodor's Choice ★ **St. Johnsbury Athenaeum.** With its polished Victorian woodwork, dramatic paneling, and ornate circular staircases, this building is both the town library (one of the nicest you're likely to ever come across) and one of the oldest art galleries in the country, housing more than 100 original works mainly of the Hudson River school. Albert Bierstadt's enormous *Domes of Yosemite* dominates the beautiful painting gallery. ✉ *1171 Main St.* ☎ *802/748–8291* 🌐 *www.stjathenaeum.org* 🎟 *Free* 🕒 *Weekdays 10–5:30, Sat. 10–3.*

OFF THE BEATEN PATH **Peacham.** Tiny Peacham, 10 miles southwest of St. Johnsbury, is on almost every tour group's list of "must-sees." With views extending to the White Mountains of New Hampshire and a white-steeple church, Peacham is perhaps the most photographed town in New England. The movie adaptation of *Ethan Frome*, starring Liam Neeson, was filmed here. Next door, the **Peacham Corner Guild** sells local handcrafts. The **Peacham Store** offers tasty soups and stews. ✉ *Peacham* 🌐 *www.peacham.net.*

WHERE TO STAY

$$$ B&B/INN 🏨 **Rabbit Hill Inn.** Few inns in New England have the word-of-mouth buzz that Rabbit Hill seems to earn from satisfied guests. **Pros:** attractive, spacious rooms; romantic; lovely grounds; good food. **Cons:** might be too quiet a setting for some. [$] *Rooms from: $210* ✉ *48 Lower Waterford Rd., 11 miles south of St. Johnsbury, Lower Waterford* 🌐 *www.rabbithillinn.com* 🛏 *19 rooms* 🕒 *Closed 1st 3 wks in Apr., 1st 2 wks in Nov.* 🍴 *Breakfast.*

4

NEW HAMPSHIRE

WELCOME TO NEW HAMPSHIRE

TOP REASONS TO GO

★ **The White Mountains:** Great for hiking and skiing, these rugged, dramatic peaks and notches are unforgettable.

★ **Lake Winnipesaukee:** Water parks, arcades, boat cruises, and classic summer camps make for a family fun summer.

★ **Fall Foliage:** Head to the Kancamagus Highway in the fall for one of America's best drives or seek out a lesser-known route that's just as stunning.

★ **Portsmouth:** Less than an hour from Boston, this great American city has coastline allure, colorful Colonial architecture, romantic dining, and fine arts and crafts.

★ **Pristine Towns:** Jaffrey Center, Walpole, Tamworth, Center Sandwich, and Jackson are among the most charming tiny villages in New England.

1 The Seacoast. You can find historical sites, hopping bars, beaches, whale-watching, and deep-sea fishing all packed in along New Hampshire's 18 miles of coastline. Hampton Beach is the center of summertime activities, while Portsmouth is a hub of nightlife, dining, art, and Colonial history.

2 Lakes Region. Throughout central New Hampshire are lakes and more lakes. The largest, Lake Winnipesaukee, has 240 miles of coastline and attracts all sorts of water sports enthusiasts, but there are many more secluded and quiet lakes with enchanting bed-and-breakfasts where relaxation is the main activity.

3 The White Mountains. Skiing, snowshoeing, and snowboarding in the winter; hiking, biking, and riding scenic railways in the summer—the Whites, as locals call their mountains, have plenty of natural wonders within a stone's throw from the roads, but other spots call for lung-busting hikes. Mt. Washington, the tallest mountain in the Northeast, can be conquered by trail, train, or car.

4 Dartmouth–Lake Sunapee. Quiet villages can be found throughout the region. Many of them are barely removed from Colonial times, but some thrive as centers of arts and education and are filled with quaint shops. Hanover, the home of 240-year-old Dartmouth College, retains that true New England college-town feel, with ivy-draped buildings and cobblestone walkways. Lake Sunapee is a wonderful place to swim, fish, or enjoy a cruise.

Lisbon
302
Woodsville
91
25
Warren
25A
Wentworth
10
118
Hanover
Enfield
89
Lebanon
4
Plainfield
Grafton
Grantham
4
Georges Mills
Lake Sunapee
11
Claremont
VERMONT
11
Newport
North Sutton
Charlestown
Goshen
10
91
Hillsboro
Walpole
Stoddard
Gilsum
Antrim
9
Bennington
Keene
Peterborough
101
Marlborough
Mt. Monadnock
Hinsdale
Troy
5
Winchester
Jaffrey
Jaffrey Center
202
91

MASSACHUSETTS

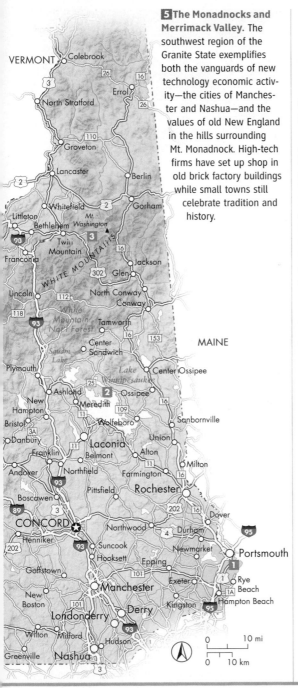

5 The Monadnocks and Merrimack Valley. The southwest region of the Granite State exemplifies both the vanguards of new technology economic activity—the cities of Manchester and Nashua—and the values of old New England in the hills surrounding Mt. Monadnock. High-tech firms have set up shop in old brick factory buildings while small towns still celebrate tradition and history.

GETTING ORIENTED

4

Although New Hampshire has three interstates running through it (I–95, I–93, and I–89), most of its regions are accessible only on smaller roads. From Boston or Portland, Maine, Interstate 95 provides the best access to Portsmouth and the beaches along the coast, though many people like to drive along Route 1A, which parallels the coast. North of Portsmouth, Route 16 leads to the White Mountains, whose precipitous peaks seem to rise out of nowhere, and the lakes region, home to Lake Winnipesaukee. From there, Interstate 93 cuts north toward Franconia and Littleton and south into Concord, Manchester, and Nashua. State roads east and north of Interstate 93 lead to Dixville Notch, which casts the first vote in presidential elections, and the Connecticut Lakes. Following the Connecticut River takes you to Hanover, home of Dartmouth College, Claremont, Charleston, Walpole, and Keene. From Concord, travelers head west to reach the Monadnock Region.

Updated by
Debbie Hagan

New Hampshire residents have often been called cantankerous, but beneath that crusty exterior is often hospitality and friendliness. The state's motto was coined by New Hampshire native General John Stark, who led the Colonial Army in its hard-fought battle of Bennington, Vermont, in 1777. "Live free or die; death is not the worst of evils," he said, in a letter written 20 years after the battle. The residents of the Granite State have taken "Live Free or Die" to heart, defining themselves by that principle for more than 200 years.

The state is often identified more by what it is not than by what it is. It lacks Vermont's folksy charm. Maine's coast is grander. But New Hampshire's independent spirit, mountain peaks, clear air, and sparkling lakes have attracted trailblazers and artists for centuries. Ralph Waldo Emerson, Henry David Thoreau, Nathaniel Hawthorne, and Louisa May Alcott all visited and wrote about the state, sparking a strong literary tradition that continues today. It also has a strong political history: it was the first colony to declare independence from Great Britain, the first to adopt a state constitution, and the first to require that constitution be referred to the people for approval.

The state's diverse terrain makes it popular with everyone from avid adventurers to young families looking for easy access to nature. You can hike, climb, ski, snowboard, snowshoe, and fish as well as explore on snowmobiles, sailboats, and mountain bikes. Natives have no objection to others enjoying the state's beauty as long as they leave some money behind. New Hampshire has long resisted both sales and income taxes, so tourism brings in much-needed revenue.

With a number of its cities consistently rated among the most livable in the nation, New Hampshire has seen considerable growth over the past decade. Longtime residents worry that the state will soon take on two personalities: one of rapidly growing cities to the southeast and the other of quiet villages to the west and north. Although newcomers have brought change, the independent nature of the people and the state's natural beauty remain constant.

PLANNING

WHEN TO GO

Summer and fall are the best times to visit most of New Hampshire. Winter is a great time to travel to the White Mountains, but most other tourist sites in the state, including the Portsmouth museums and many attractions in the Lakes Region, are closed due to snow and cold weather. In summer people flock to beaches, mountain trails, and lake boat ramps. In the cities, festivals showcase music, theater, and crafts. Fall brings leaf peepers, especially to the White Mountains and along the Kancamagus Highway (Route 112). Skiers and snowboarders take to the slopes in winter, when Christmas lights and carnivals brighten the long, dark nights. Spring's unpredictable weather—along with April's mud and late May's black flies—tends to deter visitors. Still, the season has its joys, not the least of which is the appearance of the state flower, the purple lilac, from mid-May to early June as well as colorful rhododendrons.

PLANNING YOUR TIME

Some people come to New Hampshire to hike or ski the mountains, fish and sail the lakes, or cycle along the back roads. Others prefer to drive through scenic towns, visiting museums and shops. Although New Hampshire is a small state, roads curve around lakes and mountains, making distances longer than they appear. You can get a taste of the coast, lake, and mountain areas in three to five days; eight days gives you time to make a more complete loop.

GETTING HERE AND AROUND

AIR TRAVEL

Manchester Boston Regional Airport is the state's largest and has nonstop service to more than 20 cities. Boston's Logan Airport is within one to three hours of most places in New Hampshire, as is Bradley International in Hartford, Connecticut.

CAR TRAVEL

New Hampshire is an easy drive north from Boston and serves as a good base for exploring northern New England. Many destinations are near major highways, so getting around by car is a great way to travel. Interstate 93 stretches from Boston to Littleton and on into neighboring Vermont. Interstate 89 will get you from Concord to Hanover and eventually to Burlington, Vermont. To the east, Interstate 95, which is a toll road, passes through southern New Hampshire's coastal area on its way from Massachusetts to Maine. Throughout the state are quiet backcountry lanes and winding roads that might take a little longer but can make for some of the best parts of the journey.

Speed limits on interstate and limited-access highways are usually 65 mph, except in heavily settled areas, where 55 mph is the norm. On state and U.S. routes, speed limits vary considerably. On any given stretch, the limit may be anywhere from 25 mph to 55 mph, so watch the signs carefully. Right turns on red lights are permitted unless otherwise indicated.

TRAIN TRAVEL

Amtrak. Amtrak runs its *Downeaster* service from Boston to Portland, Maine, with stops in Exeter, Durham, and Dover. ☎ *800/872–7245* ⊕ *www.amtrak.com.*

RESTAURANTS

New Hampshire prides itself on seafood—not just lobster but also salmon pie, steamed mussels, fried clams, and seared tuna. Across the state you'll find country taverns with upscale Continental and American menus, many of them embracing regional ingredients. Alongside a growing number of contemporary eateries are such state traditions as greasy-spoon diners, pizzerias, and pubs that serve hearty comfort fare. Reservations are almost never required, and dress is casual in nearly every eatery.

Prices in the reviews are the average cost of a main course at dinner or, if dinner is not served, at lunch.

HOTELS

In the mid-19th century wealthy Bostonians retreated to imposing New Hampshire country homes in summer months. Grand hotels were built across the state, especially in the White Mountains, when the area competed with Saratoga Springs, Newport, and Bar Harbor to draw the nation's elite vacationers. Today a handful of these hotel-resorts survive, with their large cooking staffs and tradition of top-notch service. Many of the vacation houses have been converted into inns and B&Bs. The smallest have only a couple of rooms and are typically done in period style. The largest contain 30 or more rooms and suites and have in-room fireplaces and even hot tubs. You'll also find a great many well-kept, often family-owned motor lodges—particularly in the White Mountains and Lakes regions. In the ski areas expect the usual ski condos and lodges. In the Merrimack River valley, as well as along major highways, chain hotels and motels prevail. There are numerous campgrounds across the state, which accommodate RVs as well. The White Mountains provide an excellent base for camping and hiking.

Prices in the reviews are the lowest cost of a standard double room in high season.

THE SEACOAST

New Hampshire's 18-mile stretch of coastline packs in a wealth of scenery and diversions. The honky-tonk of Hampton Beach gets plenty of attention, good and bad, but first-timers are often surprised by the significant chunk of shoreline that remains pristine—especially through the town of Rye. This section begins in the regional hub, Portsmouth, cuts down the coast to the beaches, branches inland to the prep-school town of Exeter, and runs back up north through Dover, Durham (home of the University of New Hampshire), and Rochester. From here it's a short drive to the Lakes Region.

OUTDOOR ACTIVITIES

Hitting the trails by boot and ski, fishing, kayaking and canoeing, biking, or just plain old walking will undoubtedly be a part of your visit.

Biking: Many ski resorts in the White Mountains offer mountain-biking opportunities, providing chairlift rides to the top and trails for all skill levels at the bottom. Some of the state's best road biking is along the Kancamagus Highway and around Lake Sunapee.

Hiking: For the more adventurous, hiking the trails in the White Mountains or along the Appalachian Trail is their reason for visiting.

For those more interested in less arduous treks, there are plenty of day hikes in the White Mountain National Forest and state parks such as Pisgah, the state's largest, in Cheshire County, the Crawford Notch and Franconia Notch state parks in the Whites, and Mt. Monadnock.

Skiing: Ski areas abound in New Hampshire—try Bretton Woods, Mt. Sunapee, Waterville Valley, or Canon Mountain. For cross-country skiing, nothing beats Gunstock Mountain Resort, with 32 miles of trails, also open for snowshoeing. Or visit Franconia Village, which has 37 miles of cross-country trails.

ESSENTIALS

Visitor Information Seacoast New Hampshire & South Coast Maine ☎ *603/427–2020* ⊕ *www.seacoastnh.com.*

PORTSMOUTH

47 miles southeast of Concord; 50 miles southwest of Portland, Maine; 56 miles north of Boston.

Fodor's Choice ★ Settled in 1623 as Strawbery Banke, Portsmouth became a prosperous port before the Revolutionary War, and, like similarly wealthy Newport, Rhode Island, it harbored many Tory sympathizers throughout the campaign. Filled with grand residential architecture spanning the 18th through early 20th centuries, this city of 23,000 has many historic homes, including the collection of 40-plus buildings that make up the Strawbery Banke Museum. With hip eateries, quirky shops, swank cocktail bars, respected theaters, and jumping live-music venues, this sheltered harbor city is a hot destination. Downtown, especially around elegant Market Square, buzzes with conviviality.

GETTING HERE AND AROUND

Interstate 95 and Route 1 run through Portsmouth. From the west, take Route 101 and from the north take Route 16. Amtrak runs through Durham, which is a short drive from the coast. Once in Portsmouth, you can walk about the downtown, though you'll want a car for farther attractions.

ESSENTIALS

Bus and Trolley COAST Bus ☎ *603/743–5777* ⊕ *www.coastbus.org.*

Taxi Anchor Taxi ☎ *603/436–1888.* **Portsmouth Taxi** ☎ *603/431–6811.*

Visitor Information **Greater Portsmouth Chamber of Commerce** ⊠ *500 Market St.* ☎ *603/610–5510* ⊕ *www.portsmouthchamber.org.*

TOURS

Prescott Park Arts Festival. This outdoor festival presents theater, dance, and musical events from June through August. ⊠ *105 Marcy St.* ☎ *603/436–2848* ⊕ *www.prescottpark.org.*

Discover Portsmouth. Part welcome center and part museum, Discover Portsmouth, operated by the Portsmouth Historical Society, is where you'll not only learn about daily events, history tours, and walking trails, but also see art and historical exhibits. Sign up here for a guided walking tour, stock up on city maps, and learn about the Portsmouth Harbour Trail, a route that passes more than 70 points of scenic and historical significance. ⊠ *10 Middle St.* ☎ *603/436–8433* ⊕ *www. portsmouthhistory.org* ▣ *Free* ⊙ *Apr.–late-Dec., daily 10–5.*

Portsmouth Black Heritage Trail. Important sites of African-American history are along the self-guided walk on the Portsmouth Black Heritage Trail. Included are the New Hampshire Gazette Printing Office, where skilled slave Primus Fowle operated the paper's printing press for some 50 years beginning in 1756, and the city's 1866 Election Hall, outside of which the city's black citizens held annual celebrations of the Emancipation Proclamation. Call about guided tours. ⊠ *Discover Portsmouth, 10 Middle St.* ☎ *603/380–1231* ⊕ *www.portsmouthhistory.org* ▣ *Donations welcome.*

EXPLORING
TOP ATTRACTIONS

Albacore Park. Built here in 1953, the USS *Albacore* is docked at this visitor center in Albacore Park. You can board the prototype submarine, which was a floating laboratory designed to test an innovative hull design, dive brakes, and sonar systems for the Navy. The nearby Memorial Garden and its reflecting pool are dedicated to those who have lost their lives in submarine service. ⊠ *600 Market St.* ☎ *603/436–3680* ⊕ *www.ussalbacore.org* ▣ *$6* ⊙ *Memorial Day–Columbus Day, daily 9:30–5; Columbus Day–Memorial Day, Thurs.–Mon. 9:30–4.*

Great Bay Estuarine National Research Reserve. Just inland from Portsmouth is one of southeastern New Hampshire's most precious assets. Amid its 10,235 acres of open and tidal waters and mudflats you can spot blue herons, ospreys, and snowy egrets, particularly during spring and fall migrations. The Great Bay Discovery Center has indoor and outdoor exhibits, a library and bookshop, and a 1,700-foot boardwalk, as well as other trails through mudflats and upland forest. ⊠ *89 Depot Rd., Greenland* ☎ *603/778–0015* ⊕ *www.greatbay.org* ▣ *Free* ⊙ *Visitor Center May–Sept., Wed.–Sun. 10–4; Oct., weekends 10–4.*

John Paul Jones House. This was a boardinghouse when the Revolutionary War hero lived here while supervising shipbuilding for the Continental Navy. The 1758 hip-roofed structure displays furniture, costumes, glass, guns, portraits, and documents from the late 18th century. The collection specializes in textiles, particularly some extraordinary embroidery samplers from the early 19th century. ⊠ *43 Middle St.* ☎ *603/436–8420* ⊕ *www.portsmouthhistory.org* ▣ *$6* ⊙ *May–Oct., daily 11–5.*

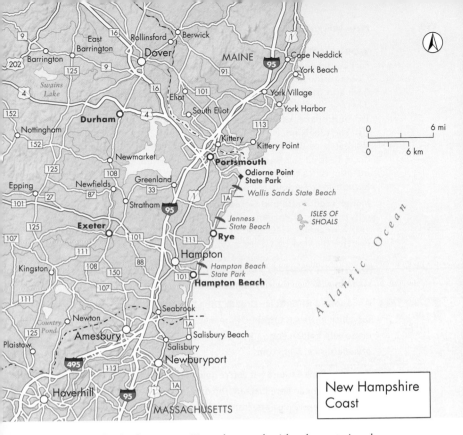

New Hampshire Coast

Redhook Ale Brewery. Tours here end with a beer tasting, but you can also stop in the Cataqua Public House for a mug of ale and a bite to eat. The grounds are home to many events during the summer, including August's Redhookfest. ⊠ *Pease International Tradeport, 1 Redhook Way* ☏ *603/430–8600* ⊕ *www.redhook.com* 🖃 *$5* ⊙ *Sun.–Thurs. 1–5, Fri. and Sat. noon–6.*

FAMILY
Fodor'sChoice
★
Strawbery Banke Museum. The first English settlers named the area around today's Portsmouth for the wild strawberries along the shores of the Piscataqua River. The name survives in this 10-acre outdoor history museum, one of the largest in New England. The compound has 46 buildings dating from 1695 to 1820—some restored and furnished to a particular period, others used for historical exhibits. Half the interior of the Drisco House, built in 1795, depicts its use as a dry-goods store in Colonial times, whereas the living room and kitchen are decorated as they were in the 1950s, showing how buildings were adapted over time. The Shapiro House has been restored to reflect the life of the Russian Jewish immigrant family who lived in the home in the early 1900s. Perhaps the most opulent house, done in decadent Victorian style, is the 1860 Goodwin Mansion, former home of Governor Ichabod Goodwin. ⊠ *14 Hancock St.* ☏ *603/433–1100* ⊕ *www.strawberybanke.org* 🖃 *$18* ⊙ *May–Oct., daily 10–5.*

WORTH NOTING

FAMILY **Fort Constitution Historic Site.** On the nearby island of New Castle, Fort Constitution was built in 1631 and then rebuilt in 1666 as Fort William and Mary, a British stronghold overlooking Portsmouth Harbor. The fort earned its fame in 1774, when patriots raided it in one of Revolutionary America's first overtly defiant acts against King George III. The rebels later used the captured munitions against the British at the Battle of Bunker Hill. Great view of Portsmouth Lighthouse, next door. Park at the Battery Farnsworth and walk into the Coast Guard installation to the fort. ⊠ *25 Wentworth Rd., next to the Coast Guard Station* ☎ *603/436–1552* ⊕ *www.nhstateparks.org* ⊠ *Free* ☉ *Daily 8–4.*

Moffatt-Ladd House and Garden. The period interior of this 1763 home tells the story of Portsmouth's merchant class through portraits, letters, and furnishings. The Colonial Revival garden includes a horse chestnut tree planted by General William Whipple when he returned home after signing the Declaration of Independence in 1776. ⊠ *154 Market St.* ☎ *603/436–8221* ⊕ *www.moffattladd.org* ⊠ *Garden and house $6, garden only $2* ☉ *Early June–mid-Oct., Mon.–Sat. 11–5, Sun. 1–5.*

QUICK BITES

Annabelle's Natural Ice Cream. Drop by Annabelle's Natural Ice Cream for a dish of New Hampshire Pure maple walnut or rich vanilla ice cream made with golden egg yolks. ⊠ *49 Ceres St.* ☎ *603/436–3400* ⊕ *www.annabellesicecream.com.*

Breaking New Grounds. If you're going out to dinner, skip the coffee and dessert and head here instead. The only problem is choosing from among the many types of sweets, from pastries to gelati. In nice weather, sit outside and soak up the street entertainment. ⊠ *14 Market Sq.* ☎ *603/436–9555* ⊕ *www.bngcoffee.com.*

Warner House. The main features of this quiet 1716 gem are the curious folk-art murals lining the hall staircase, which may be the oldest-known murals in the United States still gracing their original structure. This house, a noted example of Georgian architecture, contains original art, furnishings, and extraordinary examples of area craftsmanship. The west-wall lightning rod is believed to have been installed in 1762 under the supervision of Benjamin Franklin. ⊠ *150 Daniel St.* ☎ *603/436–5909* ⊕ *www.warnerhouse.org* ⊠ *$5* ☉ *June–Oct., Wed.–Mon. 11–4.*

Wentworth-Coolidge Mansion Historic Site. A National Historic Landmark now part of Little Harbor State Park, this was originally the residence of Benning Wentworth, New Hampshire's first royal governor (1753–70). Notable among its period furnishings is the carved pine mantelpiece in the council chamber. Wentworth's imported lilac trees bloom each May. Call ahead for house tours, offered on the hour. ⊠ *375 Little Harbor Rd., near South Street Cemetery* ☎ *603/436–6607* ⊕ *www.nhstateparks.org* ⊠ *$5* ☉ *Late May–mid-June and Sept.–mid-Oct., weekends 10–4; mid-June–Aug., Wed.–Sun. 10–4.*

OFF THE BEATEN PATH

Isles of Shoals. Many of these nine small, rocky islands (eight at high tide) retain earthy names—Hog and Smuttynose to cite but two—given them by 17th-century fishermen. A history of piracy, murder, and ghosts

Strawbery Banke Museum includes period gardens and 46 historic buildings.

surrounds the archipelago, long populated by an independent lot who, according to one writer, hadn't the sense to winter on the mainland. Celia Thaxter, a native islander, romanticized these islands with her poetry in *Among the Isles of Shoals* (1873). In the late 19th century **Appledore Island** became an offshore retreat for Thaxter's coterie of writers, musicians, and artists. **Star Island** contains a small museum, the Rutledge Marine Lab, with interactive family exhibits. From May to late October you can take a narrated history cruise of the Isles of Shoals, a day trip to Star Island, or a walking tour of Star Island with Isles of Shoals Steamship Company. ⊠ *315 Market St.* ☎ *800/441–4620* ⊕ *www.islesofshoals.com.*

Prescott Park. Picnicking is popular at this waterfront park. A large formal garden with fountains is perfect for whiling away an afternoon. The park contains Point of Graves, Portsmouth's oldest burial ground, and two 17th-century warehouses. The Prescott Park Arts Festival, a summer-long event, includes a multitude of concerts, outdoor movies, and food festivals. ⊠ *Marcy St.* ☎ *603/436–2848* ⊕ *www.prescottpark.org.*

Water Country. New Hampshire's largest water park has an tube ride, a wave pool, and 15 waterslides. ⊠ *2300 Lafayette Rd.* ☎ *603/427–1111* ⊕ *www.watercountry.com* ⊠ *$39* ☉ *Mid-June–Labor Day, hours vary.*

WHERE TO EAT

$$$
INTERNATIONAL
Fodor's Choice
★

✕ **Black Trumpet Bistro.** Award-winning chef Evan Mallett combines bold flavors from Latin America, North Africa, Turkey, and Mexico in the fare he serves in this romantic little restaurant with views of the water. The menu is constantly changing, offering such surprises as roasted allium soup, rabbit-and-mushroom enchiladas, and potato-and-cheese

A boat tour of Portsmouth Harbor is popular in warm weather, and a great introduction to the city's maritime heritage.

pierogies with smoked corn bisque and a sautéed kale–and-blueberry salad. Mallett belongs to the Heirloom Harvest Project, and brings unusual vegetables, sometimes in surprising colors, to the table. Vegetarians will always find out-of-the-ordinary entrées. The atmosphere is quiet, and walk-ins may find a table in the upstairs wine bar. [$] *Average main: $25* ✉ *29 Ceres St.* ☎ *603/431–0887* 🌐 *www.blacktrumpetbistro.com* ⌚ *No lunch.*

$$ CARIBBEAN 🍴 **Blue Mermaid Island Grill.** This fun, colorful place is good for seafood, sandwiches, and quesadillas, as well as house-cut yucca chips. Specialties include plantain-encrusted cod topped with grilled mango vinaigrette and served with grilled banana–sweet potato hash, a chipotle-and-honey-marinated sirloin, and braised short ribs with an island rub. In summer you can eat on a deck that overlooks some adorable Colonial homes. There's live music most nights. [$] *Average main: $20* ✉ *409 The Hill* ☎ *603/427–2583* 🌐 *www.bluemermaid.com.*

$$ AMERICAN FAMILY 🍴 **Friendly Toast.** The biggest and best breakfast in town is served at this funky, wildly colorful diner loaded with bric-a-brac. Coconut Cakes (buttermilk pancakes, chocolate chips, coconut, and cashews), Drunkard French toast (with a Grand Marnier–and-raspberry sauce), and hefty omelets are favorites. Also enjoy the homemade breads and muffins. The place serves lunch and dinner, and a late-night crowd gathers after the bars close. [$] *Average main: $13* ✉ *113 Congress St.* ☎ *603/430–2154* 🌐 *www.thefriendlytoast.net.*

$$$ SEAFOOD 🍴 **Jumpin' Jay's Fish Cafe.** A wildly popular downtown spot, this offbeat, dimly lighted eatery has a changing menu of fresh seafood from as far away as Iceland and Costa Rica. Try the steamed Prince Edward Island mussels with jalapeños, spicy ginger, and saffron sauce, or the haddock

with lemon, white wine, and capers. You can't go wrong with one of the fresh catches topped with one of seven different sauces. Singles like to gather at the central bar for dinner and furtive glances. $ *Average main: $25* ⊠ *150 Congress St.* ☎ *603/766–3474* ⊕ *www.jumpinjays.com.*

$$$$
STEAKHOUSE
✕ **Library Restaurant.** In this bibliophile's dream, the 12-foot hand-carved ceiling and the Spanish mahogany walls were constructed by the Pullman Car Woodworkers in 1889. Although the kitchen creates lighter dishes such as jumbo crab cakes and crispy fried shrimp in sweet chili sauce, the mainstays are thick-cut, juicy steaks and chops. The crushed-peppercorn steak is meat heaven. Choose from six different rich, creamy sauces, including hollandaise and Gorgonzola, plus an array of fresh vegetables. The English-style pub serves nearly 100 martinis made from over 250 brands of international vodkas. Sunday brunch is also popular. $ *Average main: $30* ⊠ *401 State St.* ☎ *603/431–5202* ⊕ *www.libraryrestaurant.com.*

$$
LATIN AMERICAN
✕ **Poco's Bow Street Cantina.** This casual but contemporary eatery turns out exceptional Southwestern and Latin American cuisine. Cajun red snapper tacos, fried calamari, and lobster quesadillas are among the best choices. Most tables have great views of the Piscataqua River. The downstairs bar and spacious outdoor deck are local hangouts. Try one of the craft cocktails, such as the cucumber martini. $ *Average main: $14* ⊠ *37 Bow St.* ☎ *603/431–5967* ⊕ *www.pocosbowstreetcantina. com* ⌦ *Reservations not accepted.*

WHERE TO STAY

$$$
HOTEL
⊞ **Ale House Inn.** Talk about prime location: this urban-style hotel is steps from the city's historic houses, boutiques, and restaurants. **Pros:** great location; complimentary tickets to local theater; bicycles for local jaunts. **Cons:** no breakfast. $ *Rooms from: $199* ⊠ *121 Bow St.* ☎ *603/431–7760* ⊕ *www.alehouseinn.com* ⌐ *10 rooms* ⎮◯⎮ *No meals.*

$$$
B&B/INN
⊞ **Martin Hill Inn.** You may fall in love with this adorable yellow 1815 house surrounded by flower-filled gardens. **Pros:** lovely building; central location; furnished with real antiques. **Cons:** not in historic district. $ *Rooms from: $185* ⊠ *404 Islington St.* ☎ *603/436–2287* ⊕ *www.martinhillinn.com* ⌐ *7 rooms* ⎮◯⎮ *Breakfast.*

$$$$
RESORT
Fodor'sChoice
★
⊞ **Wentworth by the Sea.** What's not to love about this white colossus overlooking the sea on New Castle Island? **Pros:** great spa; spectacular Sunday brunch; lovely oceanfront perch. **Cons:** not in downtown Portsmouth. $ *Rooms from: $429* ⊠ *588 Wentworth Rd., New Castle* ☎ *603/422–7322, 866/240–6313* ⊕ *www.wentworth.com* ⌐ *161 rooms, 31 suites* ⎮◯⎮ *No meals.*

NIGHTLIFE AND THE ARTS
THE ARTS
Music Hall. Beloved for its acoustics, the 1878 Music Hall brings the best touring events to the seacoast—from classical and pop concerts to dance and theater. The hall also screens art films. ⊠ *28 Chestnut St.* ☎ *603/436–2400* ⊕ *www.themusichall.org.*

Four of the nine rocky Isles of Shoals belong to New Hampshire; the other five belong to Maine.

NIGHTLIFE

BARS **Two Ceres Street.** This lively bar serves such original martinis as the Lumberjack, with Maker's Mark and maple syrup, and the Hammer and Sickle, with Grey Goose vodka, peperoncini, and olive juice. ⊠ *2 Ceres St.* ☎ *603/433–2373* ⊕ *www.twocerestreet.com.*

MUSIC **Portsmouth Gas Light Co.** This brick-oven pizzeria hosts local rock bands in its lounge, courtyard, and slick upstairs space. ⊠ *64 Market St.* ☎ *603/430–9122* ⊕ *www.portsmouthgaslight.com.*

The Press Room. People come from Boston and Portland just to hang out at the Press Room, which showcases folk, jazz, blues, and bluegrass performers nightly. ⊠ *77 Daniel St.* ☎ *603/431–5186* ⊕ *www. pressroomnh.com.*

The Red Door Lounge. Discover the local music scene at the Red Door Lounge, open every night except Tuesday. Indie music fans shouldn't miss Monday night's Hush Hush Sweet Harlot live music series. ⊠ *107 State St.* ⊕ *www.reddoorportsmouth.com.*

SPORTS AND THE OUTDOORS
BOAT TOURS

Gundalow Company. Sail the Piscataqua River in a flat-bottom gundalow built at Strawbery Banke. Help the crew haul up lobster traps and trawl for plankton, or buy a picnic lunch from the White Apron Café (next door to the office) and sit back and enjoy the spectacular views. Learn all about the region's history from an onboard educator. Cruises run Memorial Day to Columbus Day. ⊠ *60 Marcy St.* ☎ *603/433–9505* ⊕ *www.gundalow.org.*

Isles of Shoals Steamship Company. This company runs cruises aboard the *Thomas Laighton,* a replica of a Victorian steamship, May through October. Cruises take you to the Isles of Shoals, Portsmouth Harbor, or the nearby lighthouses. Lunches and light snacks are available on board, or you can bring your own. ⊠ *Barker Wharf, 315 Market St.* ☎ *603/431–5500, 800/441–4620* ⊕ *www.islesofshoals.com.*

Portsmouth Harbor Cruises. From May to October, Portsmouth Harbor Cruises operates tours of Portsmouth Harbor, foliage trips on the Cocheco River, and sunset cruises aboard the MV *Heritage.* ⊠ *64 Ceres Str.* ☎ *603/436–8084, 800/776–0915* ⊕ *www.portsmouthharbor.com.*

Portsmouth Kayak Adventures. Explore the Piscataqua River Basin and the New Hampshire coastline on a guided kayak tour with Portsmouth Kayak Adventures. Beginners are welcome (instruction included). Tours are run daily from June through mid-October, at 10, 2, and 6. ⊠ *185 Wentworth Rd.* ☎ *603/559–1000* ⊕ *www.portsmouthkayak.com.*

SHOPPING

Market Square, in the center of town, has gift and clothing boutiques, book and gourmet food shops, and exquisite crafts stores.

Byrne & Carlson. Watch elegant chocolates being made in the European tradition in this small shop. ⊠ *121 State St.* ☎ *888/559–9778* ⊕ *www. byrneandcarlson.com.*

Nahcotta. Stylish ceramics, jewelry, glassware, and art fill this contemporary design boutique. ⊠ *110 Congress St.* ☎ *603/433–1705* ⊕ *www. nahcotta.com.*

N.W. Barrett Gallery. Handmade jewelry, pottery, and glass are featured in this fine gallery. You'll also find one-of-a-kind lamps and rocking chairs. ⊠ *53 Market St.* ☎ *603/431–4262* ⊕ *www.nwbarrett.com.*

Piscataqua Fine Arts. This gallery mainly shows works of master wood-cutter Don Gorvett, who creates spellbinding scenes of New England's coast, particularly the Portsmouth area. There are also works by some of New England's finest printmakers, including Sidney Hurwitz, Alex deConstant, Peter Vincent, and Sean Hurley. ⊠ *123 Market St.* ☎ *603/436–7278* ⊕ *www.dongorvettgallery.com.*

Three Graces Gallery. The gallery showcases an unusual mix of paintings, sculpture, jewelry and other art; watch for monthly changing exhibitions. ⊠ *105 Market St.* ☎ *603/436–1988* ⊕ *www.threegracesgallery. com.*

RYE

8 miles south of Portsmouth.

On Route 1A as it winds south through Rye you'll pass a group of late-19th- and early-20th-century mansions known as **Millionaires' Row.** Because of the way the road curves, the drive south along this route is breathtaking. In 1623 the first Europeans established a settlement at Odiorne Point in what is now the largely undeveloped and picturesque town of Rye, making it the birthplace of New Hampshire. Today the area's main draws are a lovely state park, oceanfront beaches, and the views from Route 1A. Strict town laws have prohibited commercial development in Rye, creating a dramatic contrast with its frenetic neighbor Hampton Beach.

EXPLORING

FAMILY Fodor's Choice ★ **Odiorne Point State Park.** These 330 acres of protected land are where David Thompson established the first permanent European settlement in what is now New Hampshire. Several nature trails with informative panels describe the park's military history, and you can enjoy vistas of the nearby Isles of Shoals. The rocky shore's tidal pools shelter crabs, periwinkles, and sea anemones. Throughout the year the **Seacoast Science Center** hosts exhibits on the area's natural history. The tidal-pool touch tank and 1,000-gallon Gulf of Maine deepwater aquarium are popular with kids. There are also guided nature walks. ✉ *570 Ocean Blvd.* ☎ *603/436–8043* 🌐 *www.seacoastsciencecenter.org* 🎟 *$7* 🕒 *Science center Mar.–Oct., daily 10–5; Nov.–Feb., Sat.–Mon. 10–5.*

WHERE TO EAT

$$$ AMERICAN 🍴 **The Carriage House.** Across from Jenness Beach, this elegant cottage serves innovative dishes with a Continental flair. Standouts include penne teeming with fresh seafood, creative curries, and steak with peppercorns. Savor a hot-fudge ice-cream croissant for dessert. Upstairs is a wood-paneled tavern with ocean views. [$] *Average main: $26* ✉ *2263 Ocean Blvd.* ☎ *603/964–8251* 🌐 *www.carriagehouserye.com* 🕒 *No lunch.*

SPORTS AND THE OUTDOORS

BEACHES

Jenness State Beach. Good for swimming and sunning, this long sand beach is a favorite among locals who enjoy fewer people and nice waves for bodysurfing. Wide and shallow, Jenness Beach is a great place for kids to run and build sand castles. **Amenities:** lifeguards; parking (fee); showers; toilets. **Best for:** swimming; walking; surfing. ✉ *2280 Ocean Blvd.* ☎ *603/436–1552* 🌐 *www.nhstateparks.org* 🎟 *Parking $2 per hour May–Sept.*

Wallis Sands State Beach. This family-friendly swimmers' beach has bright white sands, a picnic area, a store, and beautiful views of the Isles of Shoals. **Amenities:** food and drink; lifeguards; parking (no fee); showers; toilets. **Best for:** swimming; walking. ✉ *1050 Ocean Blvd.* 🌐 *www.nhstateparks.org* 🎟 *$15 per car* 🕒 *June–Labor Day, weekdays 8–4, weekends 8–6.*

FISHING AND WHALE-WATCHING

Atlantic Fleet. For a full- or half-day deep-sea angling charter, try Atlantic Fleet. Whale-watching trips are also available. ✉ *1870 Ocean Blvd.* ☎ *603/964–5220, 800/942–5364* 🌐 *www.atlanticwhalewatch.com.*

Granite State Whale Watch. This outfit conducts naturalist-led whale-watching tours aboard the 100-passenger MV *Granite State* from May to mid-October. ✉ *Rye Harbor State Marina, 1860 Ocean Blvd.* ☎ *603/964–5545, 800/964–5545* 🌐 *www.granitestatewhalewatch.com* 🎟 *$36.*

HAMPTON BEACH

8 miles south of Rye.

FAMILY This is an authentic seaside amusement center—the domain of fried-dough stands, loud music, arcade games, palm readers, parasailing, and bronzed bodies. The 3-mile-long boardwalk, where kids play games and see how saltwater taffy is made, looks like a leftover from the 1940s; in fact, the whole community remains remarkably free of modern franchises. Free outdoor concerts are held on many a summer evening, and once a week there's a fireworks display. An estimated 150,000 people visit the town and its free public beach on the 4th of July, and it draws plenty of people until late September, when things close up.

GETTING HERE AND AROUND

Interstate 95 is the fastest way to get to Hampton, but the town is best seen by driving on Route 1A, which follows the coast and offers access to a number of beaches. Route 1 is the quickest way to get around, but be prepared for strip malls and stoplights.

ESSENTIALS

Visitor Information **Hampton Area Chamber of Commerce** ✉ *160 Ocean Blvd.* ☎ *603/926–8718* 🌐 *www.hamptonchamber.com.*

EXPLORING

Fuller Gardens. Away from the beach crowds is this small late-1920s estate garden designed in the Colonial Revival style by landscape architect Arthur Shurtleff. It encompasses 1,700 rosebushes, a hosta garden, a Japanese garden, and a tropical conservatory. ✉ *10 Willow Ave., North Hampton* ☎ *603/964–5414* 🌐 *www.fullergardens.org* 🎟 *$9* 🕒 *Mid-May–mid-Oct., daily 10–5:30.*

WHERE TO EAT AND STAY

$$$ AMERICAN 🍴 **Ron's Landing.** Among the motels lining Ocean Boulevard is this casually elegant restaurant. The seared ahi tuna with a citrus, chili, and soy glaze is one of the tastiest starters. Outstanding entrées include the oven-roasted salmon with a cream sauce, slivered almonds, and sliced apples, or the baked haddock stuffed with scallops and lobster and served with lemon-dill butter. From many tables you can enjoy sweeping ocean views. Brunch is popular. [$] *Average main: $28* ✉ *379 Ocean Blvd.* ☎ *603/929–2122* 🌐 *www.ronslanding.com* 🕒 *Closed Mon. Closed Tues., Sept.–June. No lunch.*

$$$$ HOTEL 🏨 **Ashworth by the Sea.** You'll be surprised how contemporary this across-from-the-beach hotel feels, even though it's been around for a century. **Pros:** center-of-town location; comfortable rooftop bar; open all year. **Cons:** breakfast not included; very busy. [$] *Rooms from: $349* ✉ *295 Ocean Blvd.* ☎ *603/926–6762, 800/345–6736* 🌐 *www.ashworthhotel.com* 🛏 *98 rooms, 7 suites* 🍽 *No meals.*

NIGHTLIFE

Hampton Beach Casino Ballroom. Despite its name, the Hampton Beach Casino Ballroom isn't a gambling establishment but a late-19th-century auditorium that has hosted everyone from Janis Joplin to Jerry Seinfeld, George Carlin, and B.B. King. Performances in the 1,800-seat space run from April to October. ✉ *169 Ocean Blvd.* ☎ *603/929–4100* ⊕ *www. casinoballroom.com.*

SPORTS AND THE OUTDOORS

BEACHES

Hampton Beach State Park. At the mouth of the Hampton River stretches this long sand beach with a boardwalk that runs along restaurants, attractions, and hotels. There's a visitor center (open year-round), multiple picnic areas, and a seasonal store. **Amenities:** food and drink; lifeguards; parking (fee); showers; toilets. **Best for:** swimming. ✉ *160 Ocean Blvd.* ☎ *603/926–3784* ⊕ *www.nhstateparks.org* 🎟 *Parking $15.*

FISHING AND WHALE-WATCHING

Several companies conduct whale-watching excursions as well as half-day, full-day, and nighttime cruises. Most leave from the Hampton State Pier on Route 1A.

Al Gauron Deep Sea Fishing. This company maintains a fleet of three boats for whale-watching cruises and fishing charters. ✉ *State Pier, 1 Ocean Blvd.* ☎ *603/926–2469, 800/905–7820* ⊕ *www.algauron.com.*

Eastman's Docks. This company offers whale-watching and fishing cruises. ✉ *River St., Seabrook* ☎ *603/474–3461* ⊕ *www.eastmansdocks.com.*

Smith & Gilmore. Enjoy half-day and full-day deep-sea fishing expeditions with Smith & Gilmore. ✉ *State Pier, Ocean Blvd.* ☎ *603/926–3503, 877/272–4005* ⊕ *www.smithandgilmore.com.*

EN ROUTE **Applecrest Farm Orchards.** At the 400-acre Applecrest Farm Orchards you can pick your own apples and berries or buy fresh fruit pies and cookies, homemade ice cream, and many other tasty treats. Fall brings cider pressing, hayrides, pumpkins, and music on weekends. Author John Irving worked here as a teenager, and his experiences inspired the book *The Cider House Rules.* ✉ *133 Exeter Rd., Hampton Falls* ☎ *603/926–3721* ⊕ *www.applecrest.com* ☉ *May–Dec., daily 8–6.*

EXETER

9 miles northwest of Hampton, 52 miles north of Boston, 47 miles southeast of Concord.

Fodor's Choice ★ During the Revolutionary War, Exeter was the state capital, and it was here amid intense patriotic fervor that the first state constitution and the first Declaration of Independence from Great Britain were put to paper. These days Exeter shares more in appearance and personality with Boston's blue-blooded satellite communities than the rest of New Hampshire—indeed, plenty of locals commute to Beantown. Cheerful cafés, coffeehouses, and shops with artisan-made wares make up this bustling town center.

GETTING HERE AND AROUND

Amtrak's *Downeaster* service stops here between Boston and Portland, Maine. On the road, it's 9 miles northwest of Hampton on Route 111. Route 101 is also a good way to get to Exeter from the east or west. The town itself is easy to walk around.

ESSENTIALS

Visitor Information Exeter Area Chamber of Commerce ✉ *24 Front St., #101* ☎ *603/772–2411* 🌐 *www.exeterarea.org.*

EXPLORING

American Independence Museum. This museum celebrates the birth of the nation. The story unfolds during the course of a guided tour focusing on the Gilman family, who lived in the house during the Revolutionary era. See drafts of the U.S. Constitution and the first Purple Heart as well as letters and documents written by George Washington and the household furnishings of John Taylor Gilman, one of New Hampshire's early governors. In July the museum hosts the American Independence Festival. ✉ *Ladd-Gilman House, 1 Governor's La.* ☎ *603/772–2622* 🌐 *www.independencemuseum.org* 🎟 *$6* 🕒 *Mid-May–Dec., Thurs.–Sat. 10–4.*

Phillips Exeter Academy. The 1,000 high school students at Phillips Exeter Academy lend energy to the town. The grounds, open to the public, resemble an elite Ivy League university campus. The Louis Kahn–designed library is the largest secondary-school library in the world. The Lamont Gallery, in the Frederick R. Mayer Art Center, offers free contemporary art exhibits. ✉ *20 Main St.* ☎ *603/772–4311* 🌐 *www.exeter.edu.*

WHERE TO EAT

$ AMERICAN 🍴 **The Green Bean.** This serve-yourself retaurant makes it easy when you can't decide between the delicious homemade soups, sandwiches, and salads. All the soups are made daily, including curried butternut squash, spicy corn chowder, and tarragon potato with peas. Perfect for dunking are sandwiches like turkey with cranberry and stuffing or veggie and walnut pesto. The early-morning menu includes breakfast burritos, French toast, and ham and eggs. It's a popular spot for those on the go, but if you have the time, sit in the delightful little courtyard for a quiet view of the town. [$] *Average main: $6* ✉ *33 Water St.* ☎ *603/778–7585* 🌐 *www.nhgreenbean.com* 🕒 *No dinner.*

$ AMERICAN 🍴 **Loaf and Ladle.** There are three components to this down-to-earth place's success: quality, price, and location. The name refers to homemade bread (more than 30 kinds) and soup (100 varieties are offered on a rotating basis). Choose a chunk of anadama bread, made with cornmeal and molasses, to go with your soup, and take your meal to one of the two decks that hover over the Exeter River. It's simple and homey. [$] *Average main: $6* ✉ *9 Water St.* ☎ *603/778–8955* ✍ *Reservations not accepted* 🕒 *Closed Tues. and Wed. No dinner.*

$$ AMERICAN 🍴 **The Tavern At River's Edge.** A convivial downtown gathering spot on the Exeter River, this downstairs tavern pulls in parents of prep-school kids, college students, and suburbanites. It may be informal, but the kitchen turns out surprisingly sophisticated meals. Start with sautéed ragout of mushrooms stewed in a Marsala cream sauce with sun-dried tomatoes, roasted shallots, garlic, and Asiago cheese, then move on to a lobster risotto with wild mushrooms and asparagus. In the bar, lighter fare is on offer. [$] *Average main: $16* ✉ *163 Water St.* ☎ *603/772–7393* 🌐 *www.tavernatriversedge.com.*

WHERE TO STAY

$$ B&B/INN **The Exeter Inn.** This elegant, brick, Georgian-style inn on the Phillips Exeter Academy campus has been the choice of visiting parents since it opened in the 1930s. **Pros:** well-designed rooms; elegant feel; near the center of town. **Cons:** a walk to the shops. [$] *Rooms from: $139* ✉ *90 Front St.* ☎ *603/772–5901, 800/782–8444* 🌐 *www.theexeterinn.com* *46 rooms, 5 suites* 🍴 *No meals.*

$$$ B&B/INN Fodor's Choice ★ **Inn by the Bandstand.** New owners have spruced up this charming B&B, located in the heart of town. **Pros:** perfect in-town location; bikes available; friendly staff. **Cons:** some ongoing renovations. [$] *Rooms from: $179* ✉ *6 Front St.* ☎ *603/772–6352, 877/239–3837* 🌐 *www.innbythebandstand.com* *9 rooms, 4 suites* 🍴 *Breakfast.*

SHOPPING

Exeter Fine Crafts. Prestigious Exeter Fine Crafts shows an impressive selection of juried pottery, paintings, jewelry, textiles, glassware, and other fine creations by more than 300 of northern New England's top artisans. ✉ *61 Water St.* ☎ *603/778–8282* 🌐 *www.exeterfinecrafts.com.*

A Picture's Worth a Thousand Words. A destination for bibliophiles, this shop offers rare books, town histories, old maps, and antique and contemporary prints. ✉ *65 Water St.* ☎ *603/778–1991* 🌐 *www.apwatw.com.*

Willow. You'll never know what you'll find at this creative shop, which stocks interesting antiques, finely stitched linens, handcrafted jewelry, woven throws, organic teas, gardening accessories, and gorgeous bags. ✉ *183 Water St.* ☎ *603/773–9666.*

DURHAM

12 miles north of Exeter, 11 miles northwest of Portsmouth.

Settled in 1635 and the home of General John Sullivan, a Revolutionary War hero and three-time New Hampshire governor, Durham was where Sullivan and his band of rebel patriots stored the gunpowder they captured from Ft. William and Mary in New Castle. Easy access to Great Bay via the Oyster River made Durham a maritime hub in the 19th century. Among the lures today are the water, farms that welcome visitors, and the University of New Hampshire, which occupies much of the town's center.

GETTING HERE AND AROUND

By car, Durham can be reached on Route 108 from the north or south and Route 4 from Portsmouth from the east or Concord from the west. The *Downeaster* Amtrak train stops here between Boston and Portland, Maine.

ESSENTIALS

Visitor Information University of New Hampshire ☎ *603/862–1234* 🌐 *www.unh.edu.*

EXPLORING

Museum of Art. Noted items in this gallery's collection include 19th-century Japanese wood-block prints, Boston expressionist works, and art of New England. It's on the campus of the University of New Hampshire. ✉ *Paul Creative Arts Center, 30 College Rd.* ☎ *603/862–3712* 🌐 *www.unh.edu/moa* 🎟 *Free* 🕒 *Sept.–May, Mon.–Wed. 10–4, Thurs. 10–8, weekends 1–5.*

WHERE TO EAT AND STAY

$$$ AMERICAN 🍴 **ffrost Sawyer Tavern.** That's not a typo, but an attempt to duplicate a quirky, obsolete spelling of the name of a former owner of this hilltop house. The eccentric stone basement tavern has its original beams, from which hang collections of mugs, hats, and—no way around it—bedpans. There's a terrific old bar. Choose from fine dinner fare, such as grilled porterhouse steak or potato-encrusted haddock. Lunch standards include burgers, pizza, and fish-and-chips. [$] *Average main: $25* ✉ *17 Newmarket Rd.* ☎ *603/868–7800* 🌐 *www.threechimneysinn.com.*

$$$ B&B/INN 🏨 **Three Chimneys Inn.** This stately yellow structure has graced a hill overlooking the Oyster River since 1649. **Pros:** intimate inn experience; afternoon social hour. **Cons:** have to walk or drive into town. [$] *Rooms from: $189* ✉ *17 Newmarket Rd.* ☎ *603/868–7800, 888/399–9777* 🌐 *www.threechimneysinn.com* 🛏 *23 rooms, 1 suite* 🍽 *Breakfast.*

NIGHTLIFE

Stone Church. Music aficionados head to the Stone Church—in an authentic 1835 former Methodist church—for its craft beers, pub grub, and live rock, jazz, blues, reggae, soul, and folk music. ✉ *5 Granite St., Newmarket* ☎ *603/659–7700* 🌐 *www.stonechurchrocks.com.*

SPORTS AND THE OUTDOORS

Wagon Hill Farm. You can hike several trails or picnic at 130-acre Wagon Hill Farm, overlooking the Oyster River. The old farm wagon on the top of a hill is one of the most photographed sights in New England. Park next to the farmhouse and follow walking trails to the wagon and through the woods to the picnic area by the water. Sledding and cross-country skiing are winter activities. ✉ *U.S. 4, across from Emery Farm.*

SHOPPING

Emery Farm. In the same family for 11 generations, Emery Farm sells fruits and vegetables in summer (including pick-your-own blueberries), pumpkins in fall, and Christmas trees in winter. The farm shop carries breads, pies, and local crafts. Children can pet the resident goats and donkey and ride on a hay wagon on some weekends in September and October. ✉ *135 Piscataqua Rd.* ☎ *603/742–8495* 🌐 *www.emeryfarm.com* 🕒 *May–Dec., daily 9–6.*

LAKES REGION

Lake Winnipesaukee, a Native American name for "smile of the great spirit," is the largest of the dozens of lakes scattered across the eastern half of central New Hampshire. With about 240 miles of shoreline of inlets and coves, it's the largest in the state. Some claim Winnipesaukee

CLOSE UP

New Hampshire Farmers' Markets

Winter squash is in season in New Hampshire from September to October.

Bedford Farmers' Market. Just outside Manchester, the Bedford Farmers' Market has a particularly rich mix of local growers and food purveyors, selling seasonal jams, pasture-raised lamb and chicken, homemade treats for dogs and cats, goats' milk soaps and balms, and even New Hampshire wines. There's usually live music and activities for children at hand. ⊠ *St. Elizabeth Seton Parish, 190 Meetinghouse Road, Bedford* ⊕ *bedfordfarmersmarket.org* ⊙ *June–Oct., Tues. 3–6 pm.*

Derry Farmers' Market. A mix of farmers, artisans, and entertainers show you what they're got at this year-round market. The summer and fall markets are held on Wednesday in the municipal parking lot. The winter market is held on Saturday mornings from early December to mid-March inside the Upper Village Hall, 53 East Derry Road. ⊠ *14 Manning St., Derry* ☎ *603/434–8974* ⊙ *Mid-July–Sept., Wed. 3–7.*

Lebanon Farmers' Market. Lebanon Farmers' Market not only draws more than 50 vendors from throughout the northern Connecticut River valley, but offers live music and concerts following the market. ⊠ *Colburn Park, 51 North Park St., Lebanon* ☎ *603/448–5121* ⊕ *www.lebanonfarmersmarket. org* ⊙ *Late May–late Sept., Thurs. 4–7 pm. Winter market, mid-Nov.-April, every third Sat., 10–1, 75 Bank St.*

Portsmouth Farmers' Market. One of the best and longest-running farmers' markets is the Portsmouth Farmers' Market, which features live music and regional treats, such as maple syrup and artisanal cheeses, in addition to seasonal produce. ⊠ *1 Junkins Ave., Portsmouth* ⊙ *May–early Nov., Sat. 8 am–1 pm.*

Seacoast Growers Association. The market is part of the Seacoast Growers Association, which also has weekly markets in Dover, Durham, Exeter, Newington, and Portsmouth. ⊕ *www.seacoastgrowers.org*

—Andrew Collins

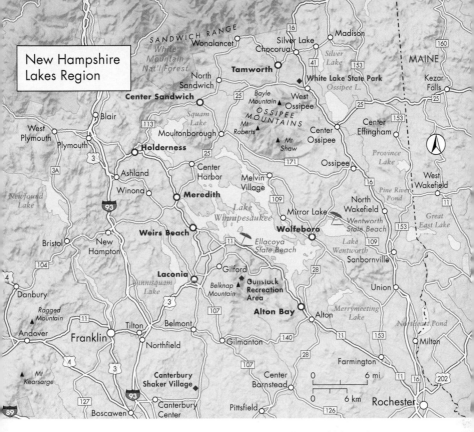

has an island for each day of the year—the total, though impressive, falls short: 274.

In contrast to Winnipesaukee, which bustles all summer long, is the more secluded Squam Lake. Its tranquillity is no doubt what attracted the producers of *On Golden Pond*; several scenes of the Academy Award–winning film were shot here. Nearby Lake Wentworth is named for the state's first royal governor, who, in building his country manor here, established North America's first summer resort.

Well-preserved Colonial and 19th-century villages are among the region's many landmarks, and you'll find hiking trails, good antiques shops, and myriad water-oriented activities. This section begins at Wolfeboro and more or less circles Lake Winnipesaukee clockwise, with several side trips.

ESSENTIALS

Visitor Information Lakes Region Association ☎ *603/286-8008, 800/605-2537* ⊕ *www.lakesregion.org.*

With 240 miles of shoreline, Lake Winnipesaukee is so much more than just the town of Wolfeboro.

WOLFEBORO

40 miles northeast of Concord, 49 miles northwest of Portsmouth.

Quietly upscale and decidedly preppy Wolfeboro has been a resort since Royal Governor John Wentworth built his summer home on the shore of the lake in 1768. The town bills itself as the oldest summer resort in the country, and its center, bursting with tony boutiques, fringes Lake Winnipesaukee and sees about a tenfold population increase each summer. The century-old, white clapboard buildings of the Brewster Academy prep school bracket the town's southern end. Wolfeboro marches to a steady, relaxed beat, comfortable for all ages.

GETTING HERE AND AROUND

Enter on the west side of Lake Winnipesaukee on Route 28. Be prepared for lots of traffic in the summertime.

ESSENTIALS

Visitor Information Wolfeboro Area Chamber of Commerce ⊠ *32 Central Ave.* ☎ *603/569–2200* ⊕ *www.wolfeborochamber.com.*

EXPLORING

New Hampshire Boat Museum. Two miles northeast of downtown, this museum celebrates New Hampshire's maritime legacy with displays of vintage wooden boats, model boats, antique engines, racing photography, trophies, and vintage marina signs. You can also take a 45-minute narrated ride on the lake in a reproduction triple-cockpit HackerCraft. ⊠ *399 Center St.* ☎ *603/569–4554* ⊕ *www.nhbm.org* ☜ *$7* ⊙ *Memorial Day–Columbus Day, Mon.–Sat. 10–4, Sun. noon–4.*

Wright Museum. Uniforms, vehicles, and other artifacts at this museum illustrate the contributions of those on the home front to the U.S. World War II effort. ⊠ *77 Center St.* ☎ *603/569–1212* ⊕ *www.wrightmuseum. org* ⚏ *$10* ⊙ *May–Oct., Mon.–Sat. 10–4, Sun. noon–4.*

QUICK BITES

Kelly's Yum Yum Shop. Picking up freshly baked breads, pastries, cookies, and other sweets in Kelly's Yum Yum Shop has been a tradition since 1948. The butter-crunch cookies are highly addictive. ⊠ *16 N. Main St.* ☎ *603/569–1919* ⊕ *www.yumyumshop.net* ⊙ *Closed Nov.–Apr.*

Lydia's Cafe. Brewster Academy students and summer folk converge upon groovy little Lydia's Cafe for espresso, sandwiches, homemade soups, bagels, and desserts. Ⓢ *Average main: $6* ⊠ *33 N. Main St.* ☎ *603/569–3991.*

SPORTS AND THE OUTDOORS

BEACH

Wentworth State Beach. Away from the hustle and bustle of Wolfeboro, this no-frills park offers a quiet beach with good fishing, picnic tables and grills, and fields for playing ball. **Amenities:** parking (no fee); showers; toilets. **Best for:** swimming; walking. ⊠ *297 Governor Wentworth Hwy.* ☎ *603/569–3699* ⊕ *www.nhstateparks.org* ⚏ *$4.*

HIKING

Abenaki Tower. A quarter-mile hike to the 100-foot post-and-beam Abenaki Tower, followed by a more rigorous climb to the top, rewards you with a view of Lake Winnipesaukee and the Ossipee mountain range. The trailhead is on Route 109 in Tuftonboro. ⊠ *Rte. 109, Tuftonboro.*

WATER SPORTS

Scuba divers can explore *The Lady*, the 125-foot-long cruise ship that sank in 30 feet of water off Glendale in 1895.

Dive Winnipesaukee Corp. This corporation runs charters out to wrecks and offers rentals, repairs, scuba sales, boat rentals, and lessons in waterskiing. ⊠ *Wolfeboro Bay, 4 N. Main St.* ☎ *603/569–8080* ⊕ *www. divewinnipesaukee.com.*

SHOPPING

The Country Bookseller. You'll find an excellent regional-history section and plenty of children's titles in this independent bookseller, where you can also do a little reading in its small café. ⊠ *23A N. Main St.* ☎ *603/569–6030* ⊕ *www.thecountrybookseller.com.*

Hampshire Pewter. The artisans at Hampshire Pewter use 16th-century techniques to make pewter tableware, accessories, and gifts. ⊠ *9 Railroad Ave.* ☎ *603/569–4944, 800/639–7704* ⊕ *www.hampshirepewter. com.*

WHERE TO EAT

$$
ASIAN

✕ **East of Suez.** In a countrified lodge on the south side of town, this friendly restaurant serves creative Asian cuisine, with an emphasis on Philippine fare, such as *lumpia* (pork-and-shrimp spring rolls with a sweet-and-sour fruit sauce) and *pancit canton* (panfried egg noodles with sautéed shrimp and pork and Asian vegetables with a sweet oyster

OUTDOOR OUTFITTERS AND RESOURCES

BIKING

Bike New England. This is an excellent resource for maps, tours, and routes for cyclists all over New England ⊕ *www.bikenewengland. com.*

Bike the Whites. From May to October, Bike the Whites organizes New Hampshire inn-to-inn bike tours. ☎ *800/421–1785* ⊕ *www. bikethewhites.com.*

HIKING

Appalachian Mountain Club. A range of hiking, biking, paddling, and climbing trips are offered at the Appalachian Mountain Club. ☎ *800/372–1758* ⊕ *amc-nh.org/ index.php.*

New England Hiking Holidays. Hike across the state with

New England Hiking Holidays. ☎ *603/356–9696, 800/869–0949* ⊕ *www.nehikingholidays.com.*

New Hampshire State Parks. Special hikes throughout the year are sponsored by New Hampshire State Parks. ⊠ *172 Pembroke Rd., Box 1856, Concord* ☎ *603/271–3556* ⊕ *www.nhstateparks.org.*

U.S. Forest Service. If you want to hike in the White Mountains, the U.S. Forest Service has all the details. ☎ *603/536–6100* ⊕ *www.fs.usda. gov/whitemountain.*

SKIING

Ski New Hampshire. Learn where the best powder is at Ski New Hampshire. ☎ *603/745–9396* ⊕ *www.skinh.com.*

sauce). You can also sample Thai red curries, Japanese tempura, and Korean-style flank steak. Gluten-free and vegan options are available. $ *Average main: $19* ⊠ *775 S. Main St.* ☎ *603/569–1648* ⊕ *www. eastofsuez.com* ⊘ *Closed Oct.–mid-May.*

WHERE TO STAY

$$$
B&B/INN

‖ **Topsides B & B.** At this stylish retreat, refined rooms convey the allure of a particular region, from Martha's Vineyard to coastal France to British fox-hunting country. **Pros:** close to downtown; appealing rooms; great service. **Cons:** some rooms are upstairs. $ *Rooms from: $195* ⊠ *209 S. Main St.* ☎ *603/569–3834* ⊕ *www.topsidesbb.com* ⇋ *5 rooms* ‖◯‖ *Breakfast.*

$$$$
B&B/INN

‖ **The Wolfeboro Inn.** This 1812 inn has a commanding lakefront location and is a perennial favorite for those visiting Lake Winnipesaukee. **Pros:** lakefront setting; interesting pub. **Cons:** no breakfast. $ *Rooms from: $279* ⊠ *90 N. Main St.* ☎ *603/569–3016, 800/451–2389* ⊕ *www. wolfeboroinn.com* ⇋ *41 rooms, 3 suites.*

ALTON BAY

10 miles southwest of Wolfeboro.

Lake Winnipesaukee's southern shore is alive with visitors from the moment the first flower blooms until the last maple sheds its leaves. Two mountain ridges hold 7 miles of the lake in Alton Bay, which is the name of both the inlet and the town at its tip. Cruise boats dock here, and small planes land year-round on the water and the ice. There's a dance pavilion, along with miniature golf, a public beach, and a Victorian-style bandstand.

EXPLORING

Mt. Major. About 5 miles north of Alton Bay, Mt. Major has a 3-mile trail up a series of challenging cliffs. At the top is a four-sided stone shelter built in 1925, but the reward is the spectacular view of Lake Winnipesaukee. ✉ *Rte. 11.*

WHERE TO EAT

$$$$ AMERICAN Fodor's Choice ★ 🍴 **The Crystal Quail.** With just four tables tucked inside an 18th-century farmhouse, this restaurant is worth the drive for the sumptuous meals prepared by longtime proprietors Harold and Cynthia Huckaby, who use free-range meats and mostly organic produce and herbs in their cooking. The prix-fixe menu changes daily but might include saffron-garlic soup, a house pâté, mushroom and herb quail, or goose confit with apples and onions. No credit cards are accepted. [$] *Average main: $75* ✉ *202 Pitman Rd., 12 miles south of Alton Bay, Center Barnstead* ☎ *603/269–4151* 🌐 *www.crystalquail.com* ✍ *Reservations essential* 💳 *No credit cards* 🕒 *Closed Mon. and Tues. No lunch* ☞ *BYOB.*

WEIRS BEACH

17 miles northwest of Alton Bay.

FAMILY Weirs Beach is Lake Winnipesaukee's center for arcade activity. Anyone who loves souvenir shops, fireworks, waterslides, hordes of children, and even a drive-in theater will feel right at home. Cruise boats also depart from here.

GETTING HERE AND AROUND

Weirs Beach is just north of Laconia and south of Meredith on Route 3.

EXPLORING

FAMILY **Funspot.** The mothership of Lake Winnipesaukee's family-oriented amusement parks, Funspot claims that its more than 500 video games make it the world's largest arcade. You can also work your way through a miniature golf course, a driving range, an indoor golf simulator, and 20 lanes of bowling. Some outdoor attractions are closed in winter months. ✉ *579 Endicott St. N* ☎ *603/366–4377* 🌐 *www.funspotnh.com* 🕒 *Mid-June–Labor Day, daily 9 am–11 pm; Labor Day–mid-June, Sun.–Thurs. 10–10, Fri. and Sat. 10 am–11 pm.*

FAMILY Fodor's Choice ★ **MS *Mount Washington*.** The 230-foot MS *Mount Washington* offers 2½-hour scenic cruises of Lake Winnipesaukee, departing from Weirs Beach and stopping in Wolfeboro, Alton Bay, Center Harbor, and Meredith (you can board at any of these stops). Evening cruises include live music and a buffet dinner, and the Sunday Champagne brunch cruise includes plenty of bubbly. The same company operates the MV *Sophie C.* ($26), which has been the area's floating post office for more than a century. The boat departs from Weirs Beach with mail and passengers and passes through parts of the lake not accessible by larger ships. The MV *Doris E.* ($18) has one- and two-hour scenic cruises of Meredith Bay throughout the summer. ✉ *211 Lakeside Ave.* ☎ *603/366–5531,*

888/843–6686 ⊕ www.cruisenh.com ✉ $29 ⊙ Mid-May–late Oct., departure times vary.

Winnipesaukee Scenic Railroad. You can board at Weirs Beach or Meredith, and the restored cars of this scenic railroad will carry you along the lakeshore on one- or two-hour rides. Special dinner trips include fall foliage and a harvest meal. ✉ *154 Main St., Meredith* ☏ *603/745–2135* ⊕ *www.hoborr.com* ✉ *$17* ⊙ *July and Aug., daily; Memorial Day–late June and Labor Day–late Oct., weekends.*

NIGHTLIFE AND THE ARTS

New Hampshire Music Festival. Attend award-winning chamber music on Tuesday, classical orchestra on Thursday, and pops concerts on alternate Saturdays from early July to mid-August. The New Hampshire Music Festival's concerts are held in the Silver Arts Center on Main Street in Plymouth. ✉ *85 Main St., Plymouth* ☏ *603/535–2787 box office* ⊕ *www.nhmf.org.*

SPORTS AND THE OUTDOORS

BEACH

FAMILY   **Ellacoya State Beach.** Families enjoy this secluded park that spans 600 feet along the southwestern shore of Lake Winnipesaukee, offering views of the Sandwich and Ossipee mountains. It's never crowded, and its shallow beach is safe for small children. The park has sheltered picnic tables and a small campground. **Amenities:** parking (no fee); toilets. **Best for:** solitude; swimming. ✉ *266 Scenic Rd., Gilford* ☏ *603/293–7821* ⊕ *www.nhstateparks.org* ✉ *$5* ⊙ *Late May–mid-June, weekends 9–6; mid-June–mid-Oct., daily 9–6.*

BOATING

Thurston's Marina. This marina rents a wide variety of boats as well as ski equipment. ✉ *18 Endicott St. N* ☏ *603/366–4811* ⊕ *www. thurstonsmarina.com.*

GOLF

Pheasant Ridge. In a bucolic setting, this 18-hole course offers great farm and mountain views. ✉ *140 Country Club Rd., Gilford* ☏ *603/524– 7808* ⊕ *www.playgolfne.com* ✉ *Greens fee: $20–$26* ⚑ *18 holes, 6,044 yards, par 70.*

SKI AREA

Gunstock Mountain Resort. High above Lake Winnipesaukee, this ski resort has invested millions to increase snowmaking capabilities, introduce more options for beginners, and add slope-side dining. Thrill Hill, a snow-tubing park, has five runs, a lift service, and 21 acres of terrain parks. The ski area has 55 trails (24 of them open for night skiing) and 32 miles of cross-country and snowshoeing trails. In summer the Mountain Adventure Park offers an adrenaline rush with ziplines, an aerial obstacle course, and scenic chairlift rides. There are also trails for mountain bikes, a skateboarding park, and paddleboats. ✉ *719 Cherry Valley Rd., Gilford* ☏ *603/293–4341* ⊕ *www.gunstock.com.*

SHOPPING

Pepi Herrmann Crystal. Watch artists at work crafting hand-cut crystal glasses, as well as contemporary tableware, ornaments, and jewelry. ⊠ *3 Waterford Pl., Gilford* ☎ *603/528–1020* ⊕ *www.handcut.com* ⊗ *Closed Sun. and Mon.*

LACONIA

4 miles west of Gilford, 27 miles north of Concord.

The arrival in Laconia—then called Meredith Bridge—of the railroad in 1848 turned the once-sleepy hamlet into the Lakes Region's chief manufacturing hub. It acts today as the area's supply depot, a perfect role given its accessibility to both Winnisquam and Winnipesaukee lakes as well as Interstate 93. It also draws bikers from around the world for Laconia Motorcycle Week in June.

GETTING HERE AND AROUND

The best way to Laconia is on Route 3 or Route 11. Scenic rides from the south include Route 106 and Route 107.

EXPLORING

Belknap Mill. Inside this 1823 textile mill you can see how cloth and clothing were made almost two centuries ago. Belknap Mill contains operating knitting machines, a 1918 hydroelectric power system, and changing exhibits. ⊠ *Mill Plaza, 25 Beacon St. E* ☎ *603/524–8813* ⊕ *www.belknapmill.org* ☞ *Free* ⊗ *Weekdays 9–5.*

OFF THE
BEATEN
PATH

Canterbury Shaker Village. Established in 1792, this village flourished in the 1800s and practiced equality of the sexes and races, common ownership, celibacy, and pacifism. The last member of the religious community passed away in 1992. Shakers invented such household items as the clothespin and the flat broom and were known for the simplicity and integrity of their designs. Engaging 60- and 90-minute tours pass through some of the 694-acre property's more than 25 restored buildings, many of them with original furnishings. Crafts demonstrations take place daily. Ask the admissions desk for a map of the many nature trails. The Shaker Box Lunch and Farm Stand offers salads, soups, and baked goods, and sells seasonal vegetables and locally produced maple syrup. A shop sells handcrafted items. ⊠ *288 Shaker Rd., 15 miles south of Laconia via Rte. 106, Canterbury* ☎ *603/783–9511, 866/783–9511* ⊕ *www.shakers.org* ☞ *$17* ⊗ *Mid-May–Oct., daily 10–5; Nov. and Dec., weekends 10–5.*

WHERE TO STAY

$$$

B&B/INN

⬚ The Lake House at Ferry Point. Four miles southwest of Laconia, this home across the street from Lake Winnisquam is a quiet retreat with a dock and small beach. Built in the 1800s as a summer retreat for the Pillsbury family of baking fame, this red Victorian farmhouse has superb views of the lake. White wicker furniture and hanging baskets of flowers grace the 60-foot-long veranda, and the gazebo by the water's edge is a pleasant place to lounge and listen for loons. **Pros:** affordable rates; lovely setting. **Cons:** away from main attractions. ⓢ *Rooms from:*

$179 ✉ *100 Lower Bay Rd., Sanbornton* ☎ *603/524–0087* 🌐 *www.lakehouseatferrypoint.com* 🛏 *8 rooms, 1 suite* 🍴 *Breakfast.*

SPORTS AND THE OUTDOORS

FAMILY **Bartlett Beach.** On Lake Winnisquam, this small but pleasant city-run park has a 600-foot-long sand beach. Here you'll find picnic tables and a playground, making it ideal for families, particularly those with small children. **Amenities:** lifeguards; parking (no fee); toilets. **Best for:** swimming. ✉ *99 Winnisquam Ave.* 🎟 *Free.*

FAMILY **Opechee Park.** Nestled in a quiet cove is this medium-sized family-friendly beach with a playground, baseball field, tennis courts, and picnic areas. **Amenities:** parking (no fee); toilets. **Best for:** swimming. ✉ *N. Main St.* 🌐 *www.city.laconia.nh.us* 🎟 *Free.*

SHOPPING

Tanger Outlets Tilton. The more than 56 stores at the Tanger Outlets Tilton include Brooks Brothers, Nike, Eddie Bauer, and Coach. ✉ *120 Laconia Rd., off I–93, Tilton* ☎ *603/286–7880* 🌐 *www.tangeroutlet.com.*

MEREDITH

11 miles north of Laconia.

Meredith is a favored spot for water sports enthusiasts and anglers. For a true taste of Meredith, take a walk down Main Street, just one block from busy Route 3, which is dotted with intimate coffee shops, salons and barber shops, family restaurants, redbrick buildings, antiques stores, and a gun shop. You can pick up area information at a kiosk across from the town docks. One caveat: on busy weekends getting into town from the west can mean sitting in traffic for 30 minutes or more.

ESSENTIALS

Visitor Information Meredith Area Chamber of Commerce ☎ *877/279–6121* 🌐 *www.meredithareachamber.com.*

WHERE TO EAT AND STAY

$$ AMERICAN 🍴 **Lakehouse Grille.** With perhaps the best lake views of any restaurant in the region, this restaurant might be forgiven for ambitious dishes that fall a bit short. Come to this upscale lodge to be near the lake, especially in the convivial bar area, and you'll leave quite happy. The best dishes are old reliables like steak, ribs, and pizza. Breakfast is offered daily, and there's brunch on Sunday. [$] *Average main: $20* ✉ *Church Landing, 281 Daniel Webster Hwy.* ☎ *603/279–5221* 🌐 *www.thecman.com.*

$$$ AMERICAN 🍴 **Mame's.** This 1820s tavern, once the home of the village doctor, now contains a warren of dining rooms with exposed-brick walls, wooden beams, and wide-plank floors. Expect a wide variety of beef, seafood, and chicken plates, but don't be afraid to order the "Luncheon Nightmare," which is pumpernickel topped with turkey, ham, broccoli, and bacon and baked in a cheese sauce. You can also find vegetarian dishes, burgers, sandwiches, and wonderful soups and salads on the menu. Save room for the bread pudding with apples and rum sauce. A cozy tavern upstairs features pub food. [$] *Average main: $23* ✉ *8 Plymouth St.* ☎ *603/279–4631* 🌐 *www.mamesrestaurant.com.*

What's your vessel of choice for exploring New Hampshire's Lakes Region: kayak, canoe, powerboat, or sailboat?

$$ B&B/INN Fodor's Choice ★ **Mill Falls at the Lake.** You have your choice of lodgings here: relaxing Church Landing and Bay Point are on the shore of Lake Winnipesaukee, and convivial Mill Falls is across the street, with a swimming pool and a 19th-century mill that's now a lively shopping area with more than a dozen unique shops. **Pros:** many lodging choices and prices; lakefront rooms; fun environment. **Cons:** expensive; two buildings do not sit on the lake. [$] *Rooms from: $150* ✉ *312 Daniel Webster Hwy., at Rte. 25* ☎ *603/279–7006, 800/622–6455* 🌐 *www.millfalls.com* 🛏 *172 rooms, 15 suites* 🍴 *Breakfast.*

THE ARTS

Interlakes Summer Theatre. Broadway musicals are presented at the Interlakes Summer Theatre during its 10-week season of summer stock. ✉ *Interlakes Auditorium, One Laker La., off Rte. 25* ☎ *888/245–6374* 🌐 *www.interlakestheatre.com.*

SPORTS AND THE OUTDOORS

BOATING

Meredith is near the quaint village of Center Harbor, another boating hub that's in the middle of three bays at the northern end of Lake Winnipesaukee.

Meredith Marina. Between May and October, you can rent powerboats and other vessels at this marina. ✉ *2 Bayshore Dr.* ☎ *603/279–7921* 🌐 *www.meredithmarina.com.*

Wild Meadow Canoes & Kayaks. Canoes and kayaks are available at Wild Meadow Canoes & Kayaks. ✉ *6 Whittier Hwy., Center Harbor Village* ☎ *603/253–7536, 800/427–7536* 🌐 *www.wildmeadowcanoes.com.*

HIKING

Red Hill. Off Route 25, Red Hill really does turn red in autumn. The reward at the end of this hiking trail is a view of Squam Lake and the mountains. ⊠ *Bean Rd., 7 miles northeast of Meredith.*

SHOPPING

Home Comfort. The owners of Lavinia's Relaxed Dining next door also operate this three-floor showroom of designer furnishings, antiques, and accessories. ⊠ *Senters Market, Rte. 25B, Center Harbor Village* ☎ *603/253–6660* ⊕ *www.homecomfortnh.com.*

Keepsake Quilting. Reputedly America's largest quilting shop, this store contains 5,000 bolts of fabric, hundreds of quilting books, and plenty of supplies. There are also gorgeous handmade quilts. ⊠ *Senters Market, 12 Main St., Center Harbor* ☎ *603/253–4026, 800/525–8086* ⊕ *www. keepsakequilting.com.*

League of New Hampshire Craftsmen. Here you'll find works by more than 250 area artisans who regularly demonstrate their skills. There are other branches in Littleton, Hanover, North Conway, and Concord. ⊠ *279 U.S. 3, next to the Inn at Church Landing* ☎ *603/279–7920* ⊕ *www. nhcrafts.org/meredith.*

Old Print Barn. This shop carries rare prints—Currier & Ives, antique botanicals, and more—from around the world. ⊠ *343 Winona Rd., New Hampton* ☎ *603/279–6479* ⊕ *www.theoldprintbarn.com.*

HOLDERNESS

8 miles northwest of Meredith.

Routes 25B and 25 lead to the prim small town of Holderness, between Squam and Little Squam lakes. *On Golden Pond,* starring Katharine Hepburn and Henry Fonda, was filmed on Squam, whose quiet beauty attracts nature lovers.

EXPLORING

FAMILY

Fodor's Choice

★

Squam Lakes Natural Science Center. A pontoon boat cruise is one of the main attractions at Squam Lakes Natural Science Center, and is the best way to tour the waterfront. Naturalists talk about the animals that make their home here, and give fascinating facts about the loon. This 230-acre property includes a ¾-mile nature trail that passes by trailside exhibits of black bears, bobcats, otters, mountain lions, red and gray foxes, and other native wildlife. The "Up Close to Animals" series in July and August lets you get a good look at these creatures. Children's activities include learning about bugs and wilderness survival skills. ⊠ *23 Science Center Rd.* ☎ *603/968–7194* ⊕ *www.nhnature.org* ⊠ *$15* ⊗ *May–Oct., daily 9:30–4:30.*

WHERE TO EAT

$$$$

AMERICAN

✕ **Manor on Golden Pond Restaurant.** Leaded-glass panes and wood paneling set a decidedly romantic tone at this wonderful inn overlooking Squam Lake. The main dining room is in the manor's original billiard room and features woodwork from 1904. Two others have very different looks: one features white linens, fresh flowers, and candlelight; the other is in the style of a Parisian bistro. The menu changes weekly,

View simple yet functional furniture, architecture, and crafts at Canterbury Shaker Village.

but might include lobster risotto, filet mignon, quail, or monkfish. Ask about the fabulous seven-course tasting menu. Breakfast is also served. [$] *Average main: $35* ✉ *31 Manor Dr., corner of U.S. 3 and Shepard Dr.* ☎ *603/968–3348* 🌐 *www.manorongoldenpond.com* ✍ *Reservations essential.*

$$ AMERICAN 🍴 **Walter's Basin.** A former bowling alley in the heart of Holderness makes an unlikely but charming setting for meals overlooking Little Squam Lake—local boaters dock right beneath the dining room. Among the specialties on this seafood-intensive menu are crostini with pan-fried rainbow trout. Burgers and sandwiches are served in the adjoining tavern. [$] *Average main: $20* ✉ *859 U.S. 3, Little Squam Lake* ☎ *603/968–4412* 🌐 *www.waltersbasin.com.*

WHERE TO STAY

$$$ B&B/INN 🏨 **Glynn House.** Pam, Ingrid, and Glenn Heidenreich operate this beautifully restored 1890s Queen Anne–style Victorian with a turret and wraparound porch and, next door, a handsome 1920s carriage house. **Pros:** luxurious rooms; well-run property; social atmosphere. **Cons:** not much to do in town. [$] *Rooms from: $171* ✉ *59 Highland St., Ashland* ☎ *603/968–3775, 866/686–4362* 🌐 *www.glynnhouse.com* 🛏 *6 rooms, 8 suites* 🍽 *Breakfast.*

$$$ B&B/INN 🏨 **Inn on Golden Pond.** Sweet-as-pie Bill and Bonnie Webb run this comfortable and informal B&B a short distance from the lake, to which they provide hiking trail maps. **Pros:** friendly innkeepers; comfortable rooms and common spaces. **Cons:** not directly on the lake; not luxurious. [$] *Rooms from: $185* ✉ *1080 U.S. 3* ☎ *603/968–7269* 🌐 *www.innongoldenpond.com* 🛏 *6 rooms, 2 suites* 🍽 *Breakfast.*

$$$$ B&B/INN Fodor's Choice ★ **The Manor on Golden Pond.** A name like this is a lot to live up to—and luckily, the Manor on Golden Pond is the most charming inn in the Lakes Region. **Pros:** wood fireplaces; comfy sitting rooms; great food; welcoming hosts. **Cons:** expensive rates. [$] *Rooms from: $285* ✉ *U.S. 3 and Shepard Hill Rd.* ☎ *603/968–3348, 800/545–2141* 🌐 *www.manorongoldenpond.com* 🛏 *21 rooms, 2 suites, 1 cottage.*

$$$ B&B/INN **Squam Lake Inn.** Graceful Victorian furnishings fill the nine stylish rooms at this peaceful farmhouse inn just a short stroll from Squam Lake. **Pros:** quiet setting; comfortable beds; big breakfasts. **Cons:** short walk to lake. [$] *Rooms from: $185* ✉ *Shepard Hill Rd.* ☎ *603/968–4417, 800/839–6205* 🌐 *www.squamlakeinn.com* 🛏 *9 rooms* 🕒 *Closed mid-Oct.–May* 🍴 *Breakfast.*

CENTER SANDWICH

12 miles northeast of Holderness on Route 103.

With Squam Lake to the west and the Sandwich Mountains to the north, Center Sandwich claims one of the prettiest settings of any Lakes Region community. So appealing are the town and its views that John Greenleaf Whittier used the Bearcamp River as the inspiration for his poem "Sunset on the Bearcamp." The town attracts artisans—crafts shops abound among its clutch of charming 18th- and 19th-century buildings.

ESSENTIALS

Visitor Information Squam Lakes Area Chamber of Commerce ☎ *603/968–4494* 🌐 *www.visitsquam.com.* **Sandwich HIstorical Society** ☎ *603/284–6269* 🌐 *www.sandwichhistorical.org.*

EXPLORING

Castle in the Clouds. Looking for all the world like a fairy-tale castle, this wonderful mountaintop estate was finished in 1914. The elaborate mansion has 16 rooms, eight bathrooms, and doors made of lead. Owner Thomas Gustave Plant spent $7 million, the bulk of his fortune, on this project and died penniless in 1941. A tour includes the mansion and the Castle Springs water facility on this high Ossippee Mountain Range property overlooking Lake Winnipesaukee; there's also hiking and pony and horseback rides. ✉ *455 Old Mountain Rd., Moultonborough* ☎ *603/476–5900* 🌐 *www.castleintheclouds.org* 🎟 *$16* 🕒 *Mid-May–early June weekends 10–4; early June–late Oct., daily 10–4.*

Loon Center. Recognizable for its eerie calls and striking black-and-white coloring, the loon resides on many New Hampshire lakes but is threatened by the gradual loss of its habitat. Two trails wind through the 200-acre Loon Center; vantage points on the Loon Nest Trail overlook the spot resident loons sometimes occupy in late spring and summer. ✉ *183 Lee's Mills Rd.* ☎ *603/476–5666* 🌐 *www.loon.org* 🎟 *Free* 🕒 *Columbus Day–Nov. and mid-May–June, Mon.–Sat. 9–5; Dec.–mid-May, Thurs.–Sat. 9–5; July–Columbus Day, daily 9–5.*

WHERE TO EAT

$$ ✕ **Corner House Inn.** In a converted barn adorned with paintings by local
AMERICAN artists, this eatery serves classic American fare. Salads with local greens
are a house specialty, but also try the chef's lobster-and-mushroom
bisque or the shellfish sauté. Lunch and Sunday brunch are served, and
on Thursday evenings there's often storytelling with dinner. $ *Average
main: $18* ✉ *22 Main St.* ☎ *603/284–6219* ⊕ *www.cornerhouseinn.com*
⊙ *No lunch mid-Oct.–mid-June.*

$$$ ✕ **Lavinia's Relaxed Dining.** Talk about relaxing: that's exactly what
AMERICAN you'll want to do in this splendidly restored mansion, built in 1820 by
John Coe for his bride Ravinia. Enjoy a glass of wine on the veranda,
then sink into a plush chairs in the dining room, where the original
French wallpaper, depicting the Seven Wonders of the World, still fills
viewers with awe. Start with pumpkin-and-mascarpone ravioli or
Gorgonzola-stuffed artichoke hearts, then try the grilled red snapper
with pineapple pico de gallo or a lobster potpie. Lighter fare can be
ordered in the upstairs lounge. For an unforgettable, romantic evening,
reserve the cupola—it seats only two. $ *Average main: $26* ✉ *Plymouth St. and Lake St., Center Harbor Village* ☎ *603/253–8617* ⊕ *www.
laviniasdining.com* ⊙ *No lunch.*

$$$ ✕ **The Woodshed.** Farm implements and antiques hang on the walls of this
AMERICAN enchanting 1860 barn. The fare is mostly traditional New England—
prime rib, rack of lamb, marinated chicken—but with some surprises,
such as Cajun-blackened pork tenderloin. Either way, the exceptionally
fresh ingredients are sure to please. $ *Average main: $26* ✉ *128 Lee
Rd., Moultonborough* ☎ *603/476–2311* ⊕ *www.thewoodshednh.com*
⊙ *Closed Mon.–Wed. mid-Oct.–June.*

SHOPPING

Old Country Store and Museum. The store has been selling maple syrup,
aged cheeses, penny candy, and other items since 1781. Much of the
equipment used in the store is antique, and the free museum displays
old farming and forging tools. ✉ *1011 Whittier Hwy.* ☎ *603/476–5750*
⊕ *www.nhcountrystore.com.*

TAMWORTH

13 miles east of Center Sandwich, 20 miles southwest of North Conway.

President Grover Cleveland summered in what remains a village of
almost unreal quaintness—it's equally photogenic in verdant summer,
during the fall foliage season, or under a blanket of winter snow. Cleve-
land's son, Francis, returned and founded the acclaimed Barnstorm-
ers Theatre in 1931, one of America's first summer theaters and one
that continues to this day. Tamworth has a clutch of villages within its
borders. At one of them—Chocorua—the view through the birches of
Chocorua Lake has been so often photographed that you may experi-
ence déjà vu. Rising above the lake is Mt. Chocorua (3,490 feet), which
has many good hiking trails.

GETTING HERE AND AROUND

The five villages of Tamworth boast six churches, which are worth a half-day's casual drive to admire their white clapboard elegance. Downtown Tamworth is tiny and can be strolled in a few minutes, but you might linger in the hope to meet one of the town's many resident poets and artists.

EXPLORING

FAMILY **Remick Country Doctor Museum and Farm.** For 99 years (1894–1993) Dr. Edwin Crafts Remick and his father provided medical services to the Tamworth area and operated a family farm. After the younger Remick died, these two houses were turned into the Remick Country Doctor Museum and Farm. The second floor of the house has been kept as it was when Remick passed away; it's a great way to see the life of a country doctor. Each season the still-working farm features a special activity such as maple-syrup making. The farm also has hiking trails and picnicking areas. ✉ *58 Cleveland Hill Rd.* ☎ *603/323–7591, 800/686–6117* 🌐 *www.remickmuseum.org* 🎟 *$5* 🕓 *Labor Day–mid-June, weekdays 10–4; mid-June–Labor Day, weekdays 10–4, Sat. 10–3.*

WHERE TO EAT AND STAY

$$ SEAFOOD FAMILY 🍴 **Jake's Seafood and Grill.** Oars and nautical trappings adorn the wood-paneled walls at this stop between West and Center Ossipee, about 8 miles southeast of Tamworth. The kitchen serves some of eastern New Hampshire's freshest and tastiest seafood, notably lobster pie, fried clams, and seafood casserole. Other choices include steak, ribs, and chicken dishes. [$] *Average main: $17* ✉ *2055 Rte. 16, West Ossipee* ☎ *603/539–2805* 🌐 *www.jakesseafoodco.com* 🕓 *Closed Apr. and Nov.*

$$ SOUTHERN FAMILY 🍴 **Yankee Smokehouse.** This down-home barbecue joint's logo depicting a happy pig foreshadows the gleeful enthusiasm with which patrons dive into the hefty sandwiches of sliced pork and smoked chicken and immense platters of baby back ribs and smoked sliced beef. Ample sides of slaw, beans, fries, and garlic toast complement the hearty fare. It serves gluten-free items, too. Even Southerners have been known to come away impressed. [$] *Average main: $17* ✉ *Rtes. 16 and 25, about 5 miles southeast of Tamworth* ☎ *603/539–7427* 🌐 *www.yankeesmokehouse.com.*

$$ B&B/INN 🏨 **Lazy Dog Inn.** If you travel with your dog, you've just found your new favorite B&B. **Pros:** mega–dog friendly; super clean; full breakfast. **Cons:** three rooms share baths. [$] *Rooms from: $120* ✉ *201 Rte. 16, Chocorua* ☎ *603/323–8350, 888/323–8350* 🌐 *www.lazydoginn.com* 🛏 *7 rooms, 4 with bath* 🍽 *Breakfast.*

THE ARTS

Arts Council of Tamworth. The Arts Council of Tamworth produces concerts—soloists, string quartets, revues, children's programs—from September through June and an arts show in late July. ✉ *77 Main St., Tamworth* ☎ *603/323–8104* 🌐 *www.artstamworth.org/.*

Barnstormers Theatre. This theater puts on eight dramatic and comedic productions during July and August. ✉ *104 Main St.* ☎ *603/323–8500* 🌐 *www.barnstormerstheatre.org.*

SPORTS AND THE OUTDOORS

White Lake State Park. The 72-acre stand of native pitch pine here is a National Natural Landmark. The park has hiking trails, a sandy beach, trout fishing, canoe rentals, and a picnic area. ⊠ *98 State Park Rd.* ☎ *603/323–7350* ⊕ *www.nhstateparks.org* ☎ *$5* ☉ *Memorial Day– Labor Day, daily dawn–dusk; Labor Day–mid-Oct., weekends dawn to dusk.*

THE WHITE MOUNTAINS

Sailors approaching East Coast harbors frequently mistake the pale peaks of the White Mountains—the highest range in the northeastern United States—for clouds. It was 1642 when explorer Darby Field could no longer contain his curiosity about one mountain in particular. He set off from his Exeter homestead and became the first European to climb what would later be called Mt. Washington. The 6,288-foot peak must have presented Field with formidable obstacles—its summit claims the highest wind velocity in the world ever recorded (231 mph in 1934) and can see snow every month of the year.

Today an auto road and a cog railway lead to the top of Mt. Washington, and people come by the tens of thousands to hike and climb, photograph the vistas, and ski. The peak is part of the Presidential Range, whose peaks are named after early presidents, and part of the White Mountain National Forest, which has roughly 770,000 acres that extend from northern New Hampshire into southwestern Maine. Among the forest's scenic notches (deep mountain passes) are Pinkham, Kinsman, Franconia, and Crawford. From the notches lead trailheads for short hikes and multiday adventures, which are also excellent spots for photographing the majestic White Mountains

This section of the guide begins in Waterville Valley, off Interstate 93, and continues to North Woodstock. It then follows portions of the White Mountains Trail, a 100-mile loop designated as a National Scenic and Cultural Byway.

ESSENTIALS

Visitor Information **White Mountains Visitors Bureau** ⊠ *200 Kancamagus Hwy., off I–93, North Woodstock* ☎ *800/346–3687* ⊕ *www.visitwhitemountains. com.* **White Mountain National Forest** ☎ *603/536–6100* ⊕ *www.fs.fed.us/r9/ forests/white_mountain.*

WATERVILLE VALLEY

60 miles north of Concord.

The first visitors began arriving in Waterville Valley in 1835. A 10-mile cul-de-sac follows the Mad River and is surrounded by mountains. The valley was first a summer resort and then more of a ski area. Although it's now a year-round getaway, it still has a small-town charm. There are inns, condos, restaurants, shops, conference facilities, a grocery store, and a post office.

GETTING HERE AND AROUND

Depot Camp is a great starting point for hiking, snowshoeing, and cross-country skiing. In town, the Schuss bus has regular stops at the shops in Village Square, the lodges and condos, the Waterville Valley Conference Center, and the ski area. There's enough to do in this small village to keep outdoors enthusiasts busy for several days.

WHERE TO STAY

$$$$ HOTEL **Black Bear Lodge.** This family-friendly property has one-bedroom suites that sleep up to six people. **Pros:** affordable rates; perfect for families. **Cons:** basic in its decor and services. [$] *Rooms from: $250* ✉ *3 Village Rd.* ☎ *603/236–4501, 800/349–2327* 🌐 *www.blackbearlodgenh.com* 🛏 *107 suites.*

$$$$ HOTEL **Golden Eagle Lodge.** Waterville's premier condominium property—with its steep roof punctuated by dozens of gabled dormers—recalls the grand hotels of an earlier era. **Pros:** most reliable accommodation in town; plenty of elbow room. **Cons:** somewhat bland architecture and decor. [$] *Rooms from: $230* ✉ *28 Packard's Rd.* ☎ *888/703–2453* 🌐 *www.goldeneaglelodge.com* 🛏 *139 condominiums.*

$ HOTEL **Snowy Owl Inn & Resort.** You're treated to afternoon wine and cheese in this hotel's atrium lobby, which has a three-story fieldstone fireplace and wonderful watercolors of its namesake. **Pros:** affordable rates; includes Continental breakfast. **Cons:** guests have access to the White Mountain Athletic Club, but pay to use. [$] *Rooms from: $99* ✉ *41 Village Rd.* ☎ *603/236–8383, 800/766–9969* 🌐 *www.snowyowlinn.com* 🛏 *85 rooms* 🍴 *Breakfast.*

SPORTS AND THE OUTDOORS

Waterville Valley Resort. Former U.S. ski-team star Tom Corcoran designed this family-oriented resort. The lodgings and various amenities are about a mile from the slopes, but a shuttle renders a car unnecessary. This ski area has hosted more World Cup races than any other in the East, so most advanced skiers will be challenged. Most of the 50 trails are intermediate: straight down the fall line, wide, and agreeably long. About 20 acres of tree-skiing add heart-pounding stimulus. Complete snowmaking coverage ensures good skiing even when nature doesn't cooperate. The Waterville Valley cross-country network, with the ski center in the town square, provides over 43 miles of groomed trails. ✉ *1 Ski Area Rd.* ☎ *603/236–8311, 800/468–2553 snow conditions, 800/468–2553 lodging* 🌐 *www.waterville.com.*

LINCOLN AND NORTH WOODSTOCK

64 miles north of Concord.

These neighboring towns at the southwestern end of the White Mountains National Forest and one end of the Kancamagus Highway (Route 112) form a lively resort area, especially for Bostonian families who can make an easy day trip straight up Interstate 93 to Exit 32. Festivals, such as the New Hampshire Scottish Highland Games in mid-September, keep Lincoln swarming with people year-round. The town itself is not much of an attraction. Tiny North Woodstock maintains more of a village feel.

The White Mountains

CANADA
QUÉBEC

MAINE

VERMONT

WHITE MOUNTAINS

Highlands
Gorham
Mt. Madison
Mt. Jefferson
Mt. Adams
Mt. Clay
Cog Railway
Observatory
Mount Washington
Mt. Washington Auto Road
Mt. Washington State Park
Pinkham Notch
Fabyan
Crawford Notch
Crawford Notch State Park
WHITE MOUNTAINS
Glen
Story Land
Bartlett
Echo Lake State Park
North Conway

4 mi
4 km

Pittsburg
First Connecticut Lake
Lake Francis
Beecher Falls
Colebrook
Dixville Notch
Dixville Notch State Park
Errol
Upton
Umbagog Lake
Aziscohos Lake
Wilsons Mills
MAINE

North Stratford
Lake Willoughby
West Burke
Maidstone Lake
Groveton
West Milan
Milan
Berlin
VERMONT
Guildhall
Lancaster
Jefferson
See Detail Above
Gorham
Gilead
Lyndonville
Lyndon
Concord
Danville
Saint Johnsbury
Whitefield
Mount Adams
Mt. Washington
Pinkham Notch
Wildcat
North Chatham
Littleton
Twin Mountain
Fabyan
Bretton Woods
WHITE MOUNTAINS
Bethlehem
Franconia
Lisbon
Franconia Notch State Park
White Mountain National Forest
Black Mountain
Jackson
Story Land
Echo Lake State Park
North Conway
Wells River
Woodsville
Barnet
Cannon Mt.
Loon Mountain
Kancamagus Hwy.
Attitash Ski Area
Glen
Bear Notch Rd.
Bartlett
Newbury
Lincoln
North Woodstock
Cranmore Mountain
Fryeburg
White Mountain Nat'l Forest
Waterville Valley
Mount Chocorua
Conway
Conway Lake
Bradford
TO HANOVER
TO CONCORD
SNOWVILLE EAST MADISON

8 mi
8 km

GETTING HERE AND AROUND

Lincoln and North Woodstock are places to spend a day shopping in their quaint shops, which are within easy walking distance of each other. It's a pleasant 1-mile stroll between the two towns. On Route 112, which connects the two villages, there is a state visitor center.

ESSENTIALS

Visitor Information Lincoln–Woodstock Chamber of Commerce ☎ *603/745–6621* ⊕ *www.lincolnwoodstock.com.*

EXPLORING

FAMILY **Clark's Trading Post.** Chock-full of hokum, this old-time amusement park is a favorite with families. There are half-hour train rides over a 1904 covered bridge, a museum of Americana inside an 1880s firehouse, a restored gas station filled with antique cars, circus performers, and an Old Man of the Mountain rock-climbing tower. In additition, there's a mining sluice where you can pan for gems. Tour guides tell tall tales and vendors sell popcorn, ice cream, and pizza. There's also a mammoth gift shop and a penny-candy store. ⊠ *110 Daniel Webster Hwy., off I–93, North Lincoln* ☎ *603/745–8913* ⊕ *www.clarkstradingpost. com* ☞ *$20* ⊗ *Mid-June–Aug. and and mid-Sept–mid-Oct., daily 9–5; mid-May–mid-June and early Sept., weekends 9–5.*

FUN TOUR **Hobo Railroad.** Newly restored vintage train cars take you along the scenic shores of the Pemigewassett River. The tours take 80 minutes. Santa Express trains run from late November to late December. ⊠ *64 Railroad St., off Kancamagus Hwy.* ☎ *603/745–2135* ⊕ *www.hoborr.com* ☞ *$16* ⊗ *July–mid-Oct., daily; May, June, and mid-Oct.–late Oct., weekends.*

Lost River Gorge in Kinsman Notch. Parents can enjoy the looks of wonder on their children's faces as they negotiate wooden boardwalks and stairs leading through a granite gorge formed by the roaring waters of the Lost River. One of the 10 caves they can explore is called the Lemon Squeezer (and it's a tight fit). Kids can also pan for gems and search for fossils, while grown-ups might prefer the attractions in the snack bar, gift shop, and nature garden. The park offers weekend lantern tours. ⊠ *1712 Lost River Rd., 6 miles west of North Woodstock, N. Woodstock* ☎ *603/745–8720, 800/346–3687* ⊕ *May, June, Sept., and Oct., daily 9–5; July and Aug., daily 9–6* ☞ *$17* ⊗ *Check Web site for hours.*

Whale's Tale Waterpark. You can float on an inner tube along a gentle river, careen down one of five waterslides, or body-surf in the large wave pool at Whale's Tale Waterpark. There's plenty here for toddlers and small children. ⊠ *491 Daniel Webster Hwy., off I–93, North Lincoln* ☎ *603/745–8810* ⊕ *www.whalestalewaterpark.net* ☞ *$34* ⊗ *Mid-June–late Aug., daily 10–6.*

Continued on page 192

HIKING THE APPALACHIAN TRAIL

Tucked inside the nation's most densely populated corridor, a simple footpath in the wilderness stretches more than 2,100 miles, from Georgia to Maine. The Appalachian Trail passes through some of New England's most spectacular regions, and daytrippers can experience the area's beauty on a multitude of accessible, rewarding hikes. *By Melissa Kim*

Running along the spine of the Appalachian Mountains, the trail was fully blazed in 1937 and designed to connect anyone and everyone with nature. Within a day's drive of two-thirds of the U.S. population, it draws an estimated two to three million people every year. Through-hikers complete the whole trail in one daunting six-month season, but all ages and abilities can find renewal and perspective here in just a few hours. One-third of the AT passes through New England, and it's safe to say that the farther north you go, the harder the trail gets. New Hampshire and Maine challenge experienced hikers with windy, cold, and isolated peaks.

Top, hiking in New Hampshire's White Mountains. Above, autumn view of Profile Lake, Pemigewasset, NH.

ON THE TRAIL

New England's prime hiking season is in late summer and early fall, when the blaze of foliage viewed from a high peak is unparalleled. Popular trails see high crowds; if you seek solitude, try hiking at sunrise, a peaceful time that's good for wildlife viewing. You'll have to curb your enthusiasm in spring and early summer to avoid mud season in late April and black flies in May and June.

With the right gear, attitude, and preparation, winter can also offer fine opportunities for hiking, snowshoeing, and cross-country skiing.

FOLLOW THE TRAIL

Most hiking trails are marked with blazes, blocks of colored paint on a tree or rock. The AT, and only the AT, is marked by vertical, rectangular 2- by 6-inch white blazes. Two blazes mark route changes; turn in the direction of the top blaze. At higher elevations, you might also see cairns, small piles of rocks carefully placed by trail rangers to show the way when a blaze might be obscured by snow or fog.

Scenic U.S. 302—and the AT—pass through Crawford Notch, a spectacular valley in New Hampshire's White Mountains.

Hikers gather outside Lakes of the Clouds Hut, near the peak of Mount Washington.

TRIP TIPS

WHAT TO WEAR: For clothes, layer with a breathable fabric like polypropylene, starting with a shirt, a fleece, and a wind- or water-resistant shell. Bring gloves, a hat, and a change of socks.

WHAT TO BRING: Carry plenty of water and lightweight high-energy food. Don't forget sunscreen and insect repellent. Bring a map and compass. Just in case: a basic first-aid kit, a flashlight or headlamp, whistle, multi-tool, and matches.

PLAN AHEAD: In your car, leave a change of clothing, especially dry socks and shoes, as well as extra water and food.

PLAY IT SAFE: Tell someone your hiking plan and take a hiking partner. Carry a rescue card with emergency contact information and allergy details.

BE PREPARED: Plan your route and check the weather forecast in advance.

REMEMBER YOUR BEGINNINGS: Look back at the trail especially at the trailhead and at tricky junctions. If you've got a digital camera, photograph trail maps posted at the trailhead or natural landmarks to help you find your way.

WHERE TO STAY

Day hikers looking to extend the adventure can also make the experience as hard or as soft as they choose. Through-hikers combine camping with overnight stays in primitive shelters, mountain huts, comfortable lodges, and resorts just off the trail.

Rustic cabins and lean-tos provide basic shelter in Maine's Baxter State Park. In Maine and New Hampshire, the Appalachian Mountain Club runs four-season lodges as well as a network of mountain huts for backcountry hikers. A hiker code of camaraderie and conviviality prevails in these huts. Experience a night and you might just find yourself dreaming of a through-hike.

FOR MORE INFORMATION

Appalachian Trail Conservancy
(🌐 www.appalachiantrail.org)

Appalachian National Scenic Trail
(🌐 www.nps.gov/appa)

Appalachian Mountain Club
(🌐 www.outdoors.org)

ANIMALS ALONG THE TRAIL

❶ Black bear

Black bears are the most common—and smallest—bear in North America. Clever and adaptable, these adroit mammals will eat whatever they can (though they are primarily vegetarian, favoring berries, grasses, roots, blossoms, and nuts). Not naturally aggressive, black bears usually make themselves scarce when they hear hikers. The largest New England populations are in New Hampshire and Maine.

❷ Moose

Spotting a moose in the wild is unforgettable: their massive size and serene gaze are truly humbling. Treasure the moment, then slowly back away. At more than six feet tall, weighing 750 to 1,000 pounds, a moose is not to be trifled with, particularly during rutting and calving seasons (fall and spring, respectively). Dusk and dawn are the best times to spot the iconic animal; you're most likely to see one in Maine, especially in and around ponds.

⚠ Black flies

Especially fierce in May and June, these pesky flies can upset the tranquility of a hike in the woods as they swarm your face and bite your neck. To ward them off, cover any exposed skin and wear light colors. You'll get some relief on a mountain peak; cold weather and high winds also keep them at bay.

❸ Bald eagles

Countless bird species can be seen and heard along the AT, but what could be more exciting than to catch a glimpse of our national bird as it bounces back from near extinction? Now it's not uncommon to see the majestic bald eagle with its tremendous wing span, white head feathers, and curved yellow beak. The white head and tail distinguish the bald from the golden eagle, a bit less rare but just as thrilling to see. Most of New England's bald eagles are in Maine, but they are now present—albeit in small numbers—in all six states.

WILDFLOWERS ALONG THE TRAIL

❹ Mountain laurel

The clusters of pink and white blooms of the mountain laurel look like bursts of fireworks. Up close, each one has the delicate detail of a lady's parasol. Blooms vary in color, from pure white to darker pink, and have different amounts of red markings. Connecticut's state flower, mountain laurel flourishes in rocky woods, blooming in May and June. Look for the shrub in southern New England; it's rare along the Appalachian trail in Vermont and Maine.

❺ Mountain avens

A member of the rose family, these showy yellow flowers abound in New Hampshire's White Mountains. You can't miss the large buttercup-like blooms on long green stems when they are in bloom from June through August. So common here, yet extremely rare: the only other place in the whole world where you can find mountain avens is on an island off the coast of Nova Scotia.

❻ Painted trillium

You might smell a trillium before you see it; these flowers have an unpleasant odor that may attract the flies that pollinate it. To identify this impressive flower, look for sets of three: three large pointed blue-green leaves, three sepals (small leaves beneath the petals), and three white petals with a brilliant magenta center. It can take four or five years for a trillium to produce one flower, which blooms in May and June in wet woodlands.

❼ Pink lady slippers

These delicate orchids can grow from 6 to 15 inches high and favor specific wet wooded areas in dappled sunlight. The slender stalk rises from a pair of green leaves, then bends a graceful neck to suspend the paper-thin pale pink closed flower. The slow-growing plant needs help from fungus and bees to survive and can live to be 20 years old. New Hampshire's state wildflower, the pink lady slipper blooms in June throughout New England.

● = Somewhat Common ● = Rare

CHOOSE YOUR DAY HIKE

MAINE

GULF HAGAS, Greenville
Difficult, 8-plus mi round-trip, 6–7 hours

This National Natural Landmark in the North Maine Woods is a spectacular sight for the adventurous day hiker. It involves a long drive on logging roads east from Greenville *(see Inland Maine section)* to a remote spot and a slippery, sometimes treacherous 8-mile hike around the rim of what's been dubbed Maine's Grand Canyon. Swimming in one of the sparkling pools under a 30-foot-high waterfall and admiring the views of cliffs, cascades, gorges, and chasms in this slate canyon, otherwise unthinkable in New England, will take your breath away.

TABLE ROCK, Bethel
Medium, 2.4 mi round-trip, 2 hours

Maine's Mahoosuc Range is thought to be one of the most difficult stretches of the entire AT, but north of Bethel at Grafton Notch State Park, day hikes range from easy walks in to cascading waterfalls to strenuous climbs up Old Speck's craggy peak. The Table Rock trail offers interesting sights—great views of the notch from the immense slab of granite that gives this trail its name, as well as one of the state's largest system of slab caves—narrow with tall openings unlike underground caves.

NEW HAMPSHIRE

ZEALAND TRAIL, Berlin
Easy, 5.6 mi round-trip, 3.5–4 hours

New Hampshire's Presidential range gets so much attention and traffic that sometimes the equally spectacular Pemigewasset Wilderness, just to its west, gets overlooked. Follow State Route 302 to the trailhead on Zealand Rd. near Bretton Woods. For an easy day hike to one of the Appalachian Mountain Club's excellent overnight huts, take the mostly flat Zealand Trail over bridges and past a beaver swamp to Zealand Pond. The last tenth of a mile is a steep ascent to the mountain retreat, where you might spot an AT through-hiker taking a well-deserved rest. (Most north-bound through-hikers reach this section around July or August.) In winter, you can get here by a lovely cross-country ski trip.

TRAIL NAMES

For through-hikers, doing the AT can be a life-altering experience. One of trail's most respected traditions is the taking of an alter ego: a trail name. Lightning Bolt: fast hiker. Pine Knot: tough as one. Bluebearee: because a bear got all her food on her very first night on the trail.

VERMONT

HARMON HILL, Bennington

Medium to difficult, 3.6 mi round-trip, 3–4 hours

This rugged hike in the Green Mountains goes south along the AT where it coincides with the Long Trail, Vermont's century-old "footpath in the wilderness." From the trailhead on Route 9 just east of Bennington, the first half mile or so is strenuous, with some rock and log staircases and hairpins. The payback is the sweeping view from the top; you'll see Mount Anthony, Bennington and its iconic war monument, and the rolling green hills of the Taconics to the west.

STRATTON MOUNTAIN, Stratton

Difficult, 6.6 mi round-trip, 5–6 hours

A steep and steady climb from the trailhead on Kelly Stand Rd. (between West Wardsboro and Arlington) up the 3,936-foot-high Stratton Mountain follows the AT and Long Trail through mixed forests. It's said that this peak is where Benton MacKaye conceived of the idea for the Appalachian Trail in 1921. An observation tower at the summit gives you a great 360-degree view of the Green Mountains. From July to October, you can park at Stratton resort and ride the gondola up (or down) and follow the .75-mi Fire Tower Trail to the southern true peak.

MASSACHUSETTS

MOUNT GREYLOCK, North Adams

Easy to difficult, 2 mi round-trip, less than 1 hour

There are many ways to experience Massachusetts's highest peak. From North Adams, follow Route 2 to the Notch Rd. trailheads. For a warm-up, try the Rounds Rock trail (Easy, 0.7 mi) for some spectacular views. Or drive up the 8-mi-long summit road and hike down the Robinson's Point trail (Difficult, 0.8 mi) for the best view of the Hopper, a glacial cirque that's home to an old-growth red spruce forest. At the summit, the impressive **Bascom Lodge**, built in the 1930s by the Civilian Conservation Corps, provides delicious meals and overnight stays (⊕ www.bascomlodge.net).

CONNECTICUT

LION'S HEAD, Salisbury

Medium, 4.6 mi round-trip, 3.5–4 hours

The AT's 52 miles in Connecticut take hikers up some modest mountains, including Lion's Head in Salisbury. From the trailhead on State Route 41, follow the white blazes of the AT for two easy miles, then take the blue-blazed Lion's Head Trail for a short, steep push over open ledges to the 1,738-foot summit with its commanding views of pastoral southern New England. Try this in summer when the mountain laurels—Connecticut's state flower—are in bloom.

Looking at Mt. Washington from Mt. Bond in the Pemigewasset Wilderness Area, New Hampshire.

Mount Washington is the Northeast's peak of superlatives: worst weather in the world, highest spot in the northeast, windiest place on Earth. It snows in the summer, there are avalanches in winter, and it's foggy 60 percent of the time. Strong 35-mile-per-hour winds are the average, and extreme winds of 100 miles per hour with higher gusts blow year-round. Here, you can literally get blown away.

Explorers, scientists, artists, and botanists have been coming to the mountain for hundreds of years, drawn by its unique geologic features, unusual plants, and exceptional climate.

WHY SO WINDY? The 6,288-foot-high treeless peak is the highest point for miles around, so nothing dampens the force of the wind. Also, the sharp vertical rise causes wind to accelerate. Dramatic changes in air pressure also cause strong, high winds. Add to that the fact that three major storm tracks converge here, and you've got a mountain that has claimed more than 135 lives in the past 150 years.

GOING UP THE MOUNTAIN

An ascent up Mount Washington is for experienced hikers who are prepared for severe, unpredictable weather. Even in summer, cold, wet, foggy, windy conditions prevail. The most popular route to the top is on the eastern face up the Tuckerman Ravine Trail. But countless trails offer plenty of moderate day hikes, like the Alpine Garden Trail, as an alternative to a summit attempt. Start at the Pinkham Notch Visitor Center on Route 16 to review your options.

BACKPACKING ON THE MOUNTAIN

Lakes of the Clouds Hut perches 5,050 feet up the southern shoulder, providing bunkrooms and meals in summer; reservations are required. On the eastern face, the **Hermit Lake Shelter Area** has shelters and tent platforms; to camp here you'll need a first-come, first-served permit from the Visitors Center. Both are operated by the **AMC** (☏ 603/466-2727; ⊕ www.outdoors.org).

NON-HIKING ALTERNATIVES

In the summer, the **Auto Road** (☎ 603/466-3988 ⊕ www.mountwashington autoroad.com) and the **Cog Railway** (☎ 800/922-8825 ⊕ www.thecog.com) present alternate ways up the mountain; both give you a real sense of the mountain's grandeur. In winter, a **SnowCoach** (☎ 603/466-2333 ⊕ www.greatglentrails. com) hauls visitors 4.5 miles up the Auto Road with an option to cross-country ski, telemark, snowshoe, or ride the coach back down.

WHERE TO EAT AND STAY

$$$

AMERICAN

FAMILY

✕ **Woodstock Inn, Station & Brewery.** If you like eateries loaded with character, don't miss this one inside the town's late-1800s train station. The walls are decorated with old maps, historic photographs, and local memorabilia. Then there are fun, curious objects, such as an old phone booth. The menu offers gluten-free items as well as the standard pub fare: pizza, burgers, steaks, and seafood. Gourmet breakfasts are served daily. A brewery on-site makes 17 different varieties; ask your server which ones are on tap. Kids will find a small game room. $ *Average main: $24* ✉ *135 Main St., off I–93, North Woodstock* ☎ *603/745–3951* ⊕ *www.woodstockinnbrewery.com.*

$$

RESORT

FAMILY

🛏 **Indian Head Resort.** The inexpensive and spacious rooms make this the place for families on a budget. **Pros:** great prices; fun for the whole family; near kid-friendly attractions. **Cons:** can be crowded; sometimes hard to get a reservation. $ *Rooms from: $169* ✉ *664 U.S. 3, 5 miles north of North Woodstock* ☎ *603/745–8000, 800/343–8000* ⊕ *www.indianheadresort.com* ⤴ *98 rooms, 40 cottages.*

$$$$

RESORT

🛏 **Mountain Club on Loon.** If you want a ski-in, ski-out stay on Loon Mountain, this is your best and only option. **Pros:** within walking distance of the lifts; on-site spa; close to the national forest. **Cons:** very busy place in winter. $ *Rooms from: $225* ✉ *90 Loon Mountain, off Kancamagus Hwy.* ☎ *603/745–2244, 800/229–7829* ⊕ *www.mtnclub.com* ⤴ *117 rooms, 117 suites.*

NIGHTLIFE AND THE ARTS

THE ARTS

FAMILY

Jean's Playhouse. A popular performing-arts venue, Jean's Playhouse is the area's year-round stage for theater and music. From July to October there's plenty here for kids. ✉ *10 Papermill Dr.* ☎ *603/745–2141* ⊕ *www.papermilltheatre.org.*

NIGHTLIFE

Black Diamond Lounge. For après-ski socializing, skiers head to the Black Diamond Lounge in the Mountain Club at the Loon Mountain ski resort. ✉ *Loon Mountain, 90 Loon Mountain Rd.* ☎ *603/745–2244* ⊕ *www.mtnclub.com.*

Thunderbird Lounge. Live music, a large dance floor, and great lake views make this a year-round hot spot. ✉ *Indian Head Resort, 664 U.S. 3, North Lincoln* ☎ *603/745–8000* ⊕ *www.indianheadresort.com.*

SPORTS AND THE OUTDOORS

Loon Mountain. Wide, straight, and consistent intermediate ski trails prevail at Loon, a modern resort on the western edge of the Pemigewasset River. The most advanced among the 61 runs are grouped on the North Peak section, with 2,100 feet of vertical skiing. Beginner trails are set apart. There's snow tubing on the lower slopes, and six terrain parks suitable for all ages and ability levels. In the base lodge are the usual dining and lounging facilities. There are 13 miles of cross-country trails, ice-skating on an outdoor rink, snowshoeing and snowshoeing tours, and a rock-climbing wall in the Loon Mountain Adventure Center. ✉ *60 Loon Mountain Rd., off the Kancamagus Hwy.* ☎ *603/745–8111, 603/745–8100 snow conditions* ⊕ *www.loonmtn.com.*

Pemi Valley Moose Tours. Eager to see a mighty moose? Embark on a moose-watching bus tour into the northernmost White Mountains. The nearly three-hour trips depart in the early evening for the best wildlife sighting opportunities. The bus is air-conditioned and screens education films about moose. Tours run late April to mid-October. ⊠ *33 Main St., off I–93* ☎ *603/745–2744* ⊕ *www.moosetoursnh.com.*

FRANCONIA

16 miles northwest of Lincoln/North Woodstock on I–93.

Travelers have long passed through the White Mountains via Franconia Notch, and in the late 18th century a town evolved just to the north. It and the region's jagged rock formations and heavy coat of evergreens have stirred the imaginations of Washington Irving, Henry Wadsworth Longfellow, and Nathaniel Hawthorne, who penned a short story about the craggy cliff known as the Old Man of the Mountain. There is almost no town proper to speak of here, just a handful of stores, touched though it is by Interstate 93 (the Franconia Notch Parkway).

Four miles west of Franconia, Sugar Hill is a town of about 500 people. It's famous for its spectacular sunsets and views of the Franconia Mountains, best seen from Sunset Hill, where a row of grand hotels and mansions once stood.

GETTING HERE AND AROUND

Franconia is a small town with not much to offer tourists, but it is an access point for many ski areas and the villages of Sugar Hill, Easton, Bethlehem, Bretton Woods, Littleton, Lincoln, and North Woodstock, towns replete with white church steeples, general stores, country inns, and picturesque farms.

ESSENTIALS

Visitor Information Franconia Notch Chamber of Commerce ☎ *603/823–5661* ⊕ *www.franconianotch.org.*

EXPLORING

Flume Gorge. This 800-foot-long chasm has narrow walls that cause an eerie echo from the gorge's running water. A visit begins at the visitor's center, followed by a stroll along a wooden boardwalk and a series of stairways winding their way to the top of the falls that thunder down the gorge. The 2-mile loop takes a little over an hour. There are also a gift shop, cafeteria, and small museum. ⊠ *853 Daniel Webster Hwy.* ☎ *603/745–8391* ⊕ *www.nhstateparks.org* ⊑ *$15* ☉ *Early May–late Oct., daily 9–5.*

The Frost Place Museum. Robert Frost's year-round home from 1915 to 1920, this is where the poet soaked up the New England life. The place is imbued with the spirit of his work, down to the rusted mailbox in front that's painted "R. Frost" in simple lettering. Two rooms contain memorabilia and signed editions of his books. Out back you can follow short trails marked with lines from his poetry. This place will slow you down and remind you of the intense beauty of the surrounding countryside. Poetry readings are scheduled during many evenings in summer. ⊠ *158 Ridge Rd.* ☎ *603/823–5510* ⊕ *www.frostplace.org* ⊑ *$5*

◷ June, daily 1–5; July–early Sept., Wed.–Mon. 1–5; mid-Sept.–Oct., Wed.–Mon. 10–5.

FAMILY **New England Ski Museum.** This small museum lets you travel back in time to see how skiing began as a sport, particularly here in New England. Here you can examine artifacts, clothing, and equipment, as well as Bode Miller's five Olympic medals. For ski enthusiasts, the museum will evoke smiles and a trip down memory lane. ✉ *Franconia Notch State Park, 135 Tramway Dr., next to Cannon Mountain Tramway* 🌐 *www.skimuseum.org* 🎟 *Free* ◷ *Memorial Day–Apr., daily 10–5.*

Old Man of the Mountain. This somber face in the rock high above Franconia Notch crumbled somewhat unexpectedly in 2003. The iconic image had defined New Hampshire, and the Old Man's "death" stunned and saddened residents. You can see photographs and learn about the history of the Old Man at the visitor center at Flume Gorge. Better yet, follow signs to a small Old Man of the Mountain Park. There you can view the iconic mountain face through newly installed steel rods that seem to literally put the beloved face back on the mountain. ✉ *Rte. 3* 🌐 *www.oldmannh.org* 🎟 *Free* ◷ *Daily 9–5.*

WHERE TO EAT AND STAY

$ AMERICAN 🍴 **Polly's Pancake Parlor.** In the Dexter family for three generations, Polly's has been serving up pancakes and waffles (from its own original recipe) since the 1930s. Since then, smoked bacon and ham, sandwiches on homemade bread, delicious baked beans, and even gluten-free items have been added to the menu. There are even desserts such as raspberry pie. Much of the food is made from grains ground on-site. The gift shop sells maple products. [$] *Average main: $11* ✉ *672 Rte. 117* ☎ *603/823–5575* 🌐 *www.pollyspancakeparlor.com* ◷ *Closed weekdays mid-Mar–mid May. No dinner.*

$$$$ AMERICAN Fodor's Choice ★ 🍴 **Sugar Hill Inn.** Inside this romantic 1789 farmhouse you'll find a very elegant dining room where memorable dinners are prepared by chef Val Fortin. Start with a trio of the chef's favorite soups or a butternut squash risotto, followed by a beet-and-anise garden salad. Main courses might include peppercorn-crusted sirloin steak with grilled mushrooms and truffle oil, or a free-range duck served three ways: breast with a bittersweet chocolate sauce, braised leg, and foie-gras ravioli. The creative desserts, such as apple dumpling with pumpkin ice cream or goat cheese crème brûlée with fruit, are all homemade. Because each meal feels individually crafted, the $63 prix-fixe menu is an excellent value. If you like it so much you don't want to leave, the inn has rooms with cozy seating areas next to woodburning fireplaces and wicker chairs on the wraparound porch. [$] *Average main: $63* ✉ *116 Rte. 117* ☎ *603/823–5621* 🌐 *www.sugarhillinn.com* ✍ *Reservations essential* ◷ *Closed Tues. and Wed. No lunch.*

$$ RESORT 🏨 **Franconia Inn.** At this 120-acre family-friendly resort, you can play tennis on four clay courts, soak in the outdoor heated pool or hot tub, hop aboard a mountain bike, or even soar on a glider. **Pros:** good for kids; amazing views; outdoor heated pool. **Cons:** may be too remote for some. [$] *Rooms from: $169* ✉ *1172 Easton Rd.* ☎ *603/823–5542,*

800/473–5299 ⊕ *www.franconiainn.com* ↘*34 rooms, 3 suites, 2 2-bedroom cottages* ◷ *Restaurant closed Apr.–mid-May.*

SPORTS AND THE OUTDOORS

SKI AREAS

Cannon Mountain. This place is rich in New England history. Here you'll find the first aerial tramway in North America, built in 1938, and the view from the top of the 4,080-foot summit (on a clear day) is spectacular. The ride is free with a ski lift ticket; otherwise it's $15. In winter you'll find classic New England ski terrain that runs the gamut from steep pitches off the peak to gentle blue cruisers. In all, Cannon has 73 trails, but beginners may want to head over to the separate Tuckerbrook family area, which offers 13 trails and four lifts. Adventurous types will want to try out the Mittersill area, which has 86 acres of lift-accessed "side country" trails and glades where the snow is au naturel. ✉ *9 Franconia Notch State Park, off Rte. 3* ☎ *603/823–8800* ⊕ *www.cannonmt.com.*

Franconia Village Cross-Country Ski Center. The cross-country ski center at the Franconia Inn has more than 40 miles of groomed and backcountry trails. One popular route leads to Bridal Veil Falls, a great spot for a picnic lunch. You can also enjoy horse-drawn sleigh rides, snowshoeing, snow tubing, and ice-skating on a lighted rink. ✉ *Franconia Inn, 1172 Easton Rd.* ☎ *603/823–5542, 800/473–5299* ⊕ *www.franconiainn.com/cross_country_ski_center.php.*

SHOPPING

Sugar Hill Sampler. In this 1815 barn set high on a hill, you'll find an old-fashioned general store filled with crafts like quilts, lamps, candles, and ornaments, along with a row of gourmet jams, sauces, and condiments. In the back, owner Barbara Serafini has set up a folksy museum with local photos, newspaper clippings, and curiosities (Bette Davis's will is among them). ✉ *71 Sunset Rd., Sugar Hill* ☎ *603/823–8478* ⊕ *www.sugarhillsampler.com.*

LITTLETON

7 miles north of Franconia and 86 miles north of Concord, on I–93.

One of northern New Hampshire's largest towns (this isn't saying much, mind you) is on a granite shelf along the Ammonoosuc River, whose swift current and drop of 235 feet enabled the community to flourish as a mill center in its early days. Later the railroad came through, and Littleton grew into the region's commerce hub. In the minds of many, it's more a place to stock up on supplies than a bona fide destination, but few communities have worked harder at revitalization. Today intriguing shops and eateries line the adorable Main Street, with its tidy 19th- and early-20th-century buildings that suggest a set in a Jimmy Stewart movie.

EXPLORING

The Rocks Estate. The rambling rock walls and beautifully restored historic buildings of The Rocks Estate, built by John Jacob Glessner of International Harvester, now serves as the 1,400-acre North Country

Conservation and Education Center for the Forest Society. The property is open year-round with a variety of natural-history programs, self-guided tours, and hiking trails with excellent views of the Presidential Range. In winter you'll find cross-country ski trails and a select-your-own Christmas tree farm. In spring, watch syrup being made in the New Hampshire Maple Experience Museum. ✉ *4 Christmas Tree La., Bethlehem* ☎ *603/444–6248* 🌐 *www.therocks.org.*

QUICK BITES

Miller's Cafe & Bakery. Next to the Riverwalk Covered Bridge, this eatery is a great breakfast or lunch stop, serving fresh salads, award-winning sandwiches, and fabulous baked goods like chocolate-pecan pie. ✉ ***16 Mill St.*** ☎ ***603/444–2146*** 🌐 ***www.millerscafeandbakery.com*** 🕒 ***Closed Mon.***

Thayers Inn. In heart of Littleton sits this former grande dame. While it still welcomes overnight guests, it functions largely as an informal museum. In the lobby and down the hall you'll find photos and memorabilia from movie star Bette Davis's huge birthday bash and artifacts from other illustrious guests, including Ulysses S. Grant, Henry Ford, P. T. Barnum, and Richard Nixon. Request a key to climb up to the cupola for 360-degree view of the town. Two rooms are open to the public: one set up as a guest room from the 1840s and one a scene from *Pollyanna,* written by Littleton native Eleanor Hodgman Porter, born in 1868. ✉ *111 Main St.* ☎ *603/444–6469* 🌐 *www.thayersinn.com.*

OFF THE BEATEN PATH

Whitefield. About 11 miles northeast of Littleton, Whitefield became a prominent summer resort in the late 19th century, when wealthy industrialists flocked to this small village in a rolling valley to play golf, ski the slopes, and hobnob with each other. The yellow clapboard Mountain View Grand Hotel, which first opened in 1865, is once again one of New England's grandest resorts. It's worth driving through the courtly Colonial-style center of town—Whitefield was settled in the early 1800s—and up Route 116 just beyond to see this magnificent structure atop a bluff overlooking the Presidentials. ✉ *Whitefield.*

WHERE TO EAT AND STAY

$$$ AMERICAN

🍴 **Tim-bir Alley.** This is a rare find in New Hampshire: an independent restaurant in a contemporary setting that's been serving customers for decades and yet still takes its food seriously. If you're in town, don't miss it. Tim Carr's menu changes weekly and uses regional American ingredients in creative ways. Main dishes might include an eggplant pâté with feta cheese, red pepper, and a tomato-herb marmalade or a basil-and-olive-oil-flavored salmon with a spinach-Brie-pecan pesto. Save room for such desserts as white chocolate–coconut cheesecake. [$] *Average main: $23* ✉ *7 Main St.* ☎ *603/444–6142* 💳 *No credit cards* 🕒 *Closed Jan.–Apr. and Mon. and Tues. No lunch.*

$$$$ B&B/INN Fodor's Choice ★

🏨 **Adair Country Inn and Restaurant.** An air of yesteryear refinement infuses Adair, a three-story Georgian Revival home that attorney Frank Hogan built as a wedding present for his daughter in 1927. **Pros:** refined, book-filled spaces; gourmet dinners; gracious service. **Cons:** removed from town. [$] *Rooms from: $245* ✉ *80 Guider La., off I–93, Bethlehem* ☎ *603/444–2600, 888/444–2600* 🌐 *www.adairinn.com* 🛏 *9 rooms, 1 cottage* 🕒 *Closed Nov. and Apr.* 🍽 *Breakfast.*

SHOPPING

Potato Barn Antiques Center. You'll find 10 dealers under one roof at Potato Barn Antiques Center. Specialties include antique lamps, vintage clothing, costume jewelry, and old tools. ⊠ *960 Lancaster Rd., 6 miles north of Lancaster, Northumberland* ☎ *603/636–2611* ⊕ *www. potatobarnantiques.com.*

Village Book Store. If you're looking for hiking maps or good books about the history of the area, you'll find them here, as well as unusual children's toys and a wide range of adult fiction and nonfiction titles. On the lower level is the League of New Hampshire Craftsmen's shop, featuring glass, prints, ceramics, fiber, and more. ⊠ *81 Main St.* ☎ *603/444–5263* ⊕ *www.booksmusictoys.com.*

4

BRETTON WOODS

14 miles southeast of Bethlehem; 28 miles northeast of Lincoln/ Woodstock.

In the early 1900s private railcars brought the elite from New York and Philadelphia to the Omni Mount Washington Hotel, the jewel of the White Mountains. A visit to the hotel, which was the site of the 1944 United Nations conference that created the International Monetary Fund and the International Bank for Reconstruction and Development (and the birth of many conspiracy theories), is not to be missed. The area is also known for its cog railway and Bretton Woods ski resort.

GETTING HERE AND AROUND

Bretton Woods is in the heart of the White Mountains on Route 302. A free shuttle makes it easy to get around the resort's various facilities. Helpful advice on how to enjoy your stay can be found at the concierge and activities desk in the main lobby of the Omni Mount Washington Hotel.

EXPLORING

FAMILY

Fodor'sChoice

★

Mount Washington Cog Railway. In 1858, Sylvester Marsh petitioned the state legislature for permission to build a steam railway up Mt. Washington. A politico retorted that he'd have better luck building a railroad to the moon. But 11 years later, the Mount Washington Cog Railway chugged its way up to the summit along a 3-mile track on the west side of the mountain. Today it's one of the state's most beloved attractions— a thrill in either direction. You'll find a small museum about the cog rail at the base. The train runs from May until early December, with varying departure times. A full trip ($64) is three hours, including one hour at the summit. ⊠ *3168 Base Station Rd., 6 miles northeast of Bretton Woods* ☎ *603/278–5404, 800/922–8825* ⊕ *www.thecog.com* 🖅 *$64.*

WHERE TO EAT

$$$$

AMERICAN

✕**Bretton Arms Dining Room.** You're likely to have the best meal in the area at this intimate setting. Though the same chef oversees the Omni Mount Washington Hotel's Main Dining Room, the latter is immense, and the Bretton Arms is cozier. Three small interconnected rooms are separated by fireplaces. The menu is seasonal and might include Georges Bank scallops with pureed celery root, baby bok choy, and

Bretton Woods is a year-round destination, and especially popular with families.

cipollini onions. Locally sourced food features prominently in all the dishes. $ *Average main: $30* ✉ *U.S. 302* ☎ *603/278–1000* 🌐 *www.mtwashingtonresort.com* 🕓 *No lunch.*

$$$$ AMERICAN 🍴 **Main Dining Room.** You'd be hard-pressed to find a larger or grander space in New Hampshire than the Omni Mount Washington Hotel's enormous octagonal Main Dining Room, which has massive windows that open onto spectacular views of the Presidential Range. Built in 1902, subtle renovations have brought it into the 21st century. Seasonal dishes are sourced from local New Hampshire farms and suppliers; thus, the menu is constantly changing. On it you might find wild salmon wrapped in buttery pastry served over lobster succotash or a rosemary-scented rack of lamb with candied beets. **■ TIP→ Appropriate evening wear is expected, meaning no shorts or sneakers.** $ *Average main: $36* ✉ *Omni Mount Washington Hotel, U.S. 302* ☎ *603/278–1000* 🌐 *www.mtwashingtonresort.com* 🕓 *No lunch.*

$$ AMERICAN FAMILY 🍴 **Fabyan's Station.** A model train circles the dining room at this former railroad station—a nod to the late 19th century, when 60 trains a day stopped here. If you're looking for an easygoing meal, Fabyan's cooks up delicious clam chowder in a bread bowl and a 16-ounce T-bone grilled to perfection. Half the restaurant is a tavern with a long bar, and the other half serves soups, sandwiches, fish, and house-smoked items. There's a kids' menu, too. $ *Average main: $17* ✉ *Rte. 302, 1 mile north of ski area* ☎ *603/278–2222* 🌐 *www.brettonwoods.com/dining/bretton_woods_dining/overview* ✍ *Reservations not accepted.*

WHERE TO STAY

$$ HOTEL — **The Lodge.** Freshly renovated throughout, this inexpensive roadside motel gives you free access to all of the resort facilities at Omni Mount Washington Hotel, including the pools, gym, and arcade, which makes it a great deal. **Pros:** inexpensive rates; access to many amenities; free ski shuttle. **Cons:** across street from resort amenities; Continental breakfast only. [$] *Rooms from: $139* ✉ *U.S. 302* ☎ *603/278–1000, 800/680–6600* 🌐 *www.mtwashington.com* 🛏 *50 rooms* 🍴 *Breakfast.*

$$$$ RESORT FAMILY Fodor's Choice ★ — **Omni Mount Washington Hotel.** The two most memorable sights in the White Mountains would have to be Mt. Washington and the Omni Mount Washington Hotel. **Pros:** beautiful resort; loads of activities; free shuttle to skiing and activities. **Cons:** kids love to run around the hotel. [$] *Rooms from: $229* ✉ *U.S. 302* ☎ *603/278–1000* 🌐 *brettonwoods.com* 🛏 *175 rooms, 25 suites* 🍴 *Multiple meal plans.*

$$$$ B&B/INN Fodor's Choice ★ — **The Notchland Inn.** Built in 1862 by Sam Bemis, America's grandfather of landscape photography, the house conveys mountain charm on a scale unmatched in New England. **Pros:** middle-of-the-forest setting; marvelous house and common rooms; good dinners. **Cons:** may seem too isolated for some. [$] *Rooms from: $265* ✉ *2 Morey Rd., Harts Location* ☎ *603/374–6131* 🌐 *www.notchland.com* 🛏 *8 rooms, 5 suites, 2 cottages* 🍴 *Breakfast.*

SPORTS AND THE OUTDOORS

SKI AREA

FAMILY Fodor's Choice ★ — **Bretton Woods.** New Hampshire's largest ski area is also one of the country's best family ski resorts. The views of Mt. Washington alone are worth the visit to Bretton Woods; the scenery is especially beautiful from the Latitude 44 restaurant, open during ski season.

This is a great place to learn to ski. Trails appeal mostly to novice and intermediate skiers, including two magic carpet lifts for beginners. There are some steeper pitches near the top of the 1,500-foot vertical and glade skiing to occupy the experts, as well as night skiing and snowboarding on weekends and holidays. Snowboarders enjoy the three terrain parks. The Nordic trail system has 62 miles of cross-country ski trails.

The Hobbit Ski and Snowplay program, for ages 3 to 5, is an introduction to skiing, and the Hobbit Ski and Snowboard School, for ages 4 to 12, has full- and half-day lessons. The complimentary Kinderwoods Winter Playground has a sled carousel, igloos, and a zip line. A snowmobile park at the base area is fun for kids ages 4 to 13. Parents can purchase interchangeable family tickets that allow them to take turns skiing while the other watches the kids—both passes come for the price of one. The ski area also offers an adaptive program for anyone with disabilities.

A recent addition is the year-round Canopy Tour, which has 9 ziplines, two sky bridges, and three rappel stations. Small groups are led by experienced guides. The tour, costing $110, is an exhilarating introduction to flora and fauna of the White Mountains. As with many activities here, kids are welcome. ✉ *U.S. 302* ☎ *603/278–3320, 603/278–1000 weather conditions* 🌐 *www.brettonwoods.com.*

EN ROUTE

Crawford Notch State Park. Scenic U.S. 302 winds through the steep, wooded mountains on either side of spectacular Crawford Notch, southeast of Bretton Woods, and passes through Crawford Notch State Park, where you can picnic and take a short hike to Arethusa Falls or the Silver and Flume cascades. The park has a number of roadside photo opportunities. The Willey House Visitor Center has a gift shop, snack bar, and picnic area. ✉ *1464 U.S. 302, Harts Location* 🌐 *www.nhstateparks.org* 🎟 *$4.*

BARTLETT

18 miles southeast of Bretton Woods.

With Bear Mountain to its south, Mt. Parker to its north, Mt. Cardigan to its west, and the Saco River to its east, Bartlett, incorporated in 1790, has an unforgettable setting. Lovely Bear Notch Road (closed in winter) has the only midpoint access to the Kancamagus Highway. There isn't much town here (dining options are in Glen). It's best known for the Attitash Ski Resort, within walking distance.

WHERE TO EAT

$$ SOUTHWESTERN

🍴 **Margarita Grill.** Après-ski types like to congregate on the enclosed, heated patio and unwind with a margarita. Here you'll find a wide assortment of Tex-Mex and Southwestern specialties, including homemade salsas, wood-fired steaks, ribs, chicken, and burgers. All ingredients are local and fresh, this being a New Hampshire farm-to-table certified restaurant. [$] *Average main: $17* ✉ *78 U.S. 302, Glen* ☎ *603/383–6556* 🌐 *www.margaritagrillnh.com* 🕒 *No lunch weekdays.*

$$ AMERICAN

🍴 **Red Parka Steakhouse & Pub.** This downtown pub has been an institution for nearly 40 years. A family-oriented menu features an all-you-can-eat locally sourced salad bar, hand-cut steaks, and barbecue ribs. The barbecue sauce is made on-site, and beer is served in mason jars. Plan to spend some time reading the dozens and dozens of license plates that adorn the walls of the downstairs pub. You'll also find open mike nights on Monday and live entertainment on Friday and Saturday. [$] *Average main: $18* ✉ *3 Station St., Glen* ☎ *603/383–4344* 🌐 *www.redparkapub.com* ✍ *Reservations not accepted* 🕒 *No lunch.*

WHERE TO STAY

$$$$ HOTEL

🏨 **Attitash Grand Summit Hotel & Conference Center.** If ski-in ski-out convenience is a must, then this is the hotel where you'll want to stay. **Pros:** great location; nice outdoor pool and hot tubs; better price with ski package. **Cons:** generally bland accommodations. [$] *Rooms from: $259* ✉ *U.S. 302* ☎ *603/374–1900, 800/223–7669* 🌐 *www.attitash.com* 🛏 *143 rooms.*

$$$ HOTEL

🏨 **Attitash Mountain Village Resort.** Hidden in a cluster of pine trees across from the ski area is a resort with guest rooms (a few are actually slopeside) that crest the top of this mountain. **Pros:** simple family place; fitness room; nice pools. **Cons:** more functional than posh. [$] *Rooms from: $199* ✉ *784 U.S. 302* ☎ *603/374–6501, 800/862–1600* 🌐 *www.mtwashingtonvalleyaccommodations.com* 🛏 *350 units.*

SPORTS AND THE OUTDOORS
SKI AREA

Attitash Ski Resort. With a vertical drop of 1,760 feet, the Attitash Ski Resort offers a total of 67 trails to explore. Not enough? The adjacent Attitash Bear Peak adds another 1,450 feet of vertical. Here you'll find traditional New England ski runs and challenging terrain, alongside wide-open cruisers that suit all skill levels. There are acres of glades, plus a progressive freestyle terrain park. The Attitash Adventure Center has a rental shop, lessons, and children's programs. ⊠ *U.S. 302* ☎ *800/223–7669* ⊕ *www.attitash.com.*

JACKSON

4

5 miles north of Glen.

Fodor's Choice Just off Route 16 via a red covered bridge, Jackson has retained its
★ storybook New England character. Art and antiques shopping, tennis, golf, fishing, and hiking to waterfalls are among the draws. When the snow falls, Jackson becomes the state's cross-country skiing capital. Four downhill ski areas are nearby. Hotels and B&Bs offer a ski shuttle. Visit Jackson Falls for a wonderful photo opportunity.

ESSENTIALS

Visitor Information Jackson Area Chamber of Commerce ☎ *603/383–9356* ⊕ *www.jacksonnh.com.*

EXPLORING

FAMILY **Story Land.** This cluster of fluorescent buildings is a theme park with life-size storybook and nursery-rhyme characters. The 22 rides include a flume ride, a river-raft ride, and a roller coaster. There's also a variety of shows when you need a break. ⊠ *850 Rte. 16, Glen* ☎ *603/383–4186* ⊕ *www.storylandnh.com* 🖃 *$32* 🕙 *Memorial Day–early Oct., hrs vary.*

SPORTS AND THE OUTDOORS
SKI AREAS

Black Mountain. Friendly, informal Black Mountain has a warming southern exposure. The Family Passport allows two adults and two kids to ski at highly discounted rates both during the week ($109) and on weekends ($139). That's a great deal, as the regular rates are considered among the lowest in the Mt. Washington Valley. The 40 trails and glades on the 1,100-foot mountain are evenly divided among beginner, intermediate, and expert. There's a nursery for kids over six months old. Enjoy guided horseback riding spring through fall. ⊠ *373 Black Mountain Rd.* ☎ *603/383–4490, 800/475–4669 snow conditions* ⊕ *www.blackmt.com.*

Fodor's Choice **Jackson Ski Touring Foundation.** Experts rate this the best-run cross-country
★ ski operation in the country. That's due to the great advice you get from the attentive staff, and also to its 60 miles of groomed trails for skiing, skate skiing, and snowshoeing. The varied terrain offers something for all abilities. Jackson Ski Touring's trails wind through covered bridges and into the picturesque village of Jackson, where you can warm up in cozy, trailside restaurants. Lessons and rentals are available. ⊠ *153 Main St.* ☎ *603/383–9355* ⊕ *www.jacksonxc.org.*

WHERE TO EAT

$$
AMERICAN
FAMILY

✕ **Red Fox Bar & Grille.** Some say this big family restaurant overlooking Wentworth Golf Club gets its name from a wily fox with a penchant for stealing golf balls off the fairway. The wide-ranging menu has burgers, barbecued ribs, and wood-fired pizzas, as well as more refined dishes such as seared sea scallops and bourbon steak tips. The Sunday breakfast buffet is very popular. Younger kids will enjoy the playroom, especially if there's a wait for a table. $ Average main: $16 ⊠ 49 Rte. 16 ☎ 603/383–4949 ⊕ www.redfoxbarandgrille.com ☉ No lunch Sat.

$$$
AMERICAN
Fodor's Choice
★

✕ **Thorn Hill.** This famous inn serves up some of New England's most memorable meals in a romantic atmosphere with low lights and piano music trickling in from the lounge. Many people enjoy dining on the heated porch, which overlooks the Presidential Range. You'll find subtle and flavorful dishes such as pan-seared trout, Peking duck on a scallion pancake with sesame bok choy, and New York sirloin in a blue cheese demi-glace. $ Average main: $26 ⊠ 42 Thorn Hill Rd. ☎ 603/383–4242, 800/289–8990 ⊕ www.innatthornhill.com ☉ No lunch.

WHERE TO STAY

$$$
B&B/INN

⬚ **Christmas Farm Inn and Spa.** Despite its wintery name, this 1778 inn is an all-season retreat. **Pros:** kids are welcome; nice indoor and outdoor pools; very close to ski area. **Cons:** can be very busy with kids. $ Rooms from: $189 ⊠ 3 Blitzen Way, off Rte. 16B ☎ 603/383–4313, 800/443–5837 ⊕ www.christmasfarminn.com ↪ 22 rooms, 12 suites, 7 cottages ⦙⊙⦙ Breakfast.

$$$
B&B/INN
Fodor's Choice
★

⬚ **Inn at Jackson.** This bright B&B is impeccably maintained and charmingly furnished. **Pros:** exceptional rooms; peaceful setting; wonderful breakfasts. **Cons:** top-floor rooms lack fireplaces. $ Rooms from: $189 ⊠ Corner of Main St. and Thorn Hill Rd. ☎ 603/383–4321, 800/289–8600 ⊕ www.innatjackson.com ↪ 14 rooms ⦙⊙⦙ Breakfast.

$$$
B&B/INN
Fodor's Choice
★

⬚ **The Inn at Thorn Hill & Spa.** With a large reception room and sweeping staircase, this inn modeled after an 1891 Stanford White Victorian is breathtaking from the minute you step inside. **Pros:** romantic setting; soothing spa. **Cons:** Wi-Fi works on main floor, but not in the rooms. $ Rooms from: $215 ⊠ 42 Thorn Hill Rd. ☎ 800/289–8990, 800/289–8990 ⊕ www.innatthornhill.com ↪ 18 rooms, 5 suites, 3 cottages ⦙⊙⦙ Some meals.

MT. WASHINGTON

20 miles northwest of Jackson.

Mt. Washington. Mt. Washington is the highest peak (6,288 feet) in the northeastern United States and the site of a weather station that recorded the world's highest winds, 231 mph, back in 1934. You can drive to the top, which climbs 4,600 feet in just over 7 miles, in the summer. A number of trailheads circle the mountain and the other peaks in the Presidential Range, but all of them are strenuous. On the summit is Extreme Mount Washington, an interactive museum dedicated to science and weather. A guided bus tour is available, or you can reach the top along several rough hiking trails. Remember that the temperatures atop Mt. Washington will be much colder than those down below—the average year-round is below freezing, and the average wind velocity is 35 mph. ☎ *603/356–2137* ⊕ *www.mountwashington.org.*

SPORTS AND THE OUTDOORS

Great Glen Trails Outdoor Center. This outdoor center at the foot of Mt. Washington is the base for year-around outdoor activities. Renowned for its dramatic 27-mile cross-country trail system, this center gives access to more than 1,100 acres of backcountry. Trees shelter most of the trails, so Mt. Washington's infamous weather isn't such a concern. You can travel to the mountain's upper reaches in nine-passenger vans that are refitted with snowmobile-like treads. You have the option of skiing or snowshoeing down or just enjoying the magnificent winter view. The center has a huge ski and sports shop, food court, climbing wall, and observation deck. In summer it's the base for hiking and biking and has programs in canoeing, kayaking, and fly-fishing. ⊠ *1 Mt. Washington Auto Rd.* ☎ *603/466–2333* ⊕ *www.greatglentrails.com.*

Pinkham Notch. Although not a town per se, scenic Pinkham Notch covers Mt. Washington's eastern side and has several ravines, including famous Tuckerman Ravine. The Appalachian Mountain Club runs a visitor center that provides year-around trail information to hikers, as well as guided hikes, outdoor skills workshops, an outdoors shop, and cafeteria. ⊠ *Appalachian Mountain Club Pinkham Notch Visitor Center, 361 Rte. 16* ☎ *603/466–2721* ⊕ *www.outdoors.org* ☯ *Daily 6:30 am–9 pm.*

Wildcat Mountain. Glade skiers favor Wildcat, with 28 acres of official tree skiing. The 49 runs include some stunning double-black-diamond trails. Experts can zip down the Lynx. Skiers who can hold a wedge should check out the 2½-mile-long Polecat, which offers excellent views of the Presidential Range. The trails are classic New England—narrow and winding—and the views are stunning. Beginners will find gentle terrain and a broad teaching slope. For an adrenaline rush, there's a terrain park. In summer you can zip to the top on the four-passenger gondola, hike the many well-kept trails, and fish in the crystal-clear streams. ⊠ *Rte. 16, Jackson* ☎ *603/466–3326, 888/754–9453 snow conditions* ⊕ *www.skiwildcat.com.*

DIXVILLE NOTCH

63 miles north of Mt. Washington, 66 miles northeast of Littleton, 149 miles north of Concord.

Just 12 miles from the Canadian border, this tiny community is known for two things: the Balsams, one of New Hampshire's oldest and most celebrated resorts, and the fact that Dixville Notch and another New Hampshire community, Hart's Location, are the first election districts in the nation to vote in presidential general elections. When the 30 or so Dixville Notch voters file into the little Balsams meeting room on the eve of Election Day and cast their ballots at the stroke of midnight, they invariably make national news.

Reward your vehicle for tackling the auto road with the obligatory bumper sticker: "This Car Climbed Mt. Washington."

TOURS

Gorham Moose Tours. One of the favorite pastimes in this area is spotting moose, those large, ungainly, yet elusive members of the deer family. These bus tours lasting up to three hours claim to have a 97% success rate in spotting moose. ✉ *69 Main St., Gorham* ☎ *603/466–2101, 877/986–6673* ⊕ *www.gorhamnh.org* 🎟 *$25* ⊙ *Memorial Day–Sept., departure times vary.*

EXPLORING

FAMILY **Poore Farm Historic Homestead.** Maybe you've visited farm museums before, but certainly not one like this. Originally built in 1825, this farm has survived almost perfectly intact because the Poore family never installed electricity or other modern conveniences. They lived here for a century and a half, and apparently saved everything. The house, barn, outbuildings, and gardens provide a rare opportunity to see how rural New Englanders actually lived, dressed, ate, farmed, and socialized. It's the perfect backdrop for farming demonstrations, music festivals, and discussions about farm life. ✉ *629 Hollow Rd., 7 miles north of Colebrook, Stewartstown* ⊕ *www.poorefarm.org* 🎟 *$5* ⊙ *June–Sept., weekdays 11–1, weekends 11–3.*

OFF THE
BEATEN
PATH

Pittsburg. In the Great North Woods, Pittsburg contains the springs that form the Connecticut River. The state's northern tip—a chunk of about 250 square miles—lies within the town's borders. Remote though it is, this frontier town teems with hunters, boaters, fishermen, hikers, and photographers from early summer through winter. Especially in the colder months, moose sightings are common. The town has more than a dozen lodges and several informal eateries. It's about a 90-minute drive from Littleton and 40 minutes from Dixville Notch.

WHERE TO EAT AND STAY

$ FRENCH Fodor's Choice ★ 🍴 **Le Rendez Vous.** You might not expect to find an authentic French pastry shop in the workaday village of Colebrook, 10 miles west of Dixville Notch, but Le Rendez Vous serves fabulous tarts and treats. Understandable, as the owners came from Paris. Drop in to this quaint café—furnished with several tables and armchairs—for hand-dipped Belgian chocolates, buttery croissants, and a tremendous variety of fresh-baked breads, as well as gourmet foods ranging from dried fruits and nuts to lentils, olive oils, and balsamic vinegar. [$] *Average main: $5* ✉ *121 Main St., Colebrook* ☎ *603/237–5150* 🌐 *www.lerendezvousbakerynh.com.*

$$$ AMERICAN 🍴 **Rainbow Grille.** Everyone loves the Rainbow Grille, whether it's for the moose antlers hanging on the pine paneling, views of the sun setting over Black Lake, or the lumberjack-sized meals. Nestled in the Tall Timber Lodge, built in 1946, this restaurant is known for its trout and salmon dishes, as well as for its mesquite-grilled prime rib. The perfect finish to any meal is a slice of bread pudding. Even though this seems like an out-of-the-way place, don't miss out on a table. Visitors reserve months in advance. [$] *Average main: $24* ✉ *609 Beach Rd., Pittsburgh* ☎ *603/538–9556* 🌐 *www.rainbowgrille.com* ✍ *Reservations essential* 🕒 *Closed Thanksgiving–Mother's Day.*

$ HOTEL 🏨 **Cabins at Lopstick.** In business since 1929, the Cabins at Lopstick have long appealed to outdoors enthusiasts. **Pros:** great views of First Connecticut Lake; full kitchens; great for summer and winter sports. **Cons:** no on-site eatery; no Wi-Fi in most cabins. [$] *Rooms from: $99* ✉ *45 Stewart Young Rd., Pittsburgh* ☎ *800/538–6659* 🌐 *www.cabinsatlopstick.com* 🛏 *43 cabins* 🍽 *No meals.*

SPORTS AND THE OUTDOORS

Dixville Notch State Park. In the northernmost notch of the White Mountains, Dixville Notch State Park has a waterfall, two mountain brooks, hiking trails, picnic areas, and restrooms. ✉ *1212 W. Rte. 26* ☎ *603/538–6707* 🌐 *www.nhstateparks.org.*

NORTH CONWAY

76 miles south of Dixville Notch; 7 miles south of Glen; 41 miles east of Lincoln/North Woodstock.

Before the arrival of the outlet stores, the town drew visitors for its inspiring scenery, ski resorts, and access to White Mountain National Forest. Today, however, the feeling of natural splendor is gone. Shopping is the big sport, and businesses line Route 16 for several miles. You'll get a close look at them because traffic slows to a crawl here. You can take scenic West Side Road from Conway to Intervale to circumvent the traffic and take in splendid views.

GETTING HERE AND AROUND

Park near the fire station on Main Street and spend half a day visiting the unique shops and restaurants in this part of town. Taxis can get you around between Conway, North Conway, and Jackson.

ESSENTIALS

Taxi Village Taxi ☎ *603/356–3602.*

Visitor Information North Country Chamber of Commerce ☎ *603/237–8939, 800/698–8939* 🌐 *www.northcountrychamber.org.*

EXPLORING

FAMILY **Conway Scenic Railroad.** Departing from historic North Conway Station, the Conway Scenic Railroad operates trips aboard vintage trains. The Notch Train to Crawford Depot (a 5-hour round-trip) or Fabyan Station (5½ hours) offers wonderful views from a domed observation coach. The Valley Train overlooks Mt. Washington during a 55-minute round-trip journey to Conway or a 1¾-hour excursion to Bartlett. Lunch is served daily from mid-June to late October, and dinner is served four evenings a week. The 1874 station displays lanterns, old tickets and timetables, and other artifacts. Reserve your spot early during foliage season. ✉ *38 Norcross Circle* ☎ *603/356–5251, 800/232–5251* 🌐 *www.conwayscenic.com* 🎟 *$16–$83* 🕒 *Mid-Apr.–mid Dec; departure times vary.*

FAMILY **Hartmann Model Railroad Museum.** All aboard! You can ride a miniature outdoor train at the Hartmann Model Railroad Museum, which also has 10 operating train layouts in scales ranging from G to Z. There's also a hobby shop on the premises. ✉ *15 Town Hall Rd., at Rte. 16, Intervale* ☎ *603/356–9922* 🌐 *www.hartmannrr.com* 🎟 *$6* 🕒 *July and Aug., daily 10–5; Sept.–June, Fri.-Mon. 10–5.*

Weather Discovery Center. Ever wonder what it's like to be in a cabin at the summit of Mt. Washington while 200 mph winds shake the rafters? This fun, interactive museum allows you to experience different weather conditions and learn about how weather affects our lives. There's a twice-daily video link with the scientists hard at work at Mt. Washington Observatory. ✉ *2779 Main St.* ☎ *603/356–2137* 🌐 *www.mountwashington.org/education/center* 🎟 *Free* 🕒 *Daily 10–5.*

WHERE TO EAT

$$ AMERICAN 🍴 **Delaney's Hole in the Wall.** This casual tavern has a real fondness for ski history, displaying early photos of local ski areas, old signs and placards, and odd bits of lift equipment. Entrées range from fajitas that come sizzling out of the kitchen to mussels and scallops sautéed with spiced sausage and Louisiana seasonings. There's an entire menu devoted to sushi. [$] *Average main: $18* ✉ *2966 White Mountain Hwy., ¼ mile north of North Conway Village* ☎ *603/356–7776* 🌐 *www.delaneys.com.*

$$ AMERICAN FAMILY 🍴 **Muddy Moose Restaurant & Pub.** This family restaurant buzzes with the sound of happy kids. The mac and cheese, blueberry-glazed ribs, and hearty burgers are a hit with the small fry, although grown-ups might prefer the pasta and seafood dishes. A unique side dish of carrots with a hint of maple syrup is a pleasant surprise. The Muddy Moose Pie, made of ice cream, fudge, and crumbled Oreos, can feed a family of four. [$] *Average main: $16* ✉ *2344 White Mountain Hwy.* ☎ *603/356–7696* 🌐 *www.muddymoose.com* ✍ *Reservations not accepted.*

$$$ ✗ **The 1785 Inn.** Visitors keep coming back to this special place, not only
AMERICAN for its outstanding food, but for its quaint New England charm and
Fodor's Choice spectacular mountain views. The main dining room is in the original
★ 1785 building with a cooking fireplace, Early American antiques, and
exposed hand-hewn beams. The restaurant is known for its gracious
service (Caesar salads are prepared table-side), extravagant desserts,
and drinks that shoot up in flames. Beyond the theatrics, the food by
chef Peter Willis is beautifully prepared and flavorful, including the
tender seared Maine scallops with a ginger, chili, coconut, and lemon-
grass sauce, and ruby trout with sweet rice and a seaweed salad. The
inn has 17 guest rooms that range from cozy to luxurious. $ *Average
main: $25* ✉ *3582 White Mountain Hwy.* ☎ *603/356–9025* ⊕ *www.
the1785inn.com* ⊗ *No lunch.*

WHERE TO STAY

$$ ⊞ **The Buttonwood Inn.** A tranquil oasis in this busy resort area, the But-
B&B/INN tonwood Inn sits on Mt. Surprise, 2 miles northeast of North Conway
Village. **Pros:** good bedding and amenities; tranquil setting; 6 acres
of grounds. **Cons:** unexciting for those not wanting a remote getaway. $ *Rooms from: $159* ✉ *64 Mt. Surprise Rd.* ☎ *603/356–2625,
800/258–2625* ⊕ *www.buttonwoodinn.com* ⇆ *10 rooms, 1 suite*
⦿ *Breakfast.*

$$ ⊞ **Darby Field Inn.** After a day in the White Mountains, warm up by the
B&B/INN fieldstone fireplace in this inn's common area. **Pros:** romantic setting; an
away-from-it-all feel. **Cons:** better for couples than families. $ *Rooms
from: $170* ✉ *185 Chase Hill, Albany* ☎ *603/447–2181, 800/426–4147*
⊕ *www.darbyfield.com* ⇆ *13 rooms* ⊗ *Closed Apr.* ⦿ *Breakfast.*

$$ ⊞ **Snowville Inn.** Journalist Frank Simonds built this gambrel-roofed
B&B/INN main house in 1916, and its nicest room has 12 windows that look out
over the Presidential Range. **Pros:** spectacular views; fine dining;
full breakfast. **Cons:** off the beaten path; Wi-Fi connection unpredictable.
$ *Rooms from: $139* ✉ *136 Stewart Rd., 6 miles southeast of Conway, Snowville* ☎ *603/447–2818, 800/447–4345* ⊕ *snowvilleinn.com*
⇆ *16 rooms, 1 suite* ⦿ *Breakfast.*

$$$ ⊞ **White Mountain Hotel and Resort.** Rooms in this hotel at the base
RESORT of Whitehorse Ledge have splendid mountain views, and the prox-
imity to White Mountain National Forest and Echo Lake State Park
makes you feel farther away from the outlet malls than you actually
are. **Pros:** scenic setting that's close to shopping; lots of activities; kids
18 and under stay free. **Cons:** two-night-minimum summer week-
ends. $ *Rooms from: $189* ✉ *2560 West Side Rd.* ☎ *800/533–6301*
⊕ *www.whitemountainhotel.com* ⇆ *69 rooms, 11 suites* ⦿ *Multiple
meal plans.*

SPORTS AND THE OUTDOORS
PARK
Echo Lake State Park. You don't have to be a rock climber to catch views
from the 700-foot White Horse and Cathedral ledges. From the top
you'll see the entire valley, including Echo Lake, which offers fish-
ing, swimming, boating, and, on quiet days, an excellent opportu-
nity to shout for echoes. ✉ *68 Echo Lake Rd., off U.S 302, Conway*

4

Sit back and enjoy the view on the Conway Scenic Railroad.

☎ 603/356–2672 ⊕ *www.nhstateparks.org* ✉ *$4* ☉ *Memorial Day–mid-Oct., daily 9–sunset.*

CANOEING AND KAYAKING

Outdoors Saco Bound. This outfitter rents stand-up paddleboards, canoes, and kayaks. It'll even provide transportation for you and your inner tubes for gentle floats down the Saco River. ✉ *2561 E. Main St., Center Conway* ☎ *603/447–2177* ⊕ *www.sacobound.com.*

FISHING

North Country Angler. One of the best tackle shops in the state, North Country Angler offers casting clinics and guided fly-fishing trips throughout the region. ✉ *2888 White Mountain Hwy.* ☎ *603/356–6000* ⊕ *www.northcountryangler.com.*

SKI AREAS

Cranmore Mountain Adventure Park. This downhill ski area has been a favorite with families since it opened in 1938. The 57 trails are fun to ski, and five glades have increased the skiable terrain. Most runs are naturally formed intermediates that weave in and out of glades. Beginners have several slopes and routes from the summit; experts must be content with a few short, steep pitches. In addition to the trails, there's snow tubing, a mountain coaster, a giant swing, and a zipline. Snowboarders have five terrain parks. Twilight skiing is offered Saturday and holidays. ✉ *1 Skimobile Rd.* ☎ *603/356–5543, 603/356–5544 snow conditions* ⊕ *www.cranmore.com.*

King Pine Ski Area at Purity Spring Resort. About 9 miles south of Conway, this family-run ski area has been going strong since 1962. King Pine's 17 gentle trails are ideal for beginner and intermediate skiers; experts won't be challenged except for a brief section of the Pitch Pine trail. There are 9 miles of cross-country ski trails. Indoors, you can enjoy a pool and fitness complex and go ice-skating. In summer the resort has every outdoor activity imaginable, including archery, waterskiing, kayaking, loon-watching, tennis, hiking, mountain biking, and fishing. ⊠ *1251 Eaton Rd., East Madison* ☎ *603/367–8896, 800/373–3754* ⊕ *www.kingpine.com.*

Mt. Washington Valley Ski Touring and Snowshoe Foundation. Nearly 30 miles of groomed cross-country trails weave through the North Conway countryside, maintained by this foundation. Membership to the Mt. Washington Valley Ski Touring Club is required, and can be purchased by the day or year. Equipment rentals are available. ⊠ *279 Rte. 16-302, Intervale* ☎ *603/356–9920* ⊕ *www.mwvskitouring.org.*

SHOPPING

ANTIQUES

Richard Plusch Antiques. This shop deals in period furniture and accessories, including glass, sterling silver, Oriental porcelains, rugs, paintings, and more. ⊠ *2584 White Mountain Hwy.* ☎ *603/356–3333.*

CLOTHING

More than 150 factory outlets—including L. L. Bean, New Balance, Orvis, Columbia, Lenox, Polo, Nike, Anne Klein, and Woolrich—line Route 16.

Joe Jones' Sun & Ski Sports. You'll find outdoor clothing and gear here, as well as the bathing suit you forgot to pack for the hot tub. Joe Jones' also offers rentals of gear and clothing. ⊠ *2709 White Mountain Hwy.* ☎ *603/356–9411* ⊕ *www.joejonessports.com.*

CRAFTS

Handcrafters Barn. This place stocks the work of 250 area artists and artisans. ⊠ *2473 White Mountain Hwy.* ☎ *603/356–8996* ⊕ *www. handcraftersbarn.com.*

Zeb's General Store. This old-fashioned country store sells specialty foods, crafts, clothing, and a range of products made in New England. ⊠ *2675 Main St.* ☎ *603/356–9294, 800/676–9294* ⊕ *www.zebs.com.*

EN ROUTE A great place to settle in to the White Mountains, take in one of the greatest panoramas of the mountains, and get visitor info is at the **Intervale Scenic Vista.** The stop, off Route 16 a few miles north of North Conway, is run by the DOT, has a helpful volunteer staff, features a wonderful large topographical map, and has terrific bathrooms.

KANCAMAGUS HIGHWAY

36 miles between Conway and Lincoln/North Woodstock.

Fodor's Choice **Kancamagus Highway.** Interstate 93 is the fastest way to the White Moun-
★ tains, but it's hardly the most appealing. The section of Route 112 known as the Kancamagus Highway passes through some of the state's most unspoiled mountain scenery—it was one of the first roads in the nation to be designated a National Scenic Byway. The Kanc, as it's called by locals, is punctuated by overlooks and picnic areas, and erupts into fiery color each fall, when photo-snapping drivers really slow things

New Hampshire's Diners

Friendly Toast. In the historic coastal city of Portsmouth, the Friendly Toast might be the most vaunted breakfast spot in the state. Creative fare like Coconut Cakes (pancakes with coconut, chocolate chips, and cashews) and the Hansel and Gretel Waffle (gingerbread waffle topped with pomegranate molasses) keep hungry bellies coming back again and again. ✉ *113 Congress St., Portsmouth* ☎ *603/430–2154* ⊕ *www.thefriendlytoast.net.*

Lou's Restaurant. Dartmouth students and professors hobnob over stellar pancakes, omelets, and breakfast tacos at Lou's Restaurant, a cheap-and-cheerful storefront diner. It serves up prodigious portions of corned-beef hash and eggs Benedict, as well as artfully decorated cupcakes and house-made cider donuts. Just beware of the long lines on weekend mornings. ✉ *30 S. Main St., Hanover* ☎ *603/643–3321* ⊕ *www.lousrestaurant.net.*

Red Arrow Diner. Once declared one of the country's "top 10 diners," the bustling Red Arrow Diner is open around the clock and caters to politicians, students, artists, and regular Janes and Joes in the heart of the Granite State's largest city. The 1922 diner's daily blue plate specials are served on actual blue plates, and you'll find such regular items as kielbasa and beans and house-brewed root beer and cream soda. There's a second location at 63 Union Square in Milford. ✉ *61 Lowell St., Manchester* ☎ *603/626–1118* ⊕ *www.redarrowdiner.com.*

Sunny Day Diner. Up in the skiing and hiking haven of Lincoln, outdoorsy souls fuel up on hearty fare like

Red Arrow Diner in Manchester.

banana-bread French toast and cherry pie à la mode at the cozy Sunny Day Diner, a handsomely restored building from the late 1950s. ✉ *U.S. 3, off I–93, Lincoln* ☎ *603/745–4833.*

Tilt'n Diner. Travelers to the state's Lakes Region have long been familiar with the flashy pink exterior and neon signage of the Tilt'n Diner, a convivial 1950s-style restaurant that's known for its omlets (served every possible way), reuben sandwiches, baked shepherd's pie, and Southern breakfasts—sausage gravy, biscuits, and baked beans with two eggs. Breakfast is served all day. ✉ *61 Laconia Rd., Tilton* ☎ *603/286–2204* ⊕ *www.thecman.com.*

—Andrew Collins
Red Arrow Diner in Manchester

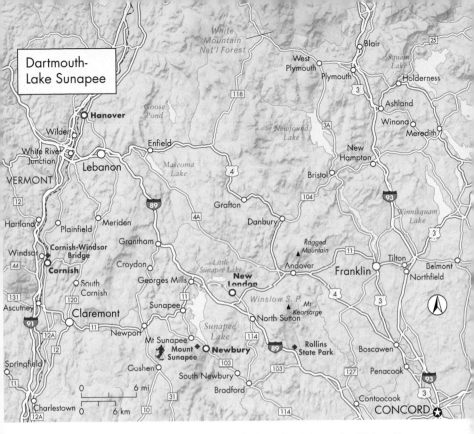

down. In bad weather, check with the White Mountains Visitors Bureau for road conditions. ⊕ *www.kancamagushighway.com.*

SPORTS AND THE OUTDOORS

Lincoln Woods Trail. A couple of short hiking trails off the Kancamagus Highway yield great rewards with relatively little effort. The Lincoln Woods Trail starts from the large parking lot of the Lincoln Woods Visitor Center, 5 miles east of Lincoln. Here you can purchase the $3 pass needed to park in any of the White Mountain National Forest lots or overlooks; stopping briefly to take photos or to use the restrooms at the visitor center is permitted without a pass. The trail crosses a suspension bridge over the Pemigewasset River and follows an old railroad bed for 3 miles along the river. ⊕ *www.fs.usda.gov/whitemountain.*

Sabbaday Falls. The parking and picnic area for Sabbaday Falls, about 15 miles west of Conway, is the trailhead for an easy ½-mile route to a multilevel cascade that plunges through two potholes and a flume. Swimming is not allowed. ✉ *Kancamagus Hwy.* ⊕ *www. kancamagushighway.com.*

DARTMOUTH–LAKE SUNAPEE

In the west-central part of the state, the towns around prestigious Dartmouth College and rippling Lake Sunapee vary from sleepy, old-fashioned outposts that haven't changed much in decades to bustling, sophisticated towns rife with cafés, art galleries, and boutiques. Among the latter, Hanover and New London are the area's main hubs, both of them increasingly popular as vacation destinations. Although distinct from the Lakes Region, greater Lake Sunapee looks like a miniature Lake Winnipesaukee, albeit with far less commercial development.

For a great drive, follow the Lake Sunapee Scenic and Cultural Byway, which runs for about 25 miles from Georges Mills (a bit northwest of New London) down into Warner, tracing much of the Lake Sunapee shoreline. When you've tired of climbing and swimming and visiting the past, look for small studios of area artists. This part of the state, along with the even quieter Monadnock area to the south, has long been an informal artists' colony where people come to write, paint, and weave in solitude.

ESSENTIALS

Visitor Information Lake Sunapee Region Chamber of Commerce
☎ *603/526–6575, 877/526–6575* ⊕ *www.sunapeevacations.com.*

NEW LONDON

16 miles northwest of Warner, 25 miles west of Tilton.

New London, the home of Colby-Sawyer College (1837), is a good base for exploring the Lake Sunapee region. A campus of stately Colonial-style buildings fronts the vibrant commercial district, where you'll find several cafés and boutiques.

GETTING HERE AND AROUND

From the south, take Exit 11 on Interstate 93 to Crockett Corner and then north on Route 114. From the north, take Exit 12 and travel south on Route 114. Mount Sunapee Ski Area offers a ski shuttle to and from many of the area hotels and B&Bs.

WHERE TO EAT AND STAY

$$
AMERICAN
✕ **Flying Goose Brew Pub & Grille.** With 12 handcrafted beers and additional seasonal varieties made with hops grown on-site, this inviting restaurant, pub, and solar-powered brewery is a hit with beer connoisseurs. Standouts include juicy ribs, paper-thin onion rings, fresh-cut steaks, and the Memphis burger with pulled pork and coleslaw piled on top. The menu changes twice a year, in the summer and fall. Enjoy live music on Thursday evening. $ *Average main: $18* ⊠ *40 Andover Rd., at the intersection of Rtes. 11 and 114* ☎ *603/526–6899* ⊕ *www. flyinggoose.com.*

$$
B&B/INN
▣ **Follansbee Inn.** Built in 1840, this quintessential country inn on the shore of Kezar Lake is the kind of place that almost automatically turns strangers into friends. **Pros:** relaxed lakefront setting; clean rooms; nice breakfast. **Cons:** not all rooms have lake views; some Wi-Fi dead zones.

[$] Rooms from: $159 ✉ 2 Keyser St., North Sutton ☎ 603/927–4221, 800/626–4221 🌐 www.follansbeeinn.com 🛏 17 rooms 🍴 Breakfast.

$$ B&B/INN 🏨 **The Inn at Pleasant Lake.** Across Pleasant Lake from majestic Mt. Kearsarge, this 1790s inn has spacious rooms filled with country antiques. **Pros:** lakefront with a small beach; kayaks and stand-up paddleboards available. **Cons:** away from town; no cell phone coverage. *[$] Rooms from: $165 ✉ 853 Pleasant St. ☎ 603/526–6271, 800/626–4907 🌐 www.innatpleasantlake.com 🛏 10 rooms 🍴 Breakfast.*

THE ARTS

New London Barn Playhouse. Broadway-style and children's plays are presented here every summer in New Hampshire's oldest continuously operating theater. *✉ 84 Main St. ☎ 603/526–6710 🌐 www.nlbarn.org.*

4

SPORTS AND THE OUTDOORS

Rollins State Park. A 3½-mile scenic route through Rollins State Park snakes up the southern slope of Mt. Kearsarge, where you can hike a ½-mile trail to the summit. The road often closes in winter due to hazardous conditions. *✉ 1066 Kearsarge Rd., off Rte. 103, Warner ☎ 603/456–3808 🌐 www.nhstateparks.org 🎟 $4.*

SHOPPING

Artisan's. This shop carries jewelry, beads, gourmet foods, clothing, and other local crafts. *✉ 11 Pleasant St. ☎ 603/526–4227 🌐 www.artisansnewlondon.com.*

NEWBURY

8 miles southwest of New London.

Newbury is on the edge of Mt. Sunapee State Park. The mountain, which rises to an elevation of nearly 3,000 feet, and the sparkling lake are the region's outdoor recreation centers. The popular League of New Hampshire Craftsmen's Fair, the nation's oldest crafts fair, is held at the base of Mt. Sunapee each August.

GETTING HERE AND AROUND

From New London, take 114 West to 103A South, which follows the eastern coast of Lake Sunapee to Newbury.

EXPLORING

The Fells Historic Estate & Gardens. John M. Hay, who served as private secretary to Abraham Lincoln, built the Fells on Lake Sunapee as a summer home in 1890. House tours offer a glimpse of early-20th-century life on a New Hampshire estate. The grounds are a gardener's delight and include a 100-foot-long perennial garden and a rock garden with a brook flowing through it. Miles of hiking trails can also be accessed from the estate. The 40-minute guided house and garden tours cost an additional $6. *✉ 456 Rte. 103A ☎ 603/763–4789 🌐 www.thefells.org 🎟 $10 🕓 Late June–Labor Day, Wed.–Sun. daily 10–4; late May–late June and Labor Day–Columbus Day, weekends 10–4.*

Sunapee Harbor. On the west side of Lake Sunapee, this an old-fashioned summer resort community with a large marina, a handful of restaurants and shops on the water, a tidy village green with a gazebo, and a small museum. A plaque outside Wild Goose Country Store details some of Lake Sunapee's attributes: for exmaple, it's one of the highest lakes in New Hampshire, and one of the least polluted. Lake Sunapee has brook and lake trout, salmon, smallmouth bass, perch, and pickerel. ✉ *Sunapee* 🌐 *www.sunapeevacations.com.*

WHERE TO EAT

$$ AMERICAN 🍴 **Anchorage at Sunapee Harbor.** Fans of this long gray restaurant with a sprawling deck overlooking Sunapee Harbor's marina come as much for the great views as for the dependable—and occasionally creative—American chow. It's as likely a place for a burger or fried seafood platter as for homemade lobster spring rolls. There's also live entertainment some nights—in fact, this is where the founders of the rock band Aerosmith first met back in the early 1970s. [$] *Average main: $18* ✉ *71 Main St., Sunapee Harbor* ☎ *603/763–3334* 🌐 *www.theanchorageatsunapeeharbor.com* 🕒 *Closed Oct.–mid-May and Mon.*

WHERE TO STAY

$$$$ RENTAL 🏨 **Sunapee Harbor Cottages.** This charming collection of six private cottages is within a stone's throw of Sunapee Harbor. **Pros:** spacious units; no minimum stays. **Cons:** no maid service; little clothes storage. [$] *Rooms from: $225* ✉ *4 Lake Ave., Sunapee Harbor* ☎ *603/763–5052, 866/763–5052* 🌐 *www.sunapeeharborcottages.com* 🛏 *6 cottages* 🍽 *No meals.*

SPORTS AND THE OUTDOORS

BEACHES

Mt. Sunapee State Park Beach. A great family spot, Sunapee State Beach has picnic areas, fishing, and a bathhouse. You can also rent canoes and kayaks, and there's a campground on-site. **Amenities:** lifeguards; parking (no fee); showers; toilets. **Best for:** swimming; walking. ✉ *86 Beach Access Rd.* ☎ *603/763–5561* 🌐 *www.nhstateparks.org* 🎟 *$5* 🕒 *Memorial Day–Labor Day, daily 9–5.*

BOAT TOURS

Lake Sunapee Cruises. Narrated cruises provide a closer look at Lake Sunapee's history and mountain scenery. They run from late May through mid-October, daily in summer and on weekends in spring and fall. ✉ *Town Dock, 81 Main St., Sunapee Harbor* ☎ *603/938–6465* 🌐 *www.sunapeecruises.com* 🎟 *$20.*

MV *Kearsarge*. Two-hour narrated sunset cruises around the lake are offered aboard the MV *Kearsarge*. With departures June to mid-October, the cruises cost $40 and include a buffet dinner. ✉ *Town Dock, 81 Main St., Sunapee Harbor* ☎ *603/938–6465* 🌐 *www.sunapeecruises.com.*

SKI AREA

Mount Sunapee. This family-friendly resort is one of New England's best-kept secrets. The owners have spent millions upgrading snowmaking and grooming equipment and turning this into a four-seasons resort. Mount Sunapee offers over 1,500 vertical feet of downhill excitement, 11 lifts (including three quads), and 66 trails and slopes for all abilities. There are four terrain parks and nine glade trails. In summer the adventure park features a canopy zipline tour, aerial challenge course, an 18-hole disc-golf course, miniature golf, and numerous hiking trails. ✉ *1398 Rte. 103* ☎ *603/763–3500, 603/763–4020 snow conditions* ⊕ *www.mtsunapee.com.*

SHOPPING
Wild Goose Country Store. On the harbor in Sunapee, the Wild Goose Country Store carries teddy bears, penny candy, pottery, and other engaging odds and ends. ✉ *77 Main St., Sunapee* ☎ *603/763–5516.*

HANOVER

12 miles northwest of Enfield; 62 miles northwest of Concord.

Eleazer Wheelock founded Hanover's Dartmouth College in 1769 to educate the Abenaki "and other youth." When he arrived, the town consisted of about 20 families. The college and the town grew symbiotically, with Dartmouth becoming the northernmost Ivy League school. Hanover is still synonymous with Dartmouth, but it's also a respected medical and cultural center for the upper Connecticut River Valley.

GETTING HERE AND AROUND
Lebanon Municipal Airport, near Dartmouth College, is served by Cape Air (in conjunction with JetBlue) from New York. By car, Interstate 91 North or Interstate 89 are the best ways to get to Lebanon, Hanover, and the surrounding area. Plan on spending a day visiting Hanover and to see all the sights on the Dartmouth campus.

Shops, mostly of the independent variety but with a few upscale chains sprinkled in, line Hanover's main street. The commercial district blends almost imperceptibly with the Dartmouth campus. West Lebanon, south of Hanover on the Vermont border, has many more shops.

ESSENTIALS
Airport Lebanon Municipal Airport ✉ *5 Airport Rd., West Lebanon* ☎ *603/298–8878* ⊕ *www.flyleb.com.*

Taxi Big Yellow Taxi ☎ *603/643–8294* ⊕ *www.bigyellowtaxis.com.*

Visitor Information Hanover Area Chamber of Commerce ✉ *Nugget Arcade Bldg., 53 S. Main St., Suite 216* ☎ *603/643–3115* ⊕ *www.hanoverchamber.org.*

EXPLORING
Dartmouth College. Robert Frost spent part of a brooding freshman semester at this Ivy League school before giving up college altogether. The buildings that cluster around the green include the **Baker Memorial Library,** which houses such literary treasures as 17th-century editions of William Shakespeare's works. The library is also well known for Mexican artist José Clemente Orozco's 3,000-square-foot murals that depict the story of civilization in the Americas. ✉ *N. Main and Wentworth Sts.* ☎ *603/646–1110* ⊕ *www.dartmouth.edu.*

QUICK BITES

Dirt Cowboy Cafe. Take a respite from museum-hopping with a cup of espresso, a ham-and-cheese scone, or a freshly baked brownie at the Dirt Cowboy, a café across from the green and beside a used-book store. ✉ *7 S. Main St.* ☎ *603/643–1323* ⊕ *www.dirtcowboycafe.com.*

DID YOU KNOW?

The Baker Memorial Library was modeled after Independence Hall in Philadelphia. Today it is the heart of the Dartmouth College campus in Hanover.

Enfield Shaker Museum. In 1782, two Shaker brothers from Mount Lebanon, New York, arrived on Lake Mascoma's northeastern side, about 12 miles southeast of Hanover. Eventually, they formed Enfield, the ninth of 18 Shaker communities in the United States, and moved it to the lake's southern shore, where they erected more than 200 buildings. The Enfield Shaker Museum preserves the legacy of the Shakers, who numbered 330 members at the village's peak. By 1923 interest in the society had dwindled, and the last 10 members joined the Canterbury community, south of Laconia. A self-guided walking tour takes you through 13 of the remaining buildings, among them an 1849 stone mill. Demonstrations of Shaker crafts techniques and numerous special events take place year-round. ☒ *447 Rte. 4A, Enfield* ☎ *603/632–4346* ⊕ *www.shakermuseum.org* 🖃 *$12* ☉ *Mon.–Sat. 10–4, Sun. noon–4.*

Hopkins Center for the Arts. If the towering arcade at the entrance to the Hopkins Center for the Arts appears familiar, it's probably because it resembles the project that architect Wallace K. Harrison completed just after designing it: New York City's Metropolitan Opera House at Lincoln Center. The complex includes a 900-seat theater for film showings and concerts, a 480-seat theater for plays, and a black-box theater for new plays. The Dartmouth Symphony Orchestra performs here. ☒ *Dartmout College, 2 East Wheelock St.* ☎ *603/646–2422* ⊕ *hop. dartmouth.edu.*

Hood Museum of Art. In addition to African, Peruvian, Oceanic, Asian, European, and American art, the Hood Museum of Art owns the Pablo Picasso painting *Guitar on a Table*, silver by Paul Revere, and a set of Assyrian reliefs from the 9th century BC. The range of contemporary works, including pieces by John Sloan, William Glackens, Mark Rothko, Fernand Léger, and Joan Miró, is particularly notable. Rivaling the collection is the museum's architecture: a series of austere, copper-roofed, redbrick buildings arranged around a courtyard. Free campus tours are available on request. ☒ *Dartmouth College, Wheelock St.* ☎ *603/646–2808* ⊕ *www.hoodmuseum.dartmouth.edu* 🖃 *Free* ☉ *Tues. and Thurs.–Sat. 10–5, Wed. 10–9, Sun. noon–5.*

OFF THE BEATEN PATH

Upper Valley. From Hanover you can make a 60-mile drive up Route 10 all the way to Littleton for a highly scenic tour of the upper Connecticut River valley. You'll have views of the river and Vermont's Green Mountains from many points. The road passes through groves of evergreens, over leafy ridges, and through delightful hamlets. Grab gourmet picnic provisions at the general store on Lyme's village common—probably the most pristine of any in the state—and stop at the bluff-top village green in historical Haverhill (28 miles north of Hanover) for a picnic amid the panorama of classic Georgian- and Federal-style mansions and faraway farmsteads.

WHERE TO EAT

$$ ✕ Canoe Club. Bedecked with canoes, paddles, and classic Dartmouth
AMERICAN paraphernalia, this festive spot presents live jazz and folk music most nights. The mood may be casual, but the kitchen presents rather imaginative food, including memorable starters like a roasted beet medley with a spiced chocolate sauce and an orange glaze, or steamed mussels

in a delectable garlic-and-herb sauce. Among the main courses, the seafood cioppino, with shrimp, scallops, onion, and sweet pepper, is a favorite. There's also a lighter, late-night menu. $ *Average main: $19* ⊠ *27 S. Main St.* ☎ *603/643–9660* ⊕ *www.canoeclub.us.*

$ ✕ **Lou's Restaurant.** One of the few places in town where students and
AMERICAN locals really mix, this place is hard to resist. A Hanover tradition since 1948, this diner-cum-café-cum-bakery serves possibly the best breakfast in the valley—a plate of *migas* (eggs, cheddar, salsa, and guacamole mixed with tortilla chips) can fill you up for the better part of the day; blueberry-cranberry buttermilk pancakes also satisfy. Or grab a seat at the old-fashioned soda fountain and order an ice cream sundae. Lou's can accommodate gluten-free diets, too. $ *Average main: $9* ⊠ *30 S. Main St.* ☎ *603/643–3321* ⊕ *lousrestaurant.net* ☾ *No dinner.*

$$ ✕ **Lui Lui.** The creatively topped thin-crust pizzas and huge portions of
ITALIAN pasta are only part of the draw at this chatter-filled eatery; the other is its dramatic setting inside a former power station on the Mascoma River. Pizza picks include the Tuscan (mozzarella topped with tomato and roasted garlic) and the grilled chicken with barbecue sauce. Pasta fans should dive into a bowl of linguine with homemade clam sauce. $ *Average main: $17* ⊠ *8 Glen Rd., West Lebanon* ☎ *603/298–7070* ⊕ *www.luilui.com.*

$$ ✕ **Murphy's On the Green.** Students, visiting alums, and locals regularly
ECLECTIC descend upon this popular pub, which has walls lined with shelves of old books. The varied menu features burgers and salads as well as meat loaf, crusted lamb sirloin, and vegetarian dishes like eggplant stuffed with tofu. Check out the extensive beer list. $ *Average main: $19* ⊠ *11 S. Main St.* ☎ *603/643–4075* ⊕ *www.murphysonthegreen.com.*

WHERE TO STAY

$$$$ 🛏 **The Hanover Inn.** If you're in town for a Dartmouth event, you'll want
HOTEL to stay on the college's—and the town's—main square. **Pros:** center of campus and town; great service; handy fitness center. **Cons:** breakfast not included; pricey rates. $ *Rooms from: $349* ⊠ *The Green, 2 S. Main St.* ☎ *603/643–4300, 800/443–7024* ⊕ *www.hanoverinn.com* ➦ *108 rooms, 15 suites* ⊙ *No meals.*

$$ 🛏 **Trumbull House.** The nicely decorated guest rooms of this white
B&B/INN Colonial-style house—on 16 acres on Hanover's outskirts—have king- or queen-size beds, feather pillows, writing desks, and other comfortable touches, as well as Wi-Fi access. **Pros:** quiet setting; lovely home; big breakfast. **Cons:** 3 miles east of town. $ *Rooms from: $169* ⊠ *40 Etna Rd.* ☎ *603/643–2370, 800/651–5141* ⊕ *www.trumbullhouse.com* ➦ *4 rooms, 1 suite, 1 cottage* ⊙ *Breakfast.*

SPORTS AND THE OUTDOORS

Ledyard Canoe Club. On the bank of the Connecticut River, the Ledyard Canoe Club of Dartmouth rents canoes, kayaks, and stand-up paddleboats by the hour. ⊠ *Cliffside Trail, near the Ledyard Bridge* ☎ *603/643–6709* ⊕ *www.dartmouth.edu/~lcc.*

The Cornish–Windsor Bridge is the second-longest covered bridge in the United States, at 460 feet.

CORNISH

22 miles south of Hanover.

Today Cornish is best known for its covered bridges and for being the home of reclusive late author J. D. Salinger, but at the turn of the 20th century the village was known primarily as the home of the country's then most popular novelist, Winston Churchill (no relation to the British prime minister). His novel *Richard Carvell* sold more than a million copies. Churchill was such a celebrity that he hosted Teddy Roosevelt during the president's 1902 visit. At that time Cornish was an enclave of artistic talent. Painter Maxfield Parrish lived and worked here, and sculptor Augustus Saint-Gaudens set up his studio and created the heroic bronzes for which he is known.

GETTING HERE AND AROUND

About 5 miles west of town on Route 44, the Cornish–Windsor Bridge crosses the Connecticut River between New Hampshire and Vermont. The Blacksmith Shop covered bridge is 2 miles east of Route 12A on Town House Road, and the Dingleton Hill covered bridge is 1 mile east of Route 12A on Root Hill Road. Cornish itself is small enough to see in one morning.

EXPLORING

Cornish-Windsor Bridge. This 460-foot bridge, 1½ miles south of the Saint-Gaudens National Historic Site, connects New Hampshire to Vermont across the Connecticut River. It dates from 1866 and is the longest covered wooden bridge in the United States. The notice on the bridge reads: "Walk your horses or pay two dollar fine." ✉ *Bridge St.*

Fodor's Choice
★

Saint-Gaudens National Historic Site. Just south of Plainfield, a small lane leads to this historic site, where you can tour sculptor Augustus Saint-Gaudens's house (with his original furnishings), studio, gallery, and 150 acres of grounds and gardens. Scattered throughout are casts of his works. The property has two hiking trails, the longer of which is the Blow-Me-Down Trail. Concerts are held every Sunday afternoon in July and August. ✉ *139 Saint-Gaudens Rd., off Rte. 12A* ☎ *603/675–2175* ⊕ *www.nps.gov/saga* ✉ *$5* ⊙ *Memorial Day–Oct., daily 9–4:30.*

SPORTS AND THE OUTDOORS

North Star Canoe Rentals. Rent a canoe, kayak, or inner tube and enjoy a lazy float down the Connecticut River, with stops en route for swimming and sunbathing. North Star Canoe will bring you back to your car. For a bigger adventure, join in one of the half- or full-day or overnight trips. ✉ *1356A Rte. 12A* ☎ *603/542–6929* ⊕ *www.kayak-canoe.com.*

THE MONADNOCKS AND MERRIMACK VALLEY

Southwestern and south-central New Hampshire mix village charm with city hustle and bustle across two distinct regions. The Merrimack River Valley has the state's largest and fastest-growing cities: Nashua, Manchester, and Concord. To the west, in the state's sleepy southwestern corner, is the Monadnock region, one of New Hampshire's least developed and most naturally stunning parts. Here you'll find plenty of hiking trails as well as peaceful hilltop hamlets that appear barely changed in the past two centuries. Mt. Monadnock, southern New Hampshire's largest peak, stands guard over the Monadnock region, which has more than 200 lakes and ponds. Rainbow trout, smallmouth and largemouth bass, and some northern pike swim in Chesterfield's Spofford Lake. Goose Pond, just north of Keene, holds smallmouth bass and white perch.

NASHUA

98 miles south of Lincoln/North Woodstock; 48 miles northwest of Boston; 36 miles south of Concord; 50 miles southeast of Keene.

Once a prosperous manufacturing town that drew thousands of immigrant workers in the late 1800s and early 1900s, Nashua declined following World War II, as many factories shut down or moved to where labor was cheaper. Since the 1970s, however, the metro area has jumped in population, developing into a charming community. Its low-key downtown has classic redbrick buildings along the Nashua River, a tributary of the Merrimack River. Though not visited by tourists as

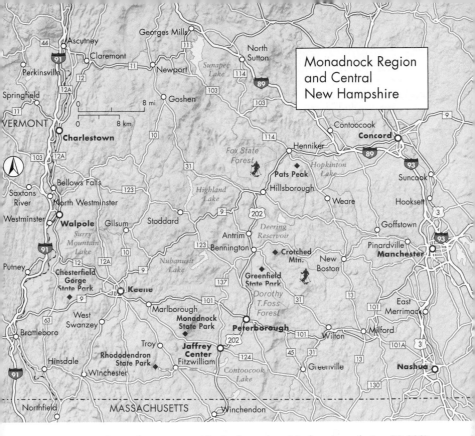

much as other communities in the region, Nashua (population 90,000) has some good restaurants and major shopping centers.

GETTING HERE AND AROUND

A good place to start exploring Nashua is at Main and High streets, where a number of fine restaurants and shops are located. Downtown Nashua has free Wi-Fi.

ESSENTIALS

Taxi D & E Taxi ☎ 603/889–3999. SK Taxi ☎ 603/882–5155.

EXPLORING

Florence Hyde Speare Memorial Museum. The city's impressive industrial history is retold at this museum that houses the Nashua Historical Society. In this two-story museum you'll find artifacts, early furnishings, photos, a vintage printing press, and a research library. Adjacent to the museum is the Federal-style **Abbot-Spalding House**, furnished with 18th- and 19th-century antiques, art, and household items. ⊠ *5 Abbott St.* ☎ *603/883–0015* ⊕ *www.nashuahistoricalsociety.org/spearemuseum* 🖾 *Free* ☉ *Mar.–late-Nov., Tues.–Thurs. 10–4.*

WHERE TO EAT

$$$ BISTRO Fodor's Choice ★ 🍴 **MT's Local Kitchen and Wine Bar.** Part hip bistro, part jazzy wine bar, MT's is so popular that even foodies from across the state line drive here. The regularly changing menu highlights local products and might include pork scaloppine with a cognac-soaked raisin pan sauce or wood-grilled Vermont chicken with marinated mushrooms. The pesto fries are legendary. Wood-fired pizzas are also a specialty—try the one topped with soppressata, stewed dates, caramelized onions, ricotta, and pecans. [$] *Average main: $26* ✉ *212 Main St.* ☎ *603/595–9334* 🌐 *www.mtslocal.com.*

$$$ ITALIAN 🍴 **Villa Banca.** On the ground floor of a dramatic, turreted building, this spot with high ceilings and tall windows specializes in traditional and contemporary Italian cooking. Start with Gorgonzola artichokes and move on to pasta Alfredo. The butternut squash ravioli is a sweet delight, and the macadamia nut–encrusted tilapia will satisfy the fish lover at your table. Note the exotic-martini menu, a big draw at happy hour. [$] *Average main: $22* ✉ *194 Main St.* ☎ *603/598–0500* 🌐 *www.villabanca.com* ⏲ *No lunch weekends.*

MANCHESTER

18 miles north of Nashua, 53 miles north of Boston.

Manchester, with 108,000-plus residents, is New Hampshire's largest city. The town grew up around the Amoskeag Falls on the Merrimack River, which fueled small textile mills through the 1700s. By 1828 Boston investors had bought the rights to the Merrimack's water power and built the Amoskeag Mills, which became a testament to New England's manufacturing capabilities. In 1906 the mills employed 17,000 people and weekly churned out more than 4 million yards of cloth. This vast enterprise served as Manchester's entire economic base; when it closed in 1936 the town was devastated.

Today Manchester is mainly a banking and business center. The old mill buildings have been converted into warehouses, classrooms, restaurants, museums, and office space. The city has the state's major airport, as well as the Verizon Wireless Arena, which hosts minor-league hockey matches, concerts, and conventions.

GETTING HERE AND AROUND

Manchester Airport, the state's largest airport, has rapidly become a cost-effective, hassle-free alternative to Boston's Logan Airport, with nonstop service to more than 20 cities. Manchester can be hard to get around, but it offers a number of taxi services.

ESSENTIALS

Airport Manchester-Boston Regional Airport ✉ *1 Airport Rd.* ☎ *603/624–6556* 🌐 *www.flymanchester.com.*

Taxi Manchester Taxi ☎ *603/623–2222.* **Queen City Taxi** ☎ *603/622–0008.*

Visitor Information Greater Manchester Chamber of Commerce ✉ *54 Hanover St.* ☎ *603/666–6600* 🌐 *www.manchester-chamber.org.*

At the Currier Museum of Art, you can enjoy European and American classics, or visit a nearby Frank Lloyd Wright house.

EXPLORING

Amoskeag Fishways. From May to mid-June, salmon, shad, and river herring "climb" the fish ladder at this spot near the Amoskeag Dam. The visitor center has an underwater viewing window and interactive exhibits and programs about the Merrimack River. ⊠ *6 Fletcher St.* ☎ *603/626–3474* ⊕ *www.amoskeagfishways.org* ☉ *May and June, daily 9–5; July–Apr., Mon.–Sat. 9–5.*

Fodor's Choice ★ **Currier Museum of Art.** This renowned art museum not only offers an astounding permanent collection of works by European and American masters, such as Claude Monet, Edward Hopper, Winslow Homer, John Marin, Andrew Wyeth, and Childe Hassam, but presents changing exhibits of contemporary works. Also run by the Currier is the nearby Frank Lloyd Wright–designed Zimmerman House, built in 1950. Wright called this sparse, utterly functional living space "Usonian," an invented term used to describe 50 such smaller homes based on his vision to create distinctly American architecture. It's New England's only Frank Lloyd Wright–designed residence open to the public. ⊠ *150 Ash St.* ☎ *603/669–6144, 603/626–4158 house tours* ⊕ *www.currier. org* ☞ *$12; $20 with Zimmerman House* ☉ *Sun., Mon., and Wed.–Fri. 11–5, Sat. 10–5.*

NIGHTLIFE AND THE ARTS

THE ARTS

The Palace Theatre. Musicals and plays are presented throughout the year at the Palace Theatre. It also hosts comedy acts, the state's philharmonic and symphony orchestras, and the Opera League of New Hampshire. ✉ *80 Hanover St.* ☎ *603/668–5588 box office* 🌐 *www.palacetheatre.org.*

NIGHTLIFE

Club 313. This popular disco's huge dance floor attracts a diverse crowd, especially gays and lesbians. It also features karaoke, a game room, and drag shows. ✉ *93 S. Maple St.* ☎ *603/628–6813* 🌐 *club313nh.com.*

The Yard. Revelers come from all over to drink at the The Yard. Saturday nights are for country line dancing featuring live music and a midnight rodeo. ✉ *1211 S. Mammoth Rd.* ☎ *603/623–3545* 🌐 *www.theyardrestaurant.com.*

WHERE TO EAT

$$ AMERICAN

🍴 **Cotton.** Inside one of the old Amoskeag Mills buildings, this eatery has mod lighting and furnishings that give it a swanky atmosphere. For warm weather there's also a patio set in an arbor. Chef Jeffrey Paige, a leader in the farm-to-table movement, specializes in putting a new spin on comfort food. Start with pan-seared crab cakes or the lemongrass chicken salad. The menu changes four times a year but might include an all-natural Delmonico steak or wood-grilled scallops with superb sweet-potato hash. The martinis here are so good they've won awards. [$] *Average main: $19* ✉ *75 Arms St.* ☎ *603/622–5488* 🌐 *www.cottonfood.com* 🕒 *No lunch weekends.*

$ AMERICAN Fodor's Choice ★

🍴 **Red Arrow Diner.** This tiny diner is ground zero for presidential hopefuls in New Hampshire come primary season. The rest of the time, a mix of hipsters and oldsters, including comedian and Manchester native Adam Sandler, favor this neon-streaked, 24-hour greasy spoon, which has been going strong since 1922. Filling fare—platters of kielbasa, French toast, liver and onions, chicken Parmesan with spaghetti, and the diner's famous panfries—keeps patrons happy. Homemade sodas and éclairs round out the menu. [$] *Average main: $10* ✉ *61 Lowell St.* ☎ *603/626–1118* 🌐 *redarrowdiner.com.*

WHERE TO STAY

$$ B&B/INN

🏨 **Ash Street Inn.** Because it's in an attractive residential neighborhood of striking Victorian homes, staying in this five-room B&B will give you the best face of Manchester. **Pros:** nicely decorated rooms; walking distance to Currier Museum. **Cons:** not a full-service hotel. [$] *Rooms from: $169* ✉ *118 Ash St.* ☎ *603/668–9908* 🌐 *www.ashstreetinn.com* 🛏 *5 rooms* 🍽 *Breakfast.*

$$$$ B&B/INN

🏨 **Bedford Village Inn.** If you've decided to sacrifice downtown conveniences to venture out to this lovely manor outside of town, its comforts and beauty will reward you. **Pros:** relaxing setting; exceptional grounds; great restaurant. **Cons:** outside of town. [$] *Rooms from: $249* ✉ *2 Olde Bedford Way, Bedford* ☎ *603/472–2001, 800/852–1166* 🌐 *www.bedfordvillageinn.com* 🛏 *12 suites, 2 apartments, 1 cottage* 🍽 *No meals.*

$$ HOTEL **Radisson Hotel Manchester Downtown.** Of Manchester's many chain properties, the 12-story Radisson has the most central location—a short walk from Amoskeag Mills and the great dining along Elm Street. **Pros:** downtown location; free airport shuttles; pets are welcome. **Cons:** fee for parking; unexciting decor. [$] *Rooms from: $159* ✉ *700 Elm St.* ☎ *603/625–1000, 800/967–9033* 🌐 *www.radisson.com/manchester-hotel-nh-03101/nhmanch* 🛏 *244 rooms, 6 suites.*

CONCORD

20 miles northwest of Manchester, 67 miles northwest of Boston, 46 miles northwest of Portsmouth.

New Hampshire's capital (population 42,000) is a quiet town that tends to the state's business but little else—the sidewalks roll up promptly at 6. Stop in town to get a glimpse of New Hampshire's State House, which is crowned by a gleaming gold, eagle-topped dome.

GETTING HERE AND AROUND

The Concord on Foot walking trail winds through the historic district, past 50 sites. Pick up a $2 map at the Greater Concord Chamber of Commerce or at stores along the way. Taxis can help get you around town, though Main Street is easy to walk about.

ESSENTIALS

Taxi Concord Cab ☎ *603/225–4222.*

Visitor Information Greater Concord Chamber of Commerce ✉ *49 S. Main St.* ☎ *603/224–2508* 🌐 *www.concordnhchamber.com.*

TOURS

Concord on Foot. The **Concord on Foot** walking trail winds through the historic district. Pick up a map at the Greater Concord Chamber of Commerce (49 S. Main St.) or stores along the trail.

The Greater Concord Chamber of Commerce. Maps for the walk can be picked up at the Greater Concord The Greater Concord Chamber of Commerce or stores along the trail. ✉ *49 S. Main St., Concord* ☎ *603/224–2508* 🌐 *www.concordnhchamber.com.*

EXPLORING

FAMILY **McAuliffe-Shepard Discovery Center.** New England's only air-and-space center offers a full day of activities that are mostly focused on the heavens. See yourself in infrared light, learn about lunar spacecraft, examine a replica of the Mercury-Redstone rocket, or experience what it's like to travel in space. You can even try your hand at being a television weather announcer. There's more, including a café and gift shop. ✉ *New Hampshire Technical Institute, 2 Institute Dr.* ☎ *603/271–7827* 🌐 *www.starhop.com* 🎟 *$9* 🕒 *Mid-June–Labor Day, Mon.–Sat. 10–5, Sun. 11:30–5; Labor Day–mid-June, Thurs.–Sat. 10–5, Sun. 11:30–5.*

New Hampshire Historical Society. Steps from the state capitol, this museum is a great place to learn about the Concord coach, a popular mode of transportation before railroads. Rotating exhibitions may include locally made quilts or historical protraits of residents. ✉ *6 Eagle*

Sq. ☎ *603/228-6688* 🌐 *www.nhhistory.org* 🎟 *$5.50* 🕒 *July–mid. Oct., Tue.–Sat. 9:30–5, Sun. noon–5; Mon. 9:30–5.*

Pierce Manse. Franklin Pierce lived in this Greek-Revival home before he moved to Washington to become the 14th U.S. president. He's buried nearby. ✉ *14 Horseshoe Pond La.* ☎ *603/225–4555* 🌐 *www.piercemanse.org* 🎟 *$7* 🕒 *Mid-June–early Sept., Tues.–Sat., 11–3; mid-Sept.–mid-Oct., Fri. and Sat, 12–3; otherwise by appt.*

Fodor's Choice ★ **State House.** Take a self-guided tour of this gilt-domed statehouse, a neoclssical treasure built in 1819. This is the oldest capitol building in the nation in which the legislature uses its original chambers. In January through June you can watch the assemblies in action once a week: the 24 senators of the New Hampshire Senate (the fourth-smallest American lawmaking body) meet once a week. In a wild inversion, the state's representatives number 400—one representative per 3,500 residents, a ratio that is a world record. Pick up tour information at the visitors center. While you're there, check out the paraphernalia from decades of presidential primaries. ✉ *104 N. Main St.* ☎ *603/271–2154* 🌐 *www.gencourt.state.nh.us/NH_Visitorcenter/default.htm* 🎟 *Free* 🕒 *Weekdays 8–4.*

WHERE TO EAT AND STAY

$ AMERICAN 🍴 **Arnie's Place.** If you need a reason to make the 1½-mile detour from Interstate 93, then more than 50 kinds of homemade ice cream should do the trick. Try the toasted-coconut, raspberry, or vanilla flavors. The chocolate shakes are a real treat for chocoholics. The lemon freeze will give you an ice cream headache in no time, but it's worth it. A small dining room is available for dishes such as a barbecue platter (smoked on the premises), hamburgers, and hot dogs, but the five walk-up windows and picnic benches are the way to go. [$] *Average main: $11* ✉ *164 Loudon Rd., off I–93, Concord Heights* ☎ *603/228–3225* 🌐 *www.arniesplace.com* 🕒 *Closed mid-Oct.–late Feb.*

$$ ECLECTIC 🍴 **Barley House.** A lively, old-fashioned tavern practically across from the capitol building and usually buzzing with a mix of politicos, business folks, and tourists, the Barley House serves dependable chow: chorizo-sausage pizzas, burgers smothered with a peppercorn-whiskey sauce, chicken potpies, beer-braised bratwurst, and Mediterranean chicken salad—it's an impressive melting pot of a menu. The bar turns out dozens of interesting beers, on tap and by the bottle, and there's also a decent wine list. It's open until 1 am. [$] *Average main: $20* ✉ *132 N. Main St.* ☎ *603/228–6363* 🌐 *www.thebarleyhouse.com* ✍ *Reservations not accepted* 🕒 *Closed Sun.*

$$ THAI 🍴 **Siam Orchid.** This dark, attractive Thai restaurant with a colorful rickshaw gracing its dining room serves spicy and reasonably authentic dishes with flair. It draws a crowd from the capitol each day for lunch. Try the fiery broiled swordfish with shrimp curry sauce or the pine-nut chicken in an aromatic ginger sauce. [$] *Average main: $18* ✉ *158 N. Main St.* ☎ *603/228–3633* 🌐 *www.siamorchid.net* 🕒 *No lunch weekends.*

$$$ · ⊞ **The Centennial.** This is the most modern hotel in New Hampshire, and
HOTEL · it's home to Granite, the state's most contemporary restaurant and bar,
making it a draw for the state's politicians and those doing business
here. **Pros:** super-sleek hotel; very comfortable and clean rooms; great
bar and restaurant. **Cons:** busy. $ *Rooms from: $189* ⊠ *96 Pleasant St.*
☎ *603/227–9000, 800/360–4839* ⊕ *www.thecentennialhotel.com* ⇌ *27
rooms, 5 suites* ⦶ *No meals.*

NIGHTLIFE AND THE ARTS

Capitol Center for the Arts. The Egyptian-motif artwork, part of the origi-
nal 1927 decor, has been restored in the Capitol Center for the Arts. The
center hosts touring Broadway shows, dance companies, and musical
acts. ⊠ *44 S. Main St.* ☎ *603/225–1111* ⊕ *www.ccanh.com.*

Hermanos Cocina Mexicana. The lounge at Hermanos Cocina Mexi-
cana stages live jazz Sunday through Thursday nights, and other
bands on Saturday nights. ⊠ *11 Hills Ave.* ☎ *603/224–5669* ⊕ *www.*
hermanosmexican.com.

SHOPPING

Capitol Craftsman Jewelers. Fine jewelry and crafts are sold at Capi-
tol Craftsman Jewelers. ⊠ *16 N. Main St.* ☎ *603/224–6166* ⊕ *www.*
capitolcraftsman.com.

Mark Knipe Goldsmiths. Near the State House, jewelry designers here cre-
ate original rings, pendants, earrings, bracelets, and more. ⊠ *2 Capitol*
Plaza, Main St. ☎ *603/224–2920* ⊕ *www.knipegold.com.*

CHARLESTOWN

70 miles northwest of Concord.

Charlestown has the state's largest historic district. About 60 homes,
handsome examples of Federal, Greek Revival, and Gothic Revival
architecture, are clustered about the town center; 10 of them were built
before 1800. Several merchants on the main street distribute brochures
that describe an interesting walking tour of the district.

GETTING HERE AND AROUND

You can reach Charlestown from Interstate 91, but it's best to follow
Route 12 North from Keene for a gorgeous scenic route. Walking about
downtown Charlestown should take only 15 minutes of your day, but
it's worth admiring the buildings in the town center. The Fort at No. 4
is less than 2 miles from downtown, north on Route 11.

EXPLORING

FAMILY · **Fort at No. 4.** In 1747 this fort was an outpost on the periphery of
Colonial civilization. That year fewer than 50 militiamen at the fort
withstood an attack by 400 French soldiers, ensuring that northern
New England remained under British rule. Today costumed interpret-
ers at this living-history museum cook dinner over an open hearth and
demonstrate weaving, gardening, and candle making. Each year the
museum holds reenactments of militia musters and battles of the French
and Indian War. ⊠ *267 Springfield Rd., ½ mile north of Charlestown*

☎ *603/826–5700 ⊕ www.fortat4.com ✉ $10 ⊗ May–Aug., Mon.–Sat. 10–4:30, Sun. 10–4; Sept. and Oct., Wed.–Fri. 10–2:30, weekends 10–4.*

SPORTS AND THE OUTDOORS

Morningside Flight Park. Here's a place for the adrenaline junkie: laser tag, ziplines, paragliding, hang gliding, and more. There are lessons too. This place is considered among the best flying areas in the country. Even if you have a fear of flying, stop and watch the bright colors of the gliders as they take off from the 450-foot peak. ✉ *357 Morningside La., off Rte. 12/11 ☎ 603/542–4416 ⊕ flymorningside.kittyhawk.com.*

WALPOLE

4

13 miles south of Charlestown.

Walpole possesses one of the state's most perfect town greens. Bordered by Elm and Washington streets, it's surrounded by homes built about 1790, when the townsfolk constructed a canal around the Great Falls of the Connecticut River and brought commerce and wealth to the area. The town now has 3,200 inhabitants, more than a dozen of whom are millionaires. Walpole is home to Florentine Films, Ken Burns's production company.

GETTING HERE AND AROUND

It's a short jaunt off Route 12, north of Keene. The small downtown is especially photogenic.

WHERE TO EAT

$$
FRENCH
Fodor'sChoice
★

✕ **The Restaurant at L. A. Burdick Chocolate.** Famous candy maker Larry Burdick, who sells his artful hand-filled and hand-cut chocolates to top restaurants around the Northeast, is a Walpole resident. This restaurant has the easygoing sophistication of a Parisian café and may tempt you to linger over an incredibly rich hot chocolate. The Mediterranean-inspired menu utilizes fresh, often local ingredients and changes daily. Of course, dessert is a big treat here, featuring Burdick's tempting chocolates and pastries. For dinner, you might start with a selection of grilled octopus or reduction trio of pâtés, followed by a house beef stew or honey-roasted duck breast. $ *Average main: $17 ✉ 47 Main St. ☎ 603/756–2882 ⊕ www.burdickchocolate.com.*

SHOPPING

Boggy Meadow Farm. At Boggy Meadow Farm you can watch the cheese process unfold, from the 200 cows being milked to the finer process of cheese-making. The farmstead's raw-milk cheeses can be sampled and purchased in the store, as well as cider donuts and root vegetables. It's worth a trip just to see the beautiful 400-acre farm. ✉ *13 Boggy Meadow Lane ☎ 603/756–3300, 877/541–3953 ⊕ www. boggymeadowfarm.com.*

KEENE

17 miles southeast of Walpole; 20 miles northeast of Brattleboro, Vermont; 56 miles southwest of Manchester.

Keene is the largest city in the state's southwest corner. Its rapidly gentrifying main street, with several engaging boutiques and cafés, is America's widest (132 feet). Each year, on the Saturday before Halloween, locals use the street to hold a Pumpkin Festival, where the small town competes with big cities such as Boston for the most jack-o'-lanterns in one place at one time.

ESSENTIALS

Visitor Information Greater Keene Chamber of Commerce ✉ *48 Central Sq.* ☎ *603/352–1303* 🌐 *www.keenechamber.com.* **Monadnock Travel Council** ☎ *800/432–7864* 🌐 *www.monadnocktravel.com.*

EXPLORING

Keene State College. The hub of the local arts community is this bustling college. The Thorne-Sagendorph Art Gallery contains a permanent collection, including works by Richard Meryman, Abbott Handerson Thayer, and Robert Mapplethorpe. ✉ *229 Main St.* ☎ *603/358–2263* 🌐 *www.keene.edu.*

QUICK BITES

Prime Roast. Serving up fine coffee, pastries, and art (covering the walls and tables), Prime Roast is a sensory experience. The beans are roasted and ground on-site, so they're absolutely fresh. It's two blocks from Keene State College. ✉ *16 Main St.* ☎ *603/352–7874* 🌐 *www.primeroastcoffee.com.*

OFF THE BEATEN PATH

Chesterfield's Route 63. If you're in the mood for a country drive, head west from Keene along Route 9 to Route 63 (about 11 miles) and turn left toward the hilltop town of Chesterfield. This is an especially rewarding journey at sunset, as from many points along the road you can see west out over the Connecticut River valley and into Vermont. The village center consists of little more than a handful of dignified granite buildings and a small general store.

WHERE TO EAT AND STAY

$$ MEDITERRANEAN Fodor's Choice ★

🍴 **Luca's.** A deceptively simple storefront bistro overlooking Keene's graceful town square, Luca's dazzles with epicurean creations influenced by Italy, France, Greece, Spain, and North Africa. Enjoy sautéed shrimp with cilantro pesto and plum tomatoes, three-cheese ravioli with artichoke hearts, or grilled salmon marinated in cumin and coriander. Don't forget to order the locally made gelato or sorbet for dessert. Luca's Market, next door, offers many of the same flavors in wraps, salads, and paninis. [$] *Average main: $20* ✉ *10-11 Central Sq.* ☎ *603/358–3335* 🌐 *www.lucascafe.com.*

$$ B&B/INN

🏨 **Chesterfield Inn.** With views of the hill in the distance, the Chesterfield Inn is nestled on a 10-acre farm. **Pros:** attractive gardens; close to the Connecticut River; includes full breakfast. **Cons:** no dinner on Sunday. [$] *Rooms from: $149* ✉ *20 Cross Rd., West Chesterfield* ☎ *603/256–3211, 800/365–5515* 🌐 *www.chesterfieldinn.com* 🛏 *13 rooms, 2 suites* 🍽 *Breakfast.*

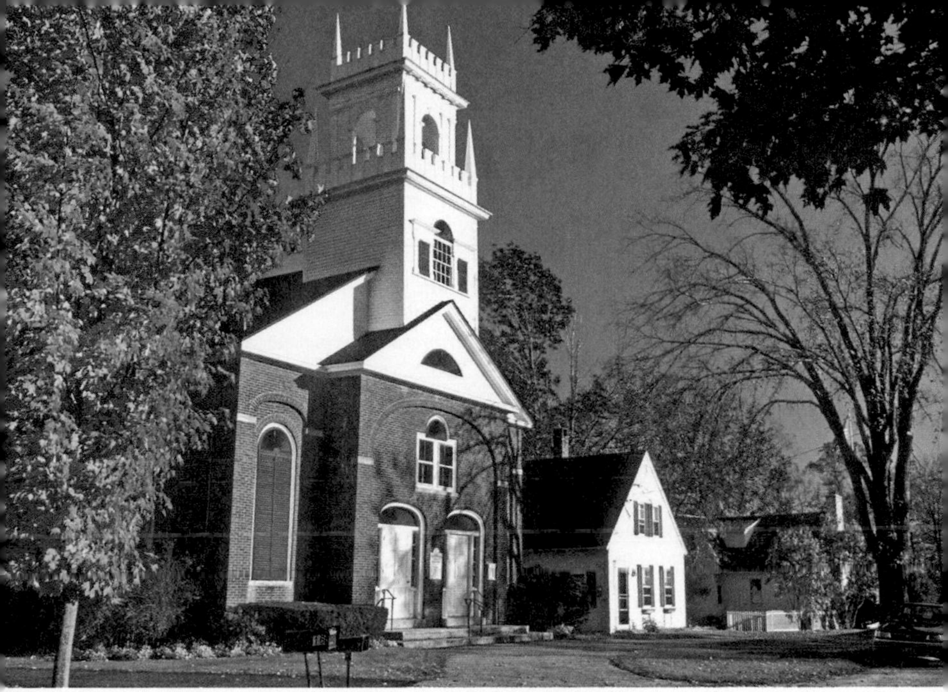

Jaffrey Center is known for its historic buildings and its proximity to Mt. Monadnock.

$$ RESORT FAMILY 🏨 **The Inn at East Hill Farm.** If you have kids who like animals, meet bliss: a family resort with daylong children's programs on a 160-acre farm overlooking Mt. Monadnock. **Pros:** rare agritourism and family resort; activities galore; beautiful setting; no TVs. **Cons:** remote location; noisy mess-hall dining. [$] *Rooms from: $128* ✉ *460 Monadnock St., 10 miles southeast of Keene, Troy* ☎ *603/242–6495, 800/242–6495* 🌐 *www.east-hill-farm.com* 🛏 *65 rooms* 🍴 *All meals.*

$ HOTEL 🏨 **The Lane Hotel.** You get a rare urban touch in the sleepy Monadnocks in this upscale boutique hotel in the middle of Main Street. **Pros:** spacious and comfortable rooms; center of town. **Cons:** no pool. [$] *Rooms from: $99* ✉ *30 Main St.* ☎ *603/354–7900, 603/347–7070* 🌐 *www.thelanehotel.com* 🛏 *33 rooms, 7 suites* 🍴 *Breakfast.*

NIGHTLIFE AND THE ARTS

Colonial Theatre. This renovated 1924 vaudeville theater is now an art movie house (with the largest movie screen in town) and a stage for comedy, music, and dance. ✉ *95 Main St.* ☎ *603/352–2033* 🌐 *www.thecolonial.org.*

Elm City Restaurant & Brewery. Located in the Colony Mill, this microbrewery is an affordable hangout for everyone from college students to families. Its menu runs the gamut: burgers, steaks, and seafood. ✉ *222 West St.* ☎ *603/355–3335* 🌐 *www.elmcitybrewing.com.*

Redfern Art Center on Brickyard Pond. At Keene State College, the Redfern Art Center on Brickyard Pond has year-round music, theater, and dance performances in two theaters and a recital hall. ✉ *Keene State College, 229 Main St.* ☎ *603/358–2168* 🌐 *www.keene.edu/racbp.*

SHOPPING

Fairgrounds Antiques. Operating for 40 years, Fairgrounds Antiques is where vintage shops get their merchandise. There are more than 70 dealers here, and if you're not afraid of a little dust, there's no telling what kind of treasure you'll find. ✉ *249 Monadnock Hwy., East Swanzey* ☎ *603/352–4420* ☉ *Daily 9–5.*

Hannah Grimes Marketplace. Shop here for locally made pottery, kitchenware, soaps, greeting cards, toys, and specialty foods. ✉ *42 Main St.* ☎ *603/352–6862* ⊕ *hannahgrimesmarketplace.com.*

JAFFREY CENTER

16 miles southeast of Keene.

Novelist Willa Cather came to Jaffrey Center in 1919 and stayed in the Shattuck Inn, which now stands empty on Dublin Road. Not far from here, she pitched the tent in which she wrote several chapters of *My Ántonia.* She returned nearly every summer thereafter until her death and was buried in the Old Burying Ground, which also contains the remains of Amos Fortune, a former slave who bought his freedom in 1863 and moved to town when he was 71. Fortune, who was a tanner, also bought the freedom of his two wives. He died at the age of 91.

GETTING HERE AND AROUND

Jaffrey Center's historic district is on Route 124 and is home to a number of brick buildings. It should take less than an hour to view it in its entirety. Two miles east of town on Route 124 can be found the Old Burying Ground, which is behind the Old Meeting House.

ESSENTIALS

Visitor Information Jaffrey Chamber of Commerce ☎ *603/532–4549* ⊕ *www.jaffreychamber.com.*

EXPLORING

Cathedral of the Pines. This outdoor memorial pays tribute to Americans who have sacrificed their lives in service to their country. There's an inspiring view of Mt. Monadnock and Mt. Kearsarge from the Altar of the Nation, which is composed of rock from every U.S. state and territory. All faiths are welcome; organ music for meditation is played at midday from Tuesday through Thursday in July and August. The Memorial Bell Tower, with a carillon of bells from around the world, is built of native stone. Norman Rockwell designed the bronze tablets over the four arches. Flower gardens, an indoor chapel, and a museum of military memorabilia share the hilltop. It's 8 miles southeast of Jaffrey Center. ✉ *10 Hale Hill Rd., off Rte. 119, Rindge* ☎ *603/899–3300* ⊕ *www.cathedralofthepines.org* ▢ *Free* ☉ *May–Oct., daily 9–5.*

SPORTS AND THE OUTDOORS

Monadnock State Park. The oft-quoted statistic about Mt. Monadnock is that it's America's most-climbed mountain—third in the world after Japan's Mt. Fuji and China's Mt. Tai. Whether this is true or not, locals agree that it's never lonely at the top. Some days more than 400 people crowd its bald peak. However, when the parking lot fills up, rangers close the park. Thus, an early morning start, especially during fall foliage, is recommended. Monadnock rises to 3,165 feet, and on a clear day the hazy Boston skyline is visible. Five trailheads branch into more than two dozen trails of varying difficulty (though all rigorous) that wend their way to the top. Allow between three and four hours for any round-trip hike. A visitor center has free trail maps as well as exhibits documenting the mountain's history. In winter you can cross-country ski along roughly 12 miles of groomed trails on the lower elevations of the mountain. ⊠ *116 Poole Rd., off Rte. 124* ☎ *603/532–8862* ⊕ *www. nhstateparks.org* ⊠ *$5* ⊘ *Daily dawn–dusk* ☞ *No pets.*

WHERE TO EAT AND STAY

$$
AMERICAN
✕ **J.P. Stephens Restaurant and Tavern.** An appealing choice for lunch or dinner, this rustic-timbered dining room overlooks a small mill pond in Rindge, about 8 miles south of Jaffrey Center. The 1790 building used to house a sawmill, a gristmill, a forge, and a blacksmith. Now it's an all-around good restaurant with live music on weekends. The Cajun-style sirloin is flavorful, and the apple brandy–and-walnut chicken is sweet and brazen. $ *Average main: $16* ⊠ *377 U.S. 202, Rindge* ☎ *603/899–3322* ⊕ *www.jpstephensrestaurant.com* ⊘ *Closed Mon.*

$$
B&B/INN
Benjamin Prescott Inn. Thanks to the dairy farm surrounding this 1853 Colonial house—with its stenciling and wide pine floors—you feel as though you're miles out in the country rather than just minutes from Jaffrey Center. **Pros:** inexpensive rates; homey and comfortable. **Cons:** some linens a little dated. $ *Rooms from: $129* ⊠ *433 Turnpike Rd.* ☎ *603/532–6637* ⊕ *www.benjaminprescottinn.com* ⊃ *7 rooms, 3 suites* ⦿| *Breakfast.*

$$
B&B/INN
The Fitzwilliam Inn. Once a stagecoach stop, the Fitzwilliam Inn has graced this picturesque town green since 1786. **Pros:** affordable rates; friendly staff; full country breakfast. **Cons:** modest furnishings for such a grand setting. $ *Rooms from: $125* ⊠ *Town Common, 62 Rte. 119 W, Fitzwilliam* ☎ *603/585–9000* ⊕ *www.fitzwilliaminn.com* ⊃ *6 rooms* ⦿| *Breakfast.*

$
B&B/INN
The Monadnock Inn. Rooms in this 1830s home are painted in lively lavenders, yellows, or peaches, a cheery presence in the heart of pristine Jaffrey Center, and a perfect place to get away from it all. **Pros:** well-lit rooms with lacy curtains; feels cozy, like grandma's house. **Cons:** limited amenities. $ *Rooms from: $110* ⊠ *379 Main St.* ☎ *603/532–7800, 877/510–7019* ⊕ *www.monadnockinn.com* ⊃ *11 rooms, 2 suites* ⦿| *Breakfast.*

$$
B&B/INN
Woodbound Inn. A favorite with families and outdoors enthusiasts, this 1819 farmhouse became an inn in 1892. **Pros:** scenic lakefront location; focus on food. **Cons:** older property; simple furnishings; no Wi-Fi service in cabins. $ *Rooms from: $159* ⊠ *247 Woodbound Rd., Rindge* ☎ *603/532–8341, 800/688–7770* ⊕ *www.woodboundinn.com* ⊃ *44 rooms, 11 cabins* ⦿| *Breakfast.*

SHOPPING

Bloomin' Antiques. Fine art and unusual antiques abound in this quaint shop overlooking the town green. ⊠ *Village Green, Fitzwilliam Center* ☎ *603/585–6688.*

PETERBOROUGH

9 miles northeast of Jaffrey Center, 30 miles northwest of Nashua, on Route 101.

Thornton Wilder's play *Our Town* was based on Peterborough. The nation's first free public library opened here in 1833. The town, which was the first in the region to be incorporated (1760), is still a commercial and cultural hub.

GETTING HERE AND AROUND

Parking is just off Main Street, with shopping, coffee, and food all close by. Stand on the bridge and watch the roiling waters of the Nubanusit River on the north end of Main Street.

ESSENTIALS

Visitor Information Greater Peterborough Chamber of Commerce ☎ *603/924–7234* 🌐 *www.peterboroughchamber.com.*

EXPLORING

FAMILY **Mariposa Museum.** You can play instruments or try on costumes from around the world and indulge your cultural curiosity at this nonprofit museum dedicated to hands-on exploration of international folk art. The three-floor museum is inside a historic Baptist church, across from the Universalist church in the heart of town. The museum hosts a number of workshops and presentations on dance and arts and crafts. There's also a children's reading nook and a library. ✉ *26 Main St.* ☎ *603/924–4555* 🌐 *www.mariposamuseum.org* 🎟 *$6* 🕒 *July and Aug., daily 11–5; Sept.–June, Wed.–Sun. 11–5.*

WHERE TO STAY

$ B&B/INN 🏨 **Birchwood Inn.** Henry David Thoreau slept here, probably on his way to climb Monadnock or to visit Jaffrey or Peterborough. **Pros:** nice tavern; pleasant rooms. **Cons:** remote small town great for some, not for others. [$] *Rooms from: $109* ✉ *340 Rte. 45, Temple* ☎ *603/878–3285* 🌐 *www.thebirchwoodinn.com* 🛏 *2 rooms, 2 suites* 🍴 *Breakfast.*

$$ B&B/INN 🏨 **The Hancock Inn.** This Federal-style 1789 inn is the real Colonial deal—the oldest in the state and the pride of this idyllic town 8 miles north of Peterborough. **Pros:** quintessential Colonial inn in a perfect New England town; cozy rooms. **Cons:** remote location. [$] *Rooms from: $165* ✉ *33 Main St., Hancock* ☎ *603/525–3318, 800/525–1789* 🌐 *www.hancockinn.com* 🛏 *13 rooms* 🍴 *Breakfast.*

THE ARTS

Monadnock Music. From early July to late August, Monadnock Music sponsors a series of solo recitals, chamber music concerts, and orchestra and opera performances by renowned musicians. Events take place throughout the area on Wednesday through Saturday evenings at 8 and on Sunday at 4. Many of the offerings are free. ✉ *2A Concord St.* ☎ *603/924–7610, 800/868–9613* 🌐 *www.monadnockmusic.org.*

Peterborough Folk Music Society. The society presents folk music concerts by artists such as John Gorka, Greg Brown, and Cheryl Wheeler. Concerts are held monthly October through April in the Peterborough

Players Theater, a fantastic repurposed old barn. ⊠ *Hadley Rd., off Middle Hancock Rd.* ☎ *603/827–2905* ⊕ *pfmsconcerts.org.*

Peterborough Players. The Peterborough Players have performed since 1933 and stage their productions in a converted barn from late June through mid-September. ⊠ *55 Hadley Rd.* ☎ *603/924–7585 box office* ⊕ *www.peterboroughplayers.org.*

SPORTS AND THE OUTDOORS

GOLF

Crotched Mountain Golf Club. At the Donald Ross–designed Crotched Mountain Golf Club you'll find a hilly, rolling 18-hole layout with nice view of the Monadnocks. ⊠ *740 Francestown Rd., Francestown* ☎ *603/588–2923* ⊕ *www.crotchedmountaingolfclub.com* ☜ *Greens fee: $49* ⌀ *18 holes, 6,111 yards, par 71.*

SKI AREA

Crotched Mountain. New Hampshire's southernmost skiing and snowboarding facility has 17 trails, half of them intermediate, and the rest divided pretty evenly between beginner and expert. There's an 875-foot vertical drop. The slopes have ample snowmaking capacity, ensuring good skiing all winter long. Crotched Mountain is famous for its night skiing—if you can stay up you will save on a lift ticket and maybe hear a few good bands. Other facilities include a 40,000-square-foot lodge with a couple of restaurants, a ski school, and a snow camp for youngsters. ⊠ *615 Francestown Rd., Bennington* ☎ *603/588–3668* ⊕ *www.crotchedmountain.com.*

SHOPPING

Depot Square. Whether you're looking for a regional book, gourmet wine and cheese, handmade gifts and crafts, or unusual gardening accessories, these 14 unique shops in the heart of town turn shoppers into treasure hunters. ⊠ *18 Depot St.* ☎ *603/924–6893* ⊕ *www.shoppeterboroughnh.com.*

Dodge Farm Antiques. Sports-related antiques, vintage kitchenware, and vintage children's toys can be found in this small but classy shop. ⊠ *7 School St.* ☎ *917/922–3910* ⊕ *www.dodgefarmantiques.com.*

Eastern Mountain Sports. The retail outlet of Eastern Mountain Sports sells everything from tents to skis to hiking boots, offers hiking and camping classes, and conducts kayaking and canoeing demonstrations. ⊠ *1 Vose Farm Rd.* ☎ *603/924–7231* ⊕ *www.ems.com.*

Sharon Arts Center. This nonprofit art center exhibits thought-provoking, yet completely accessible, edgy contemporary art. It sells the works of 180 regional artists working in media from pottery to fiber. ⊠ *20-40 Depot St.* ☎ *603/924–2787* ⊕ *www.sharonarts.org.*

INLAND MAINE

WELCOME TO INLAND MAINE

TOP REASONS TO GO

★ **Baxter State Park:** Mt. Katahdin, the state's highest peak, stands as a sentry over Baxter's forestland in its "natural wild state."

★ **Moosehead Lake:** Surrounded by mountains, Maine's largest lake—dotted with islands and chiseled with inlets and coves—retains the rugged beauty that so captivated author Henry David Thoreau in the mid-1800s.

★ **Water Sports:** It's easy to get out on the water with scheduled cruises on large inland lakes; marinas and outfitters rent boats, canoes, and kayaks throughout the region and run white-water-rafting trips on several rivers.

★ **Winter Pastimes:** Downhill skiing, snowmobiling, snowshoeing, cross-country skiing, and dogsledding are all popular winter sports.

★ **Foliage Drives:** Maine's best fall foliage is inland, where hardwoods outnumber spruce, fir, and pine trees in many areas.

1 Western Lakes and Mountains. Lakes both quiet and busy, classic New England villages, and ski resorts fit perfectly in the forested landscape. In winter this is ski country; snowmobiling and snowshoeing are also popular. In summer the woods and water draw vacationers for a cool escape. In fall, foliage drives invite exploration of the region's national forest and state parks. In spring there are no crowds, but fishermen, white-water rafters, and canoeists make their way here.

2 The North Woods. Much of the North Woods' private forestland is open for public recreation and best experienced by paddling a canoe or raft, hiking, snowshoeing, snowmobiling, or fishing. Some great destinations are mostly undeveloped: Moosehead Lake, Baxter State Park, and Allagash Wilderness Waterway. Greenville, a laid-back and woodsy resort town, is a good base for day trips—take a drive (go slow!) down a "moose alley."

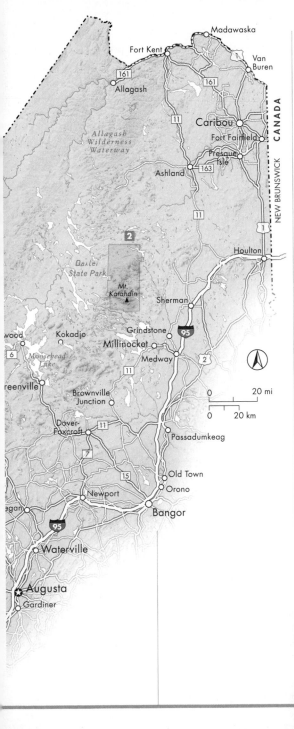

**Allagash
Wilderness
Waterway**

**Baxter
State Park**

Mt.
Katahdin

CANADA

NEW BRUNSWICK

20 mi

20 km

GETTING
ORIENTED

Though Maine is well known for its miles of craggy coastline, the inland part of the state is surprisingly vast and much less populated. Less than an hour's drive from the bays and ocean, huge swaths of forestland are dotted with lakes (sometimes called "ponds" despite their size). Summer camps, ski areas, and small villages populate the mountainous western part of the state, which stretches north along the New Hampshire border to Québec. Quiet waters are easy to find inland, but busier Sebago Lake is just north of coastal Portland, Maine's largest city. In the remote north-central part of the state, wilderness areas beckon outdoors lovers to the North Woods, which extend north and west to Canada.

5

By Mary Ruoff   Unlike Maine's more famous, more populated, and more visited coast, inland Maine is a four-season destination. With strings of lakes and rivers framed by mountainous terrain, hilly pastoral stretches, classic New England villages with restaurants and shops that entice but don't overwhelm, and the region's most extensive wilderness areas, Maine's interior lures visitors in summer, fall, winter, and spring (yes, the slow season, but canoeists, fishermen, and white-water rafters venture inland).

The most visited areas are the Western Lakes and Mountains—stretching east and north from the New Hampshire border—and the North Woods—extending north from central Maine. While much of inland Maine is remote and rugged, opportunities for outdoor recreation are plentiful and renowned, and crowds do form here, though thankfully they're scattered and don't set the tone.

Sebago and Long lakes, north of Portland and the gateway to the Western Lakes and Mountains region, hum with boaters and watercraft in the summer. Sidewalks fill and traffic slows along the causeway in the tourist hub of Naples. Baxter State Park, a 210,000-acre wilderness park in the North Woods, has Mt. Katahdin (an Abenaki Indian word for "Great Mountain"), Maine's highest peak and the terminus of the Appalachian Trail. But while you can hike in much of the park and see few other visitors even during peak season, the treeless, rocky summit of Katahdin and the trails to it are often packed with hikers in July and August and on nice weekends in September and early October.

Come winter, ski resorts wait for big snows and make snow in between. Maine often gets snow when the rest of New England doesn't, or vice versa, so track the weather here if you're coming to partake in winter sports or simply to enjoy the season's serenity. Maine's largest ski resorts, Sugarloaf and Sunday River, are in the Western Lakes and Mountains region. So are up-and-coming Saddleback Mountain in

Rangeley and Shawnee Peak in Bridgton, both family-friendly resorts. But not to worry, the lift lines don't get too long.

"Rusticators" began flocking to Maine to vacation in the mid-1800s, arriving at inland destinations by train or steamship, just as they did on Maine's coast. Escaping the summer heat and city pollution, these wealthy urbanites headed to the mountains to hike, swim, canoe, fish, hunt, and relax, staying at rustic sporting camps or at the grand hotels that cropped up in some of the most scenic spots. Moosehead Lake's Mt. Kineo—a walled outcropping north of Greenville where Indian tribes from throughout the Northeast came for flint-like stone—gave rise to one of the nation's largest and fanciest hotels in the late 1800s. Rangeley was discovered for its sport fishing in the mid-1800s and is still a haven for anglers, who come to fish for "world-class" brook trout and landlocked salmon. Modern streamer fly-fishing was born in the Rangeley region, and many of the local waters are restricted to fly-fishing.

The legacy of the rusticators and the locals who catered to them lives on at the sporting camps still found on inland Maine's remote lakes and rivers, albeit in fewer numbers. It also survives through Maine's unique system of licensed outdoor guides, known as Registered Maine Guides. These days they may lead kayak trips, hiking expeditions, white-water rafting excursions, and moose safaris as well as fishing, hunting, and canoe trips. Guides are happy to show you their license—it's the law that they have one, and some also opt to wear a badge.

PLANNING

WHEN TO GO

Inland's Maine's most popular hiking trails and lakeside beaches may get busy in warm weather, but if splendid isolation is what you crave, you can easily find it. In summer, traffic picks up but rarely creates jams, except in a few spots. Peak lodging rates apply, but moderate weather makes this a great time to visit. Inland Maine gets hotter than the coast, though less so along lakes and at higher elevations. July and August are warmest; September is less busy.

Western Maine is the state's premier destination for leaf peepers—hardwoods are more abundant here than on the coast. Late September through mid-October is peak foliage season.

Maine's largest ski areas can make their own snow; at least one of them opens its doors in mid-November and remains open until May. Inland Maine typically has snow cover by Christmas, so cross-country skiing, snowshoeing, and snowmobiling are in full swing by the end of the year. In ski towns many lodgings charge peak rates in the winter.

Snowmelt ushers in mud season in early spring. Mid-May to mid-June is black fly season; they're especially pesky in the woods but less bothersome in town. Spring is a prime time for canoeing and fishing.

PLANNING YOUR TIME

Inland Maine locales are often destinations where visitors stay their entire trip. That's certainly true of those who come to ski at a resort, fish at a remote sporting camp, or just relax at a lakeside cabin. After a day hike on a mountain trail reached by driving gravel logging roads, visitors are unlikely to hurry on to another town. Vacation rental homes and cottages often require a week's stay, as do lakeside cottage resorts. Generally speaking, the farther inland you go, the farther it is between destinations.

GETTING HERE AND AROUND

AIR TRAVEL

Two primary airports serve Maine: Portland International (PWM) and Bangor International (BGR). Portland is closer to the Western Lakes and Mountains area; Bangor is more convenient to the North Woods. Regional flying services, operating from regional and municipal airports, provide access to remote lakes and wilderness areas and offer scenic flights.

CAR TRAVEL

Because Maine is large and rural, a car is essential. U.S. 2 is the major east–west thoroughfare in Western Maine, winding from Bangor to New Hampshire. Interstate 95 is a departure point for many visitors to inland Maine, especially the North Woods. The highway heads inland at Brunswick and is a toll road, the Maine Turnpike, from the New Hampshire border to Augusta. Because of the hilly terrain and abundant lakes and rivers, inland Maine roads are often curvy. Traffic rarely gets heavy, though highways often pass right through instead of around the larger towns, which can slow your trip a bit.

There are few public roads in Maine's North Woods, though private logging roads there are often open to the public (sometimes by permit and fee). When driving these roads, always give lumber-company trucks the right-of-way; loggers must drive in the middle of the road and often can't move over or slow down for cars. Be sure to have a full tank of gas before heading onto the many private roads in the region.

RESTAURANTS

Fear not, lobster lovers: this succulent, emblematic Maine food is on the menu at many inland restaurants, from fancier establishments to roadside places. Lobster dishes are more common than boiled lobster dinners, but look for daily specials. Shrimp, scallops, and other seafood are also menu mainstays, and you may find surprises like bison burgers or steaks from a nearby farm. Organic growers and natural foods producers are planted throughout the state and often sell their food to finer restaurants nearby. Seasonal foods like pumpkins, blackberries, and strawberries make their way into homemade desserts, as do Maine's famed blueberries. Many lakeside resorts and sporting camps have a reputation for good food; some of the latter will cook the fish you catch. *Prices in the reviews are the average cost of a main course at dinner or, if dinner is not served, at lunch.*

HOTELS

Although there is a higher concentration of upscale inns on the coast than inland, you'll find well-run inns, B&Bs, and motels throughout the region, including some sophisticated lodgings. At those located near ski resorts, peak-season rates may apply in winter and summer. The two largest ski resorts, Sunday River and Sugarloaf, offer a choice of hotels and condos. Greenville has the largest selection of lodgings in the North Woods region, with both fine and homey inns. Lakeside sporting camps, from the primitive to the upscale, are popular around Rangeley and the North Woods. Many have cozy cabins heated with woodstoves and serve three hearty meals a day. Conservation organizations also operate wilderness retreats. In Maine's mountains, as on its coast, many small inns and B&Bs don't have air-conditioning. *Prices in the reviews are the lowest cost of a standard double room in high season.*

VISITOR INFORMATION

Maine Office of Tourism ☎ 888/624–6345 ⊕ www.visitmaine.com.

Maine Tourism Association ☎ 207/623–0363, 800/767–8709 ⊕ www.mainetourism.com.

5

WESTERN LAKES AND MOUNTAINS

From Sebago Lake, less than 20 miles northwest of Portland, the sparsely populated Western Lakes and Mountains region stretches north and west, bordered by New Hampshire and Québec. Each season offers different outdoor highlights: you can choose from snow sports, hiking, mountain biking, leaf peeping, fishing, swimming, and paddling. The Sebago Lake area bustles with activity in summer. Bridgton is a classic New England town, as is Bethel, in the valley of the Androscoggin River. Sunday River, a major ski resort, is nearby. The more rural Rangeley Lake area brings long stretches of pine, beech, spruce, and sky and more classic inns. Just north of Kingfield is Sugarloaf Mountain Resort, Maine's other big ski resort. Like Sunday River, it offers a host of summer activities.

SEBAGO LAKE AREA

20 miles northwest of Portland.

The shores of sprawling Sebago Lake and finger-like Long Lake are popular with water sports enthusiasts, as are Brandy Pond and many other bodies of water in the area. The Songo River links several of these lakes, forming one continuous waterway. Naples, on the causeway separating Long Lake from Brandy Pond, pulses with activity in the summer, when the area swells with seasonal residents and weekend visitors. Open-air cafés overflow with patrons, boats buzz along the water, and families parade along the sidewalk edging Long Lake. On clear days the view includes snowcapped Mt. Washington.

GETTING HERE AND AROUND

Sebago Lake, gateway to Maine's Western Lakes and Mountains, is less than 20 miles from Portland on U.S. 302.

CLOSE UP

Outdoor Activities

People visit inland Maine year-round for hiking, biking (mountain biking is big at ski resorts off-season), camping, fishing, downhill and cross-country skiing, snowshoeing, and snowmobiling.

The Kennebec and Dead rivers, which converge at The Forks in Western Maine, and the West Branch of the Penobscot River, near Millinocket in the North Woods, provide thrilling white-water rafting. Boating, canoeing, and kayaking are also possibilities.

BICYCLING
Bicycle Coalition of Maine. For information on bicycling in Maine, contact the Bicycle Coalition of Maine. ☎ 207/623–4511 ⊕ www.bikemaine. org.

FISHING
Maine Department of Inland Fisheries and Wildlife. For information about fishing licenses, contact the Maine Department of Inland Fisheries and Wildlife. ☎ 207/287–8000 ⊕ www.mefishwildlife.com.

HIKING
Maine Appalachian Trail Club. The Maine Appalachian Trail Club publishes seven Appalachian Trail maps ($8) and a Maine trail guide ($30). ⊕ www.matc.org.

Maine Trail Finder. Visitors can find Maine trails to hike, mountain bike, snowshoe, and ski on this website, which includes trail descriptions, photos, user comments, directions, links to maps, weather conditions, and more. ☎ 207/778–0900 ⊕ www. mainetrailfinder.com.

RAFTING
Maine Professional Guides Association. This association helps you find state-licensed guides to lead kayaking, canoeing, and white-water rafting trips. There are also other trips available, ranging from fishing trips to wildlife-watching excursions. ⊕ www. maineguides.org.

SKIING
Ski Maine. For alpine and cross-country skiing information, contact Ski Maine. ☎ 207/773–7669 ⊕ skimaine. com.

SNOWMOBILING
Maine Snowmobile Association. This association's excellent statewide map of about 3,500 miles of interconnected trails is available online. ☎ 207/622–6983 ⊕ www.mesnow. com.

ESSENTIALS
Vacation Rentals Krainin Real Estate ✉ 1539 Roosevelt Tr., Raymond ☎ 207/655–3811 ⊕ www.krainin.com.

Visitor Information Sebago Lakes Region Chamber of Commerce ✉ 747 Roosevelt Tr., Windham ☎ 207/892–8265 ⊕ www.sebagolakeschamber.com.

EXPLORING
Sebago Lake. This is Maine's second-largest lake, and provides Greater Portland's drinking water. Year-round and seasonal dwellings (from simple camps to sprawling showplaces) line the shores of the lake. ✉ Windham ☎ 207/892–8265 ⊕ www.sebagolakeschamber.com.

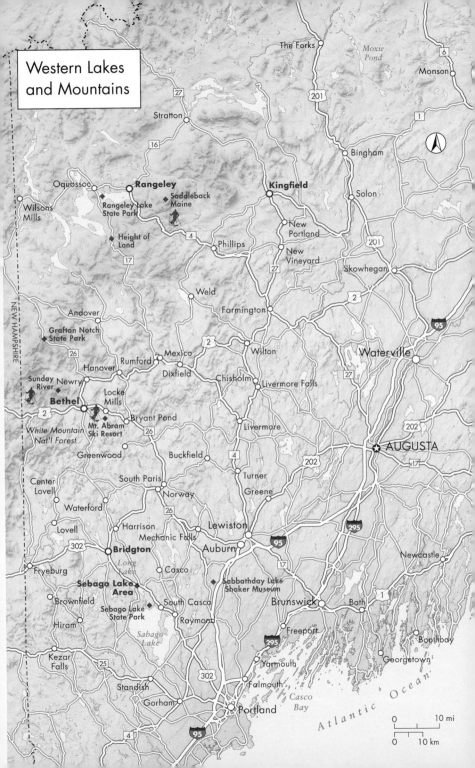

Western Lakes and Mountains

NEW HAMPSHIRE

The Forks

Moxie Pond

Monson

6

201

Bingham

Stratton

27

16

Solon

201

Oquossoc

Rangeley

Saddleback
Maine

Kingfield

Rangeley Lake
State Park

New
Portland

Height of
Land

17

Phillips

27

New
Vineyard

Skowhegan

Wilsons
Mills

4

Weld

Farmington

201

Andover

Mexico

2

Wilton

2

Waterville

95

Grafton Notch
State Park

26

Rumford

Dixfield

Chisholm

Livermore Falls

27

Hanover

Sunday
River

Newry

Bethel

Locke
Mills

Bryant Pond

Livermore

202

AUGUSTA

2

Mt. Abram
Ski Resort

26

Buckfield

4

202

17

White Mountain
Nat'l Forest

Greenwood

South Paris

Turner

Center
Lovell

Norway

Greene

Waterford

26

Lovell

Harrison

Lewiston

295

Mechanic Falls

Bridgton

302

Auburn

95

Newcastle

Fryeburg

Long
Lake

Casco

17

**Sebago Lake
Area**

Sabbathday Lake
Shaker Museum

1

Brownfield

Sebago Lake
State Park

South Casco

Brunswick

Bath

Hiram

Raymond

295

Freeport

Boothbay

Kezar
Falls

Sabago
Lake

Georgetown

25

Yarmouth

Standish

302

Falmouth

Casco
Bay

Gorham

Portland

95

4

Atlantic Ocean

0   10 mi

0   10 km

Sebago Lake State Park. This 1,400-acre park on the north shore of Sebago Lake is a great spot for swimming, boating, and fishing for both salmon and togue. A pleasant picnic area is Songo Lock State Historic Site, an operational lock along the twisty, narrow Songo River. Bicycling along the park's roads is a popular pastime in warm weather. Come winter, the park's 6 miles of hiking trails are groomed for cross-country skiing. ✉ *11 Park Access Rd., Casco* ☎ *207/693–6231* 🌐 *www.parksandlands.com* 🎟 *$6.50* 🕓 *9–sunset.*

OFF THE BEATEN PATH

Sabbathday Lake Shaker Village. Established in the late 18th century, this is the last active Shaker community in the world, with only three members. Open for guided one-hour tours are several buildings with Shaker furniture, folk art, tools, farm implements, and crafts from the 18th to the early 20th century. Besides the 1794 Meetinghouse, there's also the 1839 Ministry's Shop, where the elders and eldresses lived until the early 1900s, and the 1821 Sisters' Shop, where household goods and candies were made. The 1850 Boys' Shop has an exhibit on Shaker childhood. You can tour the herb garden on Tuesday and Thursday afternoon in July and August. If you're here in late August, don't miss the popular Maine Native American Summer Market and Demonstration. The shop sells Shaker-produced foods as well as handcrafts by area artisans. ✉ *707 Shaker Rd., near Rte. 26, New Gloucester* ☎ *207/926–4597* 🌐 *www.shaker.lib.me.us* 🎟 *Tour $10* 🕓 *Late May–Columbus Day, Mon.–Sat. 10–4:30.*

WHERE TO STAY

$$$$ RESORT FAMILY

🏨 **Migis Lodge.** Scattered under a canopy of trees along Sebago Lake, the classy pine-paneled cottages at this 125-acre resort have fieldstone fireplaces and are handsomely furnished with colorful rugs and handmade quilts. **Pros:** away-from-it-all feel; woodsy setting; evening cocktail hour. **Cons:** pricey rates; credit cards not accepted. [$] *Rooms from: $670* ✉ *30 Migis Lodge Rd., off U.S. 302, South Casco* ☎ *207/655–4524* 🌐 *www.migis.com* 🛏 *35 cottages, 6 rooms* 💳 *No credit cards* 🕓 *Closed mid-Oct.–mid-June* 🍴 *All meals.*

SPORTS AND THE OUTDOORS

U.S. 302 cuts through Naples, and in the center, at the Naples causeway, you'll find rental craft for fishing or cruising. Sebago and Long lakes are popular areas for sailing, fishing, and motorboating.

FAMILY

Songo River Queen II. Departing from the Naples causeway, *Songo River Queen II*, a 93-foot stern-wheeler, takes passengers on one- and two-hour cruises on Long Lake. ✉ *841 Roosevelt Trail, Naples* ☎ *207/693–6861* 🌐 *www.songoriverqueen.net* 🎟 *$15–$25* 🕓 *July–early Sept., daily; early May–June and early Sept.–mid-Oct., weekends; hrs vary.*

BRIDGTON

8 miles north of Naples, 30 miles south of Bethel.

Bridgton's winding Main Street (U.S. 302) passes picturesque New England townscapes at every curve. On hot summer days kids dive off the dock at the town beach tucked at the end of Highland Lake, just past storefronts with restaurants, galleries, and shops. Just steps from downtown a covered pedestrian bridge leads to 66-acre Pondicherry Park, a nature preserve with wooded trails and two streams. The town has 10 lakes that are popular for boating and fishing. Come winter, people arrive to ski at Shawnee Peak.

The surrounding countryside is a good choice for leaf peepers and outdoors lovers. A few miles north, Harrison anchors the northern end of Long Lake. Come fall, Fryeburg is home to the famed Fryeburg Fair (🌐 *www.fryeburgfair.com*), the region's largest agricultural fair.

GETTING HERE AND AROUND

U.S. 302 runs from Portland up the west side of Long Lake to Bridgton. From here it continues west to Fryeburg, where you can take Route 5 north to Center Lovell.

ESSENTIALS

Vacation Rentals Maine Lakeside Getaways ☎ *207/647–4000, 866/647–8557* 🌐 *www.mainelakesidegetaways.com.*

Visitor Information Greater Bridgton Lakes Region Chamber of Commerce ✉ *101 Portland Rd.* ☎ *207/647–3472* 🌐 *www.mainelakeschamber.com.*

5

EXPLORING

Rufus Porter Museum and Cultural Heritage Center. Local youth Rufus Porter became a leading folk artist, painting landscape and harbor murals on the walls of New England homes in the early 1800s, including those in the museum's red Cape Cod–style house. Also an inventor, Porter founded *Scientific American* magazine. Early issues are showcased, as are some of his inventions and miniature portraits. Changing exhibits feature 19th-century folk and decorative arts. By 2014 the museum will also include an 1840s house at 121 Main Street. ✉ *67 N. High St.* ☎ *207/647–2828* 🌐 *www.rufusportermuseum.org* 🎟 *$8* 🕒 *Mid-June–mid-Oct., Wed.–Sat. noon–4.*

WHERE TO EAT AND STAY

$$$ CONTEMPORARY

🍴 **Center Lovell Inn & Restaurant.** In summer the best tables for dining at this eye-catching cupola-topped 1805 property—about 15 miles northeast of Bridgton in quiet Center Lovell—are on the wraparound porch, which has sunset views of the White Mountains. Inside, one dining room has mountain views and the other an original iron fireplace that warms diners on cold nights. Herb-crusted rack of lamb, pan-seared filet mignon, and fresh swordfish are menu mainstays; fillet of bison is a welcome occasional special. Eight homey guest rooms and one two-bedroom suite (lodging is year-round) are upstairs and in the adjacent Harmon House. [$] *Average main: $28* ✉ *1107 Main St., Center Lovell* ☎ *207/925–1575, 800/777–2698* 🌐 *www.centerlovellinn.com* 🕒 *No dinner mid-Oct.–late Dec. and Mar.–mid-May.*

$$$$ B&B/INN

🏨 **Noble House Inn.** On a quiet road, this 1903 estate above Highland Lake offers a convenient location, plenty of creature comforts, and a relaxing atmosphere. **Pros:** bottomless cookie jar; ski packages available; canoeing and kayaking in summer. **Cons:** limited lake views; only suites have TVs. [$] *Rooms from: $235* ✉ *81 Highland Rd.* ☎ *207/647–3733, 888/237–4880* 🌐 *www.noblehouseinn.com* 🛏 *4 rooms, 4 suites* 🍽 *Breakfast.*

SPORTS AND THE OUTDOORS

FAMILY **Shawnee Peak.** Just a few miles from Bridgton, Shawnee Peak appeals to families and those who enjoy nighttime skiing—beginner, intermediate, and expert trails are lit most evenings. Five lifts serve 40 trails, six glades, and two terrain parks. The two base lodges have cafeterias; the main lodge also has a restaurant with an expansive deck, a ski school, and a ski shop. Summer visitors can pick blueberries or paddle a canoe on Moose Pond. ⊠ *119 Mountain Rd., off U.S. 302* ☏ *207/647–8444* ⊕ *www.shawneepeak.com.*

BETHEL

27 miles north of Bridgton; 65 miles north of Portland.

Bethel is pure New England, a town with white clapboard houses, white-steeple churches, and a mountain vista at the end of every street. The campus of Gould Academy, a college prep school founded in 1836, anchors the east side of downtown. In winter this is ski country: Sunday River, one Maine's big ski resorts, is only a few miles north in Newry. Bethel WinterFest is usually held in February. On the third weekend in July, Mollyockett Days, which includes a parade, fireworks, and frog-jumping contest, honor a Pequawket Indian renowned for her medicinal cures in the early days of white settlement.

GETTING HERE AND AROUND

From the south, both Routes 35 and 5 lead to Bethel, overlapping en route, then splitting from each other several miles south of town. Route 5 is slightly shorter from this point, and especially pretty come fall, with lots of overhanging trees. If you're coming from the west on U.S. 2, you'll pass through the White Mountain National Forest.

ESSENTIALS

Vacation Rentals Four Seasons Realty & Rentals ⊠ *32 Parkway Plaza, Suite 1* ☏ *207/824–3776* ⊕ *fourseasonsrealtymaine.com.*

Visitor Information Bethel Area Chamber of Commerce ⊠ *8 Station Pl., off Cross St.* ☏ *207/824–2282, 800/442–5826* ⊕ *www.bethelmaine.com.*

EXPLORING

Bethel Historical Society Museum of Regional History. Start your stroll in Bethel here, across from the Village Common. The center's campus comprises two buildings: the 1821 Robinson House and the 1813 Dr. Moses Mason House, both of which are listed on the National Register of Historic Places. The Robinson House has changing and permanent exhibits pertaining to the region's history. One parlor room is a gift shop with a nice book selection. The Moses Mason House has nine period rooms; the front hall and stairway are decorated with Rufus Porter School folk art murals. ⊠ *10 Broad St.* ☏ *207/824–2908, 800/824–2910* ⊕ *www.bethelhistorical.org* 🖃 *Robinson House free; Mason House $3* ⊙ *Robinson House: late Nov.–June, Sept., and Oct., Tues.–Fri. 10–4; July and Aug., Tues.–Fri. 10–4, Sat. 1–4. Mason House: July and Aug., Tues.–Sat. 1–4; Sept.–June, by appointment.*

Grafton Notch State Park. Route 26 runs through this park, which stretches along the Bear River Valley 14 miles north of Bethel and is a favorite foliage drive. It's an easy walk from roadside parking areas to Mother Walker Falls, Moose Cave, and the spectacular Screw Auger Falls. Or pick up the Appalachian Trail for a challenging 8-mile round-trip trek to the viewing platform atop Old Speck Mountain, the state's third-highest peak. Sandwiching the park are the two tracts that make up the state's 9,993-acre Mahoosuc Public Reserved Land. Trails wind through the reserve, offering stunning, if strenuous, backcountry hiking. In winter a popular snowmobile trail runs along the river through the park. ✉ *1941 Bear River Rd., Newry* ☎ *207/624–6080* 🌐 *www.parksandlands.com* 🎟 *$3* 🕒 *Daily, 9–sunset.*

White Mountain National Forest. This forest straddles New Hampshire and Maine, with the highest peaks on the New Hampshire side. The Maine section, though smaller, has magnificent rugged terrain. As for hiking, there's everything from hour-long nature loops to a day hike up Speckled Mountain. The mountain is part of the 11,000-acre Caribou-Speckled Mountain Wilderness Area, one of several in the forest, but the only one entirely within Maine. The most popular Maine access to the national forest is Route 113, which runs south from its terminus at U.S. 2 in Gilead, 10 miles from downtown Bethel. Most of the highway is the Pequawket Trail Maine Scenic Byway, and the section through the forest is spectacular come fall. This stretch is closed in winter, but is used by snowmobilers and cross-country skiers. ✉ *Route 113, off U.S. 2, Gilead* ☎ *603/466–2713* 🌐 *www.fs.fed.us/r9/white* 🎟 *Day pass $3 per car.*

5

WHERE TO STAY

$ B&B/INN 🏨 **Austin's Holidae House.** At this affordable downtown B&B it's the welcoming hospitality that keeps guests returning—everyone seems to love innkeeper Laurence Austin's British manners. **Pros:** courtesy cordials in parlor; tasty breakfasts; innkeepers help you plan day. **Cons:** some rooms have a dated feel. [$] *Rooms from: $120* ✉ *85 Main St.* ☎ *207/824–3400, 877/224–3400* 🌐 *www.holidaehouse.com* 🛏 *7 rooms* 🍴 *Breakfast.*

EN ROUTE

Artist's Bridge. In the town of Newry, make a short detour to the Artist's Bridge, located about 4 miles northwest of U.S. 2. It's the most painted and photographed of Maine's nine covered bridges. ✉ *Sunday River Rd., Newry.*

Height of Land. A direct but still stunningly scenic route from Bethel to Rangeley is U.S. 2 east to the twin towns of Rumford and Mexico. From the latter, Route 17 heads north to Oquossoc, about an hour's drive. The high point of this route is Height of Land, with its unforgettable views of mountains and the island-studded blue mass of Mooselookmeguntic Lake. In Oquossoc, continue on Route 4 to Rangeley. ✉ *Rte. 17, Rangeley.*

SPORTS AND THE OUTDOORS

MULTI-SPORT OUTFITTERS

Northwoods Outfitters. Northwoods Outfitters outfits for moose-watching, biking, skiing, snowmobiling, snowboarding, canoeing, kayaking, camping, and fishing. They lead trips for many of these activities as well as rent canoes, kayaks, bikes, snowmobiles, snowshoes, ATVs, and more. Shop, get trail advice, and kick back in the Internet café at

One of the Rangeley Lakes, Mooselookmeguntic is said to mean "portage to the moose feeding place" in the Abenaki language.

its downtown outfitters store. They also run an inn and lake rentals as well as shuttle service. ✉ *5 Lilly Bay Rd., Bethel* ☎ *207/695–3288, 866/223–1380* ⊕ *www.maineoutfitter.com.*

Sun Valley Sports. Take guided fly-fishing excursions, moose and wildlife safaris, and rent canoes and kayaks with Sun Valley Sports. ✉ *129 Sunday River Rd.* ☎ *207/824–7533* ⊕ *www.sunvalleysports.com.*

CANOEING AND KAYAKING

Bethel Outdoor Adventure. On the Androscoggin River, this outfitter rents canoes and kayaks and leads guided fishing and boating expeditions. Maine Mineralogy Expeditions is based here, offering mine tours and an open-air facility where you can sluice for precious gems. ✉ *121 Mayville Rd.* ☎ *207/824–4224, 800/533–3607* ⊕ *www.betheloutdooradventure. com.*

DOGSLEDDING

Mahoosuc Guide Service. This guide company leads day and multiday dogsledding expeditions in the Umbagog National Wildlife Refuge on the Maine–New Hampshire border. In the summer it guides canoe trips here and on rivers in northern Maine. The company runs its own lodging in nearby Newry. ✉ *1513 Bear River Rd., Newry* ☎ *207/824–2073* ⊕ *www.mahoosuc.com.*

SKI AREAS

FAMILY **Carter's Cross-Country Ski Center.** This cross-country ski center offers about 30 miles of trails for all levels of skiers. Snowshoes, skis, and sleds to pull children are available for rental. The place also rents lodge rooms and ski-in cabins. ✉ *786 Intervale Rd.* ☎ *207/824–3880, 207/539–4848* ⊕ *www.cartersxcski.com.*

CLOSE UP

Whoopie Pies

When a bill aiming to make the whoopie pie Maine's official dessert was debated in the state legislature, some lawmakers countered that blueberry pie (made with Maine wild blueberries, of course) should have the honor. In the end it did, but what could have been a civil war ended civilly, with whoopie pies designated the "official state treat." Spend a few days anywhere in Maine and you'll notice just how popular the treat is.

The name is misleading: it's a pie only in the sense of a having a filling between two "crusts"—namely, a thick layer of sugary frosting sandwiched between two saucers of rich cake,

usually chocolate. It's said to have Pennsylvania Dutch roots, and may have acquired its distinctive moniker from the jubilant yelp farmers emitted after discovering it in their lunchboxes. Many Mainers dispute this, claiming that the whoopie pie originated here. Typically, the filling is made with butter or shortening; some recipes add Marshmallow Fluff. Many bakers have indulged the temptation to experiment with flavors and ingredients, particularly in the filling but also in the cake, offering pumpkin, raspberry, oatmeal cream, red velvet, peanut butter, and more.

—Michael de Zayas

Mt. Abram. Family-friendly and very affordable, Mt. Abram has 54 trails and glade areas, five lifts, a tubing area, two base lodges, and ski lessons. It's open Thursday through Sunday during the ski season. ⊠ *308 Howe Hill Rd., off Rte. 26, Greenwood* ☎ *207/875–5000* ⊕ *www. skimtabram.com.*

FAMILY
Fodor's Choice
★

Sunday River. What was once a sleepy ski area has evolved into a sprawling resort that attracts skiers from around the world. Stretching for 3 miles, there are 16 lifts service, 135 trails, five terrain parks, and a superpipe. Sunday River has three base areas and several lodging choices, including two slope-side hotels: the family-friendly Grand Summit, located at one of the mountain bases, and the more upscale Jordan Grand, near a summit at the resort's western end. (It's really up there, several miles by vehicle from the base lodges, but during ski season there's a shuttle.) The less costly Snow Cap Inn is a short walk to the slopes. Sunday River is home to Maine Adaptive Sports & Recreation, which provides services for skiers with disabilities. The main South Ridge Base Lodge is the hub for summer activities. ⊠ *15 S. Ridge Rd., off U.S. 2, Newry* ☎ *207/824–3000, 207/824–3000 snow conditions, 800/543–2754 reservations* ⊕ *www.sundayriver.com.*

RANGELEY

66 miles north of Bethel.

Rangeley, on the north side of Rangeley Lake on Route 4, has long lured anglers and winter sports enthusiasts to its more than 40 lakes and ponds and 450 square miles of woodlands. Right behind Main Street, Lakeside Park ("Town Park" to locals) has a large swimming area and boat launch. Equally popular in summer or winter, Rangeley has a rough, wilderness feel to it. In late January the Rangeley Lakes Snowmobile Club's Snodeo offers thrilling snowmobile acrobatics, fireworks, and a chili cook-off.

GETTING HERE AND AROUND

To reach Rangeley on a scenic drive through Western Maine, take Route 17 north from U.S. 2 in Mexico to Route 4 in Oquossoc, then head east into town. Route 16 soon joins the highway and from Rangeley continues east to Sugarloaf ski resort and Kingfield.

ESSENTIALS

Vacation Rentals Morton and Furbish Vacation Rentals ✉ *2478 Main St.* ☎ *207/864-9065, 888/218-4882* 🌐 *www.rangeleyrentals.com.*

Visitor Information Rangeley Lakes Chamber of Commerce ✉ *6 Park Rd., off Main St.* ☎ *207/864-5364, 800/685-2537* 🌐 *www.rangeleymaine.com.*

EXPLORING

Rangeley Lake State Park. On the south shore of Rangeley Lake, this 869-acre park has superb lakeside scenery, swimming, picnic tables, and a boat ramp. ✉ *S. Shore Dr., off Rte. 17 or Rte. 4* ☎ *207/624-6080* 🌐 *www.parksandlands.com* 🎟 *$4.50* 🕒 *Daily 9–sunset.*

Rangeley Outdoor Sporting Heritage Museum. Spruce railings and siding on the Rangeley Outdoor Sporting Heritage Museum's facade replicate a local taxidermy shop from about 1900. Inside, the welcome center is an authentic log sporting camp from the same period, when grand hotels and full-service sporting lodges drew well-to-do "rusticators" on long stays. One of the big lures is the exhibit on local fly-tier Carrie Stevens, whose famed streamer flies increased the region's fly-fishing fame in the 1920s. ✉ *8 Rumford Rd., Oquossoc* ☎ *207/864-3091* 🌐 *www.rangeleyoutdoormuseum.org* 🎟 *$5* 🕒 *Late May–June and Sept.–mid-Oct., Fri. and Sat. 10–2; July and Aug., Wed.–Sun. 10–2.*

Wilhelm Reich Museum. The Wilhelm Reich Museum showcases the life and work of controversial physician-scientist Wilhelm Reich (1897–1957), who believed that a force called orgone energy is in all living matter and the atmosphere. The Orgone Energy Observatory exhibits biographical materials, inventions, and the equipment used in his experiments. The observatory deck has magnificent views of the countryside. In July and August, the museum offers nature programs for all ages. Trails lace the 175-acre grounds. ✉ *19 Orgonon Cir., off Rte. 4* ☎ *207/864-3443* 🌐 *www.wilhelmreichtrust.org* 🎟 *Museum $6, grounds free* 🕒 *Museum July and Aug., Wed.–Sun. 1–5; Sept., Sat. 1–5. Grounds daily 9–5.*

WHERE TO EAT AND STAY

$$$ AMERICAN 🍴 **Gingerbread House Restaurant.** With a fieldstone fireplace in the main dining room, tables scattered around the deck, and an antique marble soda fountain, there are lots of reasons to stop at what really looks like a giant gingerbread house at the edge of the woods. Sandwiches and burgers at lunch give way to crab cakes as appetizers (big enough for a meal) and such interesting entrées as lobster macaroni and cheese and barbecued ribs with a blueberry-chipotle sauce. Locals also come for baked goods or ice cream. [$] *Average main: $23* ✉ *55 Carry Rd.,*

Oquossoc ☎ *207/864–3602* 🌐 *www.gingerbreadhouserestaurant.net* 🕒 *Closed late Oct.–Nov. and Apr.; and Mon.–Thurs. Dec.–Mar., Mon. and Tues. May–late June, and Mon. early Sept.–late Oct.*

$$ B&B/INN FAMILY 🏨 **Country Club Inn.** Built in 1920 as the country club for the adjacent Mingo Springs Golf Course, this hilltop retreat has sweeping mountain and lake views and plenty of charm. **Pros:** loads of board games in living room; superhelpful staff; choice of meal plans. **Cons:** rooms in main building are smaller; no TV in rooms. [$] *Rooms from: $129* ✉ *56 Country Club Rd., off Rte. 4* ☎ *207/864–3831* 🌐 *www.countryclubinnrangeley.com* 🛏 *19 rooms* 🕒 *Closed Nov. and Apr.* 🍴 *Multiple meal plans.*

$$ HOTEL 🏨 **Rangeley Inn.** Painted eggshell blue, this three-story hotel was built around 1900 for wealthy urbanites on vacation. **Pros:** historic hotel; impressive baths (some with claw-foot tubs); canoeing and kayaking on Hayley Pond. **Cons:** no elevator; restaurant open only for dinner. [$] *Rooms from: $130* ✉ *2443 Main St.* ☎ *207/864–3341* 🌐 *www.therangeleyinn.com* 🛏 *40 rooms, 4 suites* 🕒 *Closed Apr.* 🍴 *Breakfast.*

5

SPORTS AND THE OUTDOORS

BOATING AND FISHING

Rangeley and Mooselookmeguntic lakes are good for canoeing, sailing, fishing, and motorboating. Several outfits rent equipment and provide guide service if needed. Lake fishing for brook trout and landlocked salmon is at its best in May, June, and September. The Rangeley area's rivers and streams are especially popular with fly-fishers, who enjoy the sport from May through October.

GOLF

Mingo Springs Golf Course. This popular course is known for its mountain and water views. You can also take in the views and spot wildlife on the Mingo Springs Trail & Bird Walk, an easy 3-mile loop trail through woods along the course. ✉ *43 Country Club Rd., follow signs from Rte. 4, Rangeley* ☎ *207/864–5021* 🌐 *www.mingosprings.com* 🎫 *Greens fee: $43.*

SEAPLANES

Fodor's Choice ★ **Acadian Seaplanes.** In addition to 15- to 90-minute scenic flights high above the mountains, this seaplane operator offers enticing "fly-in" excursions. You can travel by air to wilderness locales to dine at a sporting camp, spot moose in their natural habitat, or go white-water rafting on the remote Rapid River. The company also provides charter service year-round, including shuttles between Rangeley and airports in Portland, Boston, and New York. ✉ *2640 Main St.* ☎ *207/864–5307* 🌐 *www.acadianseaplanes.com.*

SKI AREAS

Rangeley Lakes Trails Center. About 35 miles of groomed cross-country and snowshoe trails stretch along the side of Saddleback Mountain. The trail network is largely wooded and leads to Saddleback Lake. In warmer weather the trails are popular with mountain bikers, hikers, and runners. A snack bar, known for its tasty soups, is open in winter. ✉ *524 Saddleback Mountain Rd., off Rte. 4, Dallas* ☎ *207/864–4309* 🌐 *www.xcskirangeley.com.*

FAMILY **Saddleback Maine.** A family atmosphere prevails at Saddleback Maine, where the lack of crowds, affordable prices, and spectacular valley views draw return visitors. The 66 trails and glades, accessed by five lifts, are divided about evenly between novice, intermediate, and advanced. A fieldstone fireplace is nestled in the post-and-beam base lodge, which has a second-story pub with views of Saddleback Lake. The resort has a ski school, rental shop, and trailside lodging. Summer guests have access to canoes on Saddleback Lake. ⊠ *976 Saddleback Mountain Rd., off Rte. 4, Dallas* ☎ *207/864–5671, 866/918–2225* ⊕ *www. saddlebackmaine.com.*

KINGFIELD

38 miles east of Rangeley.

In the shadows of Mt. Abram and Sugarloaf Mountain, home to its namesake ski resort, Kingfield has everything a "real" New England town should have: a general store, historic inns, and white clapboard churches.

ESSENTIALS

Visitor Information Franklin County Chamber of Commerce ⊠ *615 Wilton Rd., Farmington* ☎ *207/778–4215* ⊕ *www.franklincountymaine.org.*

EXPLORING

Stanley Museum. Housing a collection of original Stanley Steamer cars built by the Stanley twins—Kingfield's most famous natives—this museum also features exhibits on the glass negative business this inventive pair sold to Eastman Kodak. Also on display are their sister's wonderful photos of everyday country life at the turn of the 20th century. The museum occupies a 1903 Georgian-style former school the Stanleys built for the town. ⊠ *40 School St.* ☎ *207/265–2729* ⊕ *www. stanleymuseum.org* 🖃 *$4* ⏱ *June–Oct., Tues.–Sun. 1–4; Nov.–May., Tues.–Fri. 1–4.*

SPORTS AND THE OUTDOORS

SKI AREAS

FAMILY **Sugarloaf Mountain Resort.** An eye-catching setting, abundant natural snow, and the only above-tree-line lift-service skiing in the East have made Sugarloaf Mountain Resort one of Maine's best-known ski areas. There are 15 lifts, 153 trails and glades, a ski school, and a rental shop. There are two slope-side hotels, and hundreds of slope-side condos with ski-in ski-out access. Sugarloaf Mountain Hotel is in the ski village, while the smaller, more affordable Sugarloaf Inn is just a bit down the mountain. The Outdoor Center has more than 90 miles of cross-country ski trails, as well as snowshoeing and ice-skating. Sugarloaf has plenty for the kids, from tubing to skateboarding. Once you are here, a car is unnecessary—a shuttle connects all mountain operations. Summer is much quieter, but you can mountain bike, go hiking, or play a round on the Robert Trent Jones Jr.–designed golf course. ⊠ *5092 Access Rd., Carrabassett Valley* ☎ *207/237–2000, 800/843–5623 reservations* ⊕ *www.sugarloaf.com.*

Rafting in the North Woods

Virtually all of Maine's white-water rafting takes place on the dam-controlled Kennebec and Dead rivers, which meet at The Forks in Western Maine, and on the West Branch of the Penobscot River, near Millinocket in the North Woods. Guided excursions lasting from a day to several days run rain or shine daily from spring (mid-April on the Kennebec, May on the Dead and the Penobscot) to mid-October.

Maine is New England's premier destination for the sport, which is why thousands of people come here every year to ride the waves. The Kennebec is known for abundant big waves and splashes; the Dead has New England's

longest stretch of continuous white water, some 16 miles. The most challenging rapids are on the West Branch of the Penobscot River, a Class V river on the southern border of Baxter State Park outside Millinocket.

Many rafting outfitters operate resort facilities in their base towns. It's not uncommon for outfitters to run trips in both the Millinocket region and The Forks. In recent years operators have added family-friendly rafting trips that take you along some of the gentler stretches of these mighty rivers. North Country Rivers and New England Outdoor Center in Millinocket have many outfitters.

THE NORTH WOODS

Moosehead Lake, the four-season resort town of Greenville, Baxter State Park, and the Allagash Wilderness Waterway are dispersed within Maine's remote North Woods. This vast area in the north-central section of the state is best experienced by canoe or raft; via hiking, snowshoe, cross-country skiing, or snowmobile; or on a fishing trip. Maine's largest lake, Moosehead supplies more in the way of rustic camps, guides, and outfitters than any other northern locale. Its 400-plus miles of shorefront, three-quarters of which is owned by lumber companies or the state, are virtually uninhabited.

GREENVILLE

155 miles northeast of Portland; 70 miles northwest of Bangor.

Greenville, tucked at the southern end of island-dotted, mostly forest-lined Moosehead Lake, is an outdoors-lover's paradise. Boating, fishing, and hiking are popular in summer, while snowmobiling and ice fishing reign in winter. The town also has the greatest selection of shops, restaurants, and inns in the North Woods region. Restaurants and lodgings are also clustered 20 miles north in Rockwood, where the Moose River flows through the village and—across from Mt. Kineo's majestic cliffs—into the lake.

GETTING HERE AND AROUND

To reach Greenville from Interstate 95, get off at Exit 157 in Newport and head north, successively, on Routes 7, 23, and 15.

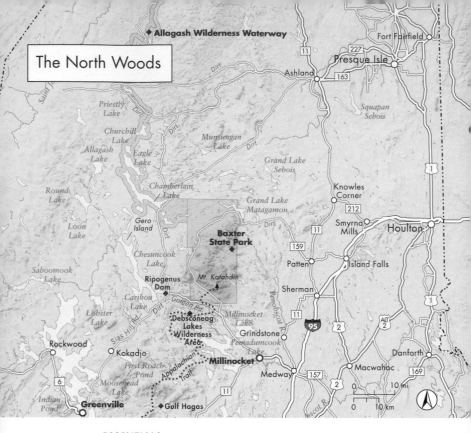

The North Woods

◆ Allagash Wilderness Waterway

ESSENTIALS

Vacation Rentals Northwoods Camp Rentals ✉ *14 Lakeview St.* ☏ *800/251–8042, 207/695–4300* ⊕ *mooseheadrentals.com.*

Visitor Information Moosehead Lake Region Chamber of Commerce ✉ *480 Moosehead Lake Rd.* ☏ *207/695–2702, 888/876–2778* ⊕ *www.mooseheadlake. org.*

EXPLORING

Lily Bay State Park. Nine miles northeast of Greenville on Moosehead Lake, this park has good lakefront swimming, a 1.6-mi walking trail with water views, two boat-launching ramps, a playground, and two campgrounds with a total of 90 sites. In winter the entrance road is plowed to access the groomed cross-country ski trails and the lake for ice fishing and snowmobiling. ✉ *State Park Rd., turn off Lily Bay Rd., Beaver Cove* ☏ *207/695–2700 mid-May–mid-Oct. only, 207/941–4014* ⊕ *www.parksandlands.com* ▭ *$4.50, Maine residents $3* ◷ *Daily 9–sunset (mid-Oct.–mid-May no staff, roads not open except on a limited basis during snow season).*

FAMILY **Moosehead Historical Society & Museums.** Guides in period costume lead
Fodor's Choice tours of the Eveleth-Crafts-Sheridan House, a late-19th-century Victo-
★ rian mansion filled with period antiques, most original to the home.

The Lumberman's Museum, about the region's logging history, is in the carriage house, while the barn next door houses a re-creation of a one-room schoolhouse and a general-store exhibit. You can savor lunch and the architecture of these meticulously maintained buildings from the art-accented Sunken Garden. A mile away in downtown Greenville, the former Universalist Church houses the Center for Moosehead History and Moosehead Lake Aviation Museum. The former has a fine exhibit of Native American artifacts from the Moosehead Lake region, dating from 9,000 BC to the 1700s, while the latter highlights the impact of aviation on the area, from early bush pilots to Greenville's annual International Seaplane Fly-in. ✉ *444 Pritham Ave., Greenville Junction* ☎ *207/695–2909* 🌐 *www.mooseheadhistory.org* 🎟 *Eveleth-Crafts-Sheridan House $5, other museums free* 🕓 *Eveleth-Crafts-Sheridan House: mid-June–mid-Oct., Wed.–Fri. 1–4; Lumberman's Museum: Tues.–Fri. 9–4; Center for Moosehead History and Moosehead Lake Aviation Museum: mid-June–mid-Oct., Thurs.–Sun. 10–4.*

WORD OF MOUTH

"Moosehead Lake and Mt. Kineo (in the Greenville area) are beautiful and in my opinion not to be missed."

—clarkgriswold

OFF THE BEATEN PATH

Mt. Kineo. Accessed primarily by steamship, Mt. Kineo House was a thriving summer resort for the wealthy set below its namesake's 800-foot cliff on an island-like peninsula north of Greenville. The last of three successive hotels with this name was built in 1884 and became America's largest inland waterfront hotel. It was torn down in 1938, but Kineo remains a pleasant day trip. There's no road access: take a 15-minute boat trip from Rockwood on the seasonal shuttle. Mt. Kineo State Park occupies most of the 1,200-acre peninsula, and you can also play a round on the Mt. Kineo Golf Course, one of the oldest in New England. ✉ *Kineo Dock, Village Rd., Rockwood* ☎ *207/534–9012* 🌐 *www.parksandlands.com* 🎟 *$3* 🕓 *Daily 9–sunset.*

WHERE TO STAY

$$$$ B&B/INN Fodor's Choice ★

🏨 **Blair Hill Inn.** Beautiful gardens and a hilltop location with marvelous views over the lake distinguish this 1891 country estate, considered one of New England's top inns. **Pros:** gorgeous rooms; amazing restaurant; 15-acre property has stone paths, wooded picnic area, and trout pond. **Cons:** pricey; no direct lake access. [$] *Rooms from: $398* ✉ *351 Lily Bay Rd.* ☎ *207/695–0224* 🌐 *www.blairhill.com* 🛏 *7 rooms, 1 suite* 🕓 *Closed Nov.–Apr.* 🍴 *Breakfast.*

$$$$ RESORT FAMILY Fodor's Choice ★

🏨 **Appalachian Mountain Club Maine Wilderness Lodges.** When you want to get away from it all, head to the Appalachian Mountain Club's 66,000 acres in Maine's 100-Mile Wilderness—you have a choice of two historic sporting camp retreats, Gorman Chairback and Little Lyford. **Pros:** great for outdoors lovers; far-from-the-crowds feel; laid-back vibe. **Cons:** winter access only by cross-country skis or snowmobile. [$] *Rooms from: $144* ✉ *Off Katahdin Iron Works Rd.* ☎ *603/466–2727* 🌐 *www.outdoors.org/lodging/mainelodges* 🛏 *Gorman Chairback: 12 cabins; Little Lyford: 9 cabins* 🕓 *Closed mid-Mar.–mid-May and late Oct.–late Dec.* 🍴 *All meals.*

5

Golden Road. For a scenic North Woods drive, travel the approximately 20-mile stretch of this private east-west logging road (named for what it cost a paper company to build it) near Baxter State Park northwest of Millinocket. Have patience with ruts and bumps and yield to logging trucks—keep right! At the western end of the drive, the West Branch of the Penobscot River drops 70-plus feet per mile through Ripogenus Gorge, giving white-water rafters a thrilling ride during scheduled releases from Ripogenous Dam. To drive across the dam on Ripogenus Lake and view the gorge, turn on Rip Dam Road (it veers right if you're traveling west). The Crib Works Rapid (Class V) overlook is on Telos Road, about a mile east of Rip Dam Road (parking is on the right after the bridge). Take photos of Baxter's Mt. Katahdin from the footbridge alongside the Golden Road's one-lane Abol Bridge—this view is famed. Park east of the bridge at Abol Bridge Campground or at the parking area west of the bridge. Also just west of the bridge is an access road for Debsconeag Lakes Wilderness Area. At North Woods Trading Post, about nine miles east of the bridge and across from Ambajejus Lake, you can cross between the Golden Road and Millinocket Lake Road (becomes Baxter State Park Road). Turn left for Baxter, right for Millinocket. West of "Rip" Dam the dirt Sias Hill Road heads south from the Golden Road on a backwoods route to Greenville through tiny Kokadjo. ⊠ *Golden Rd., Millinocket.*

SPORTS AND THE OUTDOORS

Togue (lake trout), landlocked salmon, smallmouth bass, and brook trout lure thousands of anglers to the region from ice-out in mid-May until September; the hardiest return in winter to ice fish.

MULTI-SPORT OUTFITTERS

Moose Country Safaris & Eco Tours. In the Greenville area, Moose Country Safaris & Eco Tours leads moose-spotting and bird-watching excursions. There are also snowshoe, hiking, and canoe trips, as well as late-summer meteor shower tours. Spring through fall, the itinerary includes tours of an ice cave near Baxter State Park. ⊠ *191 N. Dexter Rd., Sangerville* ☎ *207/876–4907* ⊕ *www.moosecountrysafaris.com.*

Northwoods Outfitters. This company provides all the gear you'll need for moose-watching, biking, skiing, snowmobiling, snowboarding, canoeing, kayaking, and fishing, among other activities. It also leads day and overnight trips around the region. At its base in downtown Greenville you can pick up sporting goods, get trail advice, or kick back in the Internet café. The company also has its own 16-room motel and lakeside cabin rental. ⊠ *5 Lily Bay Rd.* ☎ *207/695–3288, 866/223–1380* ⊕ *www.maineoutfitter.com.*

BOATING

Allagash Canoe Trips. Run by a husband and wife, both championship paddlers and Registered Maine Guides, this operator offers day, overnight and weeklong canoe trips on the Allagash Wilderness Waterway, the Moose and St. John rivers, and the East and West branches of the

Penobscot River. White-water canoe and kayak trips are run on the Kennebec and Dead rivers. The couple also operates clinics on white-water paddling and kayaking and canoe poling. ⊠ *156 Scammon Rd.* ☎ *207/280-1551, 207/280-0191* ⊕ *www.allagashcanoetrips.com.*

SEAPLANES

Currier's Flying Service. You can take sightseeing flights over the Moosehead Lake region with Currier's Flying Service from ice-out until the end of October. ⊠ *447 Pritham Ave., Greenville Junction* ☎ *207/695–2778* ⊕ *www.curriersflyingservice.com.*

TOURS

Katahdin Cruises. The Moosehead Marine Museum runs three- and four-and-a-half-hour afternoon trips on Moosehead Lake aboard the *Katahdin,* a 115-foot 1914 steamship converted to diesel. The longer scheduled trips skirt Mt. Kineo's cliffs. Also called *The Kate,* the ship carried resort guests to Mt. Kineo until 1938 and then was used in the logging industry until 1975. The boat and the free shoreside museum have displays about the steamships that transported people and cargo on the lake during a period of about 100 years starting in the 1830s. ⊠ *12 Lily Bay Rd.* ☎ *207/695–2716* ⊕ *www.katahdincruises. com* ⊠ *$33–$38* ⊙ *Cruises: late June–mid-Oct., Tues.–Sat. at 12:30. Museum: Mon.–Sat. 10–4.*

Gulf Hagas. Called the "Grand Canyon of the East," this National Natural Landmark has chasms, cliffs, six large waterfalls, pools, exotic flora, and rock formations. Part of the Appalachian Trail Corridor, the slate-walled gorge east of Greenville is within a remote commercial forest and accessed by gravel logging roads (always yield to trucks). An access fee is usually charged at forest checkpoints, where you can get trail maps and hiking information. From the two parking areas it's a 3- or 3½-mile round-trip hike to Stair Falls on the gorge's western end and the spectacular Screw Auger Falls on the eastern end. These are good choices for families with young children and anyone looking for a moderately difficult hike. Slippery rocks and rugged terrain make for challenging hiking along the rim; a loop route that includes the rim trail is an 8- to 9-mile trek. From the Gulf Hagas Parking Area—the one near the gorge's east end—you must ford the Pleasant River (easily done in summer, but don't attempt it in high water). From Greenville, travel 11 miles east via Pleasant Street (which eventually becomes Katahdin Iron Works Road) to the Hedgehog checkpoint. From here, follow signs to the parking areas at Head of Gulf (2½ miles) or Gulf Hagas (6½ miles). ⊠ *Accessed from Katahdin Iron Works Rd.* ⊕ *www. northmainewoods.org.*

OFF THE BEATEN PATH

5

MILLINOCKET

67 miles north of Bangor, 88 miles northwest of Greenville via Rtes. 6 and 11.

Millinocket, a paper-mill town with a population of about 4,000, is a gateway to Baxter State Park and Maine's North Woods. Although it has a smattering of motels and restaurants, Millinocket is the place to stock up on supplies, fill your gas tank, or grab a hot meal or shower before heading into the wilderness. Numerous rafting and canoeing outfitters and guides are based in the region.

GETTING HERE AND AROUND

From Interstate 95, take Route 157 (Exit 244) west to Millinocket. From here follow signs to Baxter State Park (Millinocket Lake Road becomes Baxter Park State Road), 18 miles from town.

ESSENTIALS

Visitor Information Katahdin Area Chamber of Commerce ⊠ *1029 Central St.* ☎ *207/723-4443* ⊕ *www.katahdinmaine.com.*

EXPLORING

Allagash Wilderness Waterway. A spectacular 92-mile corridor of lakes, streams, and rivers, the waterway cuts through northern Maine's vast commercial forests, beginning northwest of Baxter State Park and running north to the town of Allagash, 10 miles from the Canadian border. The Maine Bureau of Parks and Lands has campsites along the waterway, most not accessible by vehicle. From May to mid-October the Allagash is prime canoeing and camping country. It's part of the 740-mile Northern Forest Canoe Trail, which runs from New York to Maine. The complete 92-mile course requires 7 to 10 days. Novices may want to consider going with a guide, as there are many areas with strong rapids. A good outfitter can help plan your route and provide equipment and and transportation. ☎ *207/941–4014* ⊕ *www.maine. gov/allagashwildernesswaterway.*

Fodor'sChoice
★
Baxter State Park. A gift from Governor Percival Baxter, this is the jewel in the crown of northern Maine, a 210,000-acre wilderness area that surrounds **Mt. Katahdin,** Maine's highest mountain and the terminus of the Appalachian Trail. The 5,267-foot Katahdin draws thousands of hikers every year for the daylong climb to the summit and the stunning views of woods, mountains, and lakes. Three parking lot trailheads lead to its peak; some routes include the hair-raising Knife Edge Ridge. ■**TIP➔** Reserve a day-use parking space at the trailheads between May 15 and October 15. The crowds climbing Katahdin can be formidable on clear summer days and fall weekends, so if you crave solitude, tackle one of the 47 other mountains in the park, 20 of which exceed an elevation of 3,000 feet and all of which are accessible from an extensive network of trails. South Turner can be climbed in a morning, and its summit has a great view across the valley. The Owl, the Brothers, and Doubletop Mountain are good day hikes (four to five hours). A trek around Daicey Pond, or from the pond to Big and Little Niagara Falls, are good options for families with young kids. Another option if you only have a couple of hours is renting a canoe at Daicey or Togue ponds. The roads here are unpaved, narrow, and winding; there are no pay phones, gas stations, or stores. The camping is primitive at the park's 10 campgrounds; reserve. The Togue Pond Gate, the park's southern entrance, is 18 miles northwest of Millinocket. Follow signs from Route 157. ⊠ *Baxter State Park Rd.* ☎ *207/723–5140, 207/723–4636 hiking hotline* ⊕ *www.baxterstateparkauthority.com* ⊠ *$14 per vehicle* ⊙ *Mid-May–mid-Oct., 6 am–10 pm; mid-Oct.–mid-May, sunrise–sunset.*

Debsconeag Lakes Wilderness Area. Bordering the south side of the Golden Road below Baxter State Park, the Nature Conservancy's 46,271-acre Debsconeag Lakes Wilderness Area is renowned for its rare ice cave, old forests, and abundant pristine ponds—more than anywhere else in New England. The access road for the Ice Cave Trail (2-mile round-trip) and Hurd Pond is 17 miles northwest of Millinocket, just west of the Golden Road's Abol Bridge. Near here the Appalachian Trail exits the conservancy land, crossing the bridge en route to Baxter. Before hiking, paddling, fishing, or camping (no fee or reservations needed) in the remote preserve, visit the conservancy's website for directions and other information. Access roads are unmarked, but there are trail kiosks and marked trailheads within the preserve. ⊠ *Golden Road, private logging road, no fee for this section* ⊕ *www.nature.org/maine.*

SPORTS AND THE OUTDOORS
MULTI-SPORT OUTFITTERS

Katahdin Outfitters. Take canoe and kayak expeditions on the Allagash Wilderness Waterway, West Branch of the Penobscot River, and St. John River with Katahdin Outfitters. ⊠ *Millinocket Lake Rd.* ☎ *207/723–5700* ⊕ *www.katahdinoutfitters.com.*

FAMILY

Fodor'sChoice

★

New England Outdoor Center. With Baxter State Park's Mt. Katahdin rising beyond the opposite shore at both its locations, this business helps visitors enjoy Maine's pristine North Woods—whether you're relaxing with drink in hand or on a wilderness adventure. Its year-round home base, Twin Pine Camps on Millinocket Lake, 9 miles from the park's southern entrance, has rental cabins and a restaurant and offers a host of guided trips, some within the park. Older log cabins (and a few newer ones) sit beneath tall pines on a grassy nub of land that juts into Millinocket Lake, while spacious upscale "green" units are tucked among trees on a cove. Amenities include kayaks and canoes for use on the lake and a recreation center with a sauna. At the popular River Driver's Restaurant, wood for the trim, wainscoting, bar, and floors was milled from old logs salvaged from local waters. Diners enjoy views of Katahdin beyond rows of windows or the patio, and your dish may have farm-to-table fare from the center's own farm. In addition to running guided snowmobiling, fishing, canoe, kayak, hiking, and moose-watching trips, NEOC rents canoes and kayaks, gives paddling lessons, and rents snowmobiles—it's along Maine's Interconnected Trail System. Trails for hiking, cross-country skiing (11 miles groomed), and mountain biking (to open 2014) are right on the 1,400-acre property. About 2 miles from Baxter, the seasonal Penobscot Outdoor Center is the base for white-water rafting trips on the West Branch of the Penobscot River and has a wooded campground on Pockwockamus Pond. There are tent sites as well as canvas tents and simple wood-frame cabins with cots or bunks and a dim solar light. A circular fireplace anchors the open-plan base lodge, which has a snack bar, pub area, hot tub, and communal outdoor fire pit. A towering window wall provides glimpses of water through trees, and there are waterside camp sites with Katahdin views. ■ **TIP→** Nonguests can use the showers for $2 after hiking or camping at Baxter. ⊠ *30 Twin Pines Rd.* ⊹ *From Millinocket Lake Rd. turn on*

Black Cat Rd., go 1 mile to NEOC (stay left on Twin Pines Rd. shortly before NEOC) ☎ *207/723–5438, 800/634–7238* ⊕ *www.neoc.com.*

North Country Rivers. From spring to fall, North Country Rivers runs white-water rafting trips on the Dead and Kennebec rivers in The Forks in western Maine, and on the West Branch of Penobscot River outside Millinocket in the North Woods. North Country's 55-acre resort south of The Forks in Bingham has cabin and cottage rentals, a restaurant, pub, and store. Its Millinocket base is at Big Moose Inn. The outfitter also offers moose and wildlife safaris and rents snowmobiles, mountain and trail bikes, and kayaks. ⊠ *46 Main St., Bingham* ☎ *207/672–4814, 800/348–8871* ⊕ *www.northcountryrivers.com.*

6

MAINE COAST

Visit Fodors.com for advice, updates, and bookings

WELCOME TO MAINE COAST

TOP REASONS TO GO

★ **Lobster:** It's not a Maine vacation without donning a bib and digging into a steamed lobster with drawn butter for dipping.

★ **Boating:** The coastline of Maine was made for boaters. Whether it's your own boat, a friend's, or a charter, make sure you get out on the water.

★ **Wild Maine Blueberries:** They may be tiny, but the wild blueberries pack a flavorful punch in season (late July to early September).

★ **Cadillac Mountain:** Drive the winding 3½-mile road to the 1,530-foot summit in Acadia National Park for the sunrise.

★ **Perfect Souvenir:** Buy a watercolor, hand-painted pottery, or handcrafted jewelry—artists and craftspeople abound.

1 The Southern Coast. Stretching north from Kittery to just outside Portland, this is Maine's most visited region. The towns along the shore and miles of sandy expanses cater to summer visitors. Old Orchard Beach features Coney Island–like amusements, while Kittery, the Yorks, Wells, and the Kennebunks are more low-key getaways.

2 Portland. Maine's largest and most cosmopolitan city, Portland balances its historic role as a working harbor with its newer identity as a center of sophisticated arts and shopping and innovative restaurants.

3 The Mid-Coast Region. North of Portland, from Brunswick to Monhegan Island, the craggy coastline winds its way around pastoral peninsulas. Its villages boast maritime museums, antiques shops, and beautiful architecture.

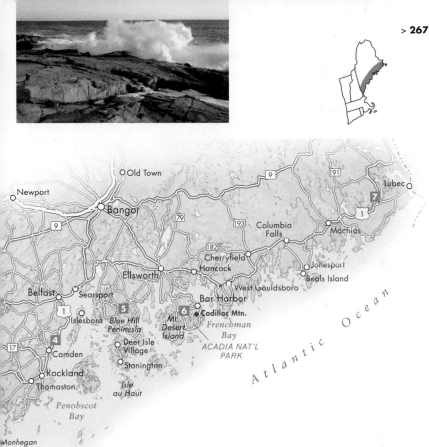

4 Penobscot Bay. This region combines lively coastal towns with dramatic natural scenery. Camden is one of Maine's most picture-perfect towns, with its pointed church steeples, antique homes, cozy harbor, and historic windjammer fleet.

5 Blue Hill Peninsula. Art galleries are plentiful here, and the entire region is ideal for biking, hiking, kayaking, and boating. For many, the peninsula defines the silent beauty of the Maine Coast.

6 Acadia National Park and Mount Desert Island. Millions come to enjoy Acadia National Park's stunning peaks and vistas of the island's mountains. Bar Harbor is more of a visitor's haven, while Southwest Harbor and Bass Harbor offer quieter retreats.

7 Way Down East. This is the "real" Maine, some say, and it unfurls in thousands of acres of wild blueberry barrens, congestion-free coastlines, and a tangible sense of rugged endurance.

GETTING ORIENTED

Much of the appeal of the Maine Coast lies in its geographical contrasts, from its long stretches of swimming and walking beaches in the south to the cliff-edged, rugged, rocky coasts in the north. And not unlike the physical differences of the coast, each town along the way reveals a slightly different character.

Updated by
Brian Kevin

As you drive across the border into Maine, a sign announces: "The way life should be." Romantics luxuriate in the feeling of a down comforter on a yellow-pine bed or in the sensation of the wind and salt spray on their faces while cruising in a historic windjammer. Families love the unspoiled beaches and safe inlets dotting the shoreline. Hikers are revived while roaming the trails of Acadia National Park, and adventure-seekers kayak along the coast.

The Maine Coast is several places in one. Portland may be Maine's largest metropolitan area, but its attitude is decidedly more big town than small city. South of Portland, Ogunquit, Kennebunkport, Old Orchard Beach, and other resort towns predominate along a reasonably smooth shoreline. North of Portland and Casco Bay, secondary roads turn south off U.S. 1 onto so many oddly chiseled peninsulas that it's possible to drive for days without retracing your route. Slow down to explore the museums, galleries, and shops in the larger towns and the antiques and curio shops and harborside lobster shacks in the smaller fishing villages. Freeport is an entity unto itself, a place where numerous name-brand outlets and specialty stores have sprung up around the retail outpost of famous outfitter L. L. Bean. And no description of the coast would be complete without mention of popular Acadia National Park, with its majestic mountains that are often shrouded in mist.

If you come to Maine seeking an untouched fishing village with locals gathered around a potbellied stove in the general store, you'll likely come away disappointed; that innocent age has passed in all but the most remote spots like Way Down East. Tourism has supplanted fishing, logging, and potato farming as Maine's number one industry, and most areas are well equipped to receive the annual onslaught of visitors. But whether you are stepping outside a cabin for a walk in the woods or watching a boat rock at its anchor, you can sense the wilderness nearby, even on the edges of the most urbanized spots.

PLANNING

WHEN TO GO

Maine's dramatic coastline and pure natural beauty welcome visitors year-round, but note that many smaller museums and attractions are open only for high season—from Memorial Day to mid-October—as are many of the waterside attractions and eateries.

Summer begins in earnest on July 4th, and many smaller inns, B&Bs, and hotels from Kittery on up to the Bar Harbor region are booked a month or two ahead on weekends through August. That's also the case come fall, when the fiery foliage draws leaf peepers. After Halloween, hotel rates drop significantly until ski season begins around Thanksgiving. Along the coast, bed-and-breakfasts that remain open will often rent rooms at far lower prices than in summer.

In spring the fourth Sunday in March is designated as Maine Maple Sunday, and farms throughout the state open their doors to visitors not only to watch sap turn into golden syrup but to sample the sweet results.

PLANNING YOUR TIME

You could easily spend a lifetime's worth of vacations along the Maine Coast and never truly see it all. But if you are determined to travel the coast from end to end, allot at least two weeks to travel comfortably.

Driving in Coastal Maine		
	Miles	Time
Boston–Portland	112	2 hours
Kittery–Portland	50	50 minutes
Portland–Freeport	18	20 minutes
Portland–Camden	80	2 hours
Portland–Bar Harbor	175	3 hours, 20 minutes

GETTING HERE AND AROUND

AIR TRAVEL

Maine has two major international airports, Portland International Jetport and Bangor International Airport, to get you to or close to your coastal destination. Manchester–Boston Regional Airport in New Hampshire is about 45 minutes away from the southern end of the Maine coastline. Boston's Logan Airport is the only truly international airport in the region; it's about 90 minutes south of the Maine border.

CAR TRAVEL

Once you are here the best way to experience the winding back roads of the craggy Maine Coast is in a car. There are miles and miles of roads far from the larger towns that have no bus services, and you won't want to miss discovering your own favorite ocean vista while on a scenic drive.

BUS TRAVEL

The Shoreline Explorer links seasonal trolleys in southern Maine beach towns from the Yorks to the Kennebunks, allowing you to travel between towns without a car.

Shoreline Explorer ☎ *207/459–2932* ⊕ *www.shorelineexplorer.com.*

TRAIN TRAVEL

Amtrak offers regional service from Boston to Portland via its Downeaster line that originates at Boston's North Station and makes six stops in Maine: Wells, Saco, Old Orchard Beach (seasonal), Portland, Freeport, and Brunswick. Greyhound and Concord Coach Lines also offer bus service from Boston to many towns along the Maine Coast. Concord has express service between Portland and Boston's Logan Airport and South Station. Both Concord and Amtrak operate out of the Portland Transportation Center at ⊠ *100 Thompson's Point Road.*

RESTAURANTS

Many breakfast spots along the coast open as early as 6 am to serve the going-to-work crowd (in fishing areas as early as 4 am). Lunch generally runs 11–2:30; dinner is usually served 5–9. Only in the larger cities will you find full dinners being offered much later than 9, although in larger towns you can usually find a bar or bistro serving a limited menu late into the evening.

Many restaurants in Maine are closed Monday, though this isn't true in resort areas in high season. However, resort-town eateries often shut down completely in the off-season. *Unless otherwise noted in reviews, restaurants are open daily for lunch and dinner.*

Credit cards are accepted for meals throughout Maine, even in some of the most modest establishments.

The one signature dinner on the Maine Coast is, of course, the lobster dinner. It generally includes boiled lobster, a clam or seafood chowder, corn on the cob, and coleslaw or perhaps a salad. Lobster prices vary from day to day, but generally a full lobster dinner should cost around $25; without all the add-ons, about $18. *Prices in the reviews are the average cost of a main course at dinner or, if dinner is not served, at lunch.*

HOTELS

Beachfront and roadside motels and historic-home B&Bs and inns make up the majority of accommodation options along the Maine Coast. There are a few large luxury resorts, such as the Samoset Resort in Rockport or the Bar Harbor Inn in Bar Harbor, but most accommodations are simple and relatively inexpensive. You will find hotel chains in larger cities and towns, including major tourist destinations like Freeport and Bar Harbor. Many properties close during the off-season—mid-October until mid-May; some that stay open drop their rates dramatically. There is an 8% state hospitality tax on all room rates. *Prices in the reviews are the lowest cost of a standard double room in high season.*

TOURS

No visit to the Maine Coast is complete without some outdoor activity—be it generated by two wheels, two feet, two paddles, or pulling a bag full of clubs.

BICYCLING

The Bicycle Coalition of Main and Explore Maine by Bike are excellent sources for trail maps and other riding information.

Bicycle Coalition of Maine. The well-regarded Bicycle Coalition of Maine's website includes where to rent bikes. ☎ *207/623–4511* ⊕ *www. bikemaine.org.*

Explore Maine by Bike. Run by the Maine Department of Transportation, this helpful website includes an exhaustive list of the state's most popular bike routes. ⊕ *www.exploremaine.org/bike.*

HIKING

Exploring the Maine Coast on foot is a quick way to acclimate to the relaxed pace of life here.

Healthy Maine Walks. Healthy Maine Walks has comprehensive listings for walks that can be done in an hour or less, from park paths to routes that follow roads and streets. ⊕ *www.healthymainewalks.com.*

KAYAKING

Nothing gets you literally off the beaten path like plying the salt waters in a graceful sea kayak.

Maine Association of Sea Kayaking Guides and Instructors. This association lists state-licensed guides and offers information about instructional classes, guided tours, and trip planning. ⊕ *www.maskgi.org.*

Maine Island Trail Association. Seasoned paddlers can join the Maine Island Trail Association ($45) for a map of and full access to Maine's famous sea trail: more than 200 islands and mainland sites, most privately owned but open to members, on a 375-mile path from the southernmost coast to the Canadian Maritimes. Member benefits also include discounts at outfitters and retailers. ☎ *207/761–8225* ⊕ *www.mita.org.*

THE SOUTHERN COAST

Maine's southernmost coastal towns—Kittery, the Yorks, Ogunquit, the Kennebunks, and the Old Orchard Beach area—present a few of the stunning faces of the state's coast, from the miles and miles of inviting sandy beaches to the beautifully kept historic towns and carnival-like attractions. There is something for every taste, whether you seek solitude in a kayak or prefer being caught up in the infectious spirit of fellow vacationers.

North of Kittery, long stretches of hard-packed white-sand beach are closely crowded by nearly unbroken ranks of beach cottages, motels, and oceanfront restaurants. The summer colonies of York Beach and Wells brim with family crowds, T-shirt and gift shops, and shorefront development; nearby wildlife refuges and land reserves promise an easy quiet escape. York Village evokes yesteryear sentiment with its acclaimed historic district, while upscale Ogunquit tantalizes visitors with its array of shops and a cliffside walk.

More than any other region south of Portland, the Kennebunks—and especially Kennebunkport—provide the complete Maine Coast experience: classic townscapes where white-clapboard houses rise from manicured lawns and gardens; rocky shorelines punctuated by sandy beaches; quaint downtown districts packed with gift shops, ice cream stands, and visitors; harbors with lobster boats bobbing alongside yachts; rustic, picnic-tabled restaurants serving lobster and fried seafood; and well-appointed dining rooms. As you continue north, the scents of fried dough and cotton candy mean you've arrived at Maine's version of Coney Island: Old Orchard Beach.

KITTERY

65 miles north of Boston; 3 miles north of Portsmouth, New Hampshire.

One of the earliest settlements in the state of Maine, Kittery suffered its share of British, French, and Native American attacks throughout the 17th and 18th centuries, yet rose to prominence as a vital shipbuilding center. The tradition continues: despite its New Hampshire name, the Portsmouth Naval Shipyard is part of Maine and has been building U.S. submarines since World War I. It was founded in 1800 and built its first warship in 1815. It's not open to the public, but those on boats can pass by and get a glimpse.

Known as the "Gateway to Maine," Kittery has become a major shopping destination thanks to its complex of factory outlets. Flanking both sides of U.S. 1 are more than 120 stores, which attract hordes of shoppers year-round. For something a little less commercial, head east on Route 103 to the hidden Kittery most people miss: the lands around **Kittery Point.** Here you can find hiking and biking trails and great views of the water. With Portsmouth, New Hampshire, across the water, Whaleback Ledge Lighthouse, and the nearby Isles of Shoals, Kittery is a picturesque place to pass some time. The isles and the light, as well as two others, can be seen from two forts along or near this winding stretch of Route 103: Fort McClary State Historic Site and Fort Foster, a town park (both closed to vehicles off-season).

GETTING HERE AND AROUND

Three bridges—on U.S. 1, U.S. 1 Bypass, and Interstate 95—cross the Piscataqua River from Portsmouth, New Hampshire to Kittery. Interstate 95 has three Kittery exits. Route 103 is a scenic coastal drive through Kittery Point to York.

ESSENTIALS

Visitor Information Greater York Region Chamber of Commerce ✉ *1 Stonewall La., off U.S. 1, York* ☎ *207/363–4422* ⊕ *www.gatewaytomaine. org.* **Kittery Visitor Information Center** ✉ *U.S. 1 and I–95* ☎ *800/767–8709* ⊕ *www.mainetourism.com.*

WHERE TO EAT

$$$
SEAFOOD
FAMILY

✕ **Chauncey Creek Lobster Pound.** From the road you can barely see the red roof hovering below the trees, but chances are you can see the cars parked at this popular outdoor restaurant along the high banks of the tidal river, beside a working pier. Brightly colored picnic tables fill the deck and an enclosed eating area. The menu has lots of fresh lobster choices and a raw bar with offerings like clams and oysters. Bring your own beer or wine if you desire alcohol. You can also bring sides and

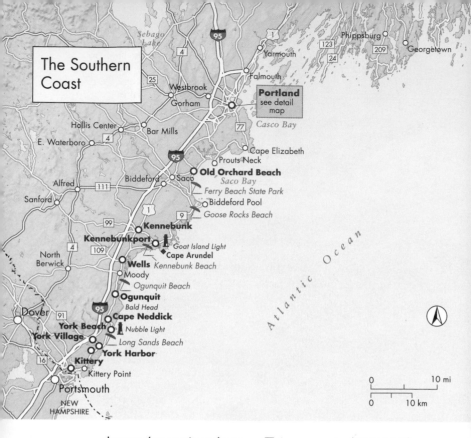

The Southern Coast

Sebago Lake

Phippsburg
Georgetown
Yarmouth
Falmouth
Westbrook
Gorham
Portland
see detail map
Casco Bay
Hollis Center
Bar Mills
E. Waterboro
Cape Elizabeth
Prouts Neck
Old Orchard Beach
Biddeford Saco
Saco Bay
Alfred
Ferry Beach State Park
Biddeford Pool
Goose Rocks Beach
Sanford
Kennebunk
North Berwick
Kennebunkport
Goat Island Light
Cape Arundel
Wells *Kennebunk Beach*
Moody
Ogunquit Beach
Ogunquit
Dover
Bald Head
Cape Neddick
York Beach
Nubble Light
York Village
Long Sands Beach
York Harbor
Kittery
Kittery Point
Portsmouth
NEW HAMPSHIRE

Atlantic Ocean

| 0 | | 10 mi |
| 0 | | 10 km |

desserts that aren't on the menu. $ *Average main: $22* ⊠ *16 Chauncey Creek Rd., Kittery Point* ☎ *207/439–1030* ⊕ *www.chaunceycreek.com* ☉ *Closed Columbus Day–mid-May. Closed Mon. Labor Day–Columbus Day.*

SPORTS AND THE OUTDOORS
HIKING AND WALKING
Cutts Island Trail. For a peek into the Rachel Carson National Wildlife Refuge, this 2-mile trail leads into the 800-acre Brave Boat Harbor Division. It's one of only a handful of trails in its 11 divisions. It's a prime bird-watching area. There's a kiosk at the trailhead. ⊠ *Seapoint Rd.* ⊕ *www.fws.gov/refuge/rachel_carson.*

YORK VILLAGE

8 miles north of Kittery via I–95, U.S. 1, and U.S. 1A.

The actual village of York is quite small, housing the town's basic components of post office, town hall, several shops and galleries, and a stretch of antique homes. As subdued as the town may feel today, the history of York Village reveals a far different character. One of the first permanently settled areas in the state of Maine, it was once witness to great destruction and fierce fighting during the French, Indian, and

British wars; towns and fortunes were sacked, yet the potential for prosperity encouraged the area's citizens continually to rebuild and start anew. Colonial York citizens enjoyed great wealth and success from fishing and lumber as well as a penchant for politics. Angered by the British-imposed taxes, York held its own little-known tea party in 1775 in protest.

GETTING HERE AND AROUND

York is Exit 7 off Interstate 95; follow signs to U.S. 1, the modern commercial strip. From here U.S. 1A winds to the village center and on to York Harbor and York Beach before looping back up to U.S. 1 in Cape Neddick.

EXPLORING

George Marshall Store Gallery. Storefront windows and bead-board trim at the George Marshall Store Gallery, built in 1867, pay homage to its past as a general store, but the focus here is on the present. Changing exhibits focus on prominent and up-and-coming regional artists. ☒ *140 Lindsay Rd.* ☎ *207/351–1083* ⊕ *www.georgemarshallstoregallery.com* ☉ *Mid-May–early Oct., Tues.–Sat. 10–5, Sun. 1–5; Apr.–mid-May and early Oct.–mid-Nov., Wed.–Sat. 10–4, Sun. 1–4; mid-Nov.–Mar., by appt.*

Museums of Old York. Nine historic 18th- and 19th-century buildings, clustered on York Street and along Lindsay Road and the York River, highlight York's rich history starting in early Colonial times. The Old York Gaol (1719) was once the King's Prison for the Province of Maine; inside are dungeons, cells, and the jailer's quarters. The many period rooms in the Emerson-Wilcox House—the main part was built in 1742—display items from daily life here in centuries past, including furniture from as early as the 1600s and an impressive ceramic dishware collection. The 1731 Elizabeth Perkins House reflects the Victorian style of its last occupants, the prominent Perkins family. Buy tickets at the Parsons Education Center, which has changing exhibits, or at the Old York Gaol. ■TIP➔ **Tickets are good for the season.** ☒ *Parsons Education Center, 3 Lindsay Rd.* ☎ *207/363–4974* ⊕ *www.oldyork. org* ☒ *$6 for one museum, $12 for all* ☉ *Memorial Day–mid-Oct., Tues.–Sat. 10–5, Sun. 1–5.*

Stonewall Kitchen. You've probably seen the kitchen's smartly labeled jars of gourmet chutneys, jams, jellies, salsas, and sauces in specialty stores back home. This complex houses the expansive flagship company store, which has a viewing area of the bottling process and stunning gardens. Sample all the mustards, salsas, and dressings you can stand, or have lunch at the café and take-out restaurant. The campus also houses a cooking school where you can join in evening or daytime courses. Reservations are required; most classes are shorter than two hours and cost $45 to $80. ☒ *2 Stonewall La., off U.S. 1* ☎ *877/899–8363* ⊕ *www. stonewallkitchen.com* ☉ *Mon.–Sat. 8–7, Sun. 9–6.*

6

SHOPPING

Bradley's Custom Framing & Gallery. Watercolors, oils, pastels, and pottery are among the artworks that can be had at Bradley's Custom Framing & Gallery, where many local artists are represented, including the photographer-owner. ⊠ *244 York St.* ☎ *207/351–3110.*

Gateway Farmers' Market. Bring a basket for morning shopping at the Gateway Farmers' Market, held in the back lot at the Greater York Region Chamber of Commerce. You'll find fresh local produce, lots of baked goods and artisanal breads, local seafood and meat, fresh flowers, and handcrafted items like soaps and candles. It's a good place to gather the makings for a beach picnic. ⊠ *1 Stonewall La., off U.S. 1* ⊕ *www.gatewayfarmersmarket.com* ⊙ *June and Sept.–Columbus Day, Sat. 9–1; July and Aug., Thurs. and Sat. 9–1.*

YORK HARBOR

1 mile from York Village via U.S. 1A.

A short trip from the village proper, York Harbor opens up to the water and offers many places to linger and explore. The harbor is busy with boats of all kinds, while the harbor beach is a good stretch of sand for swimming. Much more formal than the northward York Beach and much quieter, the area retains a somewhat more exclusive air. Perched along the cliffs on the north side of the harbor are huge "cottages" built by wealthy summer residents in the late 1800s, when the area became a premier seaside resort destination with several grand hotels.

GETTING HERE AND AROUND

After passing through York Village to York Harbor, originally called Lower Town, U.S. 1A winds around and heads north to York Beach's village center, a 4-mile trip.

EXPLORING

Sayward-Wheeler House. Built in 1718, the waterfront home was remodeled in the 1760s by Jonathan Sayward, a local merchant who had prospered in the West Indies trade. By 1860 his descendants had opened the house to the public to share the story of their Colonial ancestors. The house, accessible only by guided tour, preserves the decor of a prosperous New England family at the outset of the Revolutionary War. The parlor—considered one of the country's best-preserved Colonial interiors, with a tall clock and mahogany Chippendale-style chairs—looks pretty much as it did when Sayward lived here. ⊠ *9 Barrell La. Extension* ☎ *207/384–2454* ⊕ *www.historicnewengland.org* 🎟 *$5* ⊙ *June–mid-Oct., 2nd and 4th Sat. of month 11–5.*

WHERE TO EAT

$$$

SEAFOOD

✕**Dockside Restaurant.** On an island-like peninsula overlooking York Harbor, this restaurant has plenty of seafood on the menu, including popular dishes like haddock stuffed with Maine shrimp and "drunken" lobster—sautéed lobster, scallops, shallots, and herbs in an Irish whiskey cream. There are also treats like beef tenderloin, slow-roasted duckling, seafood chowder, or cakes of native crab and wild mushrooms. Floor-to-ceiling windows in the stair-stepped modern dinning space transport diners to the water beyond; every seat has a water view. Lighter fare is served in the cozy mahogany bar. Dockside is part of a 7-acre property with lodging rooms and suites in several buildings, from a grand 1895 summer home to condo-style quarters. [$] *Average main: $25* ✉ *22 Harris Island Rd., off Rte. 103, York* ☎ *207/363–2722* 🌐 *www.docksiderestaurant.com* 🕒 *Closed late Oct.–late May and Tues. in June and Sept.*

$$$ SEAFOOD 🍴 **Foster's Downeast Clambake.** Save your appetite for this one. Specializing in the traditional Maine clambake—a feast consisting of rich clam chowder, a pile of mussels and steamers, Maine lobster, corn on the cob, roasted potatoes and onions, and Maine blueberry crumb cake (phew!)—this massive complex provides musical entertainment as well as belly-busting meals. There are also several barbecue offerings. [$] *Average main: $28* ✉ *5 Axholme Rd., at U.S. 1A, York* ☎ *207/363–3255, 800/552–0242* 🌐 *www.fostersclambake.com* 🕒 *Closed early Sept.–late May and weekdays late May–mid-June.*

WHERE TO STAY

$$$ B&B/INN 🏨 **Inn at Tanglewood Hall.** The inn's artfully painted floors, lush wallpapers, and meticulous attention to detail are the fruits of a former designation as a designers' showcase home. **Pros:** authentic historic lodging; serene setting amid gardens; short walk to beaches. **Cons:** no water views. [$] *Rooms from: $195* ✉ *611 York St., York* ☎ *207/351–1075* 🌐 *www.tanglewoodhall.com* 🛏 *4 rooms, 2 suites* 🍽 *Breakfast.*

$$$$ B&B/INN 🏨 **Stage Neck Inn.** Since the 1870s, successive hotels have perched on this tiny rock-clad peninsula beside at York Harbor's entrance. **Pros:** elaborate full-breakfast buffet with scrumptious baked goods; poolside service and snack bar in season; rooms have balconies or deck areas. **Cons:** no suites. [$] *Rooms from: $283* ✉ *8 Stage Neck Rd., off U.S. 1A, York* ☎ *207/363–3850* 🌐 *www.stageneck.com* 🛏 *58 rooms* 🕒 *Closed for 2 wks after Jan. 1* 🍽 *Breakfast.*

$$$ B&B/INN 🏨 **York Harbor Inn.** A mid-17th-century fishing cabin with dark timbers and a fieldstone fireplace forms the heart of this historic inn, which now includes several neighboring buildings that have been added over the years. **Pros:** many rooms have harbor views; close to beaches, scenic walking trails. **Cons:** rooms vary greatly in style, size, and appeal. [$] *Rooms from: $179* ✉ *480 York St., York* ☎ *207/363–5119* 🌐 *www.yorkharborinn.com* 🛏 *60 rooms, 2 suites* 🍽 *Breakfast.*

SPORTS AND THE OUTDOORS

BIKING

Berger's Bike Shop. This former auto garage rents hybrid bikes for local excursions. ✉ *241 York St., York Village* ☎ *207/363–4070* 🌐 *www.bergersbikeshop.com.*

FISHING

Fish Tale Charters. Fish Tale Charters takes anglers on fly-fishing or light tackle charters in search of stripers or juvenile bluefin tuna; trips depart from Town Dock No. 2 in York Harbor. ✉ *Town Dock No. 2, 20 Harris Island Rd., York* ☎ *207/363–3874* 🌐 *www.maineflyfishing.net.*

Rip Tide Charters. Rip Tide Charters goes where the fish are—departure points vary, from Ogunquit to York and Portsmouth, New Hampshire.

6

It specializes in fly-fishing and light tackle for stripers, mackerel, and bluefish. ☎ *207/337–3608* ⊕ *www.mainestriperfishing.com.*

Shearwater Charters. Shearwater Charters offers light tackle and fly-fishing charters in the York River and along the shoreline from Kittery to Ogunquit. Bait-fishing trips are also available. Departures are from Town Dock #2 in York Harbor. ⊠ *Town Dock #2, 20 Harris Island Rd., York* ☎ *207/363–5324* ⊕ *www.mainestripers.net.*

HIKING AND WALKING

Cliff Walk and Fisherman's Walk. Two walking trails traverse the shore from near Harbor Beach. Just beside it in a small park, the Cliff Walk ascends its granite namesake, running past the summer "cottage" mansions at the harbor entrance. There are some steps, but as signs caution, tread carefully because of erosion. Fisherman's Walk, on the other hand, is an easy stroll. Starting across Stage Neck Road from the beach, it passes waterfront businesses, historic homes, and rocky harbor beaches on the way to York's beloved Wiggly Bridge. This pedestrian suspension bridge alongside Route 103 (there is minimal parking here) leads to Steedman Woods, a public preserve with a shaded loop trail along the York River estuary's ambling waters. You can also enter the preserve near the George Marshall Store in York Village ⊠ *Stage Neck Rd., off U.S. 1A.*

YORK BEACH

6 miles north of York Harbor via U.S. 1A.

Like many shorefront towns in Maine, York Beach has a long history of entertaining summer visitors. Take away today's bikinis and smartphones and it's easy to imagine squealing tourists adorned in the full-length bathing garb of the late 19th century. Just as they did back then, visitors today come here to eat ice cream, enjoy carnival-like novelties, and indulge in the sun and sea air.

York Beach is a real family destination, devoid of all things staid and stuffy—children are meant to be seen and heard here. Just beyond the sands of Short Sand Beach are a host of amusements, from bowling to indoor minigolf and the Fun-O-Rama arcade. Nubble Light is at the tip of the peninsula separating Long Sands and Short Sands beaches. The latter is mostly lined with unpretentious seasonal homes, though motels and restaurants are mixed in.

GETTING HERE AND AROUND

It's a scenic 6 miles to York Beach via the loop road U.S. 1A from its southern intersection with U.S. 1. Although 2 miles longer, it's generally faster to continue north on U.S. 1A to Cape Neddick and take U.S 1A south to the village center, home to Short Sands Beach. Here U.S. 1A is known as Ocean Avenue as it heads north from York Harbor along Long Sands Beach en route to York Beach village and Short Sands Beach. A trolley along U.S. 1 links the beaches in summer. You can also get from beach to beach on a series of residential streets that wind around Nubble Point between these beaches.

York Trolley Co. From late June through Labor Day, York Trolley Co.'s bright red trolleys link Short Sands Beach in York Beach village and nearby Long Sands Beach, running along U.S. 1A with a number of stops. Route maps can be picked up throughout York; fares are $1.50 one way, $3 round-trip. You can also connect with a shuttle service to Ogunquit. ☎ *207/363–9600* ⊕ *www.yorktrolley.com.*

EXPLORING

Nubble Light. On a small island just off the tip of the cape jutting dramatically into the Atlantic Ocean between Long Sands Beach and Short Sands Beach, Nubble Light is one of the most photographed lighthouses on the globe. Direct access is prohibited, but the small Sohier Park right across from the light has parking, historical placards, benches, and a seasonal information center that shares the 1879 light's history. ✉ *End of Nubble Rd., off U.S. 1A, York* ☎ *207/363–3569 Memorial Day weekend–Labor Day* ⊕ *www.nubblelight.org* ☉ *Park, daily; information center, mid-Apr.–mid-May, daily 9–4; mid-May–late Oct. 9–4.*

FAMILY **York's Wild Kingdom.** Ringed by woods, this popular zoo has an impressive variety of exotic animals and is home to the state's only white Bengal tiger. There's a nostalgic charm to the amusement park, which offers discounts for kids under 13—the target market, since there are no large thrill rides. Many York Beach visitors come just to enjoy the ocean views from the Ferris wheel and share what's advertised as the "seaboard's largest fried dough." ✉ *23 Railroad Ave., off U.S. 1* ☎ *207/363–4911, 800/456–4911* ⊕ *www.yorkzoo.com* ☜ *$14.75 for zoo; $21.25 for zoo and rides* ☉ *Zoo late May–late Sept. daily 10–5; amusement park hrs vary.*

WHERE TO EAT AND STAY

$ ✕ **The Goldenrod.** If you wanted to, you could eat nothing but the famous taffy here, made the same way today as it was back in 1896. The famous Goldenrod Kisses, some 50 tons of which are made per year, are a great attraction, and people line the windows to watch the taffy being made. Aside from the famous candy (there's penny candy, too), this eating place is family oriented, very reasonably priced, and a great place to get ice cream from the old-fashioned soda fountain. Breakfast is served all day, while the simple lunch menu of sandwiches and burgers doubles as dinner, along with a handful of entrées like baked haddock and meat loaf. $ *Average main: $10* ✉ *2 Railroad Ave.* ☎ *207/363–2621* ⊕ *www. thegoldenrod.com* ☉ *Closed mid-Oct.–mid-May.*

AMERICAN

$$$$ 🛏 **Union Bluff Hotel.** This massive, turreted structure still looks much the same as it did when it opened in the mid-19th century. **Pros:** many spectacular ocean views; in the middle of the action. **Cons:** rooms lack any charm or character befitting the inn's origins; not for those looking for a quiet getaway. $ *Rooms from: $229* ✉ *8 Beach St.* ☎ *207/363–1333, 800/833–0721* ⊕ *www.unionbluff.com* ☜ *65 rooms, 6 suites* ⊚ *No meals.*

HOTEL

6

NIGHTLIFE

Inn on the Blues. This hopping music club attracts national bands playing funk, jazz, and reggae, as well as blues. It's open April through December and weekends only in the shoulder seasons. ✉ *7 Ocean Ave., York* ☎ *207/351–3221* 🌐 *www.innontheblues.com.*

CAPE NEDDICK

1 mile north of York Beach via U.S. 1A.

Cape Neddick is one of the less developed of York's areas, but there's not much public access to the water. It has many modest homes, with a sprinkling of businesses catering to locals and visitors. There are a few restaurants and inns but no distinct village hub. Cape Neddick Harbor is at its southern end, beyond York Beach village.

GETTING HERE AND AROUND

U.S. 1A returns to U.S. 1 in Cape Neddick after its 7-mile loop down to the coast starting in southern York near Exit 7 off Interstate 95. U.S. 1 continues north to Ogunquit.

EXPLORING

Mount Agamenticus Park. A park sits atop this humble summit of 692 feet, one of the highest points along the Atlantic seaboard. That may not seem like much, but if you choose to hike to the top, you will be rewarded with incredible views all the way to the White Mountains in New Hampshire. If you don't want to hoof it (though it's not very steep), there is parking at the top. ✉ *Mountain Road, off U.S. 1* ☎ *207/361–1102* 🌐 *www.agamenticus.org* 🕒 *Daily dawn–dusk.*

WHERE TO EAT

$ AMERICAN

🍴 **Flo's Steamed Hot Dogs.** Yes, it seems crazy to highlight a hot-dog stand, but this is no ordinary place. Who would guess that a hot dog could make it into *Saveur* and *Gourmet* magazines? There is something grand about this shabby, red-shingle shack that has been dealing dogs since 1959. The line is out the door most days, but this place is so efficient that the wait isn't long. Flo has passed on, but her son and daughter-in-law keep the business going, satisfying thousands of customers each year. The classic here has mayo and the special sauce—consisting of, among other things, onions and molasses (you can buy a bottle to take home, and you'll want to). [$] *Average main: $3* ✉ *1359 U.S. 1* 🌐 *www.floshotdogs.com* 💳 *No credit cards* 🕒 *Closed Wed. No dinner.*

$$$ ECLECTIC

🍴 **Frankie & Johnny's Restaurant.** If you've had about all the fried seafood you can stand, try this hip spot that focuses on creative cuisine served with flair. There are lots of seafood, poultry, and meat options, homemade pasta choices, and always a few vegetarian dishes (special requests like gluten-free are happily accommodated). The toasted peppercorn-seared sushi-grade tuna, served with coconut risotto on gingered vegetables, is excellent. Pork served with a sweet pear-cream sauce is also a signature dish. Even the breads and most desserts are made by the chef. Entrées include really large dinner salads with fruit and nuts as well as veggies atop the greens. You're welcome to bring your own libations; only cash and checks are accepted. [$] *Average main: $28*

Ogunquit's Perkins Cove is a pleasant place to admire the boats—and wonder at the origin of their names.

⊠ *1594 U.S. 1* ☎ *207/363–1909* ⊕ *www.frankie-johnnys.com* ▭ *No credit cards* ⊗ *Closed Mon., Tues., and mid-Dec.–early Feb. Closed Wed. mid-Feb.–June and Sept.–early Dec. No lunch.*

SPORTS AND THE OUTDOORS

FISHING

Eldredge Bros. Fly Shop. This shop offers various guided fishing trips, private casting lessons, and, come June, striper and trout "schools." There are fly-tying and rod-building seminars in the off-season. Kayak rentals and rod-and-reel rentals are also available. ⊠ *1480 U.S. 1* ☎ *207/363–9269, 877/427–9345* ⊕ *www.eldredgeflyshop.com.*

KAYAKING

Excursions Coastal Maine Outfitting Co. Hop on one of the regularly scheduled guided kayak trips with Excursions Coastal Maine Outfitting Co. You can cruise along the shoreline or sign up for an overnight paddle. Reservations are recommended; trips start at $60. Classes are also offered. ⊠ *1740 U.S. 1* ☎ *207/363–0181* ⊕ *www.excursionsinmaine. com.*

SHOPPING

Jeremiah Campbell & Co. Reproductions of 18th- and 19th-century home furnishings are the specialty of Jeremiah Campbell & Co. Everything here is handcrafted, from rugs, decoys, furniture, and lighting to glassware. ⊠ *1537 U.S. 1* ☎ *207/363–8499* ⊕ *www.jeremiahcampbell.com* ⊗ *Closed Wed.*

OGUNQUIT

8 miles north of the Yorks via U.S. 1.

A resort village since the late 19th century, stylish Ogunquit gained fame as an artists' colony. Today it has become a mini Provincetown, with a gay population that swells in summer. Many inns and small clubs cater to a primarily gay and lesbian clientele. The nightlife in Ogunquit revolves around the precincts of Ogunquit Square and Perkins Cove, where people stroll, often enjoying an after-dinner ice cream cone or espresso. For a scenic drive, take Shore Road from downtown to the 175-foot Bald Head Cliff; you'll be treated to views up and down the coast. On a stormy day the surf can be quite wild here.

GETTING HERE AND AROUND

Parking in the village and at the beach is costly and limited, so leave your car at the hotel and hop the trolley. It costs $1.50 a trip and runs Memorial Day weekend until Columbus Day, with weekend-only service for the first few weeks. From Perkins Cove the trolley runs through town along Shore Road and then down to Ogunquit Beach; it also stops along U.S. 1.

ESSENTIALS

Transportation Information Ogunquit Trolley ☎ *207/646–1411* 🌐 *www.ogunquittrolley.com* 🎫 *$1.50.*

Visitor Information Ogunquit Chamber of Commerce ✉ *36 Main St.* ☎ *207/646–2939* 🌐 *www.ogunquit.org.*

EXPLORING

Perkins Cove. This neck of land off Shore Road in the lower part of Oqunquit village has a jumble of sea-beaten fish houses and buildings that were part of an art school. These have largely been transformed by the tide of tourism into shops and restaurants. When you've had your fill of browsing, stroll out along **Marginal Way,** a mile-long footpath that hugs the shore of a rocky promontory known as Israel's Head. Benches allow you to appreciate the open sea vistas. ✉ *Perkins Cove Rd., off Shore Rd.*

WHERE TO EAT AND STAY

$ AMERICAN 🍴 **Amore Breakfast.** You could hardly find a more satisfying, full-bodied breakfast than at this smart and busy joint just shy of the entrance to Perkins Cove. A lighthearted mix of retro advertising signs adorns the walls of this bright, open, and very bustling dining room. You won't find tired standards here—the only pancakes are German potato. The Oscar Madison omelet combines crabmeat with asparagus and Swiss, topped with a béarnaise sauce. For a really decadent start, opt for the Banana Foster: pecan-coated, cream cheese–stuffed French toast with a side of sautéed bananas in rum syrup. Next door, at the Cafe Amore, you can pick up sandwiches and other light fare. [$] *Average main: $10* ✉ *309 Shore Rd.* ☎ *207/646–6661* 🌐 *www.amorebreakfast.com* 🕒 *Closed mid-Dec.–early Apr. No dinner.*

$$$ HOTEL 🏨 **Ogunquit Resort Motel.** Right along U.S. 1 just a mile north of Ogunquit village, this affordable place is a great choice for families. **Pros:** Continental breakfast is included; good-size rooms; fitness center. **Cons:**

close to highway; no lawns or grounds. $ *Rooms from: $199* ⊠ *719 Main St.* ☎ *877/646–8336* ⊕ *www.ogunquitresort.com* ⤸ *77 rooms, 10 suites* ⚭ *Breakfast.*

WELLS

5 miles north of Ogunquit via U.S. 1.

Lacking any kind of noticeable village center, Wells could be easily overlooked as nothing more than a commercial stretch on U.S. 1 between Ogunquit and the Kennebunks. But look more closely—this is a place where people come to enjoy some of the best beaches on the coast. The town included Ogunquit until 1980. Today this family-oriented beach community has 7 miles of densely populated shoreline, along with nature preserves where you can explore salt marshes and tidal pools.

GETTING HERE AND AROUND

Just $1 per trip, the seasonal Shoreline Trolley serves Wells Beach and Crescent Beach and has many stops along U.S. 1 at motels, campgrounds, restaurants, and so on. You can also catch it at the Wells Transportation Center when the Downeaster (the Amtrak train from Boston to Maine) pulls in.

ESSENTIALS

Transportation Information Shoreline Trolley ☎ *207/324–5762* ⊕ *www. shorelineexplorer.com* ⚭ *$1.*

Visitor Information Wells Chamber of Commerce ⊠ *136 Post Rd.* ☎ *207/646–2451* ⊕ *www.wellschamber.org.*

EXPLORING

Rachel Carson National Wildlife Refuge. At the headquarters of the Rachel Carson National Wildlife Refuge, which has 11 divisions from Kittery to Cape Elizabeth, is the Carson Trail, a one-mile loop. The trail traverses a salt marsh and a white-pine forest where migrating birds and waterfowl of many varieties are regularly spotted, and it borders Branch Brook and the Merriland River. ⊠ *321 Port Rd.* ☎ *207/646–9226* ⊕ *www.fws.gov/northeast/rachelcarson* ☉ *Daily sunrise to sunset.*

QUICK BITES

Congdon's Doughnuts. How would you like a really superior doughnut that the same family has been making since 1945? Congdon's Doughnuts bakes about 40 different varieties, though the plain one really gives you an idea of just how good these doughnuts are. Plain, honey-dipped, and black raspberry jelly are the biggest sellers. There are drive-through and takeout windows, or you can sit inside and have breakfast or lunch. Waits can be long for breakfast in summer. ⊠ *1090 Post Rd.* ☎ *207/646–4219* ⊕ *www. congdons.com.*

WHERE TO EAT AND STAY

$$

SEAFOOD

✕ **Billy's Chowder House.** Locals and vacationers head to this classic roadside seafood restaurant in the midst of a salt marsh en route to Wells Beach. They come for the generous lobster rolls, haddock sandwiches, and chowders, but there are plenty of non-seafood choices, too. Big windows in the bright dining rooms overlook the marsh, part of the Rachel Carson National Wildlife Refuge. [$] *Average main: $15* ✉ *216 Mile Rd.* ☎ *207/646–7558* 🌐 *www.billyschowderhouse.com* 🕒 *Closed mid-Dec.–mid-Jan.*

$$ DINER 🍴 **Maine Diner.** One look at the 1953 exterior and you start craving good diner food. You'll get a little more than you're expecting—how many greasy spoons make an award-winning lobster pie? That's the house favorite, as well as a heavenly seafood chowder. There's plenty of fried seafood in addition to the usual diner fare, and breakfast is served all day. Check out the adjacent gift shop, Remember the Maine. [$] *Average main: $15* ✉ *2265 Post Rd.* ☎ *207/646–4441* 🌐 *www.mainediner.com* 🕒 *Closed at least 1 wk in Jan.*

$$$$ B&B/INN Fodor's Choice ★ 🏨 **Haven by the Sea.** Once the summer mission of St. Martha's Church in Kennebunkport, this exquisite inn has retained many of the original details from its former life as a seaside church, including cathedral ceilings and stained-glass windows. **Pros:** unusual structure with elegant appointments; tucked-away massage room. **Cons:** not an in-town location. [$] *Rooms from: $239* ✉ *59 Church St.* ☎ *207/646–4194* 🌐 *www.havenbythesea.com* 🛏 *7 rooms, 2 suites, 1 apartment* 🍽 *Breakfast.*

SPORTS AND THE OUTDOORS

BEACHES

With its thousands of acres of marsh and preserved land, Wells is a great place to spend a lot of time outdoors. Nearly 7 miles of sand stretch along the boundaries of Wells, making beachgoing a prime occupation. Tidal pools sheltered by rocks are filled with all manner of creatures awaiting discovery. During the summer season a pay-and-display (no quarters, receipt goes on dashboard) parking system is in place at the public beaches.

A summer trolley serves **Crescent Beach,** along Webhannet Drive, and **Wells Beach,** at the end of Mile Road off U.S. 1. There is another parking lot, but no trolley stop, at the north end of Atlantic Avenue, which runs north along the shore from the end of Mile Road. Stretching north from the jetty at Wells Harbor is **Drakes Island Beach** (end of Drakes Island Road off U.S. 1). Lifeguards are on hand at all the beaches, and all have public restrooms.

Crescent Beach. Lined with summer homes, this sandy beach is busy in the summer. The beach and the water are surprisingly clean, considering all the traffic. The swimming's good, and beachgoers can also explore tidal pools and look for seals on the rocks nearby. **Amenities:** food and drink; lifeguards; parking (fee); toilets. **Best for:** swimming. ✉ *Webhannet Dr., south of Mile Rd.* ☎ *207/646–5113.*

Drakes Island Beach. Smaller and quieter than the other two beaches in Wells, Drake's Island Beach is also a little wilder, with rolling sand dunes and access to salt-marsh walking trails at an adjacent estuary. The ice cream truck swings by regularly in the summer. **Amenities:** lifeguards; parking (fee); toilets. **Best for:** walking. ✉ *Island Beach Rd., 1 mile southwest of U.S. 1* ☎ *207/646–5113.*

Wells Beach. The northern end of a two-mile stretch of golden sand, Wells Beach is popular with families and surfers, who line up in the swells and preen on the boardwalk near the arcade and snack shop. The beach's northern tip is a bit quieter, with a long rock jetty perfect for strolling. **Amenities:** food and drink; lifeguards; parking (fee); toilets. **Best for:** surfing; walking. ⊠ *Atlantic Ave., north of Mile Rd.* ☎ *207/646–5113.*

Wheels and Waves. Rent bikes, surfboards, wet suits, boogie boards, kayaks, and all sorts of outdoor gear at Wheels and Waves. ⊠ *365 Post Rd.* ☎ *207/646–5774* ⊕ *www.wheelsnwaves.com.*

KENNEBUNK AND KENNEBUNKPORT

5 miles north of Wells via U.S. 1.

The town centers of Kennebunk and Kennebunkport are separated by 5 miles and two rivers, but united by a common history and a vibe of seaside affluence. Kennebunkport has been a resort area since the 19th century, but its most famous residents have made it even more popular—the presidential Bush family is often in residence in its immense home, which sits dramatically out on Walker's Point on Cape Arundel. The wealth here is as tangible as the sharp sea breezes and the sounds of seagulls overhead. Newer mansions have sprung up alongside the old; a great way to see them is to take a slow drive out along the cape on Ocean Avenue.

Sometimes bypassed on the way to its sister town, Kennebunk has its own appeal. In the 19th century the town was a major shipbuilding center; docks lined the river with hundreds of workers busily crafting the vessels that would bring immense fortune to some of the area's residents. Although the trade is long gone, the evidence that remains of this great wealth exists in Kennebunk's mansions. Kennebunk is a classic small New England town, with an inviting shopping district, steepled churches, and fine examples of 18th- and 19th-century brick and clapboard homes. There are also plenty of natural spaces for walking, swimming, birding, and biking—the Kennebunks' major beaches are here.

Kennebunk's main village sits along U.S. 1, extending west from the Mousam River. The Lower Village is along Routes 9 and 35, 4 miles down Route 35 from the main village, and the drive between the two keeps visitors agog with the splendor of the area's mansions, spread out on both sides of Route 35. To get to the grand and gentle beaches of Kennebunk, continue straight (the road becomes Beach Avenue) at the intersection with Route 9. If you turn left instead, Route 9 will take you across the Kennebunk River, into Kennebunkport's touristy downtown, called Dock Square (or sometimes just "the Port"), a commercial area with restaurants, shops, boat cruises, and galleries. Here you'll find the most activity (and crowds) in the Kennebunks.

GETTING HERE AND AROUND

Take the Intown Trolley for narrated 45-minute jaunts that run daily from Memorial Day weekend through Columbus Day. The $16 fare is valid for the day, so you can hop on and off—or start your journey—at any of the stops. The route includes Kennebunk's beaches and Lower Village and as well as neighboring Kennebunkport's scenery and sights.

6

The main stop is at 21 Ocean Avenue in Kennebunkport, around the corner from Dock Square.

ESSENTIALS

Visitor Information Intown Trolley ☎ 207/967–3686 ⊕ www.intowntrolley. com ☒ $16. **Kennebunk-Kennebunkport Chamber of Commerce** ☒ 16 Water St. ☎ 207/967–0857 ⊕ www.visitthekennebunks.com.

TOURS

To take a little walking tour of Kennebunk's most notable structures, begin at the Federal-style Brick Store Museum at 117 Main Street. Head south on Main Street (turn left out of the museum) to see several extraordinary 18th- and early-19th-century homes, including the **Lexington Elms** at No. 99 (1799), the **Horace Porter House** at No. 92 (1848), and the **Benjamin Brown House** at No. 85 (1788).

When you've had your fill of historic homes, head back up toward the museum, pass the 1773 **First Parish Unitarian Church** (its Asher Benjamin–style steeple contains an original Paul Revere bell), and turn right onto **Summer Street**. This street is an architectural showcase, revealing an array of styles from Colonial to Federal. Walking past these grand beauties will give you a real sense of the economic prowess and glamour of the long-gone shipbuilding industry.

For a guided 90-minute architectural walking tour of Summer Street, contact the museum at ☎ 207/985–4802. You can also purchase a $4.95 map that marks historic buildings or a $15.95 guidebook, *Windows on the Past*.

For a dramatic walk along Kennebunkport's rocky coastline and beneath the views of Ocean Avenue's grand mansions, head out on the **Parson's Way Shore Walk**, a paved 4.8-mile round-trip. Begin at Dock Square and follow Ocean Avenue along the river, passing the Colony Hotel and St. Ann's Church, all the way to Walker's Point. Simply turn back from here.

EXPLORING

Brick Store Museum. The cornerstone of this block-long preservation of early-19th-century commercial and residential buildings is William Lord's Brick Store. Built as a dry-goods store in 1825 in the Federal style, the building has an openwork balustrade across the roof line, granite lintels over the windows, and paired chimneys. Exhibits chronicle the Kennebunk area's history and early American decorative and fine arts. The museum leads architectural walking tours of Kennebunk's National Historic District by appointment from late May through September. For $4.95 you can also purchase a map that marks historic buildings. ☒ 117 Main St. ☎ 207/985–4802 ⊕ www.brickstoremuseum. org ☒ $7.50 ☉ Tues.–Fri. 10–4:30, Sat. 10–1.

Dock Square. Clothing boutiques, T-shirt shops, art galleries, and restaurants line this bustling square and spread out along the nearby streets and alleys. Walk onto the drawbridge to admire the tidal Kennebunk River. Cross to the other side and you are in the Lower Village of neighboring Kennebunk. ☒ Dock Sq., Kennebunkport.

First Families Kennebunkport Museum. Also known as White Columns, the imposing Greek Revival mansion with Doric columns is furnished with the belongings of four generations of the Perkins-Nott family. From mid-July through mid-October, the 1853 house is open for guided tours and also serves as a gathering place for village walking tours. It is owned by the Kennebunkport Historical Society, which has several other historic buildings a mile away at 125–135 North Street, including an old jail and schoolhouse. ⊠ *8 Maine St., Kennebunkport* ☎ *207/967–2751* ⊕ *www.kporthistory.org* ✉ *$10* ☉ *Mid-July–mid-Oct., Mon.–Sat. 11–5.*

First Parish of Kennebunk Unitarian Universalist Church. Built in 1773, just before the American Revolution, this stunning church is a marvel. The 1804 Asher Benjamin–style steeple stands proudly atop the village, and the sounds of the original Paul Revere bell can be heard for miles. The church holds Sunday services at 9:30 am in the summer (10:30 the rest of the year). ⊠ *114 Main St.* ☎ *207/985–3700* ⊕ *www.uukennebunk. org.*

Goose Rocks. Three-mile-long Goose Rocks, a 10-minute drive north of town, has plenty of shallow pools for exploring and a good long stretch of smooth sand. It's a favorite of families with small children. Pick up a $15 daily permit at Kennebunkport Town Hall. **Amenities:** parking (fee). **Best for:** walking. ⊠ *Dyke Rd., off Rte. 9, Kennebunkport.*

Kennebunk Plains. For an unusual experience, visit this 135-acre grasslands habitat that is home to several rare and endangered species. Locals call it Blueberry Plains, and a good portion of the area is abloom with the hues of ripening wild blueberries in late July. After August 1 you are welcome to pick and eat all the berries you can find. The area is maintained by the Nature Conservancy. ⊠ *Webber Hill Rd., 4½ miles northwest of town* ☎ *207/729–5181* ⊕ *www.nature.org* ☉ *Daily sunrise–sunset.*

FAMILY **Seashore Trolley Museum.** Streetcars were built here from 1872 to 1972, including trolleys for major metropolitan areas: Boston to Budapest, New York to Nagasaki, San Francisco to Sydney. Many of them are beautifully restored and displayed. Best of all, you can take a trolley ride for nearly 4 miles on the tracks of the former Atlantic Shoreline trolley line, with a stop along the way at the museum restoration shop, where trolleys are transformed from junk into gems. The outdoor museum is self-guided. ⊠ *195 Log Cabin Rd., Kennebunkport* ☎ *207/967–2712* ⊕ *www.trolleymuseum.org* ✉ *$10* ☉ *Memorial Day–Columbus Day, daily 10–5.*

WHERE TO EAT

$$ ✕ **Duffy's Tavern & Grill.** Every small town needs its own lively and
AMERICAN friendly tavern, and this bustling spot is Kennebunk's favorite, housed in a former shoe factory with exposed brick, soaring ceilings, and hardwood floors. Right outside are the tumbling waters of the Mousam River as it flows from the dam. There's a large bar with overhead televisions and plenty of seating in the main room, plus a less captivating back section. You'll find lots of comfortable standards like burgers, pizza, and the popular fish-and-chips. The tasty onion rings are hand

dipped. $ *Average main: $16* ⊠ *4 Main St.* ☎ *207/985–0050* ⊕ *www.duffyskennebunk.com.*

$$
AMERICAN

✕**Federal Jack's.** Run by the Kennebunkport Brewing Company, this two-story complex is near the bridge from Lower Village into Kennebunkport. All the beers are handcrafted on-site, including Blue Fin Stout and Goat Island Light—try the sampler if you can't decide. In the upstairs restaurant the American pub-style menu includes plenty of seafood; the clam chowder is rich and satisfying. There's also Sunday brunch buffet. The restaurant has two dining rooms and a huge deck that packs in the crowds in the summer. There's live entertainment Thursday through Saturday (Sunday in summer). $ *Average main: $14* ⊠ *8 Western Ave.* ☎ *207/967–4322* ⊕ *www.federaljacks.com.*

$$$
SEAFOOD

✕**Mabel's Lobster Claw.** Since the 1950s, Mabel's has been serving lobsters, homemade pies, and lots of seafood for lunch and dinner in this tiny dwelling out on Ocean Avenue. The decor includes paneled walls, wooden booths, autographed photos of various TV stars (plus members of the Bush family). There's outside seating, and paper place mats that illustrate how to eat a Maine lobster. The house favorite is the Lobster Savannah—split and filled with scallops, shrimp, and mushrooms and baked in a Newburg sauce. Save room for the peanut-butter ice cream pie. There's also a take-out window where you can order ice cream and food. $ *Average main: $25* ⊠ *124 Ocean Ave., Kennebunkport* ☎ *207/967–2562* ⊕ *www.mabelslobster.com* ☉ *Closed Nov.–early Apr.*

$$$
MODERN
AMERICAN

✕**Pier 77 Restaurant.** The view takes center stage at this establishment. On the ground level Pier 77 is the fine-dining portion with large windows overlooking the harbor. Every seat has a nice view at the restaurant, which serves up sophisticated fare, focusing on meats and seafood. The place is vibrant with live music in summer and a great place for cocktails on the water. Tucked down below, the tiny, tiny but oh-so-funky-and-fun Ramp Bar & Grill pays homage to a really good burger, fried seafood, and other pub-style choices. $ *Average main: $25* ⊠ *77 Pier Rd., Cape Porpoise* ☎ *207/967–8500* ⊕ *www.pier77restaurant.com.*

WHERE TO STAY

$$$$
B&B/INN

🖿 **Bufflehead Cove Inn.** On the Kennebunk River, this gray-shingle B&B sits at the end of a winding dirt road amid fields and apple trees. **Pros:** pastoral setting; riverfront location; perfect for a serene getaway. **Cons:** two-night minimum stay on weekends. $ *Rooms from: $235* ⊠ *18 Bufflehead Cove Rd.* ☎☎ *207/967–3879* ⊕ *www.buffleheadcove.com* ⟿ *4 rooms, 1 suite, 1 cottage* ☉ *Closed mid-Nov.–Apr.* ⭓*Breakfast.*

$$$$
B&B/INN

🖿 **Cape Arundel Inn.** This shingle-style 19th-century mansion, originally one of the area's many summer "cottages," commands a magnificent ocean view that takes in the Bush estate at Walker's Point. **Pros:** extraordinary views from most rooms; across the road from rockbound coast. **Cons:** not for the budget minded. $ *Rooms from: $410* ⊠ *208 Ocean Ave., Kennebunkport* ☎ *207/967–2125* ⊕ *www.capearundelinn.com* ⟿ *14 rooms, 1 suite* ☉ *Closed late Dec.–late Feb.* ⭓*Breakfast.*

$$$$
B&B/INN
Fodor's Choice
★

🖿 **The Captain Lord Mansion.** Of all the mansions in Kennebunkport's historic district that have been converted to inns, the 1814 Captain Lord Mansion is the stateliest and most sumptuously appointed. **Pros:** beautiful landscaped grounds; bikes for guests; putting green. **Cons:**

Kennebunk is a classic New England town, while Kennebunkport (pictured) has more upscale inns and shopping.

not a beachfront location. $ *Rooms from: $329* ⊠ *6 Pleasant St., Kennebunkport* ☎ *207/967–3141, 800/522–3141* ⊕ *www.captainlord.com* 🛏 *18 rooms, 2 suites* ¶◎¶ *Breakfast.*

$$$
RESORT
FAMILY
Fodor's Choice
★

🏨 **The Colony Hotel.** You can't miss this place—it's grand, white, and incredibly large, set majestically atop a rise overlooking the ocean. **Pros:** private beach; heated saltwater swimming pool; activities and entertainment for all ages. **Cons:** not intimate. $ *Rooms from: $199* ⊠ *140 Ocean Ave., Kennebunkport* ☎ *207/967–3331, 800/552–2363* ⊕ *www.colonymaine.com* 🛏 *112 rooms, 11 suites, 2 cottages* ⊙ *Closed Nov.–mid-May* ¶◎¶ *Breakfast.*

$$$$
HOTEL
FAMILY

🏨 **The Seaside.** This handsome seaside property has been in the hands of the Severance family since 1667. **Pros:** great ocean views from upper-floor rooms; tasty breakfast; rates drop significantly in winter. **Cons:** motel-style rooms; not an in-town location. $ *Rooms from: $249* ⊠ *80 Beach Ave.* ☎ *207/967–4461, 800/967–4461* ⊕ *www.kennebunkbeachmaine.com* 🛏 *22 rooms* ¶◎¶ *Breakfast.*

$$$
B&B/INN

🏨 **Waldo Emerson Inn.** The home itself is a historical gold mine, made grand with unusual maritime architectural touches by a shipbuilder in 1784. **Pros:** good base for exploring Kennebunk and Kennebunkport; authentic historic lodging; complimentary afternoon tea. **Cons:** some steep stairs; no water views or beachfront; not in town. $ *Rooms from: $170* ⊠ *108 Summer St.* ☎ *207/985–4250, 877/521–8776* ⊕ *www.waldoemersoninn.com* 🛏 *4 rooms* ¶◎¶ *Breakfast.*

$$$$
B&B/INN

🏨 **White Barn Inn.** For a romantic overnight stay, look no further than the exclusive White Barn Inn, known for its attentive, pampering service. **Pros:** about 10 minutes' walk to the beach; elegant spa offers it all; helpful concierge service. **Cons:** prices are steep. $ *Rooms from: $465*

✉ *37 Beach Ave.* ☎ *207/967–2321* ⊕ *www.whitebarninn.com* ➲ *13 rooms, 9 suites, 5 cottages* ⦿ *Breakfast.*

SPORTS AND THE OUTDOORS

BEACHES

Gooch's Beach. Kennebunk has three beaches, one following the other along Beach Avenue, which is lined with cottages and old Victorians. The most northerly, and closest to downtown Kennebunkport, is Gooch's Beach, the main swimming beach. Next is stony Kennebunk Beach, followed by Mother's Beach, which is popular with families. There's a small playground and tidal puddles for splashing, and rock outcroppings lessen the waves. **Amenities:** lifeguards; parking (fee); toilets. **Best for:** walking; swimming. ✉ *Beach Ave., south of Hwy. 9.*

FISHING

Cast-Away Fishing Charters. Find and catch fish with Cast-Away Fishing Charters. The captain also offers a lobstering trip that's fun for kids, who can help haul in the traps. ✉ *Performance Marine, 4-A Western Ave.* ☎ *207/284–1740* ⊕ *www.castawayfishingcharters.com.*

FAMILY   **Rugosa.** Lobster-trap hauling trips in the scenic waters off The Kennebunks run daily aboard the *Rugosa* from Memorial Day weekend through early October. ✉ *Nonantum Resort, 95 Ocean Ave., Kennebunkport* ☎ *207/468–4095* ⊕ *www.rugosalobstertours.com.*

WHALE-WACHING

First Chance. This company leads whale-watching cruises on 85-foot *Nick's Chance.* If you don't see a whale, you get a ticket for a free trip. Scenic lobster cruises are also offered aboard 65-foot *Kylie's Chance.* Trips run daily in summer and on weekends in the shoulder season. ✉ *Performance Marine, 4-A Western Ave.* ☎ *207/967–5507* ⊕ *www. firstchancewhalewatch.com.*

SHOPPING

Abacus. This shop sells eclectic crafts, jewelry, and furniture. ✉ *2 Ocean Ave., at Dock Sq., Kennebunkport* ☎ *207/967–0111* ⊕ *www. abacusgallery.com.*

Maine Art. Showcasing works by artists from Maine and New England, Maine Art has a two-story gallery with a sculpture garden. There's also a gallery space on Western Avenue. ✉ *10 Chase Hill Rd.* ☎ *207/967– 0049* ⊕ *www.maine-art.com.*

Mast Cove Galleries. Since 1979, Mast Cove Galleries has been selling paintings and sculpture by artists from New England and beyond. It occupies the barn and first floor of the owner's 1851 village home, which has a sculpture garden. The gallery hosts indoor jazz and blues concerts year-round. ✉ *2 Mast Cove Ln., Kennebunkport* ☎ *207/967– 3453* ⊕ *www.mastcove.com.*

EN ROUTE   For a rewarding drive that goes into the reaches of the coastline on the way to Old Orchard Beach, head out of Kennebunkport on Route 9. You'll soon come to the fishing village of Cape Porpoise, where the pier has wondrous views. Continuing on Route 9, plan to do some beach walking at Goose Rocks Beach or Fortunes Rocks Beach, both ideal for stretching your legs or just looking for shells or critters in the tide pools. (Pick up a parking permit first.) Route 9 winds through wooded areas, then heads past the charming resort villages of Camp Ellis and Ocean Park. You could pack a picnic and spend some time at Ferry Beach State Park. The varied landscapes here include forested sections, swamp, beach, a rare stand of tupelo (black gum) trees, and lots of dunes. There are a few miles of marked trails to hike.

OLD ORCHARD BEACH

15 miles north of Kennebunkport; 18 miles south of Portland.

Back in the late 19th century, Old Orchard Beach was a classic, upscale, place-to-be-seen resort area. The railroad brought wealthy families looking for entertainment and the benefits of the fresh sea air. Although a good bit of this aristocratic hue has dulled in more recent times—admittedly, the place is more than a little pleasantly tacky these days—Old Orchard Beach remains a good place for those looking for entertainment by the sea. Many visitors are French Canadian.

The center of the action is a 7-mile strip of sand beach and its accompanying amusement park. Despite the summertime crowds and fried-food odors, the atmosphere can be captivating. During the 1940s and '50s the pier had a dance hall where stars of the time performed. Fire claimed the end of the pier—at one time it jutted out nearly 1,800 feet into the sea—but booths with games and candy concessions still line both sides. In summer the town sponsors fireworks (on Thursday night). Places to stay run the gamut from cheap motels to cottage colonies to full-service seasonal hotels. You won't find free parking in town, but there are ample lots. Amtrak has a seasonal stop here.

GETTING HERE AND AROUND

From Interstate 95, get off at Exit 32 and follow signs. Traveling from the south on U.S. 1, Route 5 heads into town.

ESSENTIALS

Visitor Information Old Orchard Beach Chamber of Commerce ✉ *11 First St.* ☎ *207/934–2500, 800/365–9386* ⊕ *www.oldorchardbeachmaine.com.*

EXPLORING

Ocean Park. A world away from the beach scene lies Ocean Park, on the southwestern edge of town. Locals and visitors like to keep the separation distinct, touting their area as a more peaceful and wholesome family-style village (to that end, there are no alcohol or tobacco sales in this little haven). This vacation community was founded in 1881 by Free Will Baptist leaders as a summer assembly with both religious and educational purposes, following the example of Chautauqua, New York. The 1881 Temple, in an unusual octagon shape, is on the National Register of Historic Places. Today the community hosts an impressive variety of cultural events, from concerts to sand sculpture contests. There's even a public shuffleboard area for vacationers not interested in the neon carnival attractions about a mile up the road. Get an old-fashioned raspberry-lime rickey at the Ocean Park Soda Fountain, at Furber Park. ✉ *14 Temple Ave., Ocean Park* ☎ *207/934–9068* ⊕ *www.oceanpark.org.*

6

WHERE TO EAT

$$ ECLECTIC 🍴 **The Landmark.** In a 1910 Victorian home, this elegant eatery's tables are set either on the glassed-in porch or within high, tin-ceiling rooms. Candles and a collection of fringed Art Nouveau lamps provide a gentle light. The menu has a good selection of seafood and meats, many treated with flavors from various parts of the globe. It's the kind of menu that encourages you to try new things, and you definitely won't be disappointed. From July through Labor Day you can eat outside on the stone patio, sheltered by umbrellas, and order from an "in the rough" dinner menu, with everything cooked on the adjacent grill. Choose from clambake-style meals, charbroiled and marinated skewers, and barbecue ribs. [$] *Average main: $20* ✉ *28 E. Grand Ave.* ☎ *207/934–0156* 🌐 *www.landmarkfinedining.com* 🕘 *No lunch.*

$$$ SEAFOOD 🍴 **Yellowfin's Restaurant.** Inside this diminutive restaurant housed in an impeccably kept yellow Victorian, the atmosphere is fresh, bright, and appropriately beachy. A giant tank bubbles quietly in the background while its resident colorful fish survey the landscape of white-linen-covered tables adorned with sand and shell centerpieces. Not surprisingly, the house specialty is ahi yellowfin tuna, pan seared and treated with a wasabi glaze; other choices include seared scallops, roasted lamb, and a savory seafood *fra diavolo* (in a spicy tomato sauce). Brunch is offered Sunday year-round. It's strictly BYOB—stock up in nearby Old Orchard Beach. [$] *Average main: $23* ✉ *5 Temple Ave.* ☎ *207/934–1100* 🌐 *yellowfinsrestaurantme.com* 🕘 *No lunch.*

PORTLAND

28 miles from Kennebunk via I–95 and I–295.

Maine's largest city is considered small by national standards—its population is just 64,000—but its character, spirit, and appeal make it feel much larger. In fact, it is a cultural and economic center for a metropolitan area of 230,000 residents—almost one-quarter of Maine's entire population. It's well worth at least a day or two of exploration.

A city of many names throughout its history, including Casco and Falmouth, Portland has survived many dramatic transformations. Sheltered by the nearby Casco Bay Islands and blessed with a deep port, Portland was a significant settlement right from its start in the early 17th century. Settlers thrived on fishing and lumbering, repeatedly building up the area while the British, French, and Native Americans continually sacked it. Many considered the region a somewhat dangerous frontier, but its potential for prosperity was so apparent that settlers came anyway to tap its rich natural resources.

In 1632 Portland's first home was built on the Portland Peninsula in the area now known as Munjoy Hill. The British burned the city in 1775, when residents refused to surrender arms, but it was rebuilt and became a major trading center. Much of Portland was destroyed again in the Great Fire on July 4, 1866, when a flicked ash or perhaps a celebratory firecracker started a fire in a boatyard that grew into conflagration; 1,500 buildings burned to the ground.

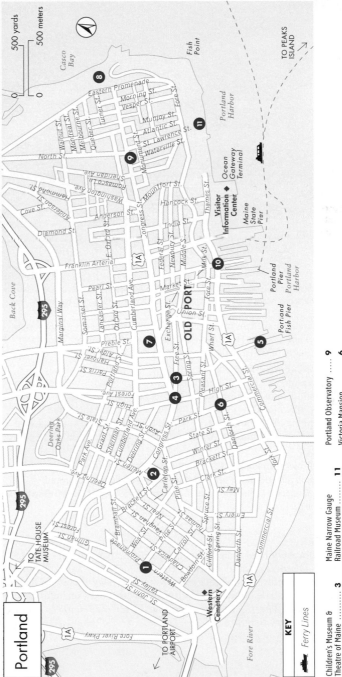

Portland

KEY

⛴ *Ferry Lines*

Children's Museum &
Theatre of Maine **3**

Eastern Promenade **8**

Harbor Fish Market **10**

Longfellow House
and Garden **7**

Maine Narrow Gauge
Railroad Museum **11**

Neal Dow Memorial **2**

Portland Fish Exchange ... **5**

Portland Museum of Art ... **4**

Portland Observatory **9**

Victoria Mansion **6**

Western Promenade **1**

Portland's busy harbor is full of working boats, pleasure craft, and ferries headed to the Casco Bay Islands.

Today, there are excellent microbrew and restaurant scenes—many visitors come here just for the food—and a great art museum. The waterfront is a lively place to walk around well into the evening.

GETTING HERE AND AROUND
From Interstate 95, take Interstate 295 to get downtown and onto the Portland Peninsula. Commercial Street runs along the harbor, Fore Street is in one block up in heart of the Old Port, and the Arts District stretches along diagonal Congress Street. Munjoy Hill is on the eastern end of the peninsula and the West End on the opposite side.

ESSENTIALS
Contacts Downtown Portland ⊠ *549 Congress St.* ☎ *207/772-6828* ⊕ *www. portlandmaine.com.* **Greater Portland Convention and Visitors Bureau** ⊠ *Visitor Information Center, 14 Ocean Gateway Pier* ☎ *207/772-5800* ⊕ *www. visitportland.com.*

TOURS
BUS TOURS
Portland Discovery Land & Sea Tours. The informative trolley tours of Portland Discovery Land & Sea Tours detail Portland's historical and architectural highlights from Memorial Day through October. Options include combining a city tour with a bay or lighthouse cruise. ⊠ *Long Wharf, 170 Commercial St.* ☎ *207/774-0808* ⊕ *www. portlanddiscovery.com* ⊠ *$22.*

WALKING TOURS

Greater Portland Landmarks. Take 1½-hour walking tours of Portland's historic West End on Friday from July through September with Greater Portland Landmarks. Tours past the neighborhood's Greek Revival mansions and grand Federal-style homes begin at the group's headquarters and cost $10. You can also pick up maps for self-guided tours of the Old Port or the Western Promenade. ⊠ *93 High St.* ☎ *207/774–5561* ⊕ *www.portlandlandmarks.org* ⊗ *Tours at 11.*

Maine Foodie Tours. Learn about Portland's culinary history and sample local delights like lobster hors d'oeuvres, organic cheese, and the famous Maine whoopie pie with Maine Foodie Tours. The culinary foot tours include stops at fish mongers, bakeries, and cheese shops that supply Portland's famed restaurants. From summer into early fall you can also take a chocolate tour, a bike-and-brewery tour, or a trolley tour with a stop at a microbrewery. Tours begin at various locales in the Old Port. ☎ *207/233–7485* ⊕ *www.mainefoodietours.com* ✉ *$39.*

Portland Freedom Trail. The Portland Freedom Trail offers a self-guided tour of sites associated with the Underground Railroad and the antislavery movement. ☎ *207/591–9980* ⊕ *www.portlandfreedomtrail.org.*

6

THE OLD PORT

Fodor's Choice A major international port and a working harbor since the early 17th
★ century, the Old Port bridges the gap between the city's historical commercial activities and those of today. It is home to fishing boats docked alongside whale-watching charters, luxury yachts, cruise ships, and oil tankers from around the globe. Commercial Street parallels the water and is lined with brick buildings and warehouses that were built following the Great Fire of 1866. In the 19th century, candle makers and sail stitchers plied their trades here; today specialty shops, art galleries, and restaurants have taken up residence.

As with much of the city, it's best to park your car and explore the Old Port on foot. You can park at the city garage on Fore Street (between Exchange and Union streets) or opposite the U.S. Custom House at the corner of Fore and Pearl streets. A helpful hint: look for the "Park & Shop" sign on garages and parking lots and get one hour of free parking for each stamp collected at participating shops. Allow a couple of hours to wander at leisure on Market, Exchange, Middle, and Fore streets. The city is very pedestrian-friendly. Maine state law requires vehicles to stop for walkers in crosswalks.

Harbor Fish Market. A Portland favorite since 1968, this freshest-of-the-fresh seafood market ships lobsters and other Maine delectables almost anywhere in the country. A bright-red facade on a working wharf opens into a bustling space with bubbling lobster pens and fish, clams, and other shellfish on ice; employees are as skilled with a fillet knife as sushi chefs. There is also a small retail store. ⊠ *9 Custom House Wharf* ☎ *207/775–0251* ⊕ *www.harborfish.com* ✉ *Free.*

FAMILY **Maine Narrow Gauge Railroad Museum.** Whether you're crazy about old trains or just want to see the sights from a different perspective, the railroad museum has an extensive collection of locomotives and rail coaches and offers scenic tours on narrow-gauge railcars. The 3-mile jaunts run on the hour and take you along Casco Bay, at the foot of the Eastern Promenade. The operating season caps off with a fall harvest ride (complete with cider). During the Christmas season there are Polar Express rides, based on the popular children's book. ⊠ *58 Fore St.* ☎ *207/828–0814* ⊕ *www.mainenarrowgauge.org* ▭ *Museum $3, train rides $10* ⊙ *May–Oct., daily 10–4.*

NEED A BREAK?

Two Fat Cats Bakery. This bakery's whoopie pies are delicately proportioned, with a smooth and light marshmallow cream filling, and conservative with flavors—no mint-chocolate-chip pies to be found here. ⊠ *47 India St., Portland* ☎ *207/347-5144* ⊕ *www.twofatcatsbakery.com.*

Portland Fish Exchange. You may want to hold your nose for this glimpse into the Old Port's active fish business when you drop by the 20,000-square-foot Portland Fish Exchange. Peek inside coolers teeming with cod, flounder, and monkfish and watch fishermen repairing nets outside. ⊠ *6 Portland Fish Pier* ☎ *207/773–0017* ⊕ *www.pfex. org* ▭ *Free* ⊙ *Daily 7–3.*

THE ARTS DISTRICT

This district starts at the top of Exchange Street, near the upper end of the Old Port, and extends west past the Portland Museum of Art. Congress Street is the district's central artery. Art galleries, specialty stores, and a score of restaurants line Congress Street. Parking is tricky; two-hour meters dot the sidewalks, but there are several nearby parking garages.

TOP ATTRACTIONS

FAMILY **Children's Museum & Theatre of Maine.** Touching is okay at Portland's small but fun Children's Museum, where kids can pretend they are lobstermen, veterinarians, shopkeepers, or actors in a play. Most exhibits, many of which have a Maine theme, are best for kids 10 and younger. An outside pirate-ship play area is a great place to have a picnic lunch, and don't miss the life-size inflatable humpback whale rising to the ceiling at the whale exhibit. Have a Ball! teaches about the science of motion, letting kids build ramps that make balls speed up, slow down, and leap across tracks. Camera Obscura, an exhibit about optics, provides fascinating panoramic views of the city. It's aimed at adults and older children, so you can purchase a separate admission. ⊠ *142 Free St.* ☎ *207/828–1234* ⊕ *www.kitetails.org* ▭ *Museum $9; Camera Obscura $4* ⊙ *Memorial Day–Labor Day, daily 10–5; Labor Day–Memorial Day, Mon.–Sat. 10–5.*

Longfellow House and Garden. The boyhood home of the famous American poet is the first brick house in Portland and the oldest building on the peninsula. It's particularly interesting because most of the furnishings, including the young Longfellow's writing desk, are original. Wallpaper, window coverings, and a vibrant painted carpet are period reproductions. Built in 1785, the large dwelling (a third floor was added in 1815) sits back from the street and has a small portico over its entrance and four chimneys surmounting the roof. It's part of the Maine Historical

Society, which includes an adjacent museum with exhibits about Maine life and a research library. After your guided tour, stay for a picnic in the Longfellow Garden; it's open to the public during museum hours. ⊠ *489 Congress St.* 🕾 *207/774–1822* ⊕ *www.mainehistory.org* 🔁 *House and museum $8, gardens free* ⊙ *House: May–Oct., Mon.–Sat. 10–5, Sun. noon–5. Museum: May–Oct., Mon.–Sat. 10–5, Sun. noon–5, Nov.– Apr., Mon.–Sat. 10–5.*

Fodor's Choice **Portland Museum of Art.** Maine's largest public art institution's collection
★ includes fine seascapes and landscapes by Winslow Homer, John Marin, Andrew Wyeth, Edward Hopper, Marsden Hartley, and other American painters. Homer's *Weatherbeaten*, a quintessential Maine Coast image, is here, and the museum owns and displays, on a rotating basis, 16 more of his paintings, plus more than 400 of his illustrations. The museum has works by Monet and Picasso, as well as Degas, Renoir, and Chagall. I. M. Pei designed the strikingly modern Charles Shipman Payson building, which fittingly displays modern art. The nearby L. D. M. Sweat Galleries showcase the collection of 19th-century American art. Special events are held in the gorgeous Federal-style 1801 McLellan House. ⊠ *7 Congress Sq.* 🕾 *207/775–6148* ⊕ *www.portlandmuseum.org* 🔁 *$12, free Fri. 5–9* ⊙ *Late May–mid-Oct., Mon.–Thurs. and weekends 10–5, Fri. 10–9; mid-Oct.–late May, Tues.–Thurs. and weekends 10–5, Fri. 10–9.*

Victoria Mansion. Built between 1858 and 1860, this Italianate mansion is widely regarded as the most sumptuously ornamented dwelling of its period remaining in the country. Architect Henry Austin designed the house for hotelier Ruggles Morse and his wife Olive. The interior design—everything from the plasterwork to the furniture (much of it original)—is the only surviving commission of New York designer Gustave Herter. Behind the elegant brownstone exterior of this National Historic Landmark are colorful frescoed walls and ceilings, ornate marble mantelpieces, gilded gas chandeliers, a magnificent 6-foot-by-25-foot stained-glass ceiling window, and a freestanding mahogany staircase. Guided tours run about 45 minutes and cover all the architectural highlights. Victorian era–themed gifts and art are sold in the museum shop. ⊠ *109 Danforth St.* 🕾 *207/772–4841* ⊕ *www. victoriamansion.org* 🔁 *$15* ⊙ *May–Oct., Mon.–Sat. 10–4, Sun. 1–5; Christmas tours day after Thanksgiving–Jan. 3, daily 11–5.*

WORTH NOTING

Eastern Promenade. Of the city's two promenades, this one, often overlooked by tourists, has by far the best view. Gracious Victorian homes, many now converted to condos and apartments, border one side of the street. On the other are 68 acres of hillside parkland that includes Fort Allen Park and, at the base of the hill, the Eastern Prom Trail and tiny East End Beach and Boat Launch. On a sunny day the Eastern Prom is a lovely spot for picnicking and people-watching. ⊠ *Extends from Washington Ave. to Fore St.*

Neal Dow Memorial. The mansion, once a stop on the Underground Railroad, was the home of Civil War general Neal Dow, who became known as the "Father of Prohibition." He was responsible for Maine's adoption of the anti-alcohol bill in 1851, which spurred a national movement. Now a museum, this majestic 1829 Federal-style home is open for guided tours that start on the hour. ⊠ *714 Congress St.* 🕾 *207/773–7773* 🖼 *$5* ⊗ *May–Dec., Mon.–Sat. 11–4; Jan.–Apr., by appt.*

FAMILY **Portland Observatory.** This octagonal observatory on Munjoy Hill was built in 1807 by Captain Lemuel Moody, a retired sea captain, as a maritime signal tower. Moody used a telescope to identify incoming ships and flags to signal to merchants where to unload their cargo. Held in place by 122 tons of ballast, it's the last remaining historic maritime signal station in the country. The guided tour leads all the way to the dome, where you can step out on the deck and take in views of Portland, the islands, and inland toward the White Mountains. ⊠ *138 Congress St.* 🕾 *207/774–5561* ⊕ *www.portlandlandmarks.org* 🖼 *$9* ⊗ *Memorial Day weekend–Columbus Day, daily 10–5; Thurs. evening sunset tours mid-July–early Sept.*

█ **OFF THE BEATEN PATH** **Tate House Museum.** Built astride rose granite steps and a period herb garden overlooking the Stroudwater River on the outskirts of Portland, this magnificent 1755 house was built by Captain George Tate. Tate had been commissioned by the English Crown to organize "the King's Broad Arrow"—the marking and cutting down of gigantic forest trees, which were shipped to England to be fashioned as masts for the British Royal Navy. The house has several period rooms, including a sitting room with some fine English Restoration chairs. With its clapboard still gloriously unpainted, its impressive Palladian doorway, dogleg stairway, unusual clerestory, and gambrel roof, this house will delight all lovers of Early American decorative arts. ⊠ *1267 Westbrook St.* 🕾 *207/774–6177* ⊕ *www.tatehouse.org* 🖼 *$10* ⊗ *Early June–mid-Oct., Wed.–Sat. 10–4, Sun. 1–4.*

THE WEST END

A leisurely walk through Portland's West End, beginning at the top of the Arts District, offers a real treat to historic architecture buffs. The neighborhood, on the National Register of Historic Places, presents an extraordinary display of architectural splendor, from High Victorian Gothic to lush Italianate, Queen Anne, and Colonial Revival.

Western Promenade. A good place to start is at the head of the Western Promenade, which has benches and a nice view. From the Old Port, take Danforth Street all the way up to Vaughn Street; take a right on Vaughn and then an immediate left onto Western Promenade. Pass by the Western Cemetery, Portland's second official burial ground, laid out in 1829 (inside is the ancestral plot of poet Henry Wadsworth Longfellow), and look for street parking. ⊠ *Extends from Danforth St. to Bramhall St.*

WHERE TO EAT

America's "Foodiest Small Town" is how one magazine described Portland, which is blessed with exceptional restaurants rivaling those of a far larger city. Fresh seafood, including the famous Maine lobster, is still popular and prevalent, but there are plenty more cuisines to be enjoyed.

Exchange Street, in the Old Port, is a popular place to explore for restaurants, shopping, and summer treats.

More and more restaurants are using local meats, seafood, and organic and local produce as much as possible; changing menus reflect what is available in the region at the moment. As sophisticated as many of these establishments have become, the atmosphere is generally casual; with a few exceptions, you can leave your jacket and tie at home.

Smoking is banned in all restaurants, taverns, and bars in Maine.

$$ ✕ **Becky's Diner.** You won't find a more local or unfussy place—or one
DINER that is more abuzz with conversation at 4 am—than this waterfront institution, way down on the end of Commercial Street. Sitting next to you at the counter or in a neighboring booth could be rubber-booted fishermen back from the sea, college students soothing a hangover, or suited business folks with BlackBerrys. From the upstairs deck you can watch the working waterfront in action. The food is cheap, generous in proportion, and has that satisfying, old-time-diner quality. $ *Average main: $14* ⊠ *390 Commercial St.* ☎ *207/773–7070* ⊕ *www. beckysdiner.com.*

$ ✕ **Duckfat.** Even in midafternoon, this small, hip sandwich shop in the
MODERN Old Port is packed. It concentrates on serving everyday farm-to-table
AMERICAN fare: the signature Belgian fries are made with Maine potatoes cooked, yes, in duck fat, and served in paper cones. Sandwiches are made with focaccia bread; choices like tuna melt with Thai chili mayo change seasonally, but the meat loaf and B.G.T. (bacon, tomato, goat cheese) are standards. Drink choices include gelato milk shakes, French-press coffee, lime-mint fountain sodas, beer, and wine. $ *Average main: $12* ⊠ *43 Middle St.* ☎ *207/774–8080* ⊕ *www.duckfat.com* ⌂ *Reservations not accepted.*

CLOSE UP

Lobster Shacks

If it's your first time to the Maine Coast, it won't be long before you stumble upon the famous and quint-essential seaside eatery, the lobster shack. Also known as a lobster "pound," especially in other parts of New England, this humble establish-ment serves only two kinds of fresh seafood—lobster and clams. Lobster shacks are essentially wooden huts with picnic tables set around the waterfront. The menu is simplicity itself: steamed lobster or clams by the pound, or a lobster roll. Sides may include potato chips, coleslaw, or corn on the cob. Some pounds are even BYOB—no, not bring your own bib; those are usually provided—but bring your own beer or refreshments.

A signature item at a lobster shack is the lobster dinner. Although this can vary from pound to pound, it generally means the works: a whole steamed lobster, steamed clams, corn on the cob, and potato chips. If the lobster dinner sounds like a bit much, then go for the classic lobster roll, a buttered New England–style hot-dog roll filled with chunks of lobster meat and a bit of mayo. Some pounds will serve it with lemon, some will serve it with butter, and some with even a touch of lettuce or herbs. Purists will serve no toppings at all (and why bother when the unadulterated taste of fresh, sweet lobster meat can't be beat). Most shacks will even have a tank with live lobsters; few will let you pick your own.

We can say this much: the best place to get a lobster dinner or lobster roll is at a shack, and the only authen-tic ones are right next to the water. There's a general sense that the "purest" pounds are the ones that are the simplest: a wooden shack, right

A lobster roll: perfection on a bun.

on the water with wooden picnic tables, and perhaps most important of all, a beautiful unobstructed view of working lobster boats in a scenic Maine harbor.

Maine Lobster Council. You can find out more about Maine lobster from the Maine Lobster Council. ☎ *207/541–9310* ⊕ *www. lobsterfrommaine.com.*

—Michael de Zayas

$$$$ MODERN AMERICAN Fodor's Choice ★ 🍴 **Five Fifty-Five.** Classic dishes are cleverly updated at this classy Congress Street spot. The menu changes seasonally to reflect ingredients available from local waters, organic farms, and food purveyors, but seared local diver scallops, served in a buttery carrot-vanilla emulsion, are an exquisite mainstay. So is the mac and cheese, which boasts artisanal cheeses and shaved black truffles. You may also find dishes such as milk-braised rabbit with Himalayan red rice and lemon-dressed local greens. You can try the $65 tasting menu, or come for Sunday brunch. The space, with exposed brick and copper accents, is a former 19th-century firehouse. A sister restaurant, Petite Jacqueline bistro in Longfellow Square, has also earned accolades and fans. [$] *Average main: $29* ✉ *555 Congress St.* ☎ *207/761–0555* 🌐 *www.fivefifty-five.com* 🕒 *No lunch.*

$$ PIZZA FAMILY 🍴 **Flatbread.** Families, students, and bohemian types gather at this popular New England chain pizza place. Two giant wood-fire ovens, where the pies are cooked, are the heart of the soaring, warehouse-like space; in summer you can escape the heat by dining on the deck overlooking the harbor. The simple menu has eight signature pizzas plus weekly veggie and meat specials; everything is homemade, organic, and nitrate-free. Be sure to order the delicious house salad with toasted sesame seeds, seaweed, blue or goat cheese, and ginger-tamarind vinaigrette. ■ **TIP→ Waits can be long on weekends and in summer, but you can call a half-hour ahead to get on the waiting list.** [$] *Average main: $13* ✉ *72 Commercial St.* ☎ *207/772–8777* 🌐 *www.flatbreadcompany.com.*

$$$$ MODERN AMERICAN 🍴 **Fore Street.** One of Maine's best chefs, Sam Hayward, opened this restaurant in a renovated warehouse on the edge of the Old Port in 1996. The menu changes daily to reflect the freshest ingredients from Maine's farms and waters. Every copper-top table in the main dining room has a view of the enormous brick oven and soapstone hearth that anchor the open kitchen, where sous-chefs seem to dance as they create such dishes as turnspit-roasted dry-rubbed pork loin, wood-grilled Maine island lamb chop with sun-root puree, and Maine mussels oven roasted in garlic and almond butter. Desserts include artisanal cheeses. In July or August, book two months in advance; otherwise, a week is usually fine. ■ **TIP→ Last-minute planners take heart: a third of the tables are reserved for walk-ins.** [$] *Average main: $30* ✉ *288 Fore St.* ☎ *207/775–2717* 🌐 *www.forestreet.biz* 🕒 *No lunch.*

$$ SEAFOOD 🍴 **Gilbert's Chowder House.** This is the real deal, as quintessential as Maine dining can be. Clam rakes and nautical charts hang from the walls of this unpretentious waterfront diner. The flavors are from the depths of the North Atlantic, prepared and presented simply: fish, clam, and seafood chowders (corn, too); fried shrimp; haddock; clam strips; and extraordinary clam cakes. A chalkboard of daily specials often features fish-and-chips. Don't miss out on the lobster roll—a toasted hot-dog bun bursting with claw and tail meat lightly dressed with mayo but otherwise unadulterated. It's classic Maine, fuss free, and presented on a paper plate. [$] *Average main: $19* ✉ *92 Commercial St.* ☎ *207/871–5636* 🌐 *www.gilbertschowderhouse.com.*

$$$$ ECLECTIC 🍴 **Hugo's.** Serving the freshest local organic foods is a high priority at Hugo's, and your server is sure to know everything about various purveyors. Updated daily, the menu at this stylish eatery is made up of

6

smartly prepared, seasonally inspired dishes like crispy-skin pork belly and crepe-wrapped arctic char. You can choose five courses for $90, or go light with two courses for $45. A 2013 renovation added an open kitchen, a handsome curved bar, and an airy, open-concept dining room. Next door is a sister business, Eventide Oyster Company, with a more casual setting. [$] *Average main: $45* ✉ *88 Middle St.* ☎ *207/774–8538* 🌐 *www.hugos.net* ⏲ *Closed Sun. No lunch.*

$$$ MEDITERRANEAN Fodor's Choice ★ 🍴 **Local 188.** There's an infectious vibe at this eclectic Arts District eatery, a foodie hot spot as well as a longtime local favorite. The 2,000-square-foot space has lofty tin ceilings and worn maple floors. Mismatched chandeliers dangle over the dining area, and a pair of antlers crown the open kitchen. Regulars chat with servers about what just-caught seafood will decorate the paella and which organic veggies are starring in the tortillas, one of several tapas choices. You'll find entrées like Casco Bay hake with herb salsa verde, poached purple potatoes, smoked aioli, and beets. Many of the 10 or so draft brews are Maine crafted; there are some 150 mostly European wines. Reservations aren't taken for the large bar side. [$] *Average main: $22* ✉ *685 Congress St.* ☎ *207/761–7909* 🌐 *www.local188.com* ⏲ *No lunch.*

$$$ ECLECTIC 🍴 **Walter's.** A fixture in the Old Port since the late 1980s, this relaxed, busy place with a chic modern interior is popular with suits and tourists alike. The seasonally changing menu nicely balances local seafood and meats with Asian and other international flavors. You'll find appetizers like calamari dressed with lemon-and-cherry-pepper aioli and such entrées as crispy duck breast served with spaetzle, baby bok choy, and plum sauce. An inviting bar has a lighter menu; try the mussels or the Greek lamb sliders. [$] *Average main: $28* ✉ *2 Portland Sq.* ☎ *207/871–9258* 🌐 *www.waltersportland.com* ⏲ *Closed Sun. No lunch Sat.*

WHERE TO STAY

As Portland's popularity as a vacation destination has increased, so have its options for overnight visitors. Though several large hotels—geared toward high-tech, amenity-obsessed guests—have been built in the Old Port, they have in no way diminished the success of smaller, more intimate lodgings. Inns and B&Bs have taken up residence throughout the West End, often giving new life to the grand mansions of Portland's wealthy 19th-century businessmen. For the least expensive accommodations, investigate the chain hotels near the Interstate and the airport.

Expect to pay from about $150 a night for a pleasant room (often with complimentary breakfast) within walking distance of the Old Port during high season, and more than $400 for the most luxurious of suites. In the height of the summer season many places are booked; make reservations well in advance, and ask about off-season specials.

$$$$ B&B/INN 🏨 **The Danforth.** A stunning showpiece, this stylish inn was one of Portland's grandest Federal-style dwellings when it was built in 1823. **Pros:** gorgeous rooms; basement billiards room; city views from cupola. **Cons:** small windows in some third-floor rooms. [$] *Rooms from: $299* ✉ *163 Danforth St.* ☎ *207/879–8755, 800/991–6557* 🌐 *www.danforthmaine.com* 🛏 *9 rooms* 🍽 *Breakfast.*

$$$
B&B/INN
Inn on Carleton. This 1869 Victorian has a curved mahogany staircase to the third floor, a bay window overlooking the street from the front parlor, and gleaming pumpkin pine floors. **Pros:** most rooms have electric fireplaces; English garden with fountain; attentive resident innkeeper. **Cons:** not an easy walk to the Old Port. *$ Rooms from: $185 ⊠ 46 Carleton St. ☎ 207/775–1910, 800/639–1770 ⊕ www. innoncarleton.com ↝ 6 rooms.*

$$$
B&B/INN
Morrill Mansion. This 19th-century townhouse has tastefully appointed rooms with well-executed color schemes: blue is a favorite hue here. **Pros:** close to arts district; parlors on each floor for relaxing. **Cons:** not on a grand block. *$ Rooms from: $200 ⊠ 249 Vaughan St. ☎ 207/774–6900, 888/566–7745 ⊕ www.morrillmansion.com ↝ 6 rooms, 1 suite ⦿ Breakfast.*

$$$$
B&B/INN
Fodor's Choice
★
Pomegranate Inn. The classic facade of this handsome 1884 Italianate in the architecturally rich Western Promenade area gives no hint of the splashy, modern surprises within. **Pros:** surprising decor; many rooms have gas fireplaces; close to Western Promenade. **Cons:** not an easy walk from Old Port. *$ Rooms from: $259 ⊠ 19 Neal St. ☎ 207/772–1006, 800/356–0408 ⊕ www.pomegranateinn.com ↝ 7 rooms, 1 suite ⦿ Breakfast.*

$$$$
HOTEL
Portland Harbor Hotel. Making luxury its primary focus, the Harbor Hotel has become a favorite with business travelers seeking meetings on a more intimate scale and vacationing guests who want high-quality service and amenities, like the free shuttle to local restaurants and sites. **Pros:** elegant extras; amid the action of the Old Port. **Cons:** smallish lobby. *$ Rooms from: $299 ⊠ 468 Fore St. ☎ 207/775–9090, 888/798–9090 ⊕ www.portlandharborhotel.com ↝ 87 rooms, 14 suites.*

$$$$
HOTEL
The Portland Regency Hotel & Spa. Not part of a chain despite the "Regency" name, this brick building in the center of the Old Port served as Portland's armory in the late 19th century. **Pros:** easy walk to sights; lots of room variety for a hotel. **Cons:** lower-than-standard ceilings in many rooms. *$ Rooms from: $279 ⊠ 20 Milk St. ☎ 207/774–4200, 800/727–3436 ⊕ www.theregency.com ↝ 85 rooms, 10 suites.*

NIGHTLIFE AND THE ARTS

THE ARTS

Art galleries and studios have spread throughout the city, infusing with new life many abandoned yet beautiful old buildings and shops. Many are concentrated along the Congress Street downtown corridor; others are hidden amid the boutiques and restaurants of the Old Port and the East End. A great way to get acquainted with the city's artists is to participate in the First Friday Art Walk, a self-guided, free tour of galleries, museums, and alternative-art venues that happens—you guessed it—on the first Friday of each month.

Merrill Auditorium. This soaring concert hall hosts numerous theatrical and musical events, including performances by the Portland Symphony Orchestra and Portland Opera Repertory Theatre. Ask about organ recitals on the the auditorium's huge 1912 Kotzschmar Memorial Organ. ⊠ 20 Myrtle St. ☎ 207/842–0800 ⊕ www.porttix.com.

WHAT'S ON TAP: MICROBREWERIES

One of the nation's microbrew hotbeds, Maine is home to around 40 breweries, and several of the larger ones—Allagash, Geary's, and Shipyard—are in and around Portland. These breweries are open for tours and tastings, but beer lovers may prefer the smaller brewpubs that make their own beer and serve it fresh from their own taps in neighborhood taverns. In the Old Port you'll find Gritty McDuff's, Sebago Brewing Company, and In'finiti Fermentation & Distillation. In Bayside there's Rising Tide and Bunker Brewing Company. If you're in town in November, check out the Maine Brewer's Festival (⊕ www. mainebrewersfestival.com). Pick up a Maine Beer Trail map from the Maine Brewers' Guild (⊕ www. mainebrewersguild.org).

Portland Stage. This company mounts theatrical productions on its two stages from September to May. ⊠ 25-A Forest Ave. ☎ 207/774–0465 ⊕ www.portlandstage.com.

Space Gallery. Space Gallery sparkles as a contemporary art gallery and alternative arts venue, opening its doors to everything from poetry readings to live music to documentary films. The gallery is open daily Wednesday to Saturday. ⊠ 538 Congress St. ☎ 207/828–5600 ⊕ www. space538.org.

NIGHTLIFE

Portland's nightlife scene is largely centered around the bustling Old Port and a few smaller, artsy spots on Congress Street. There's a great emphasis on local, live music and pubs serving award-winning local microbrews. Several hip wine bars have cropped up, serving appetizers along with a full array of specialty wines and whimsical cocktails. It's a fairly youthful scene in Portland, in some spots even rowdy and rough around the edges, but there are plenty of places where you don't have to shout over the din to be heard.

The Big Easy. To catch live local and national acts most any night of the week, try the Big Easy. Everything from blues, jazz, and soul to Grateful Dead covers are played here. ⊠ 55 Market St. ☎ 207/775–2266 ⊕ www. bigeasyportland.com.

Bull Feeney's. For nightly specials, plenty of Guinness, and live entertainment, head to Bull Feeney's, a lively two-story Irish pub and restaurant. ⊠ 375 Fore St. ☎ 207/773–7210.

Gritty McDuff's Portland Brew Pub. Maine's original brewpub serves fine ales, British pub fare, and seafood dishes. There are between six and eight ales on tap, and there's always a seasonal offering. Come on Tuesday and Saturday nights for live music. ⊠ 396 Fore St. ☎ 207/772–2739 ⊕ www.grittys.com.

Fodor'sChoice ★ **Novare Res Bier Café.** At tucked-away Novare Res Bier Café, choose from some three dozen rotating drafts and more than 300 bottled brews. Relax on an expansive deck, munch on antipasti, or share a meat and cheese plate. Craft beers from Maine occupy at least eight of the taps at any given time, and the rest span the globe, with an emphasis on Belgian and Trappist brews. ⊠ *4 Canal Plaza, off Exchange St.* ☎ *207/761–2437* ⊕ *www.novareresbiercafe.com.*

Rí Rá. Ths happening Irish pub has live music Thursday through Saturday nights. For a mellower experience, settle into a couch at the upstairs bar. ⊠ *72 Commercial St.* ☎ *207/761–4446* ⊕ *www.rira.com.*

Sonny's. In a Victorian-era bank building with arched windows overlooking an Old Port square, this stylish bar and lounge packs in the late-night crowd. It has quite a list of cocktails, many using house-infused liquors—try the chili tequila. Bluegrass and funk bands play on Thursday; there's a DJ on Saturday. The Latin American cuisine is a winner, too. At night you can order lighter fare like a poblano cheeseburger with yam fries, as well as such entrées as the braised brisket enchilada. Food is served until 10:30 on weekends. ⊠ *83 Exchange St.* ☎ *207/772–7774* ⊕ *www.sonnysportland.com.*

SPORTS AND THE OUTDOORS

When the weather's good, everyone in Portland heads outside. There are also many green spaces nearby Portland, including Fort Williams Park, home to Portland Head Light; Crescent Beach State Park; and Two Lights State Park. All are on the coast south of the city in suburban Cape Elizabeth and offer walking trails, picnic facilities, and water access. Bradbury Mountain State Park, in Pownal, has incredible vistas from its easily climbed peak. In Freeport is Wolfe's Neck Woods State Park, where you can take a guided nature walk and see nesting ospreys. Both are north of Portland.

BICYCLING

Bicycle Coalition of Maine. For state bike trail maps, club and tour listings, or hints on safety, contact the Bicycle Coalition of Maine. Maps are available at the group's headquarters in the Arts District. ⊠ *34 Preble St.* ☎ *207/623–4511* ⊕ *www.bikemaine.org.*

Cycle Mania. Rent bikes downtown at Cycle Mania. The $25 rate includes a helmet and lock. ⊠ *59 Federal St.* ☎ *207/774–2933* ⊕ *www. cyclemania1.com.*

Gorham Bike and Ski. You can rent several types of bikes, including hybrid and tandem models, starting at $25 per day. ⊠ *693 Congress St.* ☎ *207/773–1700* ⊕ *www.gorhambike.com.*

Portland Trails. For local biking information, contact Portland Trails. The staff can tell you about designated paved routes that wind along the water, through parks, and beyond. ⊠ *305 Commercial St.* ☎ *207/775–2411* ⊕ *www.trails.org.*

BOATING

Various Portland-based skippers offer whale-, dolphin-, and seal-watching cruises; excursions to lighthouses and islands; and fishing and lobstering trips. Board the ferry to see the nearby islands. Self-navigators can rent kayaks or canoes.

The Eastern Prom Trail

To experience the city's busy shoreline and grand views of Casco Bay, walkers, runners, and cyclists head out on the 2.1-mile Eastern Prom Trail.

Beginning at the intersection of Commercial and India streets, this paved trail runs along the water at the bottom of the Eastern Promenade, following an old rail bed and running alongside the still-used railroad tracks of the Maine Narrow Gauge Railroad Co. & Museum. There are plenty of places with benches and tables for a picnic break along the way. From the trailhead, it's about 1 mile to the small East End Beach.

Continuing along the trail, you'll pass underneath busy Interstate 295, and emerge at the Back Cove Trail, a popular 3½-mile loop you can connect with for a long trek. To return to the Old Port, backtrack along the trail or head up the steep path to the top of the promenade. Here you can continue along the promenade sidewalk or take the trails through this 68-acre stretch of parkland to the lovely picnic area and playground.

Continuing along the sidewalk toward the Old Port, a gazebo and several old cannons to your left indicate you're at the small Fort Allen Park. Use one of the coin-operated viewing scopes to view Civil War–era Fort Gorges, which never saw action.

Where the Eastern Prom becomes Fore Street, continue on for a few blocks to India Street and take a left, which will bring you back to where you started. Or, continue into the Old Port.

Plan at least an hour to walk the trail with brief stops, or two if you continue along the Back Cove Trail. But if can, make time for the Prom—it's truly an urban jewel.

Casco Bay Lines. Casco Bay Lines operates the ferry service to the seven bay islands with year-round populations. Summer offerings include music cruises, lighthouse excursions, and a trip to Bailey Island with a stopover for lunch. ⊠ *Maine State Pier, 56 Commercial St.* ☎ *207/774–7871* ⊕ *www.cascobaylines.com.*

Lucky Catch Cruises. You'll set sail in a real lobster boat: this company gives you the genuine experience, which includes hauling traps and the chance to purchase the catch. ⊠ *Long Wharf, 170 Commercial St.* ☎ *207/761–0941* ⊕ *www.luckycatch.com.*

Odyssey Whale Watch. From mid-May to mid-October, Odyssey Whale Watch leads whale-watching and deep-sea-fishing excursions. ⊠ *Long Wharf, 170 Commercial St.* ☎ *207/775–0727* ⊕ *www.odysseywhalewatch.com.*

Portland Discovery Land & Sea Tours. For tours of the harbor and Casco Bay, including an up-close look at several lighthouses, try Portland Discovery Land & Sea Tours. ⊠ *Long Wharf, 170 Commercial St.* ☎ *207/774–0808* ⊕ *www.portlanddiscovery.com.*

Portland Paddle. Run by a young pair of Registered Maine Guides, Portland Paddle leads introductory sea kayaking clinics along with guided trips between the Casco Bay islands. Two-hour sunset paddles

($35) are a fave, but the most unusual offering involves a four-hour paddle to the abandoned island military installation of Fort Gorges ($55), where you'll enjoy a short acoustic concert before heading back. Kayak and paddleboard rentals are available. ⊠ *Eastern Promenade, East End Beach, off Cutter St., Portland* ☎ *207/370–9730* ⊕ *www. portlandpaddle.net* ⊙ *Closed Nov.–May., appointment only in Oct.*

Portland Schooner Co. This company offers daily windjammer cruises aboard the vintage schooners *Bagheera* and *Wendameen.* You can also arrange overnight trips. Tours are offered May to October. ⊠ *Maine State Pier, 56 Commercial St.* ☎ *207/766–2500* ⊕ *www. portlandschooner.com.*

HOT-AIR BALLOON RIDES

Hot Fun First Class Balloon Flights. Hot Fun First Class Balloon Flights flies mainly sunrise trips and can accommodate up to three people. The price of $300 per person includes a post-flight champagne toast, snacks, and shuttle to the lift-off site. ☎ *207/799–0193* ⊕ *www.hotfunballoons. com.*

SHOPPING

Exchange Street is great for arts and crafts and boutique browsing, while Commercial Street caters to the souvenir hound—gift shops are packed with nautical items, and lobster and moose emblems are emblazoned on everything from T shirts to shot glasses.

ART AND ANTIQUES

Abacus. This appealing crafts gallery has gift items in glass, wood, and textiles, as well as fine modern jewelry. ⊠ *44 Exchange St.* ☎ *207/772– 7188* ⊕ *www.abacusgallery.com.*

Gleason Fine Art. This gallery exhibits sculpture and paintings by Maine and New England artists from the 19th to 21st centuries. ⊠ *545 Congress St.* ☎ *207/699–5599* ⊕ *www.gleasonfineart.com.*

Greenhut Galleries. The contemporary art at this gallery changes with the seasons. Artists represented include David Driskell, an artist and leading art scholar. ⊠ *146 Middle St.* ☎ *207/772–2693, 888/772–2693* ⊕ *www.greenhutgalleries.com.*

Portland Architectural Salvage. A fixer-upper's dream, Portland Architectural Salvage has four floors of unusual reclaimed finds from old buildings, including fixtures, hardware, and stained-glass windows, and also assorted antiques. ⊠ *131 Preble St.* ☎ *207/780–0634* ⊕ *www. portlandsalvage.com.*

BOOKS

Longfellow Books. This shop is known for its good service, author readings, and thoughtful collection of new and used books. There's a little of everything here. ⊠ *1 Monument Way* ☎ *207/772–4045* ⊕ *www. longfellowbooks.com.*

CLOTHING

Bliss. Hip boutique Bliss stocks clothing and accessories by cutting-edge designers, plus jeans by big names like J Brand and Mother. There's also a great selection of Frye boots. ⊠ *58 Exchange St.* ☏ *207/879–7129* ⊕ *www.blissboutiques.com.*

Hélène M. Photos of style icon Audrey Hepburn grace the walls of Hélène M., where you'll find classic, fashionable pieces by designers like Michael Stars, Diane von Furstenberg, and Rebecca Taylor. ⊠ *425 Fore St.* ☏ *207/772–2564* ⊕ *www.helenem.com.*

Material Objects. With an eclectic combination of good-quality consignment and new jewelry and clothing for both men and women, Material Objects makes for an affordable and unusual shopping spree. ⊠ *500 Congress St.* ☏ *207/774–1241.*

Sea Bags. At Sea Bags, totes made from recycled sailcloth and decorated with bright, graphic patterns are sewn right in the store. ⊠ *25 Custom House Wharf* ☏ *888/210–4244* ⊕ *www.seabags.com.*

HOUSEHOLD ITEMS/FURNITURE

Angela Adams. Maine islander Angela Adams specializes in simple but bold geometric motifs parlayed into dramatic rugs (custom, too), canvas totes, bedding, and other home accessories. The shop also carries sleek wood furniture from her husband's woodshop. ⊠ *273 Congress St.* ⊕ *www.angelaadams.com.*

Asia West. For reproduction and antique furnishings with a Far East feel, head to this stylish showroom on the waterfront. ⊠ *219 Commercial St.* ☏ *888/775–0066* ⊕ *www.asiawest.net.*

SIDE TRIPS FROM PORTLAND

CASCO BAY ISLANDS

The islands of Casco Bay are also known as the Calendar Islands because an early explorer mistakenly thought there was one for each day of the year (in reality there are only some 140). These islands range from ledges visible only at low tide to populous Peaks Island, a suburb of Portland. Some are uninhabited; others support year-round communities as well as stores and restaurants. Fort Gorges commands Hog Island Ledge, and Eagle Island is the site of Arctic explorer Admiral Robert Peary's home. The brightly painted ferries of Casco Bay Lines are the islands' lifeline. There is frequent service to the most populated ones, including Peaks, Long, Little Diamond, and Great Diamond.

There is little in the way of overnight lodging on the islands; the population swells during the warmer months due to summer residents. There are few restaurants or organized attractions other than the natural beauty of the islands themselves. Meandering about by bike or on foot is a good way to explore on a day trip.

GETTING HERE AND AROUND

Casco Bay Lines provides ferry service from Portland to the islands of Casco Bay. The *Nova Star*, a passenger ferry service between Portland and Yarmouth, Nova Scotia, is expected to launch in 2014.

ESSENTIALS

Transportation Information Casco Bay Lines ☎ *207/774–7871* ⊕ *www. cascobaylines.com.*

CAPE ELIZABETH

Winslow Homer painted many of his famous oceanscapes from a tiny studio on the rocky peninsula known as Prout's Neck, 12 miles south of Portland. Visitors today navigate a neighborhood of summer homes and a sprawling country-club property for a glimpse of the same dramatic coastline. Follow Highway 77 through South Portland (sometimes called "SoPo"), stopping off for bagels and coffee in its hipper residential neighborhoods. In the affluent bedroom community of Cape Elizabeth, a detour along the two-lane Shore Road shows off the famed Portland Head Light lighthouse and quite a few stunning oceanfront homes.

EXPLORING

Cape Elizabeth Light. This was the first twin lighthouse erected on the Maine coast, in 1828, and the locals still call it Two Lights, but half of the Cape Elizabeth Light was dismantled in 1924 and converted into a private residence The other half still operates, and you can get a great photo of it from the end of Two Lights Road in the surrounding state park of the same name. The lighthouse itself is closed to the public, but you can explore the tidal pools at its base for small snails known as "periwinkles." ⊠ *7 Tower Dr., Cape Elizabeth* ☎ *207/799–5871* ⊕ *www.maine.gov/twolights* ☜ *$4.50* ⊙ *Daily 9–sunset.*

Fodor's Choice ★ **Portland Head Light.** Familiar to many from photographs and the Edward Hopper's painting *Portland Head-Light* (1927), this lighthouse was commissioned by George Washington in 1787. The towering white stone structure stands over the keeper's quarters, a white home with a blazing red roof, now the Museum at Portland Head Light. The lighthouse is in 90-acre Fort Williams Park, a sprawling green space with walking paths, picnic facilities, a beach and—you guessed it—a cool old fort. ⊠ *Museum, 1000 Shore Rd., Cape Elizabeth* ☎ *207/799–2661* ⊕ *www.portlandheadlight.com* ☜ *$2* ⊙ *Memorial Day–mid-Oct., daily 10–4; Apr., May, Nov., and Dec., weekends 10–4.*

Scarborough Marsh Audubon Center. You can explore this Maine Audubon Society–run nature center on foot or by canoe on your own, or by signing up for a guided walk or paddle. The salt marsh is Maine's largest and is an excellent place for bird-watching and peaceful paddling along its winding ways. The center has a discovery room for kids, programs for all ages ranging from basket-making to astronomy, and a good gift shop. Tours include birding walks. ⊠ *Pine Point Rd., Scarborough* ☎ *207/883–5100* ⊕ *www.maineaudubon.org* ☜ *Free; guided tours* *begin at $5 ⏲ Visitor center mid-June–Labor Day, daily 9:30–5:30; Memorial Day–mid-June and Labor Day–Sept., weekends 9:30–5:30.*

Winslow Homer Studio. The great American landscape painter created many of his best-known works in this seaside home between 1883 until his death in 1910. It's easy to see how this rocky, jagged peninsula might have been inspiring. The only way to get a look is on a tour with the Portland Museum of Art, which leads 2½-hour strolls through the historic property. ✉ *Winslow Homer Rd., Scarborough* ☎ *207/775–6148* 🌐 *www.portlandmuseum.org* 🎫 *$55* ⏲ *Apr.–Nov., hrs vary.*

WHERE TO EAT AND STAY

$$ SEAFOOD 🍴 **The Lobster Shack at Two Lights.** You can't beat the location—right on the water, below the lighthouse pair that gives Two Lights State Park its name—and the food's not bad, either. Enjoy fresh lobster whole or piled into a hot-dog bun with a dollop of mayo. Other menu must-haves include chowder, fried clams, and fish-and-chips. It's been a classic spot since the 1920s. Eat inside or out. [$] *Average main: $18* ✉ *225 Two Lights Rd., Cape Elizabeth* ☎ *207/799–1677* 🌐 *www.lobstershacktwolights.com* ⏲ *Closed late Oct.–late Mar.*

$$$$ RESORT 🏨 **Black Point Inn.** Toward the tip of the peninsula that juts into the ocean at Prouts Neck stands this stylish, tastefully updated 1878 resort inn with spectacular views up and down the coast. **Pros:** dramatic setting; geothermally heated pool; discounts in shoulder seasons. **Cons:** "guest service charge" is tacked onto room rate. [$] *Rooms from: $500* ✉ *510 Black Point Rd., Scarborough* ☎ *207/883–2500* 🌐 *www.blackpointinn.com* 🛏 *20 rooms, 5 suites* ⏲ *Closed late Oct.–early May* 🍽 *Some meals.*

FREEPORT

17 miles north of Portland via I–295.

Those who flock straight to L.L. Bean and see nothing else of Freeport are missing out. The city's charming backstreets are lined with historic buildings and old clapboard houses, and there's a pretty little harbor on the south side of the Harraseeket River. It's true, many who come to the area do so simply to shop—L.L. Bean is the store that put Freeport on the map, and plenty of outlets and some specialty stores have settled here. Still, if you choose, you can stay a while and experience more than fabulous bargains; beyond the shops are bucolic nature preserves with miles of walking trails and plenty of places for leisurely ambling that don't require the overuse of your credit cards.

GETTING HERE AND AROUND

Interstate 295 has three Freeport exits and passes by on the edge of the downtown area. U.S. 1 is Main Street here.

EXPLORING

Freeport Historical Society. Pick up a village walking map and check out the historical exhibits at the Freeport Historical Society, located in Harrington House, a hybrid Federal- and Greek Revival–style home built in the 1830s. ✉ *45 Main St.* ☎ *207/865–3170* 🌐 *www.freeporthistoricalsociety.org* ⏲ *Memorial Day–Labor Day, weekdays 10–5, Sat. 10–2.*

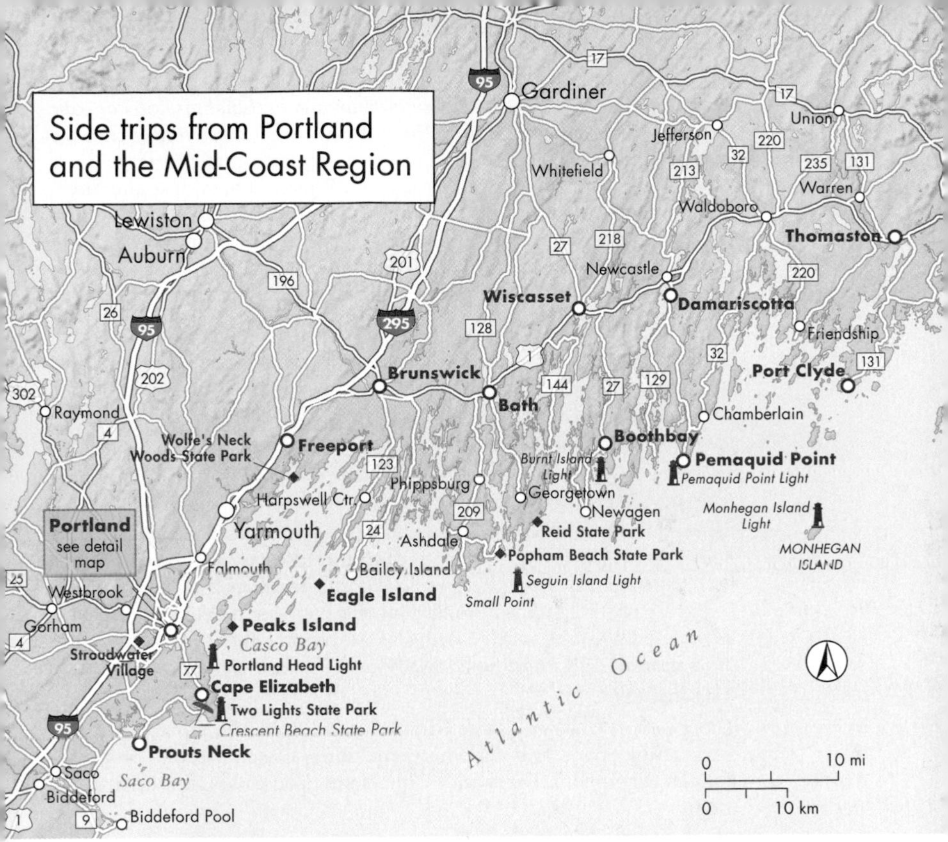
Side trips from Portland and the Mid-Coast Region
Gardiner
Jefferson
Union
Whitefield
Warren
Waldoboro
Thomaston
Lewiston
Auburn
Newcastle
Wiscasset
Damariscotta
Friendship
Brunswick
Bath
Port Clyde
Raymond
Chamberlain
Wolfe's Neck Woods State Park
Freeport
Boothbay
Burnt Island Light
Pemaquid Point
Pemaquid Point Light
Phippsburg
Georgetown
Harpswell Ctr.
Newagen
Monhegan Island Light
Portland see detail map
Yarmouth
Ashdale
Reid State Park
MONHEGAN ISLAND
Falmouth
Bailey Island
Popham Beach State Park
Seguin Island Light
Eagle Island
Small Point
Westbrook
Gorham
Peaks Island
Casco Bay
Stroudwater Village
Portland Head Light
Cape Elizabeth
Two Lights State Park
Crescent Beach State Park
Atlantic Ocean
Prouts Neck
Saco
Saco Bay
Biddeford
Biddeford Pool
0 10 mi
0 10 km

Pettengill Farm. The grounds of the Freeport Historical Society's saltwater Pettengill Farm—140 beautifully tended acres along an estuary of the Harraseeket River—are open to the public. It's about a 15-minute walk from the parking area down a farm road to the circa 1800 saltbox farmhouse, which is open by appointment. Little has changed since it was built, it has rare etchings (called sgraffitti) of ships and sea monsters on three bedroom walls. ✉ *Pettengill Rd.* ☎ *207/865–3170* 🌐 *www.freeporthistoricalsociety.org* 🕒 *Daily dawn–dusk.*

NEED A BREAK?

Cranberry Island Kitchen. This place ships nationwide, but about half of its "gourmet" whoopie pies (free-range eggs, locally churned butter) are sold at its bakery on Lower Main Street in Freeport, where the offerings include seashell-shaped whoopie pies and filling flavors like espresso chocolate chip and Chambord. ✉ ***174 Lower Main St., Freeport*** ☎ ***207/829–5200*** 🌐 ***www.cranberryislandkitchen.com.***

WHERE TO EAT AND STAY

$$ SEAFOOD

🍴 **Harraseeket Lunch & Lobster Co.** Seafood baskets and lobster dinners are the focus at this popular, bare-bones place beside the town landing in South Freeport. Order at the counter, find a seat inside or out, and expect long lines in summer. [$] *Average main: $18* ✉ *36 S. Main St., South*

Freeport ☎ *207/865–4888* 🌐 *www.harraseeketlunchandlobster.com* *Reservations not accepted* ▭ *No credit cards* ⏲ *Closed mid-Oct.–Apr.*

$$$$ HOTEL Fodor's Choice ★ **Harraseeket Inn.** Despite some modern appointments, this large hotel has a country-inn ambience throughout. **Pros:** full breakfast and afternoon tea; elevators and other modern touches; walk to shopping district. **Cons:** additions have diminished some authenticity. [$] *Rooms from: $235* ✉ *162 Main St.* ☎ *207/865–9377, 800/342–6423* 🌐 *www.harraseeketinn.com* *82 rooms, 2 suites, 9 town houses* 🍴 *Breakfast.*

NIGHTLIFE AND THE ARTS

L.L. Bean Summer Concert Series. Throughout the summer, L.L.Bean hosts free activities, including concerts, at L.L. Bean Discovery Park. It's set back from Main Street, along a side street the runs between the company's flagship and home furnishings stores. ✉ *L.L. Bean Discovery Park, 95 Main St.* ☎ *877/755–2326* 🌐 *www.llbean.com/events.*

SPORTS AND THE OUTDOORS

CLASSES **L.L. Bean Outdoor Discovery Schools.** It shouldn't come as a surprise that one of the world's largest outdoor outfitters also provides its customers with instructional adventures to go with its products. L.L. Bean's year-round Outdoor Discovery Schools offer courses in canoeing, biking, kayaking, fly-fishing, snowshoeing, cross-country skiing, and other outdoor sports. ✉ *95 Main St.* ☎ *888/552–3261* 🌐 *www.llbean.com/ods.*

SHOPPING

The *Freeport Visitors Guide* lists the more than 200 stores on Main Street, Bow Street, and elsewhere, including Coach, Brooks Brothers, Banana Republic, J. Crew, and Cole Haan. You can pick it up around town.

Edgecomb Potters. Nationally known Edgecomb Potters produces vibrantly colored, hand-thrown porcelain tableware finished with an unusual crystalline glaze. It also sells jewelry, glassware, glass sculptures, and gifts for the home, almost all made by American artisans. ✉ *8 School St.* ☎ *207/865–1705* 🌐 *www.edgecombpotters.com.*

Fodor's Choice ★ **L.L. Bean.** Founded in 1912 as a mail-order merchandiser after its namesake invented a hunting boot, L.L. Bean's giant flagship store attracts more than 3 million shoppers annually and is open 365 days a year in the heart of Freeport's outlet shopping district. You can still find the original hunting boots, along with cotton and wool sweaters; outerwear of all kinds; casual clothing, boots, and shoes for men, women, and kids; and camping equipment. Nearby are the company's home furnishings store, bike, boat, and ski store, and outlet. ✉ *95 Main St.* ☎ *877/755–2326* 🌐 *www.llbean.com.*

R. D. Allen Freeport Jewelers. This shop specializes in brightly colored tourmaline and other gemstones mined in Maine. Most of the pieces are the work of Maine artisans. Watermelon tourmaline is a specialty. ✉ *13 Middle St.* ☎ *207/865–1818, 877/837–3835* 🌐 *www.rdallen.com.*

Thos. Moser Cabinetmakers. Famed local furniture company Thos. Moser Cabinetmakers sells artful, handmade wood pieces with clean, classic lines. The store has information on tours at the workshop a half an hour away in Auburn. ⊠ *149 Main St.* ☎ *207/865–4519* ⊕ *www. thosmoser.com.*

THE MID-COAST REGION

Lighthouses dot the headlands of Maine's Mid-Coast region, where thousands of miles of coastline wait to be explored. Defined by chiseled peninsulas stretching south from U.S. 1, this area has everything from the sandy beaches and sandbars of Popham Beach to the jutting cliffs of Monhegan Island. If you are intent on hooking a trophy-size fish or catching a glimpse of a whale, there are plenty of cruises available. If you want to explore deserted beaches and secluded coves, kayaks are your best bet. Put in at the Harpswells, or on the Cushing and Saint George peninsulas, or simply paddle among the lobster boats and other vessels that ply the waters here.

Tall ships often visit Maine, sometimes sailing up the Kennebec River for a stopover at Bath's Maine Maritime Museum, on the site of the old Percy & Small Shipyard. Next door to the museum, the Bath Iron Works still builds the U.S. Navy's Aegis-class destroyers.

Along U.S. 1, charming towns, each unique, have an array of attractions. Brunswick, while a bigger, commercial city, has rows of historic brick and clapboard homes and is home to Bowdoin College. Bath is known for its maritime heritage. Wiscasset has arguably the best antiques shopping in the state. On its waterfront you can choose from a variety of seafood shacks competing for the best lobster rolls. Damariscotta, too, is worth a stop for its good seafood restaurants.

South along the peninsulas the scenery opens to glorious vistas of working lobster harbors and marinas. It's here you find the authentic lobster pounds where you can watch your catch come in off the traps. Boothbay Harbor is the quaintest town in the Mid-Coast and a busy tourist destination come summer, with lots of little stores that are perfect for window-shopping. It's one of three towns where you can take a ferry to Monhegan Island, which seems to be inhabited exclusively by painters at their easels, depicting the cliffs and weathered homes with colorful gardens.

ESSENTIALS

Visitor Information Southern Midcoast Maine Chamber ⊠ *Border Trust Business Center, 2 Main St., Topsham* ☎ *877/725–8797* ⊕ *www.midcoastmaine. com.* **State of Maine Visitor Information Center** ⊠ *1100 U.S. 1, off I–95, Yarmouth* ☎ *207/846–0833, 888/624–6345* ⊕ *www.mainetourism.com.*

BRUNSWICK

10 miles north of Freeport via U.S. 1.

Lovely brick and clapboard buildings are the highlight of Brunswick's Federal Street Historic District, which includes Federal Street and Park Row and the stately campus of Bowdoin College. From the intersection of Pleasant and Maine streets, in the center of town, you can walk in any direction and discover an impressive array of restaurants. Seafood?

German cuisine? A Chinese buffet that beats out all the competition? It's all here. So are bookstores, gift shops, boutiques, and jewelers.

Below Brunswick are Harpswell Neck and the more than 40 islands that make up the town of Harpswell, known collectively as the Harpswells. Route 123 runs down Harpswell Neck, where small coves shelter lobster boats, and summer cottages are tucked away among birch and spruce trees. On your way down from Cook's Corner to Land's End at the end of Route 24, you cross Sebascodegan Island. Heading east here leads to East Harpswell and Cundy's Harbor. Continuing straight south down Route 24 leads to Orr's Island. Stop at Mackerel Cove to see a real fishing harbor; there are a few parking spaces where you can stop to picnic and look for beach glass or put in your kayaks. Inhale the salt breeze as you cross the world's only cribstone bridge (designed so that water flows freely through gaps between the granite blocks) on your way to Bailey Island, home to a lobster pound made famous thanks in part to a Visa commercial.

GETTING HERE AND AROUND

From Interstate 295 take the Coastal Connector to U.S. 1 in Brunswick. From here Route 24 runs to Bailey Island and Route 123 down Harpswell Neck.

WHERE TO EAT

$$$ SEAFOOD FAMILY Fodor's Choice ★

🍴 **Cook's Lobster House.** What began as a lobster shack on Bailey's Island in 1955 has grown into a huge, internationally famous family-style restaurant with a small gift shop. The restaurant still catches its own seafood, so you can count on the lobster casserole and the haddock sandwich to be delectable. A shore dinner will still set you back close to $40, but you won't leave hungry after a 1¼-pound lobster with coleslaw, potato, chowder, and mussels or clams. Whether you choose inside or deck seating, you can watch the activity on the water as men check lobster pots and kayakers fan across the bay. [$] *Average main: $24* ✉ *68 Garrison Cove Rd., Bailey Island* ☎ *207/833–2818* 🌐 *www.cookslobster.com* ✍ *Reservations not accepted* 🕒 *Closed early Jan.–mid-Feb.*

SPORTS AND THE OUTDOORS

H2Outfitters. The coast near Brunswick is full of hidden nooks and crannies waiting to be explored by kayak. H2Outfitters, at the southern end of Orr's Island just before the Cribstone Bridge, is the place in Harpswell to get on the water. It provides top-notch kayaking instruction and also offers half-day, full-day, bed-and-breakfast, and camping trips in the waters off its home base and elsewhere in Maine. ✉ *1894 Harpswell Island Rd., Orr's Island* ☎ *207/833–5257, 800/205–2925* 🌐 *www.h2outfitters.com.*

BATH

11 miles north of Brunswick via U.S. 1.

Bath has been a shipbuilding center since 1607. The result of its prosperity can be seen in its handsome mix of Federal, Greek Revival, and Italianate homes along Front, Centre, and Washington streets. In the

At the Maine Maritime Museum, a boatbuilder works on a yacht tender, used to ferry people to shore.

heart of Bath's historic district are some charming 19th-century homes, including the 1820 Federal-style home at 360 Front Street, the 1810 Greek Revival mansion at 969 Washington Street, covered with gleaming white clapboards, and the Victorian gem at 1009 Washington Street, painted a distinctive shade of raspberry. All three operate as inns. An easily overlooked site is the town's City Hall. The bell in its tower was cast by Paul Revere in 1805.

The venerable Bath Iron Works completed its first passenger ship in 1890. During World War II, BIW—as it's locally known—launched a new ship every 17 days. It is still building today, turning out destroyers for the U.S. Navy. BIW is one of the state's largest employers, with about 5,600 workers. It's a good idea to avoid U.S. 1 on weekdays from 3:15 pm to 4:30 pm, when a major shift change takes place. You can tour BIW through the Maine Maritime Museum.

GETTING HERE AND AROUND
U.S. 1 passes through downtown and across the Kennebec River at Bath. Downtown is on the north side of the highway along the river.

EXPLORING

Fodor's Choice
★

Maine Maritime Museum. No trip to Bath is complete without a visit to this cluster of buildings that once made up the historic Percy & Small Shipyard. Plan on at least half a day—tickets are good for two days because there's so much to see at this museum, which examines the world of shipbuilding and is the only way to tour Bath Iron Works (May to mid-Oct.). From mid-June through Columbus Day, five nature and lighthouse boat tours cruise the scenic Kennebec River—one takes in 10 lights. The 142-foot Grand Banks fishing schooner *Sherman Zwicker*

Low tide is the perfect time to explore tidal flats, tide pools, or fish from the shore at Popham Beach State Park.

docks here during the same period. Inside the main museum building, exhibits use ship models, paintings, photographs, and historical artifacts to tell the maritime history of the region. Hour-long tours of the shipyard show how these massive wooden ships were built. In the boat shop you can watch boatbuilders wield their tools. A separate historic building houses a fascinating lobstering exhibit. It's worth coming here just to watch the 18-minute video on lobstering written and narrated by E. B. White. A gift shop and bookstore are on the premises, and you can grab a bite to eat in the café or bring a picnic to eat on the grounds. ■TIP➔ Kids ages five and younger get in free. ⊠ *243 Washington St.* ☎ *207/443–1316* ⊕ *www.mainemaritimemuseum.org* ✉ *$15 (good for 2 days within 7-day period)* ⊙ *Daily 9:30–5.*

OFF THE BEATEN PATH **Popham Beach State Park.** The park has bathhouses and picnic tables. At low tide you can walk several miles of tidal flats and also out to a nearby island, where you can explore tide pools or fish off the ledges. It's on a peninsula facing the open Atlantic, between the mouths of the Kennebec and Morse rivers. About a mile from Popham Beach State Park, the road ends at the Civil War–era Fort Popham State Historic Site, an unfinished semicircular granite fort on the sea. Enjoy the beach views at nearby Spinney's Restaurant, or grab a quick bite next door at Percy's Store, which has picnic tables and a path to the beach. **Amenities:** lifeguards; parking (no fee); showers; toilets. **Best for:** swimming; walking. ⊠ *10 Perkins Farm La., off Rte. 209, Phippsburg* ☎ *207/389–1335* ⊕ *www. parksandlands.com* ✉ *$6* ⊙ *Daily 9–sunset.*

WHERE TO EAT AND STAY

$$ BARBECUE

🍴 **Beale Street Barbecue.** Ribs are the thing at Maine's oldest (and most authentic) barbecue joint, opened in 1996. Hearty eaters should ask for one of the platters piled high with pulled pork, pulled chicken, or shredded beef. Fried calamari with habanero mayo served with corn bread is a popular appetizer. Enjoy a Maine microbrew at the bar while waiting for your table. [$] *Average main: $15* ✉ *215 Water St.* ☎ *207/442–9514* 🌐 *www.mainebbq.com.*

$$$$ RESORT Fodor's Choice ★

🏨 **Sebasco Harbor Resort.** A family-friendly resort spread across 575 acres on the water near the foot of the Phippsburg Peninsula, this place has a golf course, tennis courts, and a host of other amenities. **Pros:** good choice for families; perfect location; children's activities. **Cons:** no sand beach. [$] *Rooms from: $229* ✉ *29 Kenyon Rd., off Rte. 217, Phippsburg* ☎ *207/389–1161, 877/389–1161* 🌐 *www.sebasco.com* 🛏 *107 rooms, 8 suites, 23 cottages* 🕒 *Closed late Oct.–mid-May* 🍽 *Some meals.*

WISCASSET

6

10 miles north of Bath via U.S. 1.

Settled in 1663, Wiscasset sits on the banks of the Sheepscot River. It bills itself "Maine's Prettiest Village," and it's easy to see why: it has graceful churches, old cemeteries, and elegant sea captains' homes (many converted into antiques shops or galleries), and a good wine and specialty foods shop called Treats (stock up here if you're heading north).

Pack a picnic and take it down to the dock on Water Street, where you can watch the fishing boats or grab a lobster roll from Red's Eats or the lobster shack nearby. Wiscasset has expanded its wharf, and this is a great place to catch a breeze on a hot day.

GETTING HERE AND AROUND

U.S. 1 becomes Main Street, and traffic often slows to a crawl come summer. You'll likely have success parking on Water Street rather than Main.

WHERE TO EAT

$ FAST FOOD

🍴 **Red's Eats.** You've probably driven right past this little red shack on the Wiscasset side of the bridge if you've visited this area and seen the long line of hungry customers. Red's is a local landmark famous for its hamburgers, hot dogs, lobster and crab rolls, and crispy onion rings and clams fried in their own house-made batters. Maine-made Round Top ice cream is also sold (try blueberry or black raspberry). Enjoy views of the tidal Sheepscot River from picnic tables on the two-level deck or down on the grass by the water. [$] *Average main: $12* ✉ *41 Water St.* ☎ *207/882–6128* ✍ *Reservations not accepted* 💳 *No credit cards* 🕒 *Closed mid-Oct.–mid-Apr.*

SHOPPING

Edgecomb Potters. Not to be missed is Edgecomb Potters, which makes vibrantly colored, exquisitely glazed porcelain that is known around the country. Its store also carries jewelry, glassware, and glass

Continued on page 325

MAINE'S LIGHTHOUSES
GUARDIANS OF THE COAST By John Blodgett

Perched high on rocky ledges, on the tips of wayward islands, and sometimes seemingly on the ocean itself are the more than five dozen lighthouses standing watch along Maine's craggy and ship-busting coastline.

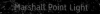
Marshall Point Light

LIGHTING THE WAY: A BIT OF HISTORY

Portland Head Light

Most lighthouses were built in the first half of the 19th century to protect the vessels from running aground at night or when the shoreline was shrouded in fog. Along with the mournful siren of the foghorn and maritime lore, these practical structures have come to symbolize Maine throughout the world.

SHIPWRECKS AND SAFETY

These alluring sentinels of the eastern seaboard today have more form than function, but that certainly was not always the case. Safety was a strong motivating factor in the erection of the lighthouses. Commerce also played a critical role. For example, in 1791 Portland Head light was completed, partially as a response to local merchants' concerns about the rocky entrance to Portland Harbor and the varying depths of the shipping channel, but approval wasn't given until a terrible accident in 1787 in which a 90-ton sloop wrecked. In 1789, the federal government created the U.S. Lighthouse Establishment (later the U.S. Lighthouse Service) to manage them. In 1939 the U.S. Coast Guard took on the job.

Some lighthouses in Maine were built in a much-needed venue, but the points and islands upon which they sat were prone to storm damage. Along with poor construction, this meant that over the years many lighthouses had to be rebuilt or replaced.

LIGHTHOUSES TODAY

In modern times, many of the structures still serve a purpose. Technological advances, such as GPS and radar, are mainly used to navigate through the choppy waters, but a lighthouse or its foghorns are helpful secondary aids, and sometimes the only ones used by recreational boaters. The numerous channel-marking buoys still in existence also are testament to the old tried-and-true methods.

Of the 66 lighthouses along this far northeastern state, 55 are still working, alerting ships (and even small aircraft) of the shoreline's rocky edge. Government agencies, historic preservation organizations, and mostly private individuals own the decommissioned lights.

KEEPERS OF THE LIGHT

Some keepers also used bells and sirens, like this Fog Signal Station on Manana Island in 1898.

Pemaquid Point's fourth-order Fresnel lens

LIFE OF A LIGHTKEEPER

One thing that has changed with the modern era is the disappearance of the lighthouse keeper. In the early 20th century, lighthouses began the conversion from oil-based lighting to electricity. A few decades later, the U.S. Coast Guard switched to automation, phasing out the need for an on-site keeper.

While the keepers of tradition were no longer needed, the traditions of these stalwart, 24/7 employees live on through museum exhibits and retellings of Maine's maritime history, legends, and lore. The tales of a lighthouse keeper's life are the stuff romance novels are made of: adventure, rugged but lonely men, and a beautiful setting along an unpredictable coastline.

The lighthouse keepers of yesterday probably didn't see their own lives so romantically. Their daily narrative was one of hard work and, in some cases, exceptional solitude. A keeper's primary job was to ensure that the lamp was illuminated all day, every day. This meant that oil (whale or coal oil and later kerosene) had to be carried about and

wicks trimmed on a regular basis. When fog shrouded the coast, they sounded the solemn horn to pierce through the damp darkness that hid their light. Their quarters were generally small and often attached to the light tower itself. The remote locations of the lights added to the isolation a keeper felt, especially before the advent of radio and telephone, let alone the Internet. Though some brought families with them, the keepers tended to be men who lived alone.

THE LIGHTS 101

Over the years, Fresnel (fray-NELL) lenses were developed in different shapes and sizes so that ship captains could distinguish one lighthouse from another. Invented by Frenchman Augustin Fresnel in the early 19th century, the lens design allows for a greater transmission of light perfectly suited for lighthouse use. Knowing which lighthouse they were near helped captains know which danger was present, such as a submerged ledge or shallow channel. Some lights, such as those at Seguin Island Light, are fixed and don't flash. Other lights are colored red.

DID YOU KNOW?

A lighthouse's personality shines through its flash pattern. For example, Bass Harbor Light (pictured) blinks red every four seconds. Some lights, such as Seguin Island Light, are fixed and don't flash.

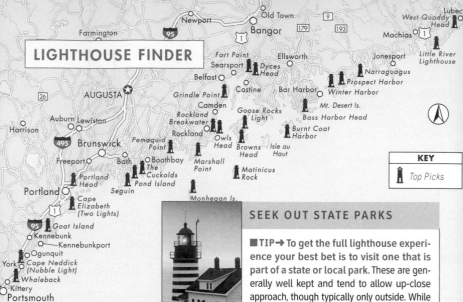

LIGHTHOUSE FINDER

Farmington
Newport
Old Town
Bangor
West Quoddy Head
Lubec
Machias

95
1
179
193
9

AUGUSTA
26
Fort Point
Searsport
Dyces Head
Belfast
Ellsworth
Jonesport
Little River Lighthouse
Narraguagus
Prospect Harbor

Auburn Lewiston
Harrison
Grindle Point
Castine
Bar Harbor
Winter Harbor
Mt. Desert Is.
Bass Harbor Head
Burnt Coat Harbor

Camden
Rockland Breakwater
Rockland
Goose Rocks Light

495
Brunswick
Pemaquid Point
Owls Head
Browns Head
Isle au Haut

Freeport
Bath
Boothbay
The Cuckolds
Pond Island
Marshall Point
Matinicus Rock

Portland Head
Portland
Seguin
Monhegan Is.

Cape Elizabeth (Two Lights)

95
Goat Island
Kennebunk
Kennebunkport
Ogunquit
York
Cape Neddick (Nubble Light)
Whaleback
Kittery
Portsmouth

KEY

⚑ Top Picks

West Quoddy Head

SEEK OUT STATE PARKS

■ **TIP →** To get the full lighthouse experience your best bet is to visit one that is part of a state or local park. These are generally well kept and tend to allow up-close approach, though typically only outside. While you're at the parks you can picnic or stroll on the trails. Wildlife is often abundant in and near the water; you might spot sea birds and even whales in certain locations (try West Quoddy Head, Portland Head, or Two Lights).

VISITING MAINE'S LIGHTHOUSES

As you travel along the Maine Coast, you won't see lighthouses by watching your odometer—there were no rules about the spacing of lighthouses. The decision as to where to place a lighthouse was a balance between a region's geography and its commercial prosperity and maritime traffic.

Lighthouses dot the shore from as far south as York to the country's easternmost tip at Lubec. Accessibility varies according to location and other factors. A handful are so remote as to be outright impossible to reach (except perhaps by kayaking and rock climbing). Some don't allow visitors according to Coast Guard policies, though you can enjoy them through the zoom lens of a camera. Others you can walk right up to and, occasionally, even climb to the top. Lighthouse enthusiasts and preservation groups restore and maintain many of them. All told, approximately 30 lighthouses allow some sort of public access.

MUSEUMS, TOURS, AND MORE

Most keeper's quarters are closed to the public, but some of the homes have been converted to museums, full of intriguing exhibits on lighthouses, the famous Fresnel lenses used in them, and artifacts of Maine maritime life in general. Talk to the librarians at the **Maine Maritime Museum** in Bath (⊕ *www.mainemaritimemuseum.org*) or sign up for one of the museum's daily lighthouse cruises to pass by no fewer than ten on the Lighthouse Lovers Cruise. In Rockland, the **Maine Lighthouse Museum** (⊕ *www.mainelighthousemuseum.org*) has the country's largest display of Fresnel lenses. The museum also displays keepers' memorabilia, foghorns, brassware, and more. Maine Open Lighthouse Day is the second Saturday after Labor Day; you can tour and even climb lights usually closed to the public.

For more information, check out the lighthouse page at Maine's official tourism site: ⊕ *www.visitmaine.com/attractions/sightseeing_tours/lighthouse.*

SLEEPING LIGHT: STAYING OVERNIGHT

Goose Rocks, where you can play lighthouse keeper for a week.

Want to stay overnight in a lighthouse? There are several options to do so. ■ TIP→ Book lighthouse lodgings as far in advance as possible, up to one year ahead.

Our top pick is **Pemaquid Point Light** (*Newcastle Square Vacation Rentals* ☎ *207/563–6500* ⊕ *www.mainecoast-cottages.com*) because it has one of the most dramatic settings on the Maine coast. Two miles south of **New Harbor**, the second floor of the lighthouse keeper's house is rented out on a weekly basis early May through mid-November to support upkeep of the grounds. When you aren't enjoying the interior, head outdoors: the covered front porch has a rocking-chair view of the ocean. The one-bedroom, one-bath rental sleeps up to a family of four.

Situated smack dab in the middle of a major maritime thoroughfare between two Penobscot Bay islands, **Goose Rocks Light** (☎ *203/400–9565* ⊕ *www.beacon-preservation.org*) offers lodging for the adventuresome—the 51-foot "spark plug" lighthouse is completely surrounded by water. Getting there requires a ferry ride from Rockland to nearby **North Haven**, a 5- to 10-minute ride by motorboat, and then a climb up an iron-rung ladder from the pitching boat—all based on high tide and winds, of course. There's room for up to eight people. It's a bit more cushy experience than it was for the original keepers: there's a flat-screen TV with DVD player and a selection of music and videos for entertainment. In addition, a hammock hangs on the small deck that encircles the operational light; it's a great place from which to watch the majestic windjammers and the fishing fleet pass by.

Little River Lighthouse (☎ *207/259–3833* ⊕ *www.littleriverlight.org*), along the far northeastern reaches of the coast in **Cutler**, has three rooms available for rent in July and August. You're responsible for food and beverages, linens, towels, and other personal items (don't forget the bug spray), but kitchen and other basics are provided. The lighthouse operators will provide a boat ride to the island upon which the lighthouse sits.

TOP LIGHTHOUSES TO VISIT

BASS HARBOR LIGHT

Familiar to many as the subject of countless photographs is Bass Harbor Light, at the southern end of **Mount Desert Island.** It is within Acadia National Park and 17 miles from the town of Bar Harbor. The station grounds are open year-round.

CAPE ELIZABETH LIGHT

Two Lights State Park is so-named because it's next to two lighthouses. Both of these **Cape Elizabeth** structures were built in 1828. The western light was converted into a private residence in 1924; the eastern light, Cape Elizabeth Light, still projects its automated cylinder of light. The grounds surrounding the building and the lighthouse itself are closed to the public, but the structure is easily viewed and photographed from nearby at the end of Two Lights Road.

CAPE NEDDICK LIGHT

More commonly known as Nubble Light for the smallish offshore expanse of rock it rests upon, Cape Neddick Light sits a few hundred feet off a rock point in **York Beach.** With such a precarious location, its grounds are inaccessible to visitors, but close enough to be exceptionally photogenic, especially during the Christmas season.

MONHEGAN ISLAND LIGHT

Only the adventuresome and the artistic see this light, because **Monhegan Island** is accessible by an approximately one-hour ferry ride. To reach the lighthouse, you have an additional half-mile walk uphill from the ferry dock. The former keeper's quarters is home to the Monhegan Museum, which has exhibits about the island. The tower itself is closed to the public.

PORTLAND HEAD LIGHT

One of Maine's most photographed lighthouses (and its oldest), the famous Portland Head Light was completed in January 1791. At the edge of Fort Williams Park, in **Cape Elizabeth,** the towering white stone lighthouse stands 101 feet above the sea. The Coast Guard operates it and it is not open for tours. However the adjacent keeper's dwelling is now a museum.

WEST QUODDY HEAD LIGHT

Originally built in 1808 by mandate of President Thomas Jefferson, West Quoddy Head Light sits in **Lubec** on the easternmost tip of land in the mainland United States. The 49-foot-high lighthouse with distinctive red and white stripes, is part of Quoddy Head State Park.

Cape Neddick

Portland Head

West Quoddy Head

sculptures. ⊠ *727 Boothbay Rd., Edgecomb* ☎ *207/882–9493* ⊕ *www. edgecombpotters.com.*

Sheepscot River Pottery. This shop boasts beautifully glazed kitchen tiles as well as kitchenware and home accessories, including sinks. Jewelry and other items by local artisans are also on sale. ⊠ *34 U.S. 1, Edgecomb* ☎ *207/882–9410* ⊕ *www.sheepscot.com.*

BOOTHBAY

10 miles south of Wiscasset via Rte. 27.

The town of Boothbay includes the village center, Boothbay Harbor, as well as East Boothbay. The shoreline of the Boothbay Peninsula is a craggy stretch of inlets where pleasure craft anchor alongside trawlers and lobster boats. Boothbay Harbor is like a smaller version of Bar Harbor—touristy but friendly and fun—with pretty, winding streets and lots to explore. Commercial Street, Wharf Street, Townsend Avenue, and the By-Way are lined with shops and ice cream parlors.

GETTING HERE AND AROUND

In season, boat trips to Monhegan Island leave from the piers off Commercial Street. Drive out to Ocean Point in East Boothbay for some incredible scenery. Boothbay is 13 miles south of Wiscasset via U.S. 1 and Route 27.

6

EXPLORING

Coastal Maine Botanical Garden. Set aside a couple of hours to stroll among the roses, lupines, and rhododendrons at the 248-acre Coastal Maine Botanical Garden. In the summer free docent-led tours leave from the visitor center at 11 and 1 on Thursdays and Saturdays. The "children's garden" is a wonderland of stone sculptures, rope bridges, and even a hedge maze. ⊠ *132 Botanical Gardens Dr., off Rte. 27, Boothbay* ☎ *207/633–4333* ⊕ *www.mainegardens.org* ⌖ *$14 Apr.– Oct., free Nov.–March.* ⊗ *9–5.*

WHERE TO EAT AND STAY

$$$

SEAFOOD

✕ **Boat House Bistro.** The multitiered rooftop terrace (complete with an outdoor bar) stays crowded all summer at the Boat House Bistro. Austrian-born chef Karin Guerin dishes up tapas-style small plates ranging from mango empanadas to sweet-potato latkes. For those seeking the full-on Maine experience, there are plenty of seafood options, too, including a different paella each day. The waitstaff is young, friendly, and just as diverse as the menu. Ⓢ *Average main: $21* ⊠ *12 By-Way, Boothbay Harbor* ☎ *207/633–0400* ⊕ *www.theboathousebistro.com* ⊗ *Closed mid-Oct.–mid-Apr.*

$$$$

B&B/INN

⌂ **Topside Inn.** The Adirondack chairs on the immense lawn of this historic, hilltop B&B have what is probably the best bay view in town. **Pros:** knockout views; plenty of green space for croquet; easy walk downtown. **Cons:** more guests coming and going than at your average B&B; walls are a bit thin in the annexes. Ⓢ *Rooms from: $330* ⊠ *60 McKown St., Boothbay Harbor* ☎ *207/633–5404* ⊕ *www.topsideinn. com* ⇆ *25 rooms* ⊗ *Closed mid-Oct.–mid-May* ⦿⍜ *Breakfast.*

DAMARISCOTTA

8 miles north of Wiscasset via U.S. 1.

The Damariscotta region comprises several communities along the rocky coast. The town itself sits on the water and is a lively place filled with attractive shops and restaurants.

Just across the bridge over the Damariscotta River is the town of Newcastle, between the Sheepscot and Damariscotta rivers. Newcastle was settled in the early 1600s. The earliest inhabitants planted apple trees, but the town later became an industrial center, home to several shipyards and a couple of mills. The oldest Catholic church in New England, St. Patrick's, is here, and it still rings its original Paul Revere bell.

Bremen, which encompasses more than a dozen islands and countless rocky outcrops, has many seasonal homes along the water, and the main industries in the small community are fishing and clamming. Nobleboro, a bit north of here on U.S. 1, was settled in the 1720s by Colonel David Dunbar, sent by the British to rebuild the fort at Pemaquid. Neighboring Waldoboro is situated on the Medomak River and was settled largely by Germans in the mid-1700s. You can still visit the old German Meeting House, built in 1772. The Pemaquid Peninsula stretches south from Damariscotta to include Bristol, South Bristol, Round Pond, New Harbor, and Pemaquid.

GETTING HERE AND AROUND

In Newcastle, U.S. 1B runs from U.S. 1 across the Damariscotta River to Damariscotta. From this road take Route 129 south to South Bristol and Route 130 south to Bristol and New Harbor. From here you can return to U.S. 1 heading north on Route 32 through Round Pond and Bremen. In Waldoboro, turn off U.S. 1 on Jefferson Street to see the historic village center.

ESSENTIALS

Visitor Information Damariscotta Region Chamber of Commerce ☎ *207/563–8340* 🌐 *www.damariscottaregion.com.*

NEED A BREAK? **Moody's Diner. This diner makes whoopie pies of considerable size, prized for their filling above all.** ✉ ***1885 Atlantic Hwy., Waldoboro*** ☎ ***207/832–7785*** 🌐 ***www.moodysdiner.com.***

WHERE TO EAT AND STAY

$$ AMERICAN 🍴 **King Eider's Pub & Restaurant.** The classic pub right downtown bills itself as having the finest crab cakes in New England. Start with the fresh local oysters that the Damariscotta region is known for, then move on to entrées like steak-and-ale pie, sea scallop florentine, or sautéed haddock with chips. With exposed-brick walls and low wooden beams, it's a cozy place to enjoy your favorite ale. Stop by on Thursday nights for live music. [$] *Average main: $18* ✉ *2 Elm St.* ☎ *207/563–6008* 🌐 *www.kingeiderspub.com.*

$$$ B&B/INN 🏨 **Newcastle Inn.** A riverside location, tasteful decor, and lots of common areas (inside and out) make this a relaxing country inn. **Pros:** guests can order beer or wine; one suite-like room and two suites with sitting areas. **Cons:** not an in-town location. [$] *Rooms from: $190* ✉ *60 River Rd.,*

Lobster trap buoys are popular decorations in Maine; the markings represent a particular lobsterman's claim.

Newcastle ☎ 207/563–5685 ⊕ *www.newcastleinn.com* ⇨ *12 rooms, 2 suites* ❙◯❙ *Breakfast.*

PEMAQUID POINT

10 miles south of Damariscotta via U.S. 1, U.S. 1B, and Rte. 130.

Pemaquid Point is the tip of the Pemaquid Peninsula, bordered by Muscongus and Johns bays. It's home to the famous lighthouse of the same name and its attendant fog bell and tiny museum. Also at the bottom of the peninsula, along the Muscongus Bay, is the Nature Conservancy's Rachel Carson Salt Pond Preserve.

GETTING HERE AND AROUND

From U.S. 1, take U.S. 1B into Damariscotta and head south on Route 130 to Pemaquid Point.

EXPLORING

FAMILY **Pemaquid Point Light.** At the end of Route 130, this lighthouse at the tip of the Pemaquid Peninsula looks as though it sprouted from the ragged, tilted chunk of granite that it commands. Most days in the summer you can climb the tower to the light. The former keeper's cottage is now the Fishermen's Museum, which displays historic photographs, scale models, and artifacts that explore commercial fishing in Maine. Also here are the original fog bell and bell house. Pemaquid Art Gallery, on-site, mounts exhibitions by area artists in the summer. There are restrooms and picnic tables. ✉ *3115 Bristol Rd., Pemaquid* ☎ *207/677–2492* ⊕ *www.bristolparks.org* 🎟 *$2* ◷ *Museum: early May–Oct., daily 9–5.*

WHERE TO EAT AND STAY

$$ SEAFOOD 🍴 **Moscungus Bay Lobster Co.** The food here is practcially guaranteed to be fresh: the lobsters come in off the boat at one of the pier, and the restaurant is at the other. Grab a picnic table and be careful not to hit your head on the colorful, dangling wooden buoys. It's fun to watch the lobstermen unload their catch over lunch. [$] *Average main: $18* ✉ *28 Town Landing Rd., Round Pond* ☎ *207/529–2251* 🌐 *www.mainefreshlobster.com* 🕒 *Closed mid-May–mid-Oct.*

$$ SEAFOOD 🍴 **Round Pond Fisherman's Coop.** Sheltered Moscungus Bay is where you'll find this down-home lobster shack, on the pier so you have pleasant views of the water. Competition with the neighboring Moscungus Bay Lobster Co. keeps the prices low for fresh-off-the-boat lobster and steamers. [$] *Average main: $18* ✉ *25 Town Landing Rd., Round Pond* ☎ *207/529–5725* 🕒 *Closed Labor Day–mid-May.*

$$ B&B/INN 🏨 **Christmas Cove Inn.** If you're traveling with a dog, you'll find few more accommodating spots in Maine than this out-of-the-way place on Rutherford Island. **Pros:** great if you're traveling with dogs; great views from lookout. **Cons:** dogs on premises. [$] *Rooms from: $150* ✉ *53 Coveside Rd., South Bristol* ☎ *207/644–1502, 866/644–1502* 🌐 *www.christmascoveinn.com* 🛏 *7 rooms* 🍽 *No meals.*

SPORTS AND THE OUTDOORS

Hardy Boat Cruises. Mid-May through mid-October, you can take a cruise to Monhegan with Hardy Boat Cruises. The company also offers seal- and puffin-watching trips and lighthouse and fall coastal cruises. ✉ *Shaw's Wharf, 132 State Rte. 32, New Harbor* ☎ *207/677–2026, 800/278–3346* 🌐 *www.hardyboat.com.*

THOMASTON

10 miles northeast of Waldoboro, 72 miles northeast of Portland.

Thomaston is a delightful town, full of beautiful sea captains' homes and dotted with antiques and specialty shops. A National Historic District encompasses parts of High, Main, and Knox streets. The town is the gateway to the two peninsulas; you will see water on both sides as you arrive.

GETTING HERE AND AROUND

U.S. 1 is Main Street through Thomaston. Route 131 runs down the St. George Peninsula from here and Route 97 leads down the Cushing Peninsula and to Friendship.

WHERE TO EAT

$$ AMERICAN 🍴 **Thomaston Cafe.** This is a great place to stop on the long, slow drive up U.S. 1. Works by local artists adorn the walls of this small downtown café, which uses local ingredients as much as possible. It serves an excellent breakfast, including homemade corned beef hash. For lunch there's scrumptious haddock chowder and delicious sandwiches. Try the panfried haddock sandwich lightly breaded with panko bread crumbs, or a salad and crab cakes (sold at breakfast, too). Entrées include lobster ravioli and filet mignon with béarnaise sauce. Sunday

brunch is popular. [$] *Average main: $20* ✉ *154 Main St.* ☎ *207/354–8589* 🌐 *www.thomastoncafe.com* 🕒 *Closed Mon. No dinner Sun.–Wed.*

$$ SEAFOOD 🍴 **Waterman's Beach Lobster.** This place in South Thomaston is authentic, inexpensive, and scenic, overlooking islands in the Atlantic. You can eat lunch or dinner under the pavilions right next to the beach and pier, or get even closer to the water at picnic tables. In addition to the seafood favorites, Waterman's also sells freshly baked pies and locally made ice cream. It's strictly BYOB. [$] *Average main: $18* ✉ *343 Waterman's Beach Rd., South Thomaston* ☎ *207/596–7819, 207/594–7518* 🌐 *www.watermansbeachlobster.com* 🕒 *Closed Oct.–mid-June.*

PORT CLYDE

5 miles south of Tenants Harbor via Rte. 131.

The fishing village of Port Clyde sits at the end of the St. George Peninsula. The road leading here meanders along the St. George River, passing meadows and farmhouses and winding away from the river to the east side of the peninsula, which faces the Atlantic Ocean. Shipbuilding and granite quarrying were big industries here in the 1800s. Later, seafood canneries opened here; you can still buy Port Clyde sardines. Lobster fishing is an economic anchor today, and the quiet village is a haven for artists, with a number of galleries. Marshall Point Lighthouse, right in the harbor, has a small museum.

6

EXPLORING

Monhegan Island Light. Getting a look at this squat stone lighthouse—from land, anyway—requires a slightly steep, half-mile walk uphill from the island's ferry dock. The lighthouse was automated in 1959, and the former keeper's quarters became the Monhegan Museum shortly thereafter. The tower is open sporadically throughout the summer for short tours. Exhibits at the museum have as much to do with life on the island as they do with the lighthouse itself. ✉ *Lighthouse Hill Rd., ½ mile east of dock, Monhegan* ☎ *207/596–7003* 🕒 *Museum July and Aug., daily 11:30–3:30; June and Sept., daily 1:30–3:30.*

PENOBSCOT BAY

Few could deny that Penobscot Bay is one of Maine's most dramatically beautiful regions. Its more than 1,000 miles of coastline is made up of rocky granite boulders, often undeveloped shores, a sprinkling of colorful towns, and views of the sea and islands that are a photographer's dream.

Penobscot Bay stretches 37 miles from Port Clyde in the south to Stonington, the little fishing village at the tip of Deer Isle, in the north. The bay begins where the Penobscot River, New England's second-largest river system, ends, near Stockton Springs, and terminates in the Gulf of Maine, where it is 47 miles wide. It covers an estimated 1,070 square miles and is home to more than 1,800 islands.

Initially, shipbuilding was the primary moneymaker here. In the 1800s, during the days of the great tall ships (or Down Easters, as they were often called), more wooden ships were built in Maine than any other state in the country, and many were constructed along Penobscot Bay. This golden age of billowing sails and wooden sailing ships came to an end with the development of the steam engine. By 1900, sailing ships were no longer a viable commercial venture in Maine. However, as you will see when traveling the coast, the tall ships have not entirely disappeared—some, albeit tiny in number compared to the 1800s heyday, have been revived as recreational boats known as windjammers. Today, once again, there are more tall ships along Penobscot Bay than anywhere else in the country.

ROCKLAND

3 miles north of Thomaston via U.S. 1.

The town is considered the gateway to Penobscot Bay and is the first stop on U.S. 1 offering a glimpse of the often sparkling and island-dotted blue bay. Though once merely a place to pass through on the way to tonier ports like Camden, Rockland now gets attention on its own, thanks to a trio of attractions: the renowned Farnsworth Museum, the increasingly popular summer Lobster Festival, and the lively North Atlantic Blues Festival. Specialty shops and galleries line the main street, and one of the restaurants, Primo (between Camden and the little village of Owls Head), has become nationally famous. The town is still a large fishing port and the commercial hub of this coastal area.

Rockland Harbor bests Camden by one as home to the largest fleet of Maine windjammers. The best place in Rockland to view these beautiful vessels as they sail in and out of the harbor is the mile-long granite breakwater, which bisects the outer portion of Rockland Harbor. To get there, from U.S. 1, head east on Waldo Avenue and then right on Samoset Road; follow this short road to its end.

GETTING HERE AND AROUND
U.S. 1 runs along Main Street here, while U.S. 1A curves through the residential neighborhood west of the business district, offering a faster route if you are passing through.

Visitor Information Penobscot Bay Regional Chamber of Commerce
✉ *Visitor Center, 1 Park Dr.* ☎ *207/596–0376, 800/223–5459* ⊕ *www. therealmaine.com.*

EXPLORING

Fodor$Choice **Farnsworth Art Museum.** One of the most important small museums in the
★ country, much of its collection is devoted to Maine-related works of the famous Wyeth family: N. C. Wyeth, an accomplished illustrator whose works were featured in many turn-of-the-20th-century books; his late son Andrew, one of the country's best-known painters; and Andrew's son James, also an accomplished painter, who like his elders before him summers nearby. Galleries in the main building always display some of Andrew Wyeth's works, such as *The Patriot, Witchcraft,* and *Turkey Pond.* The **Wyeth Center,** a former church, shows art by his father and son. The museum's collection also includes works by Fitz Henry Lane, George Bellows, Frank W. Benson, Edward Hopper (as watercolors,

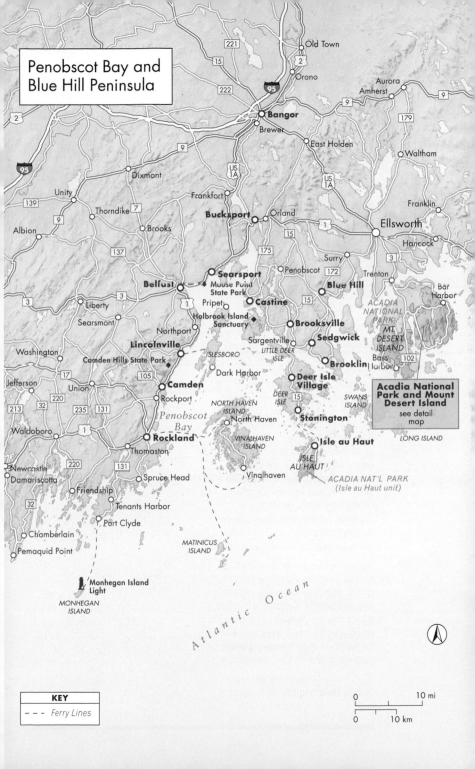

CLOSE UP

Windjammer Excursions

A windjammer cruise gives you a chance to admire Maine's dramatic coast from the water.

Nothing defines the Maine coastal experience more than a sailing trip on a windjammer. Windjammers were built all along the East Coast in the 19th and early 20th centuries. Designed primarily to carry cargo, these beauties (most are wood hulled) have a rich past—the *Nathaniel Bowditch* served in World War II, while others plied the waters in the lumbering, granite, fishing, and oystering trades or served as pilot boats. They vary in size but can be as small as 46 feet and hold six passengers (plus a couple of crew members) or more than 130 feet and hold 40 passengers and 10 crew members. During a windjammer excursion passengers are usually able to participate in the navigation, be it hoisting a sail or playing captain at the wheel.

During the Camden Windjammer Festival, held Labor Day weekend, crowds gather to watch the region's fleet sail into the harbor, and most boats are open for tours. The schooner-crew talent show later in the weekend is a bit more irreverent than the majestic arrival ceremony.

Cruises can be anywhere from one to eight days, and day trips usually involve a tour of the harbor and some lighthouse sightseeing. The price, ranging from $230 to $1,100, depending on length of trip, includes all meals. Trips leave from Camden, Rockland, and Rockport. You can get information on the fleets by contacting one of two windjammer organizations:

Maine Windjammer Association ☎ *800/807–9463* ⊕ *www.sailmainecoast.com*. **Maine Windjammer Cruises** ☎ *207/236–2938, 800/736–7981* ⊕ *www.mainewindjammercruises.com*.

they may be "resting"), Louise Nevelson, and Fairfield Porter. Changing exhibits are shown in the **Jamien Morehouse Wing.** The **Farnsworth Homestead,** a handsome circa-1850 Greek Revival dwelling that's part of the museum, retains its original lavish Victorian furnishings and is open late June through mid-October.

In Cushing, a tiny town about 10 miles south of Thomaston on the St. George River, the museum operates the **Olson House,** which is depicted in Andrew Wyeth's famous painting *Christina's World,* as well as in other works by the artist. It's accessible by guided tour only. ⊠ *16 Museum St.* ☎ *207/596–6457* ⊕ *www.farnsworthmuseum.org* ✉ *$12* ۞ *Jan.–Mar., Wed.–Sun. 10–5; Apr., May, Nov., and Dec., Tues.–Sun. 10–5; June–Oct., Sat.–Tues. and Thurs., 10–5, Wed. and Fri. 10–8.*

FAMILY **Maine Lighthouse Museum.** The lighthouse museum has more than 25 Fresnel lighthouse lenses, as well as a collection of lighthouse artifacts and Coast Guard memorabilia. Permanent exhibits spotlight topics like lighthouse heroines—women who manned the lights when the keepers couldn't—and lightships. ⊠ *1 Park Dr.* ☎ *207/594–3301* ⊕ *www. mainelighthousemuseum.org* ✉ *$5* ۞ *June–Oct., weekdays 9–5, weekends 10–4; Nov., Dec., and Mar.–May, Thurs. and Fri. 9–5, Sat. 10–4.*

6

WHERE TO EAT

$$$$ ✕ **Primo.** Award-winning chef Melissa Kelly and her world-class restau-
MEDITERRANEAN rant have been written up in *Gourmet, Bon Appétit,* and *O Magazine.*
Fodor's Choice The upstairs in this restored Victorian home has a funky vibe; down-
★ stairs is fancier. Wherever you eat it's farm-to-table here: the eatery raises chickens and pigs, cures meats, produces eggs, and grows produce. Combining fresh Maine ingredients with Mediterranean influences, the daily-changing menu includes dishes like kale salad with creamy garlic dressing, house-made pasta with local squid, and duck with sweet-and-sour rhubarb chutney. Pastry chef Price Kushner creates delectable desserts like cannoli featuring crushed pistachios and amarena cherries. Ⓢ *Average main: $35* ⊠ *2 S. Main St.* ☎ *207/596–0770* ⊕ *www.primorestaurant.com* ۞ *No lunch.*

$$ ✕ **Rockland Cafe.** It may not look like much from the outside, but Rock-
DINER land Cafe is one of the most popular eateries in town. It's famous for the size of its breakfasts—don't pass up the fish cakes, also available for lunch and dinner. If you're a late riser, don't worry: breakfast is served until noon (until 4 November to April). At dinner, the seafood combo of shrimp, scallops, clams, and haddock is excellent, or there's also classic liver and onions. Ⓢ *Average main: $15* ⊠ *441 Main St.* ☎ *207/596–7556* ⊕ *www.rocklandcafe.com.*

WHERE TO STAY

$$$ ☷ **Berry Manor Inn.** Originally the residence of Rockland merchant
B&B/INN Charles H. Berry, this 1898 shingle-style B&B sits in Rockland's National Historic District. **Pros:** quiet neighborhood; within walking distance of downtown and the harbor; rooms have TVs. **Cons:** not much of a view. Ⓢ *Rooms from: $195* ⊠ *81 Talbot Ave.* ☎ *207/596–7696, 800/774–5692* ⊕ *www.berrymanorinn.com* ➴ *12 rooms* ۞ *Breakfast.*

$$ ☷ **LimeRock Inn.** In the center of town in Rockland's National Historic
B&B/INN District, the LimeRock Inn puts you within easy walking distance of

the Farnsworth Museum and many restaurants. **Pros:** all rooms have TVs and DVD players; large in-town lot with gazebo. **Cons:** not on the water. [$] *Rooms from: $159* ✉ *96 Limerock St.* ☎ *207/594–2257, 800/546–3762* 🌐 *www.limerockinn.com* 🛏 *8 rooms* 🍴 *Breakfast.*

$$$$ RESORT Fodor's Choice ★ 🏨 **Samoset Resort.** Occupying 230 waterfront acres on the Rockland–Rockport town line, this all-encompassing resort offers luxurious rooms and suites with private balconies overlooking the water or the grounds. **Pros:** full-service spa; children's programs; activities from basketball to croquet. **Cons:** no beach. [$] *Rooms from: $359* ✉ *220 Warrenton St., Rockport* ☎ *207/594–2511, 800/341–1650* 🌐 *www.samoset.com* 🛏 *160 rooms, 18 suites, 4 cottages, 72 condos* 🍴 *Breakfast.*

NIGHTLIFE AND THE ARTS

Maine Lobster Festival. Rockland's annual Maine Lobster Festival, held in early August, is the region's largest annual event. About 10 tons of lobsters are steamed in a huge lobster cooker—you have to see it to believe it. The festival, held in Harbor Park, includes a parade, live entertainment, food booths—and, of course, the crowning of the Maine Sea Goddess. ✉ *Harbor Park, Main St., south of Rte. 1* ☎ *207/596–0376* 🌐 *www.mainelobsterfestival.com.*

FAMILY **North Atlantic Blues Festival.** About a dozen well-known musicians gather for the North Atlantic Blues Festival, a two-day affair held the first full weekend after July 4th. The show officially takes place at the public landing on Rockland Harbor Park, but it also includes a "club crawl" through downtown Rockland on Saturday night. Admission to the festival is $25 in advance, $35 at the gate. ✉ *Harbor Park, Main St.* ☎ *207/691–2248* 🌐 *www.northatlanticbluesfestival.com.*

SPORTS AND THE OUTDOORS

Nathaniel Bowditch. A racing yacht built in 1922 and rebuilt in 1971, the *Nathaniel Bowditch* leads chartered trips lasting from a single afternoon up to four days. ☎ *800/288–4098* 🌐 *www.windjammervacation.com.*

Schooner *Heritage.* The newest windjammer in Maine's fleet offers three- to six-day cruises, and Captain Doug Lee is a storyteller and author of nautical histories. ✉ *North End Shipyard, 11 Front St., Rockland* ☎ *207/594–8007, 800/648–4544* 🌐 *www.schoonerheritage.com.*

Schooner *Summertime.* Built with a pointed stern in a pre-Revolutionary War style known as a "pinky" schooner, the *Summertime* heads out on three- to six-day cruises from Rockland (with day sails limited to its home port on Blue Hill Bay, farther up the coast). ✉ *Rockland* ☎ *800/562–8290* 🌐 *www.schoonersummertime.com.*

CAMDEN

8 miles north of Rockland.

Fodor's Choice ★ More than any other town along Penobscot Bay, Camden is the perfect picture-postcard of a Maine coastal village. It is one of the most popular destinations on the Maine Coast, so June through September the town is crowded with visitors, but don't let that scare you away; Camden is worth it. Just come prepared for busy traffic on the town's

THE PRETTIEST WALK IN THE WORLD

A few years ago *Yankee,* the quintessential magazine of New England, did a cover story on what it called "The Prettiest Walk in the World." The two-lane paved road, which winds up and down, with occasional views of the ocean and the village of Rockport, connects this town with Camden. To judge the merits of the journey of a few miles or so for yourself, you can travel on foot or by car. Begin at the intersection of U.S. 1 and Pascal Avenue. Take a right off U.S. 1 toward Rockport Harbor, then cross the bridge and go up the hill to Central Street. One block later, bear right on Russell Avenue, which becomes Chestnut Street at the Camden town line.

Take this all the way to downtown Camden. Lining the way are some of the most beautiful homes in Maine, surrounded by an abundance of flora and fauna. Keep an eye out for Aldermere Farm and its Belted Galloway cows, as well as views of the sparkling ocean. For those who may not know, these rare cows get their name from the foot-wide white "belt" around their middles. The walk or drive is beautiful at any time of the year, but in fall it's breathtaking. Like the rest of New England, the coast of Maine gets a large number of fall-foliage "leaf peepers," and the reds and golds of the chestnut, birch, and elm trees along this winding route are especially beautiful.

Main Street (U.S. 1) and make reservations for lodging and restaurants well in advance.

Camden is famous not only for its geography, but also for its large fleet of windjammers—relics and replicas from the age of sailing—with their romantic histories and great billowing sails. At just about any hour during the warm months you're likely to see at least one windjammer tied up in the harbor. The excursions, whether for an afternoon or a week, are best from June through September.

The town's compact size makes it perfect for exploring on foot: shops, restaurants, and galleries line Main Street, as well as side streets and alleys around the harbor. Especially worth inclusion on your walking tour is Camden's residential area. It is quite charming and filled with many fascinating old period houses from the time when Federal, Greek Revival, and Victorian architectural styles were the rage among the wealthy. Many of them are now B&Bs. The Chamber of Commerce, at the Public Landing, can provide you with a walking map. Humped on the north side of town are the Camden Hills. Drive or hike to the summit at Camden Hills State Park to enjoy mesmerizing views of the town, harbor, and island-dotted bay.

GETTING HERE AND AROUND

U.S. 1 runs right through Camden. Take Route 90 west from U.S. 1 and rejoin it in Warren to bypass Rockland—this is the quickest route south.

ESSENTIALS

Visitor Information Penobscot Bay Regional Chamber of Commerce
✉ *Visitor Center, 2 Public Landing* ☎ *207/236–4404, 800/223–5459* ⊕ *www. mainedreamvacation.com.*

WHERE TO EAT

$$$
SEAFOOD
⊁ Atlantica. Right on the water's edge, the Atlantica is in a classic weathered shingled building. Its lower deck is cantilevered over the water, offering a romantic setting with great views, and the interior decor is a mix of red walls and contemporary paintings. Fresh seafood with international accents is the specialty here. Favorites include pan-roasted split lobster tails with lemon butter, lobster stuffed with scallops, and pan-roasted king

salmon. Everything is made from scratch, including the breads and desserts. There are small plates and lighter offerings like fish tacos. $ *Average main: $27 ⊠ 9 Bayview Landing ☎ 207/236–6011, 888/507–8514 ⊕ www.atlanticarestaurant.com ⌂ Reservations essential ⊗ Closed Nov.–Apr. No lunch.*

$$
SEAFOOD
⊁ Cappy's Chowder House. As you would expect from the name, Cappy's clam "chowdah" is the thing to order here—it's been written up in the *New York Times* and *Bon Appétit*—but there are plenty of other seafood specials at this restaurant. Don't be afraid to bring the kids—they'll love the "Crow's Nest" upper level. $ *Average main: $13 ⊠ 1 Main St. ☎ 207/236–2254 ⊕ www.cappyschowder.com ⌂ Reservations not accepted.*

$$$$
MODERN
AMERICAN
⊁ Natalie's Restaurant. One of the most sought-after dining spots in Camden, Natalie's is the creation of Dutch owners Raymond Brunyanszki and Oscar Verest, who brought in executive chef Jon Gaboric in 2013. Located in the Camden Harbour Inn, the restaurant is fine dining with a distinctly Maine flair. Seasonal ingredients set the tone. Choose from two prix-fixe menus (a three-course à la carte for $68 or a seven-course chef's choice for $97), which might feature cabbage-wrapped Maine monkfish or local lamb with root veggies. There's also a five-course lobster tasting menu that may include lobster with peaches and wasabi cream and grilled lobster with carrot puree. In the lounge, you can order small tapas-style dishes or enjoy a predinner cocktail in front of the big fireplace. $ *Average main: $72 ⊠ Camden Harbour Inn, 83 Bay View St. ☎ 207/236–7008 ⊕ www.nataliesrestaurant.com ⌂ Reservations essential ⊗ Closed Mon. Nov.–May. No lunch.*

WHERE TO STAY

$$$
B&B/INN
⊞ Camden Hartstone Inn. This 1835 mansard-roofed Victorian home has been turned into a plush and sophisticated retreat and a fine culinary destination. **Pros:** luxury in the heart of town; extravagant breakfasts; some private entrances. **Cons:** not on water. $ *Rooms from: $199 ⊠ 41 Elm St. ☎ 207/236–4259, 800/788–4823 ⊕ www.hartstoneinn.com ⌔ 12 rooms, 9 suites ⊠ Breakfast.*

$$$$
HOTEL
⊞ Lord Camden Inn. If you want to be in the center of town and near the harbor, look for this handsome brick building with the bright blue-and-white awnings. **Pros:** large Continental breakfast; suite-like

The view from Camden Hills is a great way to see Penobscot Bay and the town of Camden.

"premier" rooms have balconies and sitting areas. **Cons:** traffic noise in front rooms. $ *Rooms from: $239* ✉ *24 Main St.* ☎ *207/236–4325, 800/336–4325* ⊕ *www.lordcamdeninn.com* ⤴ *34 rooms, 2 suites* ❢⊙❢ *Breakfast.*

$$$$
B&B/INN
Fodor'sChoice
★

❖ **Norumbega Inn.** This welcoming B&B is the one of the most photographed pieces of real estate in Maine, and once you get a look at its castle-like facade, you'll understand why. **Pros:** eye-popping architecture; beautiful views; close to town. **Cons:** stairs to climb. $ *Rooms from: $239* ✉ *63 High St.* ☎ *207/236–4646, 877/363–4646* ⊕ *www.norumbegainn.com* ⤴ *9 rooms, 2 suites* ❢⊙❢ *Breakfast.*

$$$
B&B/INN

❖ **Whitehall Inn.** The oldest part of the Whitehall is an 1834 white-clapboard sea captain's home, and much of the rest of this historic lodging was built in the early 1900s. **Pros:** short walk to downtown and harbor; breakfast entrée choices. **Cons:** no good water views. $ *Rooms from: $175* ✉ *52 High St.* ☎ *207/236–3391, 800/789–6565* ⊕ *www.whitehall-inn.com* ⤴ *37 rooms, 4 suites* ☾ *Closed mid-Oct.–mid-May* ❢⊙❢ *Breakfast.*

NIGHTLIFE AND THE ARTS

FAMILY **Windjammer Weekend.** One of the biggest and most colorful events of the year is the Camden Windjammer Festival, which takes place over Labor Day weekend. The harbor is packed with historic vessels, and there are lots of good eats. Visitors can tour the ships. ☎ *207/236–4404* ⊕ *www.camdenwindjammerfestival.com.*

SPORTS AND THE OUTDOORS

Angelique. Captain Mike and Lynne McHenry have more than three decades of experience on the high seas. Three- to six-day cruise options aboard the *Angelique* include photography workshops and meteor-watching trips. ⊠ *Camden Harbor* ☎ *800/282–9899* ⊕ *www. sailangelique.com.*

Heron. This schooner, which had a cameo in the movie *The Rum Diary*, offers lunchtime sails, wildlife-watching trips, and sunset cruises. ⊠ *Rockport Marine Park, Pascal Ave., Rockport* ☎ *207/236–8605, 800/599–8605* ⊕ *www.sailheron.com.*

Mary Day. Sailing for more than 50 years, the *Mary Day* is the first schooner in Maine built specifically for vacation excursions. Meals are cooked on an antique wood-fired stove. ⊠ *Camden Harbor, Atlantic Ave.* ☎ *800/992–2218* ⊕ *www.schoonermaryday.com.*

Olad. Captain Aaron Lincoln runs two-hour trips on both the *Olad* and a smaller sailing vessel, spotting lighthouses, coastal mansions, the occasional seal, and the red-footed puffin cousins known as guillemots. Either boat can also be chartered for longer trips. ⊠ *Camden Harbor, Bay View St.* ☎ *207/236–2323* ⊕ *www.maineschooners.com.*

SHOPPING

Camden's downtown area is a shopper's paradise, with lots of interesting places to spend money. Most of the shops and galleries are along Camden's main drag. From the harbor, turn right on Bay View, and walk to Main/High Street. U.S. 1 has lots of names as it runs through Maine. Three are within Camden's town limits—it starts as Elm Street, changes to Main Street, then becomes High Street.

Lily, Lupine & Fern. This full-service florist offers a wonderful array of gourmet foods, chocolates, wines, imported beers, and cheeses. It stocks cigars, too. There's a small deck where you can enjoy harbor views and a cup of coffee. ⊠ *11 Main St.* ☎ *207/236–9600* ⊕ *www.lilylupine.com.*

Planet. In this storefront shop you'll find unique clothing, lots of books, and quality toys, many of them made in Maine. ⊠ *10 Main St.* ☎ *207/236–4410.*

LINCOLNVILLE

6 miles north of Camden via U.S. 1.

Lincolnville's area of most interest—where there are a few restaurants, the ferry to Islesboro, and a swimming beach that attracts folks from neighboring Camden and Belfast—is Lincolnville Beach. The village is tiny; you could go through it in less than a minute. Still, it has a history going back to the Revolution, and you can see a small cannon on the beach here (never used) that was intended to repel the British in the War of 1812.

GETTING HERE AND AROUND

Lincolnville Beach is on U.S. 1, and the town of Lincolnville Center is inland on Route 173.

WHERE TO EAT

$$$ ✕**Lobster Pound Restaurant.** If you're looking for an authentic place to
SEAFOOD enjoy your Maine lobster dinner, this is it. This large restaurant has
FAMILY rustic wooden picnic tables outside, an enclosed patio, and two din-
ing rooms with a gift shop in between. Hundreds of live lobsters are
in swimming tanks out back, so feel free to pick your own. There's
a full bar, and the wine list includes some local vintages. The classic
"shore dinner deluxe" consists of lobster stew or fish chowder, steamed
clams or mussels, fried clams, and a 1½-pound lobster, along with side
dishes and dessert. Because this is such a big place, you won't have to
wait long, even if it's busy. Right on U.S. 1, next to a small beach, the
restaurant has beautiful views. $ *Average main: $22* ✉ *2521 Atlan-
tic Hwy.* ☎ *207/789–5550* ⊕ *www.lobsterpoundmaine.com* ☽ *Closed
mid-Oct.–mid-Apr.*

BELFAST

13 miles north of Lincolnville via U.S. 1.

A number of Maine coastal towns, such as Wiscasset and Damariscotta,
like to think of themselves as the prettiest little town in Maine, but Bel-
fast (originally to be named Londonderry) may be the true winner of
this title. It has a full variety of charms: a beautiful waterfront; an old
and interesting main street climbing up from the harbor; a delightful
array of B&Bs, restaurants, and shops; and a friendly population. The
downtown even has old-fashioned streetlamps, which set the streets
aglow at night.

GETTING HERE AND AROUND

U.S. 1 runs through Belfast as it travels up the coast. From Interstate
95, take U.S. 3 in Augusta to get here. The highways join in Belfast
heading north. The information center has a large array of magazines,
guidebooks, maps, and brochures that cover the entire Mid-Coast. It
also can provide you with a free walking-tour brochure that describes
the various historic buildings.

ESSENTIALS

Visitor Information Belfast Area Chamber of Commerce ✉ *14 Main St.*
☎ *207/338–5900* ⊕ *www.belfastmaine.org.*

EXPLORING

In the mid-1800s Belfast was home to a number of wealthy business
magnates, ship builders, ship captains, and so on. Their mansions still
stand along High Street and in the residential area above it, offering
excellent examples of Greek Revival and Federal-style architecture. In
fact, the town has one of the best showcases of Greek Revival homes
in the state. Don't miss the "White House" where High and Church
streets merge several blocks south of downtown.

WHERE TO EAT

$$$ ✕**Darby's Restaurant and Pub.** This charming, old-fashioned restaurant
AMERICAN and bar is very popular with locals. With pressed-tin ceilings, it has
been a bar or a restaurant since it was built in the 1890s. On the walls
are works for sale by local artists and old murals of Belfast scenes. Pad

thai and chicken with chili and cashews are signature dishes. The menu also has hearty homemade soups and sandwiches and classic fish-and-chips. $ *Average main: $23* ⊠ *155 High St.* ☎ *207/338–2339* ⊕ *www. darbysrestaurant.com.*

$$$
SEAFOOD
Fodor'sChoice
★

✕ **Young's Lobster Pound.** The corrugated-steel building looks more like a fish cannery than a restaurant, but it's one of the best places for an authentic Maine lobster dinner. It sits right on the water's edge, across the harbor from downtown Belfast. When you first walk in, you'll see tanks and tanks of live lobsters of varying size. The traditional meal here is the "shore dinner," consisting of clam chowder or lobster stew, steamed clams or mussels, a 1½-pound boiled lobster, corn on the cob, and chips. Order your dinner at the counter, then find a table inside or on the deck. Surf-and-turf dinners and hot dogs are popular, too. It's BYOB. ■TIP→ Don't leave your outdoor table unattended—seagulls love lobster. $ *Average main: $25* ⊠ *2 Mitchell St., off U.S. 1* ☎ *207/338–1160* ⊕ *youngslobsterpound.webs.com* ☉ *Takeout only Jan.–Mar.*

NIGHTLIFE AND THE ARTS

Rollie's Bar & Grill. Up a bit from the harbor, Rollie's Bar & Grill has been in business since 1972. The vintage bar is from a 19th-century sailing ship. Rollie's is the town's most popular watering hole, especially with the TVs for watching the big game. It just may serve the best hamburgers in the state, which is why you'll see families here through the dinner hour. Food is served until midnight on Friday and Saturday. ⊠ *37 Main St.* ☎ *207/338–4502* ⊕ *www.rollies.me.*

SEARSPORT

6 miles north of Belfast via U.S. 1.

Searsport is well known as the antiques and flea-market capital of Maine, and with good reason: the Antique Mall alone, on U.S. 1 just north of town, contains the offerings of 70 dealers, and flea markets during the visitor season line both sides of U.S. 1.

Searsport also has a rich history of shipbuilding and seafaring. In the early to mid-1800s there were 10 shipbuilding facilities in Searsport, and the population of the town was about 1,000 people more than it is today because of the ready availability of jobs. By the mid-1800s Searsport was home to more than 200 sailing-ship captains.

GETTING HERE AND AROUND

Downtown Searsport is right along U.S. 1, as is much of the town, which doesn't have lots of side streets. Just north of here in Stockton Springs U.S. 1A leads to Bangor.

EXPLORING

FAMILY
Fodor'sChoice
★

Penobscot Marine Museum. Just off Main Street, this downtown museum explores the maritime culture of the Penobscot Bay region. Exhibits, artifacts, and paintings are in six nearby buildings, most from the first half of the 19th century. One of the former sea captain's homes has period rooms. Outstanding marine art includes a notable collection of works by Thomas and James Buttersworth. There are photos of

Learn about Maine's seafaring heritage at the Penobscot Marine Museum.

local sea captains, model ships, lots of scrimshaw, navigational instruments, and tools from the area's history of logging, granite mining, and ice cutting. There are also exhibits just for the kids. ⊠ *5 Church St.* ☎ *207/548–2529* ⊕ *www.penobscotmarinemuseum.org* ▦ *$12* ☉ *Late May–third weekend in Oct., Mon.–Sat. 10–5, Sun. noon–5.*

SHOPPING

Searsport Antique Mall. The area's biggest collection of antiques is in the Searsport Antique Mall, which has more than 70 dealers. ⊠ *149 E. Main St.* ☎ *207/548–2640* ⊕ *www.searsportantiquemall.com.*

BUCKSPORT

9 miles north of Searsport via U.S. 1.

The new Penobscot Narrows Bridge, spanning the Penobscot River, welcomes visitors to Bucksport, a town founded in 1763 by Jonathan Buck. Bucksport was the site of the second-worst naval defeat in American history (the first was Pearl Harbor), in 1779, when a British Armada defeated the fledgling American Navy. It became known as "the disaster on the Penobscot." You can learn more about it at the museum in Bucksport or at the Penobscot Marine Museum in Searsport. Fort Knox, Maine's largest historic fort, overlooks the town from across the river. There are magnificent views of the imposing granite structure from the pleasant riverfront walkway downtown.

GETTING HERE AND AROUND

U.S. 1 crosses a bridge into Bucksport; turn left for downtown and right to continue on the highway. Route 15 heads north to Bangor from here.

EXPLORING

FAMILY

Fodor's Choice

★

Penobscot Narrows Bridge & Observatory Tower/Fort Knox Historic Site. An "an engineering marvel" is how experts describe the 2,120-foot-long Penobscot Narrows Bridge, which opened in 2006. It's certainly beautiful to look at—from the surrounding countryside it pops up on the horizon like the towers of a fairy-tale castle. Spanning the Penobscot River across from Bucksport, the bridge's 437-foot observation tower is the highest in the world. An elevator shoots you to the top. Don't miss it—the panoramic views, which take in the hilly countryside and the river as it widens into Penobscot Bay, are breathtaking.

Also here is Fort Knox, the largest historic fort in Maine. It was built between 1844 and 1869, when despite a treaty with Britain settling boundary disputes, invasion was feared—the Brits controlled this region during the Revolutionary War and again during the War of 1812. The fort never saw any actual fighting, but it was used for troop training and as a garrison during the Civil War and the Spanish-American War. Visitors are welcome to explore the passageways and many rooms. Guided tours are given daily during the summer and several days a week in the shoulder seasons. ⊠ *711 Ft. Knox Rd., off U.S. 1, Prospect* ☎ *207/469–6553* ⊕ *www.fortknox.maineguide.com* ⊠ *$7 observatory and fort, $4.50 fort only* ⊙ *Observatory May, June, Sept., and Oct., daily 9–5; July and Aug., daily 9–6. Fort May–Oct., daily 9–5.*

BANGOR

122 miles north of Portland via I–95, 19 miles north of Bucksport via Rte. 15.

The state's second-largest metropolitan area (Portland is the largest), Bangor is about 20 miles from the coast and is the unofficial capital of northern Maine. Back in the 19th century the most important product and export of the "Queen City" was lumber from the state's vast North Woods. Now, because of its airport, Bangor has become a gateway to Mount Desert Island, Bar Harbor, and Acadia National Park. Along the revitalized waterfront, the American Folk Festival draws big crowds on the last full weekend in August, and an outdoor stage attracts top bands and musicians throughout the summer.

GETTING HERE AND AROUND

Interstate 95 has five Bangor exits, 45 to 49. U.S. 1A loops up to Bangor from Stockton Springs and Ellsworth, near Bar Harbor, and connects with Interstate 395 on the western side of the Bangor area.

ESSENTIALS

Visitor Information Greater Bangor Convention & Visitors Bureau ⊠ *33 Harlow St.* ☎ *207/947–5205, 800/916–6673* ⊕ *www.bangorcvb.org.*

EXPLORING

FAMILY

Maine Discovery Museum. Three floors with more than 60 interactive exhibits let kids explore the state's ecosystem in Nature Trails, learn about other cultures in TradeWinds, step into classic children's books like *Charlotte's Web*—all written by Maine authors—in Booktown, and unearth dinosaur "bones" in DINO Dig. There are also a drop-in art studio and daily programs on art and other topics. ■ TIP→ Visitors to Acadia National Park often head here on a rainy day. ⊠ *74 Main St.* ☎ *207/262–7200* ⊕ *www.mainediscoverymuseum.org* 🖾 *$7.50* ☺ *June–Sept., Mon.–Sat. 10–5, Sun. noon–5; Oct.–May, Tues.–Sat. 10–5, Sun. noon–5.*

NEED A BREAK? **Friars' Bakehouse.** Locals say this place has the best whoopie pies in the Bangor area. The bakery and restaurant is run by three Franciscan friars, one of whom spent time in highly regarded culinary programs. ⊠ *21 Central St., Bangor* ☎ *207/947–3770.*

Governor's Restaurant & Bakery. The old family-friendly standby Governor's Restaurant and Bakery, with six locations, including Bangor, is famed for its peanut butter whoopie pies as well as the old reliable standard, and can accommodate special flavor combinations by request with 24-hour notice. ⊠ *643 Broadway, Bangor* ☎ *207/827–7630* ⊕ *www.governorsrestaurant.com.*

WHERE TO STAY

$$ ⛰ **Lucerne Inn.** Nestled in the mountains, the Lucerne Inn overlooks
HOTEL beautiful Phillips Lake. **Pros:** golf course across the road. **Cons:** some dated rooms. Ⓢ *Rooms from: $149* ⊠ *2517 Main Rd., Dedham* ☎ *207/843–5123, 800/325–5123* ⊕ *www.lucerneinn.com* ⛊ *21 rooms, 10 suites* ⦿| *Breakfast.*

THE BLUE HILL PENINSULA

If you want to see unspoiled Down East Maine landscapes, explore art galleries, savor exquisite meals, or simply enjoy life at an unhurried pace, you should be quite content on the Blue Hill Peninsula.

The large peninsula juts south into Penobscot Bay. Not far from the mainland are the islands of Little Deer Isle, Deer Isle, and, at the latter's tip, the picturesque fishing town of Stonington. A twisting labyrinth of roads winds through blueberry barrens and around picturesque coves, linking the towns of Blue Hill, Brooksville, Sedgwick, and Brooklin. Blue Hill and Castine are the area's primary business hubs. Painters, photographers, sculptors, and other artists are drawn to the area. You can find more than 20 galleries on Deer Isle and in Stonington and at least half as many on the mainland. With its small inns, charming B&Bs, and outstanding restaurants scattered across the area, the Blue Hill Peninsula may just persuade you to leave the rest of the coastline to the tourists.

VISITOR INFORMATION

Contacts **Blue Hill Peninsula Chamber of Commerce** ⊠ *16 South St., Blue Hill* ☎ *207/374–3242* ⊕ *www.bluehillpeninsula.org.* **Deer Isle–Stonington Chamber of Commerce** ⊠ *Main St., at Church St., Deer Isle* ☎ *207/348–6124* ⊕ *www.deerisle.com.*

CASTINE

18 miles north of Bucksport via U.S. 1 and Rtes. 175 and 166.

A summer destination for more than 100 years, Castine is a well-preserved seaside village rich in history. The French established a trading post here in 1613, naming the area Pentagoet. A year later Captain John Smith claimed the area for the British. The French regained control of the peninsula with the 1667 Breda Treaty, and Jean Vincent d'Abbadie de St. Castin obtained a land grant in the Pentagoet area, which would later bear his name. Castine's strategic position on Penobscot Bay and its importance as a trading post meant there were many battles for control until 1815. In the 19th century Castine was an important port for trading ships and fishing vessels. Larger ships, the Civil War, and the advent of train travel brought its prominence as a port to an end, but by the late 1800s some of the nation's wealthier citizens had discovered Castine as a pleasant summer retreat.

GETTING HERE AND AROUND

From U.S. 1 in Orland, near Bucksport, Route 175 heads south along the Penobscot River toward Castine. Continue on Route 166 at the crossroads of West Penobscot and after a bit you have the option of taking Route 166A into the village. The roads form a loop; the latter is especially scenic, passing expansive Wadsworth Cove at the mouth of the river as it enters its namesake bay.

EXPLORING

Federal- and Greek Revival–style architecture, rich history, and spectacular views of Penobscot Bay make Castine an ideal spot to spend a day or two. Explore its lively harbor front, two small museums (the Wilson Museum and the Castine Historical Society), and the ruins of a British fort. You can't miss the oversized historical signs throughout the village. An excellent self-guided walking tour is available at local businesses and the historical society. For a nice stroll, park your car at the landing and walk up Main Street toward the white Trinitarian Federated Church. Turn right on Court Street and go one block to the town common. Among the white-clapboard buildings ringing this green space are the Ives House (once the summer home of poet Robert Lowell), the Adams School, the former Abbott School (home to the historical society), and the Unitarian Church, capped by a whimsical belfry. From lower Main Street, head out Perkins Street on foot or by bike or car. You'll pass summer "cottage" mansions and the Wilson Museum on the way to Dyces Head Lighthouse (private), where a path leads to cliffs (careful here) fronting Penobscot Bay, site of a major Revolutionary War battle. You can return on Battle Avenue to make a loop.

WHERE TO EAT

$$

AMERICAN

✕ **Dennett's Wharf.** Originally built as a sail-rigging loft in the early 1800s, this longtime favorite is a good place for oysters and fresh seafood of all kinds. The waterfront restaurant also serves burgers, sandwiches, and light fare. There are 23 microbrews on tap, including the tasty Dennett's Wharf Rat Ale. Eat in the dining room or outside on the deck—there are covered and open sections, another bar, and Adirondack chairs if you just stop by for a brew. $ *Average main:*

$18 ✉ *15 Sea St.* ☎ *207/326–9045* 🌐 *www.dennettswharf.net* 🕒 *Closed Nov.–mid-Apr.*

SPORTS AND THE OUTDOORS

Castine Kayak International Adventures. At Eaton's Wharf, Castine Kayak Adventures operates tours run by owner Karen Francoeur, a Registered Maine Guide. Sign up for a half day of kayaking along the shore, a full day of kayaking in Penobscot Bay, or nighttime bioluminescent trips—paddling stirs up a type of phytoplankton, causing them to light up like fireflies as they shoot through the water. The company also offers overnight kayak camping trips and rents mountain bikes and kayaks. ✉ *Eaton's Wharf, 17 Sea St.* ☎ *207/866–3506* 🌐 *www.castinekayak.com.*

BLUE HILL

20 miles east of Castine via Rtes. 166, 175, and 176.

Snuggled between 943-foot Blue Hill Mountain and Blue Hill Bay, the village of Blue Hill sits cozily beside its harbor. Originally known for its granite quarries, copper mines, and shipbuilding, today the town is known for its pottery and galleries, bookstores, antiques shops, and studios that line its streets. The Blue Hill Fair (🌐 *www.bluehillfair.com*), held Labor Day weekend, is a tradition in these parts, with agricultural exhibits, food, rides, and entertainment. A charming little park with a great playground is tucked away on the harbor downtown.

6

GETTING HERE AND AROUND

From U.S. 1 in Orland, Route 15 heads south to Blue Hill. To continue north on the highway, take Route 172 north to Ellsworth.

WHERE TO EAT AND STAY

$$$$ MODERN AMERICAN Fodor's Choice ★

🍴 **Arborvine.** Glowing gas fireplaces, period antiques, exposed beams, and hardwood floors covered with Oriental rugs adorn the four candlelit dining areas in this renovated Cape Cod–style house. Begin with a salad of mixed greens, sliced beets, and pears with blue cheese crumbled on top. For your entrée, choose from seasonal dishes such as crispy duck with rhubarb and lime glaze or roasted rack of lamb with a basil-and-pine-nut crust. The fresh fish dishes are also superb. Save room for desserts; the ice cream (chocolate chili!) is homemade. Return when you're in a more casual mood: like the restaurant, the adjacent nautical-theme DeepWater Brew Pub serves dishes made with organic ingredients, as well as its own beer. It's housed in an inviting, historic barn that opens to lawn seating come summer. [$] *Average main: $31* ✉ *33 Tenney Hill* ☎ *207/374–2119* 🌐 *www.arborvine.com* 🕒 *No lunch.*

$$$$ B&B/INN

🏨 **Blue Hill Inn.** One side of this 1830 Federal-style inn was built as a home, but it soon became an inn, adding a wing with a matching facade in the 1850s. **Pros:** plenty of charm; modern suites with kitchens in separate building. **Cons:** some small rooms. [$] *Rooms from: $225* ✉ *40 Union St.* ☎ *207/374–2844, 800/826–7415* 🌐 *www.bluehillinn.com* 🛏 *10 rooms, 3 suites* 🕒 *Closed Nov.–mid-May* 🍽 *Breakfast.*

SHOPPING
ART GALLERIES
Blue Hill Bay Gallery. This gallery sells oil and watercolor landscapes and seascapes of Maine and New England from the 19th through the 21st centuries. It also carries the owner's photography. ⊠ *11 Tenny Hill* ☎ *207/374–5773* ⊕ *www.bluehillbaygallery.com.*

POTTERY
North Country Textiles. Huge windows fill this colorful corner store with light, adding to the delight of browsing the handcrafted rag rugs, ornate cotton jackets, felt puppets, knitted items, and dyed artisanal yarns. Almost everything sold at this shop in downtown's Levy Building is handcrafted in Maine. ⊠ *36 Main St.* ☎ *207/374–2715* ⊕ *www. northcountrytextiles.com.*

Rackliffe Pottery. In business since 1969, this shop sells colorful pottery made with lead-free glazes. You can choose between water pitchers, serving platters, tea-and-coffee sets, and sets of canisters, among other lovely items. ⊠ *126 Ellsworth Rd.* ☎ *207/374–2297* ⊕ *www. rackliffepottery.com.*

WINE
Blue Hill Wine Shop. In a restored barn at the rear of one of Blue Hill's earliest houses, the Blue Hill Wine Shop carries more than 1,200 carefully selected wines. Coffee, tea, cheeses, and prewrapped sandwiches are also available. ⊠ *123 Main St.* ☎ *207/374–2161* ⊕ *www. bluehillwineshop.com.*

SEDGWICK, BROOKLIN, AND BROOKSVILLE

Winding through the hills, the roads leading to the villages of Sedgwick, Brooklin, and Brooksville take you past rambling farmhouses, beautiful coves, and blueberry barrens studded with occasional masses of granite.

GETTING HERE AND AROUND
From Blue Hill, Route 175 runs along the bottom of the Blue Hill Peninsula, heading first to Brooklin, then through Sedgwick and Brooksville on its way to U.S. 1 in Orland. Route 176 traverses Sedgwick and Brooksville as it heads west from Blue Hill across the middle of the peninsula. Because this wide peninsula has lots of capes, points, and necks, take care when driving to make sure you're continuing on the right road and not unintentionally looping around. Use a map (don't rely on GPS)—there's a good one in the Blue Hill Peninsula Chamber of Commerce's visitors guide.

Brooklin. The village of Brooklin, originally part of Sedgwick, established itself as an independent town in 1849. Today it's home to the world-famous Wooden Boat School, a 60-acre oceanfront campus offering courses in woodworking, boatbuilding, and seamanship. A small park-like area on the waterfront has a long pier and affords spectacular views of the area's chiseled coast. The school is off the road to Naskeag Point, a sleepy, serenely beautiful spot at the end of the peninsula road with a small rock beach, teeny park, and a home peeking through the trees on the island across the harbor.

Brooksville. The town of Brooksville, incorporated in 1817, is almost completely surrounded by water, with Eggemoggin Reach, Walker Pond, and the Bagaduce River marking its boundaries. Cape Rosier, remote and cove-lined even for this off-the-beaten-path peninsula, is home to Holbrook Island Sanctuary, a state park with hiking trails and a gravel beach.

Sedgwick. Incorporated in 1789, Sedgwick runs along much of Eggemoggin Reach, the body of water separating the mainland from Deer Isle, Little Deer Isle, and Stonington.

WHERE TO EAT

$ SEAFOOD FAMILY Fodor's Choice ★

🍴 **Bagaduce Lunch.** This tidy fried-fish specialist sits next to the reversing falls on the Bagaduce River. About 10 miles west of Blue Hill, it's the perfect place for an outdoor lunch (no indoor seating). Picnic tables dot this nub of land with water on three sides, and there's a pier to tie up your kayak or boat, or to walk out on to enjoy the lovely view. Clam, shrimp, haddock, or scallop baskets come with onion rings or chips; there are also hot dogs, burgers, and fried chicken fingers. Seals, bald eagles, and ospreys provide natural entertainment in this rich tidal estuary. At low tide kids explore along the shore. [$] *Average main: $12* ✉ *145 Franks Flat Rd., Penobscot* ☎ *207/326–4197* 💳 *No credit cards* ⏲ *Closed mid-Sept.–late Apr. No dinner Wed.*

$$$ CONTEMPORARY

🍴 **Brooklin Inn.** At this small B&B restaurant, in a 1920s bungalow-style building that was the dining room for a long-gone resort, the ambience is pleasantly yesteryear. In summer it expands to include seating on the classic glass-enclosed wraparound porch. The changing menu embraces traditional New England fare without clinging to the past, and all the produce, meats, poultry, and fish are local and often organic. You'll find dishes like crispy duckling with a rhubarb and lime glaze and Frenchman Bay mussels in a Dijon herb cream reduction. There's also an Irish pub downstairs with a menu of oysters, pizza, and sandwiches. The inn has five homey guest rooms. [$] *Average main: $22* ✉ *22 Reach Rd., Brooklin* ☎ *207/359–2777* 🌐 *www.brooklininn.com* 🛏 *5 rooms, 3 with bath* ⏲ *Closed Mon. and Tues. mid-Oct.–late May. No lunch.*

DEER ISLE VILLAGE

16 miles south of Blue Hill via Rtes. 176 and 15.

Around Deer Isle Village, thick woods give way to tidal coves. Stacks of lobster traps populate the backyards of shingled houses, and dirt roads lead to secluded summer cottages. This region is prized by artists, and studios and galleries are plentiful.

GETTING HERE AND AROUND

From Sedgwick, Route 15 crosses a 1930s suspension bridge onto Little Deer Isle and continues on to the larger Deer Isle.

EXPLORING

Edgar M. Tennis Preserve. Enjoy several miles of woodland and shore trails at the Edgar M. Tennis Preserve. Look for hawks, eagles, and ospreys and wander among old apple trees, fields of wildflowers, and ocean-polished rocks. ⊠ *Tennis Rd., Deer Isle* ☏ *207/348–2455* ⊕ *www.islandheritagetrust.org* ✉ *Free* ☉ *Daily dawn–dusk.*

Haystack Mountain School of Crafts. Want to learn a new craft? This school 6 miles from Deer Isle Village offers one- and two-week courses for people of all skill levels in crafts such as blacksmithing, basketry, print-making, and weaving. Artisans from around the world present free evening lectures throughout summer. ⊠ *89 Haystack School Dr., off Rte. 15* ☏ *207/348–2306* ⊕ *www.haystack-mtn.org* ✉ *$5 for tours* ☉ *Tours June–Aug., Wed. at 1.*

SHOPPING

Nervous Nellie's Jams and Jellies. Jams and jellies are made right on the property at Nervous Nellie's. There is a tearoom with homemade goodies and also a fanciful sculpture garden with everything from knights to witches to a lobster and a flamingo. They are the works of sculptor Peter Beerits, who operates Nervous Nellie's with his wife. ⊠ *598 Sunshine Rd., off Rte. 15, Deer Isle* ☏ *207/348–6182, 800/777–6845* ⊕ *www.nervousnellies.com.*

STONINGTON

6 miles south of Deer Isle.

Stonington is at the southern end of Route 15, which has helped it retain its unspoiled small-town flavor. The boutiques and galleries lining Main Street cater mostly to out-of-towners, though the town remains a fishing and lobstering community at heart. The principal activity is at the waterfront, where boats arrive with the day's catch. The sloped island that rises to the south is Isle au Haut, which contains a remote section of Acadia National Park.

GETTING HERE AND AROUND

From Deer Isle village, Route 15 runs all the way to Stonington at the tip of the island. There is a ferry from here to Isle au Haut.

EXPLORING

Deer Isle Granite Museum. This tiny museum documents Stonington's quarrying tradition. The museum's centerpiece is a working model of quarrying operations on Crotch Island and the town of Stonington at the turn of the last century. Granite was quarried here for Rockefeller Plaza in New York City and the John F. Kennedy Memorial in Arlington National Cemetery, among other well-known structures. ⊠ *51 Main St.* ☏ *207/367–6331* ⊕ *www.deerislegranitemuseum.wordpress.com* ✉ *Free* ☉ *July and Aug., Thurs.–Tues. 9–5.*

SPORTS AND THE OUTDOORS

Old Quarry Ocean Adventures. Departing from Webb Cove and passing Stonington Harbor en route to the outer islands, Captain Bill Baker's refurbished lobster boat takes visitors on puffin-watching, whale-watching, sunset, and lighthouse trips. There's also a three-hour Sightseeing and Natural History Eco-Cruise that goes by Crotch Island, which has one of the area's two active stone quarries, and stops at Green Island, where you can take a dip in a water-filled quarry. There are all-day day trips to bike or kayak on nearby islands, including Isle au Haut. ⊠ *130 Settlement Rd.* ☎ *207/367–8977* ⊕ *www.oldquarry.com.*

ISLE AU HAUT

6 miles south of Stonington via ferry.

Isle au Haut thrusts its steeply ridged back out of the sea south of Stonington. French explorer Samuel D. Champlain discovered Isle au Haut—or "High Island"—in 1604, but heaps of shells suggest that native populations lived on or visited the island prior to his arrival. The island is accessible only by mail boat, but the 45-minute journey is well worth the effort. A section of Acadia National Park is here, with miles of trails, and the boat will drop visitors off there in peak season. The island has some seasonal rentals but no inns. With only three stores, you wouldn't think folks would come here to shop. But some do, as the island is home to Black Dinah Chocolatiers (☎ *207/335–5010* ⊕ *www. blackdinahchocolatiers.com*), which makes artful high-end chocolates and has a small café.

GETTING HERE AND AROUND

There's one main road here: it circles the island and goes through the Acadia National Park section. Locals give sections of the road a name. Isle au Haut Boat Services (☎ *207/367–5193* ⊕ *www.isleauhaut.com*) operates daily ferry service between Stonington and Isle au Haut. During the summer season trips increase from two to five Monday through Saturday and one to two on Sunday. From mid-June until late September the boat also stops at Duck Harbor, in the island section of Acadia National Park (it will not unload bicycles, kayaks, or canoes). Ferry service is scaled back in the fall, then returns to the regular or "winter" schedule.

QUICK BITES

Maine Lobster Lady. Come summer, this former island innkeeper sells yummy quick-eats, many of them made with fish from the local waters and her own organic garden produce. Her "food truck" (actually a tow trailer) is parked near the ranger's station at the Acadia National Park section on Isle au Haut. There are lobster rolls of course, or try a shrimp-salad sandwich with paprika-dill mayo on a homemade roll, or shrimp puffs served in a paper cone. ⊠ *Off Main Rd., Isle au Haut* ☎ *207/335–5141* ⊕ *www. mainelobsterlady.com.*

ACADIA NATIONAL PARK AND MOUNT DESERT ISLAND

With some of the most dramatic and varied scenery on the Maine Coast and home to Maine's only national park, Mount Desert Island (pronounced "Mount Dessert" by locals) is Maine's most popular tourist destination, attracting well over 2 million visitors a year. Much of the approximately 12-by-15-mile island belongs to Acadia National Park. The rocky coastline rises starkly from the ocean, appreciable along the

Acadia National Park and Mount Desert Island

Marlboro

Union River Bay

230

3

Trenton

East Lamonie

Lamoine State Park

Eastern Bay

Frenchman Bay

230

Salisbury Cove

3

Hulls Cove Visitor Center

3

Western Bay

Town Hill

198

BAR IS.

Bar Harbor

SEASONAL FERRY TO WINTER HARBOR

233

Park Loop Road

Eagle Lake

Wild Gardens of Acadia

Somesville

BARTLETT ISLAND

Pretty Marsh

Somes Sound

ACADIA NATIONAL PARK

Abbe Museum at Sieur de Monts Spring

Cadillac Mountain

Park Loop Rd.

The Bubbles

Bubble Pond

Echo Lake

3

Jordan Pond

Sand Beach

198

Loop Rd.

Thunder Hole

Long Pond

Valley Cove

102

Otter Point

Seal Cove Pond

Park

102

Seal Harbor

3

Seal Cove

Northeast Harbor

Southwest Harbor

BEAR ISLAND

Eastern Way

West Tremont

Manset

SUTTON ISLAND

Islesford

LITTLE CRANBERRY ISLAND

Bernard

Bass Harbor

GREAT CRANBERRY ISLAND

Cranberry Isles

BAKER ISLAND

Blue Hill Bay

Ship Harbor Nature Trail

Bass Harbor Head Light

Atlantic Ocean

Atlantic

SWANS ISLAND

FERRY TO FRENCHBORO
↓

0   2 mi

0   2 km

scenic drives. Trails for hikers of all skill levels lead to the rounded tops of the mountains, providing views of Frenchman and Blue Hill bays and beyond. Ponds and lakes beckon you to swim, fish, or boat. Ferries and charter boats provide a different perspective on the island and a chance to explore the outer islands, all of which are part of Maine but not necessarily of Mount Desert. A network of old carriage roads lets you explore Acadia's wooded interior, filled with birds and other wildlife.

Mount Desert Island has four different towns, each with its own personality. The town of Bar Harbor is on the northeastern corner of the island and includes the little villages of Hulls Cove, Salisbury Cove, and Town Hill. The park aside, Bar Harbor is the major tourist destination, with plenty of accommodations, restaurants, and shops. The town of Mount Desert, in the middle of the island, has four main villages: Somesville, Seal Harbor, Otter Creek, and Northeast Harbor, a summer haven for the very wealthy. Southwest Harbor includes the smaller village of Manset south of the village center. Tremont is at the southernmost tip of the island and stretches up the western shore. It includes the villages of Bass Harbor, Bernard, and Seal Cove. Yes, Mount Desert Island is a place with three personalities: the hustling, bustling tourist mecca of Bar Harbor; the "quiet side" on the western half; and the vast natural expanse that is Acadia National Park. But though less congested and smaller, Northeast Harbor and Southwest Harbor are home to inns, campgrounds, restaurants, ferries, galleries, and small museums.

Sponsored by several Mount Desert Island communities as well as Acadia National Park, the Mt. Desert Island Information Center is along Route 3 just before it crosses to Mount Desert Island. The center is loaded with pamphlets about island tours, restaurants, inns, and attractions, including Acadia National Park. You can buy park passes here, and the staff includes a park ranger.

ESSENTIALS

Visitor Information Bar Harbor Chamber of Commerce ⊠ *1201 Bar Harbor Rd., Trenton* ☎ *800/345–4617* ⊕ *www.barharborinfo.com.* **Bar Harbor Information Center** ⊠ *2 Cottage St., Bar Harbor* ☉ *Early May–late Oct.* **Mount Desert Chamber of Commerce** ⊠ *18 Harbor Dr., Northeast Harbor* ☎ *207/276–5040* ⊕ *www.mountdesertchamber.org.* **Mt. Desert Island Information Center at Thompson Island** ⊠ *1319 Bar Harbor Rd., Trenton* ☎ *207/288–3411* ☉ *Mid-May–mid-June, daily 8–5; late June–Aug., daily 8–6; Sept.–mid-Oct., daily 8–5:30.*

BAR HARBOR

34 miles from Blue Hill via Rte. 172 and U.S. 1.

A resort town since the 19th century, Bar Harbor is the artistic, culinary, and social center of Mount Desert Island. It also serves visitors to Acadia National Park with inns, motels, and restaurants. Around the turn of the last century the island was known as the summer haven of the very rich because of its cool breezes. The wealthy built lavish mansions throughout the island, many of which were destroyed in a huge fire that devastated the island in 1947, but many of those that survived have been converted into businesses. Shops are clustered along Main, Mount Desert, and Cottage streets. Take a stroll down West Street, a National Historic District, where you can see some fine old houses.

The island and the surrounding Gulf of Maine are home to a great variety of wildlife: whales, seals, eagles, falcons, ospreys, and puffins (though not right offshore here), and forest dwellers such as deer, foxes, coyotes, and beavers.

THE EARLY BIRD GETS THE SUN

During your visit to Mount Desert, pick a day when you are willing to get up very early, such as 4:30 or 5 am. Drive with a friend to the top of Cadillac Mountain in Acadia National Park. Stand on the highest rock you can find and wait for the sun to come up. When it does, have your friend take a photo of you looking at it and label the photo something like "The first person in the country to see the sun come up on June 1, 2014."

GETTING HERE AND AROUND

In Ellsworth, Route 3 leaves U.S. 1 and heads to Bar Harbor. In season, free Island Explorer buses (🌐 *www.exploreacadia.com* ☎ *207/667–5796*) take visitors to Acadia National Park and other island towns. There is also a passenger ferry to Winter Harbor across Frenchman Bay.

EXPLORING

Abbe Museum. This small museum dedicated to Maine's indigenous tribes—collectively known as the Wabanaki—is the state's only Smithsonian-affiliated facility. The year-round archaeology exhibit displays spear points, bone tools, and other artifacts found around Mount Desert Island. Rotating exhibits often feature contemporary Native American art, and there are frequent demonstrations of everything from boatbuilding to basket weaving. Call on rainy days for impromptu children's activities. A second location, inside the park at Sieur de Monts Spring, features artifacts from the earliest digs around the island. ✉ *26 Mount Desert St.* ☎ *207/288–3519* 🌐 *www.abbemuseum.org* 🎫 *$6* 🕒 *Late May–early Dec., daily 10–5.*

WHERE TO EAT AND STAY

$$$ SEAFOOD Fodor's Choice ★

🍴 **Burning Tree.** One of the top restaurants in Maine, this easy-to-miss gem with a festive dining room is on Route 3 between Bar Harbor and Otter Creek. The seasonal menu emphasizes freshly caught seafood, and seven species of fish are offered virtually every day, all from the Gulf of Maine. There is always monkfish; you may find it pan-sautéed, glazed with sweet chili sauce, and served with Thai-flavored eggplant and coconut rice. Oven-poached cod and stuffed gray sole are signature dishes. There are always two or three vegetarian options using organic produce, much of it from the owners' garden. [$] *Average main: $22* ✉ *69 Otter Creek Dr., Otter Creek* ☎ *207/288–9331* 🕒 *Closed mid-Oct.–mid-June. No lunch.*

$$$$ HOTEL Fodor's Choice ★

🏨 **Bar Harbor Inn & Spa.** Originally established in the late 1800s as a men's social club, this waterfront inn has rooms spread among three buildings on well-landscaped grounds. **Pros:** at the harbor; some two-level suites. **Cons:** not right near Acadia National Park. [$] *Rooms from:*

Long ramps on Maine's many docks make it easier to access boats at either high tide or low tide.

$209 ⊠ *Newport Dr., 1 Newport Dr.* ☎ *207/288–3351, 800/248–3351* ⊕ *www.barharborinn.com* ⇆ *138 rooms, 15 suites* ☉ *Closed late Nov.– mid-Mar.* ⧘ *Breakfast.*

SPORTS AND THE OUTDOORS

AIR TOURS

Acadia Air Tours. This outfit provides sightseeing flights over Bar Harbor and Acadia National Park. Most tours run from 15 minutes to an hour and range from $150 to $450 for two people. The sunset tour is $50 extra. ⊠ *968 Bar Harbor Rd., Trenton* ☎ *207/667–7627* ⊕ *www. acadiaairtours.com.*

BICYCLING

Acadia Bike. With mountain bikes and hybrids, Acadia Bike rents models that are good for negotiating the carriage roads in Acadia National Park. ⊠ *48 Cottage St.* ☎ *207/288–9605, 800/526–8615* ⊕ *www. acadiabike.com.*

Bar Harbor Bicycle Shop. Rent bikes by the half or full day at the Bar Harbor Bicycle Shop. ⊠ *141 Cottage St.* ☎ *207/288–3886, 800/824–2453* ⊕ *www.barharborbike.com.*

Coastal Kayaking Tours. This outfitter has been leading trips in the scenic waters off Mount Desert Island since 1982. Rentals are provided through its sister business, Acadia Outfitters, on the same downtown street. Trips are limited to no more than 12 people. The season is May through October. ⊠ *48 Cottage St.* ☎ *207/288–9605, 800/526–8615* ⊕ *www.acadiafun.com.*

Downeast Sailing Adventures. Take two-hour and sunset cruises for $35 with six passengers or $50 with fewer. Departures are from Upper Town Dock in Southwest Harbor and several other locations. ⊠ *Upper Town Dock, Clark Point Rd., Southwest Harbor* ☎ *207/288–2216* ⊕ *www. downeastsail.com.*

FAMILY **Margaret Todd.** The 151-foot four-masted schooner *Margaret Todd* operates 1½- to 2-hour trips three times a day among the islands of Frenchman's Bay The sunset sail has live music, and the 2 pm trip is narrated by an Acadia National Park ranger. Trips are $37.50 and depart from from mid-May to October. ⊠ *Bar Harbor Inn pier, Newport Dr.* ☎ *207/288–4585* ⊕ *www.downeastwindjammer.com.*

WHALE-WATCHING

FAMILY **Bar Harbor Whale Watch Co.** This company has four boats, one of them a 140-foot jet-propelled double-hulled catamaran with spacious decks. It's one of two large catamarans used for whale-watching trips, some of which go at sunset or include a side trip to see puffins. The company also offers lighthouse, lobstering, and seal-watching cruises, and a trip to Acadia National Park's Baker Island. ⊠ *1 West St.* ☎ *207/288–2386, 800/942–5374* ⊕ *www.barharborwhales.com.*

SHOPPING
ART
Alone Moose Fine Crafts. The oldest made-in-Maine gallery in Bar Harbor, Alone Moose Fine Crafts offers bronze wildlife sculptures, jewelry, pottery, and watercolors. ⊠ *78 West St.* ☎ *207/288–4229* ⊕ *www. finemainecrafts.com.*

Eclipse Gallery. The Eclipse Gallery carries handblown glass, ceramics, wood and metal furniture, and home decor items like mirrors and lamps. The gallery is open from mid-May through October. ⊠ *12 Mount Desert St.* ☎ *207/288–9088* ⊕ *www.eclipsegallery.us.*

Island Artisans. this shop sells basketry, pottery, fiber work, and jewelry created by about 150 Maine artisans. ⊠ *99 Main St.* ☎ *207/288–4214* ⊕ *www.islandartisans.com.*

Native Arts Gallery. Silver and gold jewelry is a specialty at Native Arts Gallery, open from May through October. ⊠ *99 Main St.* ☎ *207/288– 4474* ⊕ *www.nativeartsgallery.com.*

SPORTING GOODS
Cadillac Mountain Sports. One of the best sporting-goods stores in the state, Cadillac Mountain Sports has developed a following of locals and visitors alike. You can find top-quality climbing, hiking, boating, paddling, and camping equipment. In winter you can rent cross-country skis, ice skates, and snowshoes. ⊠ *26 Cottage St.* ☎ *207/288–4532* ⊕ *www.cadillacmountainsports.com.*

ACADIA NATIONAL PARK

3 miles from Bar Harbor via U.S. 3.

Fodor's Choice ★ With about 49,000 acres of protected forests, beaches, mountains, and rocky coastline, Acadia National Park is the second-most-visited national park in America (after the Great Smoky Mountains National

Park). According to the National Park Service, 2 million people visit Acadia each year. The park holds some of the most spectacular scenery on the Eastern Seaboard: a rugged coastline of surf-pounded granite and an interior graced by sculpted mountains, quiet ponds, and lush deciduous forests. Cadillac Mountain (named after a Frenchman who explored here in the late 1600s and later founded

> ### BOOK A CARRIAGE RIDE
>
> If you would like to take a horse-drawn carriage ride down one of the park's roads, you can do so from mid-June to mid-October by making a reservation with Wildwood Stables (☎ 877/276-3622). One of the carriages can accommodate wheelchairs.

Detroit) the highest point of land on the East Coast, dominates the park. Although it's rugged, the park also has graceful stone bridges, miles of carriage roads (popular with walkers, runners, and bikers as well as horse-drawn carriages), and the Jordan Pond House restaurant (famous for its popovers).

The 27-mile Park Loop Road provides an excellent introduction, but to truly appreciate the park you must get off the main road and experience it by walking, hiking, biking, sea kayaking, or taking a carriage ride. If you get off the beaten path, you can find places you'll have practically to yourself. Mount Desert Island was once a preserve of summer homes for the very rich (and still is for some), and, because of this, Acadia is the first national park in the United States that was largely created by donations of private land. There are two smaller parts of the park: on Isle au Haut, 15 miles away out in the ocean, and on the Schoodic Peninsula, on the mainland across Frenchman Bay from Mt. Desert.

PARK ESSENTIALS

ADMISSION FEE

A user fee is required May through October—unless arriving on the Island Explorer buses that serve the park and island villages from June 23 through Columbus Day. They are free to ride and also offer free admittance to the park. The per-vehicle fee is $20 for a seven-consecutive-day pass from May through October. You can walk or ride in (bike or motorcycle) on a $5 individual pass, also good for seven days. Or you can use your National Park America the Beautiful Pass, which allows entrance to any national park in the United States. Check ⊕ *www.nps.gov* for details.

ADMISSION HOURS

The park is open 24 hours a day, year-round, but roads are closed from December to mid-April except for the Ocean Drive section of Park Loop Road and a small part of the road that provides access to Jordan Pond.

PARK CONTACT INFORMATION

Acadia National Park ☎ *207/288-3338* ⊕ *www.nps.gov/acad.*

GETTING HERE AND AROUND

Route 3 leads to the island and Bar Harbor from Ellsworth and circles the eastern part of the island. Route 102 is the major road on the west side. Free Island Explorer buses serve the main villages and the park from June 23 through Columbus Day. There are scheduled stops; they also pick up and drop off passengers anywhere along the park it is safe to stop.

EXPLORING

SCENIC DRIVES AND STOPS

Fodor's Choice ★ **Cadillac Mountain.** At 1,530 feet, this is one of the first places in the United States to see the sun's rays at break of day. It is the highest mountain on the eastern seaboard north of Brazil. Dozens of visitors make the trek to see the sunrise or, for those less inclined to get up so early, sunset. From the smooth summit you have an awesome 360-degree

> **ACADIA LEAF PEEPING**
>
> The fall foliage in Maine can be spectacular. Because of the moisture, it comes later along the coast, around the middle of October, than it does in the interior of the state. The best way to catch the colors along the coast is travel on the Acadia National Park Loop Road. For up-to-date information, go to ⊕ *www.mainefoliage.com.*

view of the jagged coastline that runs around the island. A small gift shop and some restrooms are the only structures at the top. The road up the mountain is closed from December through mid-May. ⊠ *Cadillac Summit Rd.*

FAMILY
Fodor's Choice ★ **Park Loop Road.** This 27-mile road provides a perfect introduction to the park. You can drive it in an hour, but allow at least half a day so that you can explore the many sites along the way. The route is served by the free Island Explorer buses, which will also pick and drop off anywhere along the route. Traveling south on Park Loop Road toward Sand Beach, you'll reach a small ticket booth, where, if you haven't already, you will need to pay the park entrance fee between May and October. Traffic is one way from the Route 233 entrance to the Stanley Brook Road entrance south of the Jordan Pond House. The section known as Ocean Drive is open year-round, as is a small section that provides access to Jordan Pond from Seal Harbor.

VISITOR CENTER

FAMILY **Hulls Cove Visitor Center.** This is a great spot to get your bearings. A large relief map of Mount Desert Island gives you the lay of the land, and you can watch a free 15-minute video about everything the park has to offer. Pick up guidebooks, maps of hiking trails and carriage roads, schedules for ranger-led tours, and recordings for drive-it-yourself tours. Don't forget to grab a schedule of ranger-led programs, which include guided hikes and other interpretive events. Junior-ranger programs for kids, nature hikes, photography walks, tide-pool explorations, and evening talks are all popular. The Acadia National Park Headquarters, off Route 233 near the north end of Eagle Lake, serves as the park's visitor center during the off-season. ⊠ *Rte. 3, Hulls Cove* ☎ *207/288–3338* ⊕ *www.nps.gov/acad* ☉ *Mid-May–Sept., daily 9–5; Oct., daily 8–4:30.*

SPORTS AND THE OUTDOORS

The best way to see Acadia National Park is to get out of your vehicle and explore on foot or by bicycle or boat. There are more than 45 miles of carriage roads that are perfect for walking and biking in the warmer months and for cross-country skiing and snowshoeing in winter. There are 125 miles of trails for hiking, numerous ponds and lakes for canoeing or kayaking, two beaches for swimming, and steep cliffs for rock climbing.

HIKING

Acadia National Park maintains more than 125 miles of hiking trails, from easy strolls around lakes and ponds to rigorous treks with climbs up rock faces and scrambles along cliffs. Although most hiking trails are on the east side of the island,

> **CAUTION**
>
> Every few years someone falls off one of the park's trails or cliffs and is swept out to sea. There is a lot of loose, rocky gravel along the shoreline, and sea rocks can often be slippery—so watch your step.

the west side also has some scenic trails. For those wishing for a long climb, try the trails leading up Cadillac Mountain or Dorr Mountain. Another option is to climb Parkman, Sargeant, and Penobscot mountains. Most hiking is done from mid-May to mid-November. Snow falls early in Maine, so from as early as late November to the end of March cross-country skiing and snowshoeing replace hiking. Volunteers groom most of the carriage roads if there's been 4 inches of snow or more. ■TIP➔ You can park at one end of any trail and use the free shuttle bus to get back to your starting point.

Distances for trails are given for the round-trip hike.

Fodor's Choice
★ **Acadia Mountain Trail.** If you're up for a challenge, this is one of the area's best trails. The 2½-mile round-trip climb up Acadia Mountain is steep and strenuous, but the payoff is grand: views of Somes Sound. If you want a guided trip, look into the ranger-led hikes for this trail. ⊠ *Rte. 102* ☎ *207/288–3338* ⊕ *www.nps.gov/acadia.*

Fodor's Choice
★ **Ocean Path Trail.** This easily accessible 4.4-mile round-trip trail runs parallel to the Ocean Drive section of the Park Loop Road from Sand Beach to Otter Point. It has some of the best scenery in Maine: cliffs and boulders of pink granite at the ocean's edge, twisted branches of dwarf jack pines, and ocean views that stretch to the horizon. Be sure to save time to stop at **Thunder Hole,** named for the sound the waves make as they thrash through a narrow opening in the granite cliffs, into a sea cave, and whoosh up and out. Steps lead down to the water, where you can watch the wave action close up, but use caution here (access may be limited due to storms), and if venturing onto the outer cliffs along this walk. ⊠ *Ocean Dr. section of Park Loop Rd.*

SWIMMING

The park has two swimming beaches, Sand Beach and Echo Lake Beach. Sand Beach, along Park Loop Road, has changing rooms, restrooms, and a lifeguard on duty from the first full week of June to Labor Day. Echo Lake Beach, on the western side of the island just north of Southwest Harbor, has much warmer water, as well as changing rooms, restrooms, and a lifeguard on duty throughout the summer.

Echo Lake Beach. A quiet lake surrounded by woods in the shadow of Beech Mountain, Echo Lake draws swimmers to its sandy southern shore. The lake bottom is bit muckier than the ocean beaches nearby, but the water is considerably warmer. The surrounding trail network skirts the lake and ascends the mountain. The beach is 2 miles north of

6

Southwest Harbor. **Amenities:** lifeguards; toilets. **Best for:** swimming. ⊠ *Echo Lake Beach Rd., off Hwy. 102.*

Sand Beach. This pocket beach is hugged by two picturesque rocky out-croppings, and the combination of the crashing waves and the chilly water (peaking at around 55°F) keeps most people on the beach. You'll find some swimmers at the height of summer, but the rest of the year this is a place for strolling and snapping photos. In the shoulder season you'll have the place to yourself. **Amenities:** lifeguards; parking; toilets. **Best for:** sunrise; solitude; walking. ⊠ *Ocean Dr. section of Park Loop Rd., 3 miles south of Hwy. 3.*

NORTHEAST HARBOR

12 miles south of Bar Harbor via Rtes. 3 and 198.

The summer community for some of the nation's wealthiest families, Northeast Harbor has one of the best harbors on the coast, which fills with yachts and powerboats during peak season. Some summer residents rebuilt here after Bar Harbor's Great Fire of 1947 destroyed mansions there.

It's a great place to sign up for a cruise around Somes Sound or to the Cranberry Isles. Other than that, this quiet village has a handful of restaurants, inns, boutiques, and art galleries.

SOMESVILLE

7 miles north of Northeast Harbor via Rte. 198.

Most visitors pass through Somesville on their way to Southwest Harbor, but this well-preserved village, the oldest on the island, is more than a stop along the way. Originally settled by Abraham Somes in 1761, this was once a bustling commercial center with shingle, lumber, and wool mills; a tannery; a varnish factory; and a dye shop. Today Route 102, which passes through the center of town, takes you past a row of white-clapboard houses with black shutters and well-manicured lawns.

SOUTHWEST HARBOR

6 miles south of Somesville via Rte. 102.

Across from Northeast Harbor, Southwest Harbor sits on the south side of the entrance to Somes Sound, which cuts up the center of the island. The town makes for a mellower Acadia base camp than Bar Harbor, with handsome yachts and towering sailboats along the waterfront throughout the summer. Just north of town, trailheads at Echo Lake Beach and Fernald Point access some of the park's less-traveled trails.

BASS HARBOR

10 miles south of Somesville via Rtes. 102 and 102A.

Bass Harbor is a tiny lobstering village with a relaxed atmosphere and a few accommodations and restaurants. If you're looking to get away from the crowds, consider using this hardworking community as your base. Although Bass Harbor does not draw as many tourists as other villages, the Bass Harbor Head Light in Acadia National Park is one of the region's most popular attractions and is undoubtedly one of the most photographed lighthouses in Maine. From Bass Harbor you can hike on the Ship Harbor Nature Trail or take a ferry to Frenchboro or Swans Island.

GETTING HERE AND AROUND

From Bass Harbor the Maine State Ferry Service operates a ferry, the *Captain Henry Lee,* carrying both passengers and vehicles to Swans Island (40 minutes, round-trip $17.50 per person and $49.50 per car with driver) and Frenchboro (50 minutes, round-trip $11.25 per person and $32.25 per car with driver). The Frenchboro ferry doesn't run daily; there's also a passenger-only trip on a smaller boat (same price) from April through November. Round-trip excursions (you don't get off the boat) are $10.

ESSENTIALS

Transportation Information Maine State Ferry Service ✉ *114 Granville Rd* ☎ *207/244–3254* 🌐 *www.maine.gov/mdot/msfs.*

6

EXPLORING

Fodor's Choice ★ **Bass Harbor Head Light.** Built in 1858, this lighthouse is one of the most photographed lights in Maine. Now automated, it marks the entrance to Blue Hill Bay. The grounds and residence are Coast Guard property, but two trails around the facility provide excellent views. It's within Acadia National Park, and there is parking. **■ TIP→ The best place to take a picture is from the rocks below—but watch your step, as they can be slippery.** ✉ *Lighthouse Rd., off Rte. 102A* 🎟 *Free* 🕒 *Daily 9–sunset.*

WHERE TO EAT

$$ SEAFOOD 🍴 **Thurston's Lobster Pound.** Right on Bass Harbor, looking across to the village, Thurston's is easy to spot because of its bright yellow awning. You can buy fresh lobsters to go or sit at covered outdoor tables. Order everything from a grilled-cheese sandwich, soup, or hamburger to a boiled lobster served with clams or mussels. [$] *Average main: $20* ✉ *Steamboat Wharf, 9 Thurston Rd., Bernard* ☎ *207/244–7600* 🌐 *www.thurstonslobster.com* 🕒 *Closed mid-Oct.–mid-May.*

WAY DOWN EAST

Slogans such as "The Real Maine" ring truer Way Down East. The raw, mostly undeveloped coast in this remote region is more accessible than it is farther south. Even in summer here you're likely to have rocky beaches and shady hiking trails to yourself. The slower pace is as calming as a sea breeze.

One innkeeper relates that visitors who plan to stay a few days often opt for a week after learning more about the region's offerings, which include historic sites; museums on local history, culture, and art; national wildlife refuges; state parks and preserves; and increasingly, conservancy-owned public land. Cutler's Bold Coast, with its dramatic granite headlands, is protected from development. Waters near Eastport

have some of the world's highest tides. Lakes perfect for canoeing and kayaking are sprinkled inland, and rivers snake through marshland as they near the many bays. Boulders are strewn on blueberry barrens. Rare plants thrive in coastal bogs and heaths, and dark-purple and pink lupines line the roads in late June.

VISITOR INFORMATION

Many chambers of commerce in the region distribute free copies of the pamphlet "Maine's Washington County: Just Off the Beaten Path," which is several cuts above the usual tourist promotion booklet.

Contacts DownEast and Acadia Regional Tourism ✉ *87 Milbridge Rd., Cherryfield* ☎ *207/546–3600, 888/665–3278* ⊕ *www.downeastacadia.com.*

SCHOODIC PENINSULA

25 miles east of Ellsworth via U.S. Rte. 1 and Rte. 186.

The landscape of Schoodic Peninsula's craggy coastline, towering evergreens, and views over Frenchman Bay are breathtaking year-round. A drive through the well-to-do summer community of Grindstone Neck shows what Bar Harbor might have been like before so many of its mansions were destroyed in the Great Fire of 1947. Artists and artisans have opened galleries in and around Winter Harbor. Anchored at the foot of the peninsula, Winter Harbor was once part of Gouldsboro, which wraps around it. The southern tip of the peninsula is home to the Schoodic section of Acadia National Park.

GETTING HERE AND AROUND

From U.S. 1, Route 186 loops around the peninsula. Route 195 runs from U.S. 1 to Prospect Harbor and on to its end in Corea.

ESSENTIALS

Visitor Information Schoodic Chamber of Commerce ⊕ *www.acadia-schoodic.org.*

EXPLORING

Within Gouldsboro on the Schoodic Peninsula are several small coastal villages. You drive through Wonsqueak and Birch Harbor after leaving the Schoodic section of Acadia National Park. Near Birch Harbor you can find Prospect Harbor, a small fishing village nearly untouched by tourism. In Corea, there's little to do besides watch the fishermen at work, wander along stone beaches, or gaze out to sea.

Fodor's Choice   **Acadia National Park.** The only section of Maine's national park that sits
★   on the mainland is at the southern end of the Schoodic Peninsula in the town of Winter Harbor. The park has a scenic 6-mile loop that edges along the coast and yields views of Grindstone Neck, Winter Harbor, Winter Harbor Lighthouse, and, across the water, Cadillac Mountain. At the tip of the point, huge slabs of pink granite lie jumbled along the shore, thrashed unmercifully by the crashing surf, and jack pines cling to life amid the rocks. Fraser Point, at the beginning of the loop, is an ideal place for a picnic. Work off lunch with a hike up Schoodic Head for the panoramic views up and down the coast. During the summer season you can take a passenger ferry to Winter Harbor from Bar

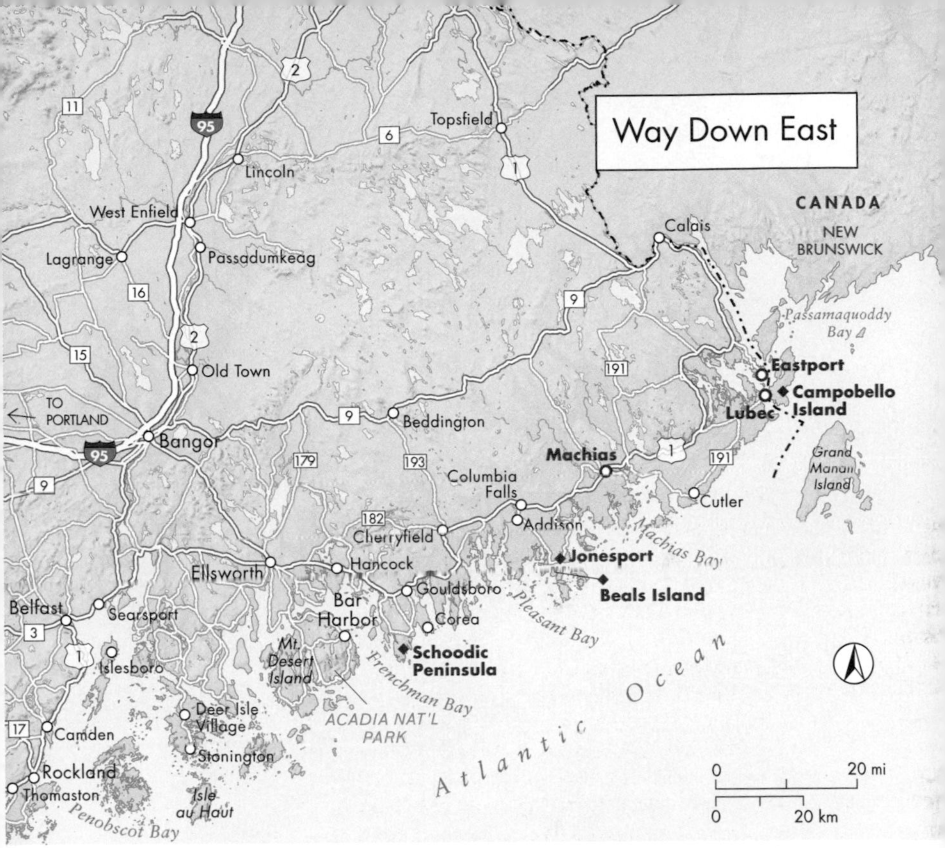

Harbor, then catch the free Island Explorer bus, which stops throughout the park. ✉ *End of Moore Rd., off Rte. 186* ☎ *207/288–3338* 🌐 *www.nps.gov/acad* 🕒 *Daily 24 hrs.*

Schoodic Education and Research Center. In the Schoodic Peninsula section of Acadia National Park, this center offers lectures, workshops, and kid-friendly events about nature. It's worth a drive by just to see the Rockefeller Building, a massive 1935 French Eclectic and Renaissance-style structure with a stone and half-timber facade that housed naval offices and housing. In 2013 the building reopened as a visitor center after an extensive renovation. ✉ *64 Acadia Dr., off Park Loop Rd., 3 miles south of park entrance* ☎ *207/288–1310* 🌐 *www.sercinstitute.org*

WHERE TO EAT AND STAY

$ SEAFOOD 🍴 **Chase's Restaurant.** The orange booths may remind you of a fast-food joint, but this family restaurant has a reputation for serving good, basic fare—in this region that means a lot of fish. There are large and small fried seafood dinners and several more expensive seafood platters. Try the sweet-potato fries as a side. Lunch fare, sold all day, includes wraps and burgers. It's also open for breakfast. [$] *Average main: $10* ✉ *193 Main St.* ☎ *207/963–7171.*

$ B&B/INN FAMILY 🏨 **Bluff House Inn.** This homey, modern inn is on a secluded hillside with expansive views of Frenchman Bay. **Pros:** good value; largest room has

DID YOU KNOW?

Almost unrelated to the
bloated berries at most
grocery stores, Maine's
small and flavor-packed
wild blueberries are a must
in season, from late July
to early September. Try a
handful fresh, in pancakes,
or a pie.

Wild for Blueberries

There's no need to inquire about the cheesecake topping if you dine out in August when the wild blueberry crop comes in. Anything but blueberries would be unthinkable.

Way Down East, wild blueberries have long been a favorite food and a key ingredient in cultural and economic life. Maine produces about a third of the commercial harvest, which totals about 80 million pounds annually, Canada supplying virtually all the rest. Washington County yields more than half of Maine's total crop, which is why the state's largest blueberry processors are here: Jasper Wyman & Son and the predecessor of what is now Cherryfield Foods were founded shortly after the Civil War.

Wild blueberries, which bear fruit every other year, thrive in the region's cold climate and sandy, acidic soil. Undulating blueberry barrens stretch for miles in Deblois and Cherryfield ("the Blueberry Capital of the World") and are scattered throughout Washington County. Look for tufts among low-lying plants along the roadways. In spring the fields shimmer as the small-leaf plants turn myriad shades of mauve, honey orange, and lemon yellow. White flowers appear in June. Fall transforms the barrens into a sea of red.

Amid Cherryfield's barrens, a plaque on a boulder lauds the late J. Burleigh Crane for helping advance an industry that's not as wild as it used to be. Honeybees have been brought in to supplement native pollinators, fields are irrigated, and barrens are burned and mowed to rid plants of disease and insects, reducing the need for pesticides. Most of the barrens in and around Cherryfield are owned by the large blueberry processors.

About 80% of Maine's crop is now harvested with machinery. That requires moving boulders, so the rest continues to be harvested by hand with blueberry rakes, which resemble large forks and pull the berries off their stems. Years ago, year-round residents did the work. Today migrant workers make up 90% of this seasonal labor force.

Blueberries get their dark color from anthocyanins, believed to provide antioxidants. Wild blueberries have more of these anti-aging, anticancer compounds than their cultivated cousins. Smaller and more flavorful than cultivated blueberries, wild ones are mostly used in packaged foods. Less than 1% of the state's crop—about 500,000 pints—is consumed fresh, mostly in Maine. Look for fresh berries (sometimes starting in late July and lasting until early September) at roadside stands, farmers' markets, and supermarkets.

Wild Blueberry Land in Columbia Falls sells everything blueberry, from muffins and candy to socks and books. Find farm stores, stands, and markets statewide, many selling blueberries and blueberry jams and syrups, at ⊕ www.getrealmaine.com, a Maine Department of Agriculture site that promotes Maine foods.

—Mary Ruoff

a sitting area with pullout couch. **Cons:** only two rooms have good water views. [$] *Rooms from: $95* ✉ *57 Bluff House Rd., turn off Rte. 186, Gouldsboro* ☎ *207/963–7805* 🌐 *www.bluffinn.com* 🛏 *8 rooms, 1 suite* 🍴 *Breakfast.*

$$ B&B/INN FAMILY Fodor's Choice ★ **Oceanside Meadows Inn.** A must for nature lovers, this lodging sits on a 200-acre preserve dotted with woods, streams, salt marshes, and ponds. **Pros:** one of region's few sand beaches; staff share info about the area over tea. **Cons:** need to cross road to beach. [$] *Rooms from: $149* ✉ *202 Corea Rd., Prospect Harbor* ☎ *207/963–5557* 🌐 *www.oceaninn.com* 🛏 *13 rooms, 2 suites* 🕓 *Closed mid-Oct.–late-May* 🍴 *Breakfast.*

SPORTS AND THE OUTDOORS

KAYAKING

SeaScape Kayaking. Led by a Registered Maine Guide, SeaScape's morning and afternoon kayak tours include an island stop and a blueberry snack. The company also rents canoes, kayaks, and bikes from its location in Birch Harbor. ✉ *Birch Harbor, 18 E. Schoodic Dr.* ☎ *207/963–5806* 🌐 *www.seascapekayaking.com.*

SHOPPING

ANTIQUES AND MORE

U.S. Bells. Hand-cast bronze doorbells and wind chimes are among the items sold at U.S. Bells. You can also buy finely crafted quilts and wood-fired pottery made by the owner's family. Ask for a tour of the foundry. ✉ *56 W. Bay Rd., Prospect Harbor* ☎ *207/963–7184* 🌐 *www.usbells.com.*

ART GALLERIES

Lee Fusion Art Glass. Window glass is fused in a kiln at Lee Fusion Art Glass to create unusual glass dishware. Colorful enamel accents depict birds, lighthouses, flowers, and designs made from doilies. The store is open Memorial Day weekend through Columbus Day. ✉ *679 S. Gouldsboro Rd., Gouldsboro* ☎ *207/963–7280* 🌐 *www.leefusionartglass.com.*

JONESPORT AND BEALS ISLAND

48 miles northeast of Winter Harbor via Rte. 186, U.S. Rte. 1, and Rte. 187; 20 miles southwest of Machias.

The birding is superb around Jonesport and Beals Island, a pair of fishing communities joined by a bridge over Moosabec Reach. A handful of stately homes ring Jonesport's Sawyer Square, where Sawyer Memorial Congregational Church's exquisite stained-glass windows are illuminated at night. But the towns are less geared to travelers than those on the Schoodic Peninsula. Lobster traps are still piled in the yards, and lobster-boat races near Moosabec Reach are the highlight of the community's annual Independence Day celebration. Right next to Beals Island, Great Wass Island, connected to it by a bridge, is home to a namesake preserve with rugged trails to the coast.

GETTING HERE AND AROUND

In Columbia Falls Route 187, a loop road, heads down to Jonesport, where a bridge leads to Beals Island. Route 187 returns to U.S. 1 in Jonesboro.

MACHIAS

20 miles northeast of Jonesport.

The Machias area—Machiasport, East Machias, and Machias, the Washington County seat—lays claim to being the site of the first naval battle of the Revolutionary War, which took place in what is now Machiasport. Despite being outnumbered and out-armed, a small group of Machias men under the leadership of Jeremiah O'Brien captured the armed British schooner *Margaretta.* That battle, fought on June 12, 1775, is now known as the "Lexington of the Sea." The town's other claim to fame is wild blueberries. On the third weekend in August the annual Machias Wild Blueberry Festival is a community celebration complete with parade, crafts fair, concerts, and plenty of blueberry dishes.

ESSENTIALS

Visitor Information **Machias Bay Area Chamber of Commerce** ✉ *85 Main St., Suite 2* ☎ *207/255–4402* 🌐 *www.machiaschamber.org.*

EXPLORING

Burnham Tavern Museum. It was in this gambrel-roofed tavern home that the men of Machias laid the plans that culminated in the capture of the *Margaretta* in 1775. After the Revolutionary War's first naval battle, wounded British sailors were brought here. Tour guides highlight exhibits and tell colorful stories of early settlers. Period furnishings and household items show what life was like in Colonial times. On the National Register of Historic Places, the dwelling is among the 21 in the country deemed most important to the Revolution. ✉ *14 Colonial Way* ☎ *207/255–6930* 🌐 *www.burnhamtavern.com* 🎟 *$5* 🕒 *Mid-June–Sept., weekdays 9:30–4.*

WHERE TO EAT

$$$ MODERN AMERICAN 🍴 **Riverside Inn & Restaurant.** A bright yellow exterior invites a stop at this delightful restaurant in a former sea captain's home perched on the bank of the Machias River, as are the restaurant's vegetable and herb gardens. Ask for a table in the sunroom, which has water views and opens to the other dining room. You can enjoy a drink on the deck. The chef-owner brings a special flair to traditional dishes, such as pork served with a pistachio crust. His signature dish is salmon stuffed with crabmeat and shrimp. In summer months the menu includes dressed-up dinner salads—try pairing one with standout appetizers like hake cakes and red-tuna wontons. Also an inn with Victorian touches, Riverside has two guest rooms in the main house and two suites in the coach house. [$] *Average main: $28* ✉ *608 Main St., East Machias* ☎ *207/255–4134, 888/255–4344* 🌐 *www.riversideinn-maine.com* 🕒 *Closed Jan. and Mon. Closed Tues. and Wed. in Feb.–May, Nov., and Dec. No lunch.*

LUBEC

28 miles northeast of Machias via U.S. 1 and Rte. 189.

Lubec is one of the first places in the United States to see the sunrise. A popular destination for outdoors enthusiasts, it offers plenty of

opportunities for hiking and biking, and the birding is renowned. It's a good base for day trips to New Brunswick's Campobello Island, reached by a bridge—the only one to the island—from downtown Lubec. The main attraction there, Roosevelt Campobello International Park, operates a visitor center that also provides information about the region generally on the U.S. side of the border. It's in Whiting at the corner of U.S. 1 and Route 189, the road to Lubec. The village is perched at the end of a narrow strip of land at the end of Route 189, so you often can see water in three directions in this special off-the-beaten-path place.

GETTING HERE AND AROUND

In summer you can take a water taxi from here to Eastport—about a mile by boat, but 40 miles by the circuitous northerly land route. From U.S. 1 in Whiting, Route 189 leads to Lubec; it's about 13 miles to the village.

SPORTS AND THE OUTDOORS

West Quoddy Head Light. The easternmost point of land in the United States is marked by candy-striped West Quoddy Head Light. In 1806 President Thomas Jefferson signed an order authorizing construction of a lighthouse on this site. You can't climb the tower, but the former lightkeeper's house has a museum with a video showing the interior and displays on Lubec's maritime past. A gallery displays works by artists who live or summer in the area. A mystical 2-mile path along the cliffs at Quoddy Head State Park, one of five trails, yields magnificent views of Canada's cliff-clad Grand Manan Island. Whales can often be sighted offshore. The 540-acre park has a picnic area. ✉ *973 S. Lubec Rd., off Rte. 189* ☎ *207/733–0911* 🌐 *www.parksandlands.com* 🎟 *$3* 🕒 *Daily, 9–sunset.*

WHERE TO EAT AND STAY

$$ SEAFOOD 🍴 **Uncle Kippy's.** There isn't much of a view from the picture windows, but locals don't mind—they come here for the satisfying seafood. The dining room is large and has a bar. Entrées include seafood dinners and combo platters and some chicken and meat dishes. There are burgers, too, and the fresh-dough pizza is popular. You can order from the lunch or dinner menu. A take-out window and ice-cream bar are open May through September. [$] *Average main: $16* ✉ *170 Main St.* ☎ *207/733–2400* 🌐 *www.unclekippys.com.*

$ B&B/INN 🏨 **Peacock House.** Five generations of the Peacock family lived in this 1860 sea captain's home before it was converted into an inn. **Pros:** piano and fireplace in living room; lovely garden off deck; think-of-everything innkeepers direct guests to area's tucked-away spots. **Cons:** not on the water. [$] *Rooms from: $103* ✉ *27 Summer St.* ☎ *207/733–2403, 888/305–0036* 🌐 *www.peacockhouse.com* 🛏 *3 rooms, 4 suites* 🕒 *Closed Nov.–Apr.* 🍽 *Breakfast.*

CAMPOBELLO ISLAND, CANADA

28 miles east of Machias.

A popular excursion from Lubec, New Brunswick's Campobello Island has two fishing villages, Welshpool and Wilson's Beach. The only bridge is from Lubec, but in summer a car ferry shuttles passengers from Campobello Island to Deer Island, where you can continue on to the Canadian mainland.

GETTING HERE AND AROUND

After coming across the bridge from Lubec, Route 774 runs from one end of the island to the other, taking you through the two villages and to Roosevelt Campobello International Park.

EXPLORING

Roosevelt Campobello International Park. Neatly manicured Campobello Island has always had a special appeal for the wealthy and famous. It was here that President Franklin Roosevelt and his family spent summers. You can take a self-guided tour of the 34-room Roosevelt Cottage that was presented to Eleanor and Franklin as a wedding gift. The wicker-filled structure looks essentially as it did when the family was in residence. A visitor center has displays about the Roosevelts and Canadian-American relations. Eleanor Roosevelt Teas are held at 11 and 3 daily in the neighboring Hubbard Cottage. A joint project of the American and the Canadian governments, this park is crisscrossed with interesting hiking trails. Groomed dirt roads attract bikers. Eagle Hill Bog has a wooden walkway and signs identifying rare plants. **■ TIP→ Note that the Islands are on Atlantic Time, which is an hour later than EST.** ✉ *459 Rte. 774, Welshpool, New Brunswick, Canada* ☎ *506/752–2922, 877/851–6663* 🌐 *www.fdr.net* 🎟 *Free* 🕐 *House and visitor center: Memorial Day weekend–Columbus Day, daily 10–6.*

6

WHERE TO EAT

$$ SEAFOOD FAMILY 🍴 **Family Fisheries.** Seafood lovers know that fried fish doesn't have to be greasy. That's why people keep heading across the international bridge to eat at this family establishment in Wilson's Beach. The freshest seafood is delivered to the restaurant, where you can bring your own wine ($2 corking fee). Order fried haddock, scallops, shrimp, or clams alone or as part of a platter. Eat in the large dining room or near the playground at picnic tables or in a screened room. Lobsters are cooked outside and also sold live or steamed to go. You can buy ice cream at the take-out window, and the restaurant serves breakfast in July and August. [$] *Average main: C$15* ✉ *1977 Rte. 774, Wilson's Beach, New Brunswick, Canada* ☎ *506/752–2470* 🌐 *www.family-fisheries.webs.com* 🕐 *Closed late Oct.–early Apr.*

EASTPORT

39 miles northeast of Lubec via Rte. 189, U.S. 1, and Rte. 190; 109 miles north of Ellsworth via U.S. 1 and Rte. 190.

Connected by a granite causeway to the mainland at Pleasant Point Reservation, Eastport has wonderful views of the nearby islands, and you can sometimes spot whales from the waterfront because the harbor is so deep. Known for its diverse architecture, the island city was one of the nation's busiest seaports in the early 1800s. On the weekend after Labor Day the Eastport Pirate Festival brings folks out in pirate attire for a ship race, parade, fireworks, cutlass "battles" by reenactors, and other events, including a children's breakfast and schooner ride with pirates.

Get downtown early to secure a viewing spot for Maine's largest July 4th parade. On the weekend of the second Sunday in August, locals celebrate Sipayik Indian Days at the Pleasant Point Reservation. This festival of Passamaquoddy culture includes canoe races, dancing, drumming, children's games, fireworks, and traditional dancing.

GETTING HERE AND AROUND

From U.S. 1 Route 190 leads to the Island City. Continue on Washington Street to the water. You can also take a water taxi from here to Lubec—1 mile or so by boat but about 40 by land—in the summer.

ESSENTIALS

Visitor Information Eastport Area Chamber of Commerce ☎ *207/853–4644* 🌐 *www.eastport.net.*

WHERE TO EAT

$$ SEAFOOD FAMILY 🍴 **Chowder House.** Just north of downtown Eastport, this expansive waterfront eatery sits on the pier next to where the ferry docks. Built atop an old cannery foundation, it has original details such as wood beams and a stone wall. Eat in the downstairs pub, upstairs in the dining room, or on the large deck. The house specialties include a smoked fish appetizer and seafood pasta in a wine-and-cheese sauce. Lunch, served until 4, includes fried seafood plates, burgers, wraps, and sandwiches. [$] *Average main: $17* ✉ *167 Water St.* ☎ *207/853–4700* 🌐 *eastportchowderhouse.org* 🕒 *Closed mid-Oct.–mid-May.*

TRAVEL SMART MAINE, VERMONT, AND NEW HAMPSHIRE

GETTING HERE AND AROUND

New England's largest and most cosmopolitan city, Boston, is the region's major transportation center for reaching Maine, Vermont, and New Hampshire. A secondary hub is Portland, Maine and there are also sizeable airports in Burlington, Vermont and Manchester, New Hampshire. Your best bet for exploring is to travel by car—flying within the region is expensive and driving distances between most attractions are short. Inside most cities, public transportation is a viable—and often preferable—means for getting around. Passenger ferry service is available to outlying islands (some vessels accommodate vehicles).

See the Getting Here and Around section at the beginning of each chapter for more transportation information.

■ AIR TRAVEL

Due to the costs and lack of major airports, generally most travelers visiting Northern New England head for a major gateway, such as Boston, Manchester, or Portland and then rent a car to explore the region. The New England states form a fairly compact region, with few important destinations more than six hours apart by car.

Boston's Logan Airport is one of the nation's most important domestic and international airports, with direct flights arriving from all over North America and internationally. New England's other major airports receive few international flights (mostly from Canada) but do offer a wide range of direct domestic flights to East Coast and Midwest destinations and, to a lesser extent, to the western United States. Some sample flying times to Boston are: from Chicago (2½ hours), London (6½ hours), and Los Angeles (6 hours). Times from U.S. destinations are similar, if slightly shorter, to Albany and Hartford, assuming you can find direct flights.

AIRPORTS

The main gateway to Maine, Vermont, and New Hampshire is Boston's Logan International Airport (BOS). Manchester Boston Regional Airport (MHT), in New Hampshire, is a lower-cost alternative to Logan. Additional New England airports served by major carriers include Portland International Jetport (PWM) in Maine and Burlington International Airport (BTV) in Vermont. Other airports are in Albany, New York (ALB, near Vermont) and Bangor, Maine (BGR)

Airport Information Albany International Airport ⊠ *737 Albany Shaker Rd., Albany, New York* ☎ *518/242-2200* ⊕ *www.albanyairport. com.* **Bangor International Airport** ⊠ *287 Godfrey Blvd., Bangor, Maine* ☎ *207/992-4600* ⊕ *www.flybangor.com.* **Burlington International Airport** ⊠ *1200 Airport Dr, South Burlington, Vermont* ☎ *802/863-1889* ⊕ *www. burlingtonintlairport.com.* **Logan International Airport** ⊠ *1 Harborside Dr., Boston, Massachusetts* ☎ *800/235-6426* ⊕ *www.massport. com.* **Manchester Boston Regional Airport** ⊠ *1 Airport Rd., Manchester, New Hampshire* ☎ *603/624-6539* ⊕ *www.flymanchester. com.* **Portland International Jetport** ⊠ *1001 Westbrook St., Portland, Maine* ☎ *207/874-8877* ⊕ *www.portlandjetport.org.* **Westchester County Airport-White Plains** ⊠ *240 Westchester Airport County Rd., White Plains, New York* ☎ *914/995-4850* ⊕ *airport. westchestergov.com.*

FLIGHTS

Numerous airlines fly to and from Boston; additionally, the discount carrier Southwest Airlines flies to Albany, Boston, and Manchester, New Hampshire. Smaller or discount airlines serving Boston include AirTran, Cape Air, and JetBlue. You can fly to Burlington from New York City on JetBlue, and you can fly to Boston from Atlantic City, Myrtle Beach, and Fort Lauderdale on Spirit Airlines.

Airline Contacts AirTran Airways ☎ *800/247-8726* ⊕ *www.airtran.com.*

American Airlines ☎ 800/433–7300 ⊕ www.aa.com. **Cape Air** ☎ 800/352–0714 ⊕ www.capeair.com. **Delta Airlines** ☎ 800/221–1212 ⊕ www.delta.com. **JetBlue** ☎ 800/538–2583 ⊕ www.jetblue.com. **New England Airlines** ☎ 800/243–2460 ⊕ www.block-island.com/nea. **Southwest Airlines** ☎ 800/435–9792 ⊕ www.southwest.com. **Spirit Airlines** ☎ 801/772–7117 ⊕ www.spirit.com. **United Airlines** ☎ 800/864–8331 ⊕ www.united.com. **US Airways** ☎ 800/428–4322 ⊕ www.usairways.com.

▮ BOAT TRAVEL

Principal ferry routes in Northern New England provide access to many islands off the Maine Coast. Ferries cross Lake Champlain between Vermont and upstate New York. International service between Portland, Yarmouth, and Bar Harbor, Maine, and Nova Scotia, is also available. With the exception of the Lake Champlain ferries—which are first-come, first-served—car reservations are advisable.

▮ BUS TRAVEL

Regional bus service is relatively plentiful throughout New England. It can be a handy and affordable means of getting around, as buses travel many routes that trains do not.

Concord Coach runs buses between Boston and Concord, New Hampshire, Portland, Maine, and Bangor, Maine. C&J sends Wi-Fi–equipped buses up the New Hampshire coast to Newburyport, Massachusetts, Dover, New Hampshire, Durham, New Hampshire, and Portsmouth, New Hampshire, and also provides service to New York City. Concord and C&J both leave from Boston's South Station (which is connected to the Amtrak station) and Logan Airport.

Information C&J ☎ 800/258–7111 ⊕ www.ridecj.com. **Concord Coach** ☎ 800/639–3317 ⊕ www.concordcoachlines.com.

With fares starting at just $1 if you reserve early enough, BoltBus runs buses with Wi-Fi and electrical outlets between Boston, New York, Philadelphia, and Washington, D.C. Megabus also offers low fares, and its Wi-Fi–equipped buses serve New York City and many other points on the East Coast. BoltBus and Megabus use Boston's South Station.

Bus Information BoltBus ☎ 877/265–8287 ⊕ www.boltbus.com. **Megabus** ☎ 877/462–6342 ⊕ us.megabus.com.

▮ CAR TRAVEL

In Maine, Vermont, and New Hampshire public transit options are limited and a car is necessary. Areas in the interior are largely without heavy traffic and congestion. Coastal New England is more congested (especially getting to and from Cape Cod during the summer) and parking can be hard to find in cities and the many smaller resort towns along the coast. Still, a car is typically the best way to get around even on the coast (though you may want to park it at your hotel and use it as little as possible). If you rent a car at Logan International Airport, allow plenty of time to return it—as much as 60 minutes to be on the safe side.

GASOLINE

Gas stations are easy to find along major highways and in most communities throughout the region. At this writing, the average price of a gallon of regular unleaded gas in Northern New England is $3.59. However, prices vary from station to station within any city. The majority of stations are self-serve with pumps that accept credit cards, though you may find a holdout full-service station on occasion. Tipping is not expected at these.

PARKING

In large cities, finding a spot on the street can be time-consuming. Your best bet is to park in a garage, but the rates are upward of $20 a day. In smaller cities, street parking is usually simpler, though parking garages are convenient and less expensive than their big-city counterparts. Pay attention to signs—some cities allow only residents to park on certain streets. In most small towns parking is not a problem, though some beach and lake parking areas are reserved for those with resident stickers.

ROAD CONDITIONS

Major state and U.S. routes are generally well maintained, with snowplows at the ready during the winter to salt and plow road surfaces soon after the flakes begin to fall. Traffic is heaviest around Boston and Portland , especially during rush hour. Secondary state routes and rural roads can be a mixed bag; generally, Route 1 is well maintained, but with slower traffic that can get locally congested in even the smallest coastal towns.

Boston motorists are notorious for driving aggressively. Streets in the Boston area are confusing, so a GPS unit can be very helpful.

ROADSIDE EMERGENCIES

Throughout Northern New England, call 911 for any travel emergency, such as an accident or a serious health concern. For breakdowns, dial a towing service.

RULES OF THE ROAD

On city streets the speed limit is 30 mph unless otherwise posted; on rural roads the speed limit ranges from 40 to 50 mph unless otherwise posted. Interstate speeds range from 50 to 65 mph, depending on how densely populated the area is. Throughout the region, you're permitted to make a right turn on red except where posted. Be alert for one-way streets in congested communities.

State law requires that drivers and all passengers wear seat belts at all times. Always strap children under age five or 40 pounds into approved child-safety seats.

You will encounter many traffic circles/rotaries if you drive in Northern New England. Remember that cars entering traffic circles must yield to cars that are already in the circle. Some rotaries have two lanes, which complicates things. If you're leaving the rotary at the next possible exit, enter from the right lane. If you're leaving the rotary at any exit after the first possible exit, enter from the left lane (which becomes the inner lane of the circle); you can also exit the circle directly from this lane—though check your right side so you don't sideswipe a driver who's incorrectly in the right lane.

CAR RENTAL

Because a car is the most practical way to get around Northern New England, it's best to rent one if you're not bringing your own. The major airports serving the region all have on-site car-rental agencies. If you're traveling to the area by bus or train, you might consider renting a car once you arrive. A few train or bus stations have one or two major car-rental agencies on-site.

Rates at the area's major airport, Boston's Logan Airport, begin at around $50 a day and $200 a week for an economy car with air-conditioning, automatic transmission, and unlimited mileage. The same car might go for around $70 a day and $300 a week at a smaller airport such as Portland International Jetport. These rates do not include state tax on car rentals, which varies depending on the airport but generally runs 12% to 15%. Generally, it costs less to rent a car outside of an airport, but factor into the value whether it is easy or difficult to get there with your luggage.

Most agencies won't rent to you if you're under the age of 21 and several major agencies will not rent to anyone under 25. When picking up a rental car, non-U.S. residents need a voucher for any prepaid reservation that was made in their home country, a passport, a driver's license, and a travel policy that covers each driver. Boston's Logan Airport is large, spread out, and usually congested, so if you will be returning a rental vehicle there, make sure to allow plenty of time to take care of it before heading for your flight.

Major Rental Agencies Alamo
☎ *877/222–9075* ⊕ *www.alamo.com.* **Avis**
☎ *800/331–1212* ⊕ *www.avis.com.* **Budget**
☎ *800/527–0700* ⊕ *www.budget.com.* **Hertz**
☎ *800/654–3131* ⊕ *www.hertz.com.* **National**
Car Rental ☎ *877/222–9058* ⊕ *www.*
nationalcar.com.

▌ TRAIN TRAVEL

Amtrak offers frequent daily service along
its Northeast Corridor route from Washington, D.C., Philadelphia, and New York
to Boston. Amtrak's high-speed Acela
trains link Boston and Washington, with
stops at New York, Philadelphia, etc.,
along the way. The *Downeaster* connects
Boston with Portland, Maine, with stops
in coastal New Hampshire.

Other Amtrak services include the *Ver-*
monter between Washington, D.C., and
St. Albans, Vermont, the *Ethan Allen*
Express between New York and Rutland, Vermont, and the *Lake Shore Lim-*
ited between Boston and Chicago, with
stops at Pittsfield, Springfield, Worcester,
and Framingham, Massachusetts. These
trains run on a daily basis. Allow 15 to 30
minutes to make train connections.

Information Amtrak ☎ *800/872–7245*
⊕ *www.amtrak.com.*

ESSENTIALS

■ ACCOMMODATIONS

In Northern New England you can bed down in a basic chain hotel or a luxurious grande dame, but unless you're staying in a city, this is really bed-and-breakfast land. Charming—and sometimes historic—inns, small hotels, and B&Bs dot the region and provide a glimpse of local life.

⇨ *Prices in the reviews are the lowest cost of a standard double room in high season.*

BED-AND-BREAKFASTS

Historic B&Bs and inns are found throughout Northern New England. In many less touristy areas B&Bs offer an affordable alternative to chain properties. In most major towns, expect to pay about the same or more for a historic inn. Many of the region's finest restaurants are attached to country inns, so you often don't have to go far for the best meal in town. Quite a few inns and B&Bs serve substantial breakfasts.

Reservation Services Bed & Breakfast.com ☎ *512/322–2710, 800/462–2632* ⊕ *www. bedandbreakfast.com.* **Bed & Breakfast Inns Online** ☎ *800/215–7365* ⊕ *www.bbonline. com.* **BnB Finder.com** ☎ *888/469–6663* ⊕ *www.bnbfinder.com.*

HOUSE AND APARTMENT RENTALS

In New England you are most likely to find a house, apartment, or condo rental in areas in which ownership of second homes is common, such as beach resorts and ski country. Home-exchange directories sometimes list rentals as well as exchanges. Another good bet is to contact real-estate agents in the area in which you are interested.

Contacts Home Away ☎ *512/782–0805* ⊕ *www.homeaway.com.* **Interhome** ☎ *800/882–6864* ⊕ *www.interhomeusa. com.* **Villas International** ☎ *415/499–9490, 800/221–2260* ⊕ *www.villasintl.com.*

HOTELS

Major hotel and motel chains are amply represented in Northern New England. The region is also liberally supplied with small, independent motels, which run the gamut from the tired to the tidy. Don't overlook these mom-and-pop operations; they frequently offer cheerful, convenient accommodations at lower rates than the chains.

Reservations are always a good idea, particularly in summer and in winter resort areas; in college towns in September and at graduation time in spring; and at areas renowned for autumn foliage.

Most hotels and motels will hold your reservation until 6 pm; call ahead if you plan to arrive late. All will hold a late reservation for you if you guarantee your reservation with a credit-card number.

Note that in Massachusetts, by state law, all hotels are no-smoking. All hotels listed have private baths unless otherwise noted.

Information New England Inns & Resorts Association ☎ *603/964–6689* ⊕ *www. newenglandinnsandresorts.com.*

■ CHILDREN IN NORTHERN NEW ENGLAND

Throughout Northern New England you'll have no problem finding comparatively inexpensive kid-friendly hotels and family-style restaurants—as well as some museums, beaches, parks, planetariums, and lighthouses. Keep in mind that B&Bs are not always suitable for kids—many flat-out refuse to accommodate children. Also, some of the quieter and more rural areas lack child-oriented attractions.

Favorite destinations for family vacations in Northern New England include the White Mountains, Stowe, Vermont, and coastal Maine, but in general, the entire region has plenty to offer families.

LODGING

New England has many family-oriented resorts with lively children's programs. You'll also find farms that accept guests and can be lots of fun for children. Rental houses and apartments abound, particularly around ski areas. In the off-season, these can be economical as well as comfortable. Some country inns, especially those with a quiet, romantic atmosphere and those furnished with antiques, are less enthusiastic about little ones.

Most hotels in Northern New England allow children under a certain age to stay in their parents' room at no extra charge, but others charge for them as extra adults; find out the cutoff age. Note that in Maine hotels and inns cannot put age restrictions on children unless they have five or fewer rooms.

Most lodgings that welcome infants and small children will provide a crib or cot, but remember to give advance notice so that one will be available for you. Many family resorts make special accommodations for small children during meals.

TRANSPORTATION

Each Northern New England state has specific requirements regarding age and weight requirements for children in car seats. If you will need a car seat, make sure your rental-car agency provides them and reserve well in advance.

▌COMMUNICATIONS

INTERNET

Most major chain hotels and many smaller motels throughout Northern New England now offer wired or wireless Internet access (often both). Many have a desktop computer available for guest use. Access is often free, but be sure to ask about possible fees when you book. Many coffee shops offer Wi-Fi, as do most libraries. Cybercafes lists more than 4,000 Internet cafés worldwide.

Contacts Cybercafes ⊕ *www.cybercafes.com.*

▌EATING OUT

Although certain ingredients and preparations are common to the region as a whole, Northern New England's cuisine varies greatly from place to place. In urban centers like Portland, upscale resort areas such as Manchester, Vermont and Stowe, Vermont, as well as Portsmouth, New Hampshire, and coastal Maine, you can expect to find stellar restaurants, many of them with culinary luminaries at the helm and a reputation for creative—and occasionally daring—menus.

Elsewhere, restaurant food tends more toward the simple, traditional, and conservative. Towns, collegiate communities, and other sophisticated areas also have a great variety of international restaurants, especially excellent Italian, French, Japanese, Indian, and Thai eateries. There are also quite a few diners, which typically present patrons with page after page of inexpensive, short-order cooking and often stay open until the wee hours.

The proximity to the ocean accounts for a number of restaurants, often tiny shacks, serving very fresh seafood. The area's numerous boutique dairy, meat, and vegetable suppliers account for other choice ingredients. In fact, menus in the more upscale and tourism-driven communities often note which Vermont dairy or New Hampshire produce farm a particular goat cheese or heirloom tomato came from.

For information on food-related health issues, see Health below.

MEALS AND MEALTIMES

For an early breakfast, pick places that cater to a working clientele. City, town, and roadside establishments specializing in breakfast for early workers often open their doors at 5 or 6 am. At country inns and B&Bs, breakfast is seldom served before 8 am; if you need to get an earlier start, ask ahead of time. Lunch generally runs from around 11 am to 2:30 pm; dinner is usually served from 6 to 9 pm (with early-bird specials sometimes beginning at

5). Only in the larger cities will you find dinner much later than 9 pm. Many restaurants in New England are closed Monday and sometimes Sunday or Tuesday, although this is never true in resort areas in high season. However, resort-town eateries often shut down completely in the off-season.

Unless otherwise noted, the restaurants listed *in this guide* are open daily for lunch and dinner.

PAYING

Credit cards are accepted for meals throughout Northern New England in all but the most modest establishments. *Prices in the reviews are the average cost of a main course at dinner or, if dinner is not served, at lunch.*

RESERVATIONS AND DRESS

It's a good idea to make a reservation if you can. We only mention them specifically when reservations are essential (there's no other way you'll ever get a table) or when they are not accepted. For popular restaurants, book as far ahead as you can (often 30 days) and reconfirm as soon as you arrive. (Large parties should always call ahead to check the reservations policy.) We mention dress only when men are required to wear a jacket or a jacket and tie.

WINE, BEER, AND SPIRITS

Northern New England is no stranger to microbrews. Following the Sam Adams lead in offering hearty English-style ales and special seasonal brews are breweries such as Vermont's Long Trail, Maine's Shipyard, and New Hampshire's Smutty-nose Brewing Co. Green Mountain Cidery makes Woodchuck hard cider in Middlebury, Vermont.

New England is beginning to earn some respect as a wine-producing region. Vermont is getting into the act with the Snow Farm Vineyard in the Lake Champlain Islands and Boyden Valley Winery in Cambridge.

Although a patchwork of state and local regulations affect the hours and locations

of places that sell alcoholic beverages, Northern New England licensing laws are fairly liberal. State-owned or -franchised stores sell hard liquor in New Hampshire, Maine, and Vermont; many travelers have found that New Hampshire offers the region's lowest prices. Look for state-run liquor "supermarkets" on Interstate highways in the southern part of New Hampshire.

▌ HEALTH

Lyme disease, so named for its having been first reported in the town of Lyme, Connecticut, is a potentially debilitating disease carried by deer ticks. They thrive in dry, brush-covered areas, particularly in coastal areas. Always use insect repellent; the potential for outbreaks of Lyme disease makes it imperative that you protect yourself from ticks from early spring through summer. To prevent bites, wear light-color clothing and tuck pant legs into socks. Look for black ticks about the size of a pinhead around hairlines and the warmest parts of the body. If you have been bitten, consult a physician, especially if you see the telltale bull's-eye bite pattern. Flu-like symptoms often accompany a Lyme infection. Early treatment is imperative.

Northern New England's two greatest insect pests are black flies and mosquitoes. The former are a phenomenon of late spring and early summer and are generally a problem only in the densely wooded areas of the far north.

Mosquitoes, however, are a nuisance just about everywhere. The best protection against both pests is repellent containing DEET; if you're camping in the woods during black fly season, you'll also want to use fine mesh screening in eating and sleeping areas and even wear mesh headgear. A particular pest of coastal areas, especially salt marshes, is the greenhead fly. Their bite is nasty, they are hard to kill, and they are best repelled by a liberal application of Avon Skin So Soft or a similar product.

Coastal waters attract seafood lovers who enjoy harvesting their own clams, mussels, and even lobsters; permits are required and casual harvesting of lobsters is strictly forbidden. Amateur clammers should be aware that Northern New England shellfish beds are periodically visited by red tides, during which microorganisms can render shellfish poisonous. To keep abreast of the situation, inquire when you apply for a license (usually at town halls or police stations) and pay attention to red tide postings as you travel.

▌ HOURS OF OPERATION

Hours in Northern New England differ little from those in other parts of the United States. Within the region, shops and other businesses tend to keep slightly later hours in larger cities and along the coast, which is generally more populated than interior New England.

Most major museums and attractions are open daily or six days a week (with Monday being the most likely day of closing). Hours are often shorter on Saturday and especially Sunday, and some prominent museums stay open late one or two nights a week, usually Tuesday, Thursday, or Friday. New England also has quite a few smaller museums—historical societies, small art galleries, highly specialized collections—that open only a few days a week and sometimes only by appointment in winter or slow periods.

▌ MONEY

It costs a bit more to travel in most of Northern New England than it does in the rest of the country, with the most costly areas along the coast. There are also a fair number of somewhat posh inns and restaurants in parts of Vermont and New Hampshire. ATMs are plentiful and larger denomination bills (as well as credit cards) are readily accepted in tourist destinations during the high season.

Prices throughout this guide are given for adults. Substantially reduced fees are almost always available for children, students, and senior citizens.

CREDIT CARDS

Major credit cards are readily accepted throughout New England, though in rural areas you may encounter difficulties or the acceptance of only MasterCard or Visa (also note that if you'll be making an excursion into Canada, many outlets there accept Visa but not MasterCard).

Reporting Lost Cards American Express ☎ 800/528-4800 ⊕ www.americanexpress. com. **Diners Club** ☎ 800/234-6377 ⊕ www. dinersclub.com. **Discover** ☎ 800/347-2683 ⊕ www.discover.com. **MasterCard** ☎ 800/627- 8372 ⊕ www.mastercard.us. **Visa** ☎ 800/847- 2911 ⊕ usa.visa.com.

▌ PACKING

The principal rule on weather in Northern New England, is that there are no rules. A cold, foggy morning in spring can and often does become a bright, 60°F afternoon. A summer breeze can suddenly turn chilly and rain often appears with little warning. Thus, the best advice on how to dress is to layer your clothing so that you can peel off or add garments as needed for comfort. Showers are frequent, so pack a raincoat and umbrella. Even in summer you should bring long pants, a sweater or two, and a waterproof windbreaker, for evenings are often chilly and sea spray can make things cool.

Casual sportswear—walking shoes and jeans or khakis—will take you almost everywhere, but swimsuits and bare feet will not: shirts and shoes are required attire at even the most casual venues. Dress in restaurants is generally casual, except at some of the distinguished restaurants of Maine Coast towns such as Kennebunkport. Upscale resorts, at the very least, will require men to wear collared shirts at dinner, and jeans are often frowned upon.

In summer, bring a hat and sunscreen. Remember also to pack insect repellent; to prevent Lyme disease you'll need to guard against ticks from early spring through summer (⇨ *Health*).

▌ SAFETY

Rural New England is one of the country's safest regions, so much so that residents often leave their doors unlocked. In the cities observe the usual precautions. You should avoid out-of-the-way or poorly lighted areas at night; clutch handbags close to your body and don't let them out of your sight; and be on your guard in subways and buses, not only during the deserted wee hours but in crowded rush hours, when pickpockets are at work. Keep your valuables in hotel safes. Try to use ATMs in busy, well-lighted places such as bank lobbies.

If your vehicle breaks down in a rural area, pull as far off the road as possible, tie a handkerchief to your radio antenna (or use flares at night—check if your rental agency can provide them), and stay in your car with the doors locked until help arrives. Don't pick up hitchhikers. If you're planning to leave a car overnight to make use of off-road trails or camping facilities, make arrangements for a supervised parking area if at all possible. Cars left at trailhead parking lots are subject to theft and vandalism.

The universal telephone number for crime and other emergencies throughout Northern New England is 911.

TIPPING GUIDELINES FOR NEW ENGLAND	
Bartender	$1 to $5 per round of drinks, depending on the number of drinks
Bellhop	$1 to $2 per bag, depending on the level of the hotel
Hotel Concierge	$5 or more, if he or she performs a service for you
Hotel Doorman	$1–$2 if he helps you get a cab
Hotel Maid	$1–$3 a day (either daily or at the end of your stay, in cash)
Hotel Room-Service Waiter	$1 to $2 per delivery, even if a service charge has been added
Porter at Airport or Train Station	$1 per bag
Skycap at Airport	$1 to $3 per bag checked
Taxi Driver	15%–20%, but round up the fare to the next dollar amount
Tour Guide	15% of the cost of the tour
Valet Parking Attendant	$1–$2, but only when you get your car
Waiter	15%–20%, with 20% being the norm at high-end restaurants; nothing additional if a service charge is added to the bill
Other Attendants	Restroom attendants in more expensive restaurants expect some small change or $1. Tip coat-check personnel at least $1–$2 per item checked unless there is a fee, then nothing.

▌ TAXES

Sales taxes in New England are as follows: Maine 5.5%; Vermont 6%. No sales tax is charged in New Hampshire. Some states and municipalities levy an additional tax (from 1% to 10%) on lodging or restaurant meals. Alcoholic beverages are sometimes taxed at a higher rate than that applied to meals.

TIME

New England operates on Eastern Standard Time and follows daylight saving time. When it is noon in Boston it is 9 am in Los Angeles, 11 am in Chicago, 5 pm in London, and 3 am the following day in Sydney. When taking a ferry to Nova Scotia, remember that the province operates on Atlantic Standard Time and, therefore, is an hour ahead.

TOURS

Insight Vacations offers a selection of fall foliage tours. Contiki Vacations, specialists in vacations for 18- to 35-year-olds, has a few tours available that pass through parts of New England as well as the rest of the Northeast.

Recommended Companies Contiki Vacations ☎ 866/266–8454 ⊕ contiki.com. **Insight Vacations** ☎ 888/680–1241 ⊕ www.insightvacations.com/us.

SPECIAL-INTEREST TOURS

BICYCLING AND HIKING

Contacts Bike New England ☎ 978/979–6598 ⊕ www.bikenewengland.com. **TrekAmerica** ☎ 800/873–5872 ⊕ www.trekamerica.com. **Urban Adventures** ☎ 617/670–0637 ⊕ www.urbanadventours.com.

CULINARY

Contacts Creative Culinary Tours ☎ 888/889–8681 ⊕ www.creativeculinarytours.com.

CULTURE

Contacts New England Vacation Tours ☎ 800/742–7669 ⊕ www.newenglandvacationtours.com. **Northeast Unlimited Tours** ☎ 800/759–6820 ⊕ www.newenglandtours.com. **Wolfe Adventures & Tours** ☎ 888/449–6533 ⊕ www.wolfetours.com.

SKIING

Contacts New England Action Sports ☎ 800/477–7669 ⊕ www.skitrip.net.

VISITOR INFORMATION

Each Northern New England state provides a helpful free information kit, including a guidebook, map, and listings of attractions and events. All include listings and advertisements for lodging and dining establishments. Each state also has an official website with material on sights and lodgings; most of these sites have a calendar of events and other special features.

Contacts Maine Office of Tourism ☎ 888/624–6345 ⊕ www.visitmaine.com. **New Hampshire Division of Travel and Tourism Development** ☎ 603/271–2665 ⊕ www.visitnh.gov. **Vermont Department of Tourism and Marketing** ☎ 802/828–3237, 800/837–6668 ⊕ www.vermontvacation.com.

ONLINE RESOURCES

Check out the official home page of each Northern New England state for information on state government as well as links to state agencies with information on doing business, working, studying, living, and traveling in these areas. GORP is a terrific general resource for just about every kind of recreational activity. You can narrow your search using the "Park Finder" for a wide range of topics, ranging from backpacking to sailing to nature viewing.

Yankee, New England's premier regional magazine, also publishes an informative travel website. Another great Web resource is Visit New England.

Online Info GORP ⊕ www.gorp.com. **Visit New England** ⊕ www.visitnewengland.com. **Yankee** ⊕ www.yankeemagazine.com/travel.

INDEX

PHOTO CREDITS

NOTES

NOTES

NOTES

NOTES

NOTES

NOTES

NOTES

ABOUT OUR WRITERS

Born and raised in Burlington, Vermont, **Mike Dunphy** (*www.michaeldunphy.com*) got the travel bug while studying at the University of Kent in Canterbury, England. Following graduation, he joined the Peace Corps and worked for the next ten years as a teacher, trainer, and water park attendant in Europe and Turkey. It was in Istanbul that he began his career in journalism as a writer for *Time Out* magazine. On returning to the United States he earned a master's degree in publishing and writing at Emerson College. Today he lives in New York City and makes his living as a writer and editor for several Web and print publications—but always misses Vermont, which he updated for this edition.

Debbie Hagan is a magazine writer and former editor of *Art New England*. She is an avid international traveler and skier, who has spent most of her adult life exploring ski trails and inns in New England and the Alps. She currently lives in northern Massachusetts and teaches writing classes at New Hampshire Institute of Art in Manchester. She updated the New Hampshire chapter.

Brian Kevin lives in Damariscotta, Maine, where he's a contributing editor to *Down East* magazine. He also contributes periodically to publications such as *Outside*, *Men's Journal*, and *Travel + Leisure*, and is the author of *The Footloose American: Following the Hunter S. Thompson Trail Across South America*. Brian updated the Maine Coast chapter.

Josh Rogol, a native of Stamford, Connecticut, has spent many summers broadcasting minor league baseball and traveling throughout New England. He is a licensed New York City tour guide and a freelance writer and sports broadcaster. For this edition, Josh updated Experience Maine, Vermont, and New Hampshire; Travel Smart; and "A Celebration of Color." A veteran of countless road trips, he composed drives that showcase the best of New England. Josh also contributes to *Fodor's New York City*.

As a freelance writer in Belfast, Maine, **Mary Ruoff** covers travel and other subjects. She is an award-winning former newspaper reporter and a graduate of the School of Journalism at the University of Missouri-Columbia. One of her sources on all things Maine is her husband, Michael Hodsdon, a mariner and lifelong Mainer. They enjoy exploring the state with their son, Dima. For this edition, Mary updated the Inland Maine chapter.